THE DEMIURGE IN ANCIENT THOUGHT

CW00820117

How was the world generated and how does matter continue to be ordered so that the world can continue functioning? Questions like these have existed as long as humanity has been capable of rational thought. In antiquity, Plato's *Timaeus* introduced the concept of the Demiurge, or Craftsman-god, to answer them. This lucid and wide-ranging book argues that the concept of the Demiurge was highly influential on the many discussions operating in Middle Platonist, Gnostic, Hermetic and Christian contexts in the first three centuries AD. It explores key metaphysical problems such as the origin of evil, the relationship between matter and the First Principle and the deployment of ever-increasing numbers of secondary deities to insulate the First Principle from the sensible world. It also focuses on the decreasing importance of demiurgy in Neoplatonism, with its postulation of procession and return.

CARL SÉAN O'BRIEN is Alexander von Humboldt Fellow in the Department of Philosophy at Ruprecht-Karls-Universität Heidelberg and Research Associate, Centre for the Study of the Platonic Tradition, Trinity College, Dublin.

THE DEMIURGE IN ANCIENT THOUGHT

Secondary Gods and Divine Mediators

CARL SÉAN O'BRIEN

CAMBRIDGE
UNIVERSITY PRESS

CAMBRIDGE
UNIVERSITY PRESS

University Printing House, Cambridge CB2 8BS, United Kingdom

One Liberty Plaza, 20th Floor, New York, NY 10006, USA

477 Williamstown Road, Port Melbourne, VIC 3207, Australia

314-321, 3rd Floor, Plot 3, Splendor Forum, Jasola District Centre, New Delhi - 110025, India

79 Anson Road, #06-04/06, Singapore 079906

Cambridge University Press is part of the University of Cambridge.

It furthers the University's mission by disseminating knowledge in the pursuit of education, learning and research at the highest international levels of excellence.

www.cambridge.org
Information on this title: www.cambridge.org/9781107428096

First published 2015
First paperback edition 2018

A catalogue record for this publication is available from the British Library

ISBN 978-1-107-07536-8 Hardback
ISBN 978-1-107-42809-6 Paperback

For my mother, Gloria, who first placed me upon the path of scholarship

Contents

Acknowledgements

There is perhaps no more pleasant task to turn to than thanking those who have enabled a project to come to fruition. This monograph resulted from my PhD thesis at the School of Classics/Centre for the Study of the Platonic Tradition at Trinity College, Dublin and I am deeply grateful to my doctoral supervisor, Professor John M. Dillon, as well as to my academic advisor at Fribourg, Professor Dominic J. O'Meara, for guiding me through this thesis and for their advice and assistance, which went far beyond the call of duty. I have also benefitted from the comments of my doctoral examiners, Professor Vasilis Politis and Professor Jan Opsomer.

I am grateful to the Board of Trinity College, Dublin, for the award of a Postgraduate Studentship, which I held from 2003–4 and again from 2005–6, as well as the subsequent award of a Long Room Hub Fellowship in 2010, which permitted me to work once again with Professor Dillon and develop the monograph further. I am also grateful to the Eidgenössische Stipendienkommission für ausländische Studierende in Bern for a Swiss Confederation Scholarship which permitted me to conduct research with Professor O'Meara in the idyllic surroundings of the University of Fribourg from 2004–5, as well as to the Irish Research Council for the Humanities and Social Sciences for the award of a Government of Ireland Scholarship from 2006–7. My thanks also go to the staff of the Embassy of Switzerland in Dublin, especially the Ambassador of Switzerland to Ireland, HE Mr Josef Doswald and the Counsellor, Mr Ernst Balzli, for their assistance in the course of arranging my research stay in Switzerland. It is difficult to imagine a more pleasant way of conducting research than in a medieval city against the backdrop of the snow-clad Alps. My sincerest thanks go to the Alexander von Humboldt Foundation at Bonn for the award of a research fellowship to continue my work on the Demiurge at Heidelberg under the supervision of Professor Jens Halfwassen; I would also like to thank Professor Halfwassen for having kindly supplied me with a large number of his publications regarding the Demiurge, as well as his support and advice throughout the course of my fellowship at Heidelberg.

Due to the hospitality and *Gastfreundlichkeit* of numerous academics, it was possible to present parts of this research at various international fora: my thanks go to Professor Gunnar af Hällström and his research group at the Faculty of Theology, Åbo Akademi University, to Dr Euree Song at the Institute of Humanities, Seoul National University, to Professor Kevin Corrigan at Emory University, to Professor Michael Erler and Professor Christian Tornau at the University of Würzburg and to Professor Troels Engberg-Pederson and the Naturalism and Christian Semantics research group at the Faculty of Theology, University of Copenhagen. I benefitted greatly from the comments of the participants, especially Dr Stefan Svendson, who kindly supplied me with access to his unpublished research. I would also like to thank the School of Classics at Trinity and the Department of Philosophy at Fribourg for having generously funded my attendance at a conference in Switzerland to present my research, as well as Dr Frieda Klotz and the Hellenic Society of the University of London for the opportunity to attend a conference on Plutarch's *Quaestiones Convivales*. I am extremely grateful to Professor Gabriele Cornelli and Professor Anastácio Borges de Araújo Júnior for the opportunity to deliver a paper at the Federal University of Pernambuco, Recife.

In a world in which the liberal arts are increasingly under pressure, it was a great privilege to have been able to study, as well as to subsequently teach, at a Jesuit college and to have the opportunity to study the classical languages as part of a vibrant culture, rather than simply as an historical artifact. In particular, my deepest gratitude goes to my former Headmaster at Belvedere College, Rev. Fr Leonard Moloney SJ for his support and encouragement throughout the course of my career.

I am grateful to all of my lecturers at Trinity: Professor Damien Nelis, Dr Christine Morris, Professor Brian McGing, Professor Judith Mossman, Professor Monica Gale, Dr Hazel Dodge, Mr Jean Martin Deniau and Mr David Hodgkinson. My thanks go to other members of the Platonic Centre at Dublin during my time there for numerous stimulating discussions, especially Dr Barry Dixon, Dr Brendan O'Byrne, Dr Sarah Klitenic Wear, Professor Andrew Smith, Professor Francis O'Rourke and Dr Patrick Quinn; sadly Professor John Cleary cannot read my thanks in print. At Fribourg, I wish to thank the other members of my research group: Dr Valérie Cordonier, Dr Marlis Colloud-Streit, Professor Pascal Mueller-Jourdan and Professor Alexandrine Schniewind, as well as Professor Christoph Flüeler.

Much of the final revision of this manuscript was carried out while I was a lecturer in the Department of Classics, National University of Ireland, Maynooth. I am grateful to all of my colleagues there, especially to Dr William Desmond for always being on hand to supply advice on technical matters, as well as to Dr Kieran McGroarty, my Head of Department, and to Professor David Scourfield. My thanks also go to Professor Keith Sidwell of the University of Calgary and John and Carmel Barry and Dr David O'Sullivan at University College, Cork. I have benefitted from discussions of various aspects of this topic with Professor Michele Abbate, Professor Luc Brisson, Professor Franco Ferrari, Professor John Finamore, Rev. Professor Gary Gurtler SJ, Dr Christina Manolea, Professor Menahem Luz, Professor Emily Kutash, Professor David Runia and Professor Harold Tarrant.

At Heidelberg, I am grateful to numerous colleagues in many different ways: I would particularly like to thank Dr Javier Álvarez-Vázquez, Dr Emanuele Castelli (for advice on numerous textual matters), Dr István Czachesz, Dr Dirk Cürsgen, Dr Tobias Dangel, Professor Anton Friedrich Koch, Professor Charlotte Köckert, Dr Young Woo Kwon, Professor Peter McLaughlin, Dr Luisa Orsaria, Dr Tommaso Pierini, Omar Rodriguez and Dr Doris Weber. I would also like to thank Dr Michael Sharp, commissioning editor at Cambridge University Press, and Elizabeth Hanlon, the production editors, Sarah Payne and Dave Morris, the copy editor Kate Ollerenshaw, as well as the anonymous reviewers of the Press, for numerous invaluable suggestions. A special word of thanks also goes to the entire team at the Press for working behind the scenes to make this volume possible.

On a personal note, I would like to thank my parents, Gloria and Raymond, and my sister, Dr Zeldine O'Brien (University College, Dublin), for their encouragement and support.

Carl S. O'Brien
Heidelberg

Abbreviations

Abr.	Philo, *De Abrahamo*
Acad.	Cicero, *Academica*
Adv. Haer.	Irenaeus, *Adversus Haereses*
Aet.	Philo, *De Aeternitate Mundi*
Agr.	Philo, *De Agricultura*
CCels.	Origen, *Contra Celsum*
CE	Gregory of Nyssa, *Contra Eunomium*
CH	*Corpus Hermeticum*
Charm.	Plato, *Charmides*
Cher.	Philo, *De Cherubim*
CMt.	Origen, *Commentary on Matthew*
Comm in Met.	Alexander of Aphroisias, *Commentary on Aristotle's Metaphysics*
Comm. Jn.	Origen, *Commentary on John*
Conf.	Philo, *De Confusione Linguarum*
Decal.	Philo, *De Decalogo*
De Comm. Notit.	Plutarch, *De Communibus Notitiis adversus Stoicos*
De Fato	Pseudo-Plutarch, *De Fato*
De Mund.	Aristotle, *De Mundo*
De Plat.	Apuleius, *De Platone*
De An. Proc.	Plutarch, *De Animae Procreatione in Timaeo*
De Stoic. Rep.	Plutarch, *De Stoicorum Repugnantiis*
Det.	Philo, *Quod Deterius Potiori Insidiari Solet*
Deus	Philo, *Quod Deus Sit Immutabilis*
De Vir. Inl.	Jerome, *De Viris Illustribis*
Didasc.	Alcinous, *Didaskalikos*
DK	Diels-Kranz

DL	Diogenes Laertius, *Lives and Opinions of Eminent Philosophers*
Ebr.	Philo, *De Ebrietate*
Enn.	Plotinus, *Enneads*
Epist. Philipp. Ap. Dem.	Demosthenes, *Reply to Philip*
Euthph.	Plato, *Euthyphro*
Fug.	Philo, *De Fuga et Inventione*
GA	Aristotle, *De Generatione Animalium*
Gig.	Philo, *De Gigantibus*
Her.	Philo, *Quis Rerum Divinarum Heres Sit*
Hom. Gen.	Origen, *Homilies on Genesis*
IG9	*Inscriptiones Graecae* vol. IX
In Tim.	Calcidius, *Commentary on Timaeus*
Leg. All.	Philo, *Legum Allegoriae*
Mut.	Philo, *De Mutatione Nominum*
ND	Cicero, *De Natura Deorum*
NHC	Nag Hammadi Corpus
Opif.	Philo, *De Opificio Mundi*
Or.	Dio Chrysostom, *Orationes*
PA	Aristotle, *De Partibus Animalium*
Phileb.	Plato, *Philebus*
Phys.	Simplicius, *On Aristotle's Physics*
Plant.	Philo, *De Plantatione*
Post.	Philo, *De Posteritate Caini*
Praep. Ev.	Eusebius, *Praeparatio Evangelica*
Princ.	Origen, *De Principiis*
Prov.	*Book of Proverbs*
Ps.-Plutarch Plac.	Pseudo-Plutarch, *De Placitis Philosophorum*
QE	Philo, *Quaestiones in Exodum*
QG	Philo, *Quaestiones et Solutiones in Genesim*
Ref.	Pseudo-Hippolytus, *Refutatio omnium haeresium (= Philosophumena)*
Rep.	Plato, *Republic*
Somn.	Philo, *De Somniis*
Soph.	Plato, *Sophist*
Spec.	Philo, *De Specialibus Legibus*
Stat.	Plato, *Statesman*
SVF	*Stoicorum Veterum Fragmenta*
Sym.	Plato, *Symposium*
Theaet.	Plato, *Theaetetus*

Theol. Arith.	Iamblichus, *The Theology of Arithmetic*
Thuc.	Thucydides, *History of the Peloponnesian War*
Tim.	Plato, *Timaeus*
TLG	*Thesaurus Linguae Graecae*
TP	Proclus, *Platonic Theology*

CHAPTER I

Demiurgy and other approaches to world-generation

The theoretical background

Speculation on world-generation has existed as long as humanity has been capable of rational thought. Indeed, if one considers the existence of various cosmological myths spanning different cultures, it precedes the existence of any sort of 'scientific methodology'. The search for an explanation of the generation of the world can be found both at the beginning of Greek science and philosophy in the speculations of the pre-Socratics, and in early Greek literature, exemplified by Hesiod's *Theogony*. The present study examines the distinctly Platonic concept of demiurgy and its influence five to seven centuries after the dialogue in which it first appeared was composed. My main approach is diachronic: I firstly analyse Plato's concept of the Demiurge as expressed in the *Timaeus*, and the interpretation of the dialogue by Aristotle, the Old Academy and modern commentators (Chapter 2). I also consider the principal philosophical problems which Plato bequeathed to his successors, before turning to the chief period under discussion, the first to third centuries AD (Chapters 3–9). This allows the principal metaphysical challenges posed by the *Timaeus* to be identified before considering the responses of subsequent interpreters. My policy throughout has been to structure the discussion around individual texts, rather than an intra-traditional organisation adopting a more thematic approach. This allows greater consideration of the aims of the text and the context in which it was composed than would otherwise be possible. A thematic approach might have a potentially distorting effect by not adequately evaluating the reliability of textual transmission (Numenius' fragments and Origen's *Peri Archôn* are good examples) or obscuring the nature of a work. (In the case of the *De Iside et Osiride*, for example, it is important to note that Plutarch's comments are made in the context of an exegesis of Egyptian myth.)

It is fitting, though, firstly to elaborate the theoretical framework of the study here. In spite of Baltes' *Die Weltentstehung des platonischen Timaios nach den antiken Interpreten* (1976)[1] and the research of Jan Opsomer and Franco Ferrari, there is an issue of whether demiurgy can be said to exist as a concept or whether we are simply dealing with unrelated and independent speculations relating to the generation of the cosmos, particularly since the Demiurge disappears from view under Plato's successors. The first task facing us is to demonstrate that it is possible to trace the influence of the *Timaeus* upon concepts of world-generation, and to suggest the reasons underlying its return to popularity during the first to third centuries AD.

Demiurgy can be described as world-generation via the ordering of pre-existent matter by an entity, sometimes represented as endowed with only limited abilities, according to some sort of model, so that the activity is generally regarded as intellective, as opposed to the *creatio ex nihilo* envisaged in the Judaeo–Christian concept of creation, where God creates simply by willing it to happen. There are naturally some complexities in attempting to delineate both approaches to world-generation, which shall be dealt with later. I further contend that there are a range of subdivisions of demiurgy, depending on the sect by which, and the period in which, they were applied, even if historically dependent upon each other and all ultimately stemming from Plato's myth in the *Timaeus*. So, for example, Neoplatonic demiurgy differs from its Middle Platonist counterpart in positing multiple demiurges, which function within triads. These demiurges are assigned a highly circumscribed role, such as responsibility for partial or universal demiurgy at the encosmic or hypercosmic level. Even if this can be viewed as simply the development of already existent trends, it differs from what is found in Middle Platonist philosophers, since the system of world-generation posited by Plotinus is one of 'procession' and 'return'. So the One does not generate as the result of conscious activity, in the same way that the Demiurge does, but rather overflows, producing the next ontological level, which orders itself in response to the One above. Similarly, the Gnostic conception differs in regarding the Demiurge as either evil or ignorant and placing him in opposition to the First Principle. In Numenius, by contrast, the Demiurge collaborates with the First Principle. Admittedly, the Gnostic version is in many ways the ultimate development of Numenius' insistence on a distinction between the

---

[1] Baltes and Dörrie also collected and commented upon relevant Bausteine: especially relevant in this context are Bausteine 125–35 on the Theory of Forms, Bausteine 136–45 (the generation of the world) and Bausteine 146–50 (the elements) in Dörrie and Baltes 1998 and Baustein 159 (the generation of soul) in Dörrie and Baltes 2002.

First God, who is the First Principle and the Second God, who is the Demiurge.

The situation is further complicated by the appropriation of aspects of demiurgy by members of the Judaeo–Christian tradition as a mechanism for providing a 'scientific' exegesis of the creational account of *Genesis*. The two most notable proponents are Philo and Origen, although St Basil is also influenced by demiurgy in his *Hexaemeron* and he, like Calcidius in his great commentary on the *Timaeus*, is more heavily influenced by the Middle Platonist variant, rather than by Neoplatonism.[2] Since a dichotomy even between Judaeo–Christian creation and Platonic demiurgy has not been observed, how then do we set about defining the concept?

The first question is the issue of terminology. The noun *demiourgos*, 'craftsman', and the verb *demiourgein*, 'to labour like a craftsman', are both frequently used by thinkers influenced by this concept. St Basil describes the world as *demiourgia* or craftsmanship. Since this term before Plato would have been somewhat strange to use in reference to God, we can identify in such terminology the influence of the *Timaeus*. This does not help with our definition, since it could be argued that Plato's influence merely helped to develop a common language, without necessarily referring to an identical concept, and furthermore that this had simply become part of the philosophical heritage of the period, rather than as the result of any more extensive legacy. Indeed not all accounts which are influenced by demiurgy refer to their instrumental cause as a Demiurge. Numenius clearly posits a demiurgic figure, even though he refers to him as a Second God. Philo's demiurgic entity is called the *Logos* and Origen's instrumental cause is the Son-*Logos* (although he applies the title of 'Demiurge' to the Father and describes the Son as the 'immediate Demiurge'). Calcidius also never uses the Latin loan-word *demiurgus* to translate the Greek *demiourgos* and in both his translation and his commentary prefers to use words like *opifex* or *fabricator*. Using the imagery of craftsmanship to represent a divine entity when describing world-generation might seem like a more promising definition. That runs into difficulties when one considers that God in the creation accounts of *Genesis* (*Gen.* 1:1–2:4a and *Gen.* 2:4b*ff*) is described as a potter or builder and clearly we are not dealing with either the ordering of pre-existent matter or a text influenced by the *Timaeus*.

In spite of this, analysis of the texts reveals a shared heritage, not just amongst Middle Platonist thinkers, but even in the Christian and

---

[2] St Basil uses the demiurgic image to highlight God's sympathy for artisans, since He is one too and presents the Son as the demiurgic power, while the Father is the final cause, much like Origen, even if elsewhere in the *Hexaemeron* he adopts an anti-philosophical stance. See O'Brien, C. S.: 2011.

Gnostic traditions. However, beyond stating that the Demiurge performs the intellective activity of ordering matter, which is pre-existent, according to a model which is also pre-existent and that this ordering takes place on rational lines, i.e. according to geometric or mathematical principles, there is no coherent system of demiurgy. What can be demonstrated is that the thinkers surveyed here are influenced by the *Timaeus*, rather than presenting unrelated speculations on world-generation. Clearly Philo and Origen's understanding of the Creation does not derive entirely from the spontaneous sort of activity described in the Biblical accounts, and their attempt to integrate a noetic realm with the *Genesis* account can only have arisen under Platonic influence.

Demiurgy cannot be reduced to a single, coherent pattern, since the motif was exploited by such a range of thinkers. Even within Platonism, Plutarch and Atticus do not demote the Demiurge to a second-rank figure as Numenius does. However, the unity of my thesis is that while there are different representations of demiurgy, this is as a result of divergent readings of the *Timaeus*. Therefore, the present study is justified, not just because it examines the *Nachleben* of one of Western philosophy's most influential works, but because it reveals the use made of Plato to solve an important question: how did the world as we know it come to be?[3] However, that does not mean a range of atomised opinions. Certain trends emerge. Frequently, for example, the Demiurge produces the world as the result of his goodness. He desires that the world should be as good as possible, and achieves this by bringing order to the disordered elements. The Demiurge may also function as an intermediary between the higher, noetic world and the sublunar, material realm.[4] However, any attempt at a definition does not exhaust the complexity of the demiurgic notion or truly account for the various ways in which it is exploited. It is also misleading to represent those who exploit the motif as conceiving demiurgy as part of a coherent system; rather they respond differently to the questions raised and the intellectual challenges posed by the *Timaeus*. Modern exegeses of the dialogue have similarly failed to reach a consensus.

Influence of the Stoic Logos

Having attempted to define demiurgy and having at least managed to delineate some of its most pervasive features, the next step is to consider

---

[3] The *Timaeus* also raises the subsidiary question: why was it designed that way?
[4] O'Brien, C. S.: 2007b, 60

why such an approach to world-generation should prove inconsequential in the Old Academy, only to re-emerge again in the first century AD. Demiurgy ceased to be of interest within the Old Academy, since it no longer favoured the Theory of Forms, without which there is not much need for a Demiurge to instantiate Forms in the material realm. The Demiurge's return to prominence, on the other hand, may be traced to the fact that he proved useful in the academic climate of the first to third centuries, as a means of accommodating dualistic systems which were popular during this period.

In any case, the Demiurge did not simply disappear, but persisted in the Stoic concept of the *Logos*, as a rational divine element which assisted with the better ordering of the world. This Stoic contribution to the interpretation of the *Timaeus* has been conclusively demonstrated by Gretchen Reydams-Schils' 1999 study *Demiurge and Providence*. It might appear counterintuitive to suggest that the Stoics played an important role in cosmological theory, since they displayed such limited interest in the area in the period following Posidonius. However, this is mainly due to their reliance on the doxographical codification of their viewpoints, and, as Lapidge points out, the resultant lack of an adequate expertise in cosmology to respond to the criticisms of figures like Plutarch leaves us with a highly biased account of the technical level of Stoic cosmology.[5] The Stoics were also less interested in cosmology once it seemed to be less important for achieving their ethical objectives. Cosmology could be justified if the *telos* of life was to bring oneself into harmony with the cosmos, but as the Stoics began to adopt an increasingly more realistic understanding of the minor role which man played in the cosmos as a whole, interest in this discipline waned. The Stoics, though, are an important intermediary stage in the development and transmission of demiurgy.

Plato in the *Timaeus* presents world-generation in two different ways, the more famous of which is the account of a Craftsman-god toiling at fashioning the universe, and the description of Reason and Necessity can be regarded as complementary to this. The second, less celebrated image is a biological one – the Receptacle is described as the mother and nurse of all. The Stoics use the language of the technological image, but ultimately reject it in favour of the biological one, which is enriched with appropriations from Aristotle's theory of sexual generation. In his important article 'Nature as Craftsman in Greek Thought', Friedrich Solmsen demonstrates that both images of world-generation, that of craftsmanship and procreation,

---

[5] Lapidge: 1973, 240

actually precede Plato, but the primary model in Greek cosmogony is the biological one. This is illustrated by the marriages of various deities in the earliest Greek cosmogony which we possess: Hesiod's *Theogony*. However, it should be noted that both there and in the *Works and Days*, Hephaestus fashions the first woman, meaning that both technical and biological concepts co-exist from the beginning of Greek speculations in this area.

Empedocles too uses an image that can be regarded as demiurgic in his description of earth 'receiving in broad melting pots two portions of water and four of fire'.[6] Plato's Demiurge echoes elements of Anaxagoras' *Nous* to the extent that they are both ordering Intellects. As Anaxagoras comments 'mind also devised this orderly revolution in which now the stars, the sun and the moon revolve'.[7] Despite this, Solmsen concludes that 'the Demiurge of Plato's *Timaeus* is a conception much too original to be explained as a synthesis of earlier thinkers' ideas'.[8] It is not that Plato's Demiurge is merely a Mind that orders, rather he is capable of deliberately pursuing rational choices in order to further his objectives. For example, he chooses a skull constructed of bone, rather than flesh, as this will endow humans with greater rational capacity, thereby furthering his objective of a cosmos with increased order and intelligibility (*Tim.* 75b).

The Stoics distinguish between an active and a passive principle, which can be described in various ways – as God or *Logos* and matter or as fire and moisture. Despite this, the Stoics adopt a monistic approach, similar to that of the pre-Socratics. Their two principles do not exist independently of each other and the distinction is essentially just one which is made in thought, rather than observable in actuality. While it may seem evident that that which acts could not possibly have much of a role to play without that which is acted upon, such an argument provides another weapon in the arsenal of those engaged in polemical attacks against the Stoics, who are already vulnerable as a result of what appears to be a failure to differentiate properly between principles, such as God and matter, and elements, such as fire and water.

In any case, the Stoics account for two of the principles of the *Timaeus*, but positively reject its third principle, the Forms. In their version, God is immanent:

> The Stoics also criticise Plato for having said that since the models of all
> things exist in a venerable, pre-existent and ancient substance, the sensible

[6] Fr. 31b Diels-Kranz, trans. Solmsen.
[7] Fr. 59b12 Diels-Kranz, trans. Solmsen.   [8] Solmsen: 1963, 480

world was made by God according to an immortal model. For, in fact, there is no need for an immortal model, according to them, since the seminal reason, which pervades another nature, which takes hold of it and apprehends it, has brought forth the whole world and everything which is in it. (Calcidius, *In Tim.*, 294, p. 296, 11–162)

The Stoic model is a different one: there is no separation between God and his product, since Reason works from within Matter. Once Matter is regarded as passive, it detracts somewhat from God's accomplishment. He no longer has to labour at world-generation and it becomes an effortless activity. This immanence can be regarded as a failure to distinguish between God and Matter: 'The Stoics believed that God is either matter or is even an inseparable quality of matter and that he passes through matter just as semen through the genitals' (Calcidius, *In. Tim.* 294, p. 296, 19–297.3 (= *SVF* 1.87)). The terminology does, however, reveal the influence of the Platonist demiurgic image. One has to only consider passages such as 'fire, functioning as a craftsman [*technikôs*] proceeds on a course towards genera-tion' (*SVF* 1.171 = DL 7.156; *cf.* *SVF* 2.1027), fire referring to God or nature. Similarly, God is described as 'producing like a craftsman (δημιουργεῖν) every single thing throughout all matter' (DL 7.134). As Zeno comments: 'whatever in the execution of our craftsmanship is carried out by hand, Nature accomplishes much more skilfully, by the crafting fire, so to speak, the teacher of the remaining crafts' (*SVF* 1.171 = Cicero, *ND* 11.57).

The parallel in the Stoic mind between cosmogony and procreation is evident: 'just as the sperm is contained in the engendering fluid, in such a manner does God, as the generative *logos* (reason/forming principle) of the cosmos, remain behind in the moisture making matter easy to work for Him for the subsequent generation' (DL 7.136). An important mediator between the technological and biological images is Aristotle, who referred to the sperm as a craftsman at *GA* 1.22.730b5–32.[9] He also compares the seed to a moving tool which can bring form to matter through its motion (though by this Aristotle means the actualisation of a potentiality). Aristotle notes 'it does not make a difference to say "engendering fluid" or "movement responsible for the growth of each of the parts". For the *logos* (formative principle) of the movement is the same' (*GA* 4.3.767b18–20). Despite Aristotle's criticism of the demiurgic model, he everywhere betrays its influence. He distinguishes between Reason and Necessity, as Plato does, and numerous details, such as the diaphragm serving as a partition between the exalted and more degraded parts of the body are clearly drawn from

---

[9] Todd: 1978, 144; Hahm: 1977, 73.

the *Timaeus*.[10] Aristotle compares *pneuma* to a multifunctional instrument (*polychreston organon*) in *GA* 5, where it is also described as a hammer or anvil.[11] As Solmsen notes, even in his disagreements with Plato, Aristotle betrays his influence: Plato asserts at *Tim.* 74a7–d2 that flesh was produced as a protective covering for bone, whereas Aristotle at *PA* 2.9 inverts this by claiming that bone was designed as a support for flesh.[12]

For Aristotle, there was no need to posit a craftsman who worked upon nature, but rather nature itself was capable of directing itself towards a teleological function: 'wherever there is an end (*telos*), the preceeding and subsequent steps are undertaken for the sake of this end. For just as in (human) undertakings, so too in nature, and as it is in nature, so it is in (human) undertakings, if nothing prevents it. And (human) undertakings aim at an end and nature too aims at an end' (Arist. *Phys.* 2.8.199a8*ff.*). Even though there is no need for the image of a Demiurge, nature itself in Aristotle's account is envisaged as working like a craftsman, with analogies drawn from a variety of occupations. As Solmsen notes, each of these analogies tends to be self-contained; there is no attempt to assemble them within a coherent overarching scheme, as Plato does with the Demiurge. To be more accurate, it is not that nature works like a craftsman, but that craftsmen imitate nature (as stated at *Phys.* 2.8.199a15*ff.*)[13] and also at *Phys.* 2.8.199a12*ff.*: 'if a house were made by nature, it would come into being as now it does by craftsmanship and if those things which nature produces were not generated only by nature, but also by craftsmanship, they would be generated just as they are by nature.' This does not imply that nature considers the 'end' of its productions, as Plato's Demiurge does; the spider does not do so when it weaves a web or the swallow when it builds its nest.[14] Solmsen sees a further trace of Aristotle's Academic heritage in his choice of the term ὕλη to mean matter, although the term literally means wood, but this is an obvious choice for the material of a craftsman, particularly if one envisages him as a carpenter fabricating a bed, as Plato does at *Rep.* x.

Aristotle applied this conception of nature to his theory of sexual genera-tion. The father does not supply any material content to his offspring; that is supplied by the mother. The father's contribution is to shape this material 'just as from the carpenter nothing passes into the timber, his material, and no physical part of the art of carpentry is present in the product, what is

---

[10] Solmsen: 1963 cites numerous examples of these similarities: On the distinction between Reason and Necessity, 'Nature is in the class of purpose clauses', Arist. *Phys.* 2.198b10*ff.*

[11] *GA* 5.8.789b6–13   [12] Solmsen: 1963, 486

[13] As Solmsen points out (Solmsen: 1963, 488) a similar attitude is expressed in Democritus 68B154.

[14] Solmsen: 1963, 488

due to the carpenter is the shape and form...' (*GA* 1.22.730b9–15, trans. Solmsen).

By using this biological theory, the Stoics can present world-generation in terms of sexual intercourse:

> Zeus, mindful of Aphrodite and genesis, grew softer and having arrived at this point and having extinguished much of his light, he turned himself into fiery air of a milder fire. And having engaged in intercourse with Hera... he ejected the complete engendering fluid of the universe. And he made the substance (*ousia*) wet, a single seed of the universe, running through it himself, just like the moulding and demiurgic breath (*pneuma*) in the engendering fluid. At this point, he is composed so as to resemble most closely the other living beings, since he might be accurately said to be composed of soul and body. He then easily shaped and moulded the remaining things, having poured the smooth and soft substance around himself. (*SVF* 2.622 = Dio Chrysost. *Or.* xxxvi §55)

So the Stoics drew not just upon Aristotelian biological theory and the biological theory of the *Timaeus*, but also upon the Greek cosmogonical tradition, to form their cosmobiology. After all, the idea of equating fire with *Logos* can be found in Heraclitus. While they reject a demiurgic model, the imprint of the *Timaeus* can easily be observed. Plato too regards the cosmos as a living being. Like Plato, the Stoics also drew a distinction between two cosmic levels. Again, it is problematic to see how one might draw such a divide in a pantheistic system, if God is meant to be immanent in all of matter, although the Stoics are able to explain it through parallelism with the human soul: 'mind pervades every part of it, just as the soul pervades our bodies. But some parts it pervades to a greater extent and others less. Some parts it passes through as a '*hexis*' or bond, just like the bones and sinews and through other parts like mind, just like the command centre' (*SVF* 2.634 = DL 7.138).

This command centre or *hēgemonikon* is the Stoic equivalent of the Platonic intellect, where *pneuma*, used as an equivalent of God or *Logos* in certain contexts, occurs in such a concentration that it provides the ability to think.[15] It therefore exists in the human soul (*SVF* 2.458), meaning that for the Stoics, as for Plato, the human soul is a microcosm of the world. The idea of the world being regulated by a *pneuma* is clearly influenced by the notion of the Platonic World-Soul, which is the metaphysical system Plato posits in the *Timaeus*, if one decides to demythologise the Demiurge. Zeno drew a distinction between heavenly fire, where he located God (*SVF*

---

[15] Lapidge: 1973, 171

1.154) and the sublunar realm, and Chrysippus too observed a distinction, even if his pronouncements are a little confusing, locating God both in the *aether* (*SVF* 2.579) and in the purest part of the *aether* (*SVF* 2.644), though naturally both of these statements can be regarded as consistent.

So the basic Stoic position is that a πῦρ τεχνικόν, a crafting-fire, transforms part of itself into water or matter and that subsequently acting upon this it produces the four elements, and at the end of the cosmic cycle the universe dissolves back again into a πῦρ τεχνικόν which consumes it. It is easy to see that such a position creates numerous problems: (1) How can fire and water be regarded as principles and subsequently as elements? (2) The Stoic concept of *ekpyrosis* resolves an issue that Plato had left live in the *Timaeus*, namely why God should spontaneously decide to generate the world, by contextualising it as an event within a cosmic cycle, but it does not manage to escape from related weaknesses. What does God do in the period between *ekpyrosis* and world-generation? (3) From a Platonist perspective, there is a difficulty with God's immanence in the world and his operation directly upon matter, without mediation.

To be fair, the Stoic system does have the advantage of ensuring that if Providence is immanent in the world, the way the cosmos is ordered is the best sort of arrangement,[16] (or if one wishes to be pessimistic, it is a matter of indifference, but any other arrangement would equally be a matter of indifference). Plato, admittedly, regards the Demiurge as producing the best possible world, but it is a world where the Demiurge is constrained by factors outside of his control. As Cicero's Epicurean at *De Natura Deorum* 1.19 comments in a mocking reference to the Platonists, it does appear to be beneath God's dignity to have to labour at world-generation. The Demiurge seems to be a particularly unfortunate image, when one of the advantages of positing a Demiurge in the first place is that it can be used to avoid placing the First Principle in parts of the cosmos which might be regarded as beneath its dignity to go:

> For you yourselves are accustomed to say that there is nothing which is impossible for a god to achieve, and without any labour, just as the limbs of a man are moved without a struggle by his mind and desire, in this way you say that the power of the gods can shape and move and change things. And you do not say this as a superstition or old wives' tale, but as a scientific and consistent account; for the matter of things, from which and in which all things are, is entirely flexible and changeable, so that there is nothing which cannot, however suddenly, be formed and changed out of it and the shaper

---

[16] Long: 2010, 47

and the regulator of this universal material is divine providence, therefore wherever Providence moves it is able to achieve whatever it wishes. (Cicero, *ND* 3.92)

The influence of the Stoic *Logos* can be clearly seen in Philo, Plutarch and Origen's conception of the Demiurge (even if in the case of Plutarch it can be conceived of as a reaction against the Stoics).

Additionally, the Demiurge in the first to third centuries is represented as an intermediate entity, midway between matter and the Forms. For Plato, the Demiurge is a paradigm himself, even though he looks to a model. He fashions the cosmos like himself (*Tim.* 29e), and in the procession of souls in the *Phaedrus* (252d), each soul follows the god who is its paradigm. As Doherty points out, though, there is an ambiguity in Plato concerning whether the paradigm exists in the mind of the artisan or whether it is an external model.[17] For example, at *Rep.* VI.501b, the legislator uses nature and just men as his models, yet at 561e, the democratic man has the models of different sorts of constitutions within himself. The issue seems to become more of a problem under Aristotelian influence. For Aristotle, the paradigm referred to the *Logos* immanent in the mind of the artisan at *Physics* (194b24) and *Metaphysics* (1013a27).[18] So irrespective of whether the Forms are considered as a separate noetic world, or as the thoughts of God (as the Middle Platonists would have it), the Demiurge 'must possess them intentionally in order to act efficiently'.[19] So only once these Forms enter into the mind of the Demiurge can he function as a Demiurge. This aspect of the Demiurge's activity is illustrated by his contemplation of the Forms, as found, for example, in Numenius. This intermediate role is relevant in accounting both for the Demiurge's original activity of world-generation (if one posits a temporal creation) and the mechanics of demiurgy (the manner in which the Demiurge engages in the continuous ordering of matter to ensure the functioning of the world). It is particularly problematic for Christian thinkers, who adopt the Demiurge, to explain the Demiurge's intermediate status, before the exact position of Christ within the Trinity had been defined.

The Christian aspect

Alongside the twin models of demiurgy and biology, Stoicism and Platonism both display the attempt to grapple with the issues of God's transcendence or immanence. To put it simply, the more involved in the world

---

[17] Doherty: 1960, 62   [18] Doherty: 1960, 63   [19] Kroll, 1902. *Cf.* Doherty: 1960, 58

God is, the more his 'otherness' and separation from the world becomes obscured, whereas the more one emphasises his transcendence, the greater the difficulty in explaining how God works on the world and the greater the risk of regarding him as completely isolated from us and with little concern for the material realm. This problem perplexed not just Greek philosophers, but caused even greater difficulty for Christian thinkers, who are faced with the Incarnation as a radical divine intervention in the material realm. It has still proved difficult to explain Christ's involvement in creation to the present day: the term 'cosmic Christ', which can refer to Christ as an 'instrument in God's creative activity' (amongst other meanings), only goes back to the 1960s and its antecedents to the 1830s.[20] This belies a history of attempts to reconcile God's creative activity with 'scientific' theories; the endeavours of Origen to explain it in terms of Greek cosmology can be regarded as the antecedent for the work of the French Jesuit Pierre Teilhard de Chardin, who similarly sought to develop a Christology which would take account of contemporary cosmological views.[21] (The comparison is made more poignant by the hostility which they both faced within the Church, as well as the attempts to suppress their work.)

The Christians are further forced to explain Jesus' relationship to God. Did he remain God, but simply appear human (Docetism), in which case he never suffered, but only appeared to, undermining the nature of his sacrifice and denying his humanity? Perhaps he was just a man (Ebionitism), although one can claim that he was adopted by God during his baptism at the Jordan?[22] Here one either denies Christ's divinity or if one regards his divinity as accorded by God through Adoptionism, it means that Jesus was not divine by nature. If there is an advantage to asserting that Jesus is either a man or God (but not both), it is that it allows his nature to be explained without having recourse to metaphysics.[23]

It is easy to see why Christians might not be keen to embrace either position. Jesus' humanity and divinity are both core Christian beliefs, stressed in the New Testament writers, and to emphasise either one at the expense of the other seems to undermine Biblical authority. If Jesus is truly regarded as the Son of God (rather than interpreting this as a title), the Son must have existed before the Incarnation (since Christians, amongst others,

---

[20] Lyons: 1982, 1   [21] Lyons: 1982, 5

[22] By regarding Jesus as adopted as lord of the angels, the Ebionites clearly regard Jesus as more than an ordinary man, although the term Ebionitism is probably applied in Christological discourse in an historically inaccurate sense, which also implies that they had no metaphysical ideas. *Cf.* Spence: 2008, 11–12.

[23] Spence: 2008, 12

believe in the immutability of God).[24] This difficulty explains the appeal of a figure such as the Demiurge, particularly once Justin Martyr identified the Son with the *Logos* of God, a concept already existing in Jewish thought. Such an identification has numerous advantages. The *Logos*, according to Justin, had revealed the nature of God to pagan thinkers (to a limited extent) in the past and by becoming Incarnate, had made him known to those who embraced Christianity. It explained both the pre-existence of the Son and how the Son could be related to the godhead and yet preserve monotheism. Just as when someone utters a word, it can be viewed as having a separate existence and yet remaining part of him, the same is the case with the Word of God. The Hebrew term is *dabar*, meaning both 'word' and 'deed' – this allows both concepts to be more firmly united:[25] God revealed himself through his Word, but also his act (the Incarnation).

However, such an identification can be regarded as creating problems of its own: 'it gave metaphysical significance to an historical faith, it drew into the domain of cosmology and religious philosophy a person who had appeared in time and space . . . Most of us regard this identification as inadmissible, because the way in which we perceive the world and ethics does not point to the existence of any *logos* at all.'[26] Spence essentially refers to a similar problem when he comments in reference to Christians worshipping both one God and an historical figure that 'most Jews and Muslims regard such devotion to an historical person as both absurd and impious, if not blasphemous. Christians seem generally far less conscious of just how odd or paradoxical their religion looks from the outside.'[27] (Christians can, of course, turn this to their advantage. The *Logos* was involved in the material realm during creation and in making God known, to a limited extent, to the Jews and pagans before Christ. The Incarnation becomes just a continuation of this divine activity, rather than a manifestation of the divine nature's alteration.)

Once such an identification is made, theories concerning Christ need to explore metaphysical options. It also means that the figure of the Demiurge was of interest to those attempting to explain Christ's interaction on the world. Since Philo had already posited the *Logos* as a mediating instrument, drawing upon Jewish thought, as well as the Stoic concept of the *logos spermatikos* and the Platonic Demiurge, there was already a basis for explaining Christ's activity in terms of a secondary, mediating entity, once the Son and *Logos* had been identified (as in Origen's Son-*Logos*). This

---

[24] Actually Tertullian avoids this when he states 'God can change into all things and still remain as he is' (*De Carne Christi* 3.4–6).

[25] Smulders: 1968, 8   [26] von Harnack: 1900, 128   [27] Spence: 2008, 3

also allowed Christian thinkers to draw upon Platonic formulations for preserving God's transcendence, while explaining his interaction on the world (through the form of divine mediators).

There is of course an overlap in methodology between the approaches of those operating within a Biblical tradition, such as Philo and Origen, and pagans such as Numenius. Philo with his theories concerning God and the *Logos*, Origen with his *epinoiai* and Numenius in his doctrine of three gods posit modes of divinity; the positing of hypostases was an important technique during the first to third centuries.[28] In many ways, it is a natural mechanism for preserving divine transcendence while explaining demiurgic activity upon matter. This modalistic approach allows greater cohesion: as Numenius puts it 'all is in all, but in each appropriately to its nature.'[29] As Kenny notes, this 'telescoping' of metaphysical levels into each other, coupled with the connections posited between them helps to maintain the relationship between them.[30] This technique has obvious utilty for those committed to a monotheistic world-view and explains its popularity amongst those of a Jewish or Christian background. Rather than each mode representing a separate god, it can be used as a mechanism to distinguish between degrees of divinity.[31] Obviously, in Gnosticism, the opposite tendency prevails and the Demiurge is completely separated from the godhead.

Thinkers investigated and criteria for selection

In tracing the development of this concept, my aim has been to consider thinkers from a range of traditions who taken as a group illustrate the variety of speculations on world-generation underpinned by the *Timaeus*. This explains the perhaps surprising inclusion of Maximus of Tyre. Although he deals with the topic in a superficial manner, he does provide good evidence for the understanding of demiurgy in Middle Platonism. The *Chaldean Oracles*, though replete with a satisfying, complex system of divine mediators, such as Teletarchs, Connectors and Iynges, have not been included, precisely because, although figures such as Porphyry or Damascius regarded them as carrying the same authority as Plato's *Timaeus*, their significance is felt to a greater extent on these later Neoplatonists than upon the period in question, contrasting with the situation regarding Gnosticism.

---

[28] Kenny: 1991, 58*ff.*   [29] Fr. 41, trans. Kenny.
[30] Kenny: 1991, 65–6   [31] Kenny: 1991, 72

It suffices to note some points of interest regarding the *Chaldean Oracles*. Firstly, the Chaldean supreme God resembles the Numenian First God in so far as he is a self-contemplating intellect. Secondly, while the tortuous ontological scheme parallels the same phenomenon in Gnosticism, these divine mediators are evocative of the Platonic world of the Forms. For example, the Iynges resemble the thoughts of God. Despite the points of Middle Platonist re-evaluation of Plato's metaphysics illustrated by the *Chaldean Oracles*, it has seemed preferable to focus rather on the Gnostic and Hermetic traditions.

A further investigation on the influence of the *Timaeus* upon Philo after Runia's magisterial monograph might seem to require justification. However, an analysis of the development of the demiurgic concept in Middle Platonism could not be said to be complete without an analysis of the originality (or lack thereof) of Philo's contribution. This is more evidently the case in a study of demiurgy in the Christian, Gnostic and Hermetic traditions, since Philo can to a certain extent be viewed as a link between these 'Biblical' or 'pseudo-Biblical' traditions and mainstream Greek philosophy. Philo is treated in his chronological position, which has resulted in him being somewhat separated from other interpreters of *Genesis*, but also helps to highlight his somewhat unusual position and the rather strange circumstance that the first witness to the notion of demiurgy in later Platonism is not, strictly speaking, a Platonist at all.

It might be felt (and with a certain degree of reason, I might add) that not enough attention has been paid to the role of soul in world-generation and its interaction with the sensible realm.[32] Such a topic would be extensive enough to form the basis for a monograph in its own right. Although the Demiurge does produce (or distills) soul and then inserts it into matter (assuming that one accepts the demiurgic myth), Plato never concerns himself excessively with the interaction of soul upon matter. Although soul is assigned a central role in *Laws* x, a detailed account of the manner in which it fulfils its functions is not supplied. It has also been less of concern amongst the thinkers assembled here, though Origen does consider the matter and Plutarch in the *De Iside et Osiride* appears to touch upon it. In my defence, I have focused upon the issues which most exercised the interest of 'the heirs of Plato', to borrow Dillon's phrase, which I examine here: issues such as the causality of the Demiurge and the functioning of secondary gods and divine mediators within their metaphysical systems.

---

[32] For the development of the doctrine of soul in the Platonic tradition, see Dillon and El-Kaisy-Friemuth: 2009, Deuse: 1985 and Dörrie and Baltes: 1998.

On the issue of soul, Plato was more concerned with the role it played in relation to Time and Eternity than upon matter, but this issue is largely ignored by the Middle Platonist period, although it did influence the Neoplatonic theory of soul.

I have identified the following main areas where the influence of the Demiurge of the *Timaeus* may be most strongly discerned: (1) the relation of the Demiurge to the First Principle, (2) the actual causality of the Demiurge and his interaction with matter, (3) the ontological status of the Forms, (4) the question of the origin of evil and (5) other factors which limit the influence of the Demiurge (such as Providence, Necessity or other entities). However, it is not always practical to deal with each of these aspects in the precise order outlined above.

Indeed, this schema is perhaps somewhat misleading since it implies a degree of systematisation in theorising about the Demiurge, which could not be said to be present in each of the instances examined. Most notable in this regard are the Gnostic and Hermetic traditions, inclusion of which requires some justification, since it would seem to stray beyond the boundaries of philosophy or classical philology into the realm of heresiology or comparative religion. However, the increase of our knowledge of Gnosticism and Hermetism has been one of the most exciting twentieth-century developments in this area. While the Nag Hammadi Library was discovered in 1945, it was only as recently as 1977 that publication commenced. Even the great works of Festugière (1950) and Jonas (1958 and 1963) were unable to wholly take into account the Nag Hammadi corpus, and it has fallen to a new generation of Gnostic scholars to consider the full impact of these works. Indeed, academic prejudice and a quasi-religious disdain for 'heretical' texts considerably undermined research into this area and the only thoroughly 'modern' studies of Gnosticism with implications for Platonism have been Pétrement's *A Separate God* (1991)[33] and the 1997 study edited by Van den Broek and Hanagraaf: *Gnosis and Hermetism – From Antiquity until Modern Times.* Bentley Layton and John Turner have not only been important commentators, contextualising the Gnostic phenomenon within its intellectual milieu, but have also played a major role in making these texts available; one has only to think of Layton's *The Gnostic Scriptures* (1987) or Turner's valuable translations and commentaries for *The Nag Hammadi Library in English* (1977) or *The Coptic Gnostic Library* (1990).[34]

---

[33] The original French study was published in 1984.
[34] Turner's translations and commentaries include *The Book of Thomas the Contender, the Interpretation of Knowledge, A Valentinian Exposition, Allogenes, Hypsiphrone* and *The Trimorphic Protennoia*, in

The same phenomenon can be observed with the *Corpus Hermeticum*, which dropped out of the ambit of classical scholarship after Casaubon discovered that it was not as old as it claimed to be. This changed when a Coptic version found at Nag Hammadi forced a reappraisal. To a certain extent, justifying the Gnostic and Hermetic traditions as a serious subject of academic study would appear to be a moot point after John Dillon's *The Middle Platonists* (1977), which rehabilitated the 'Platonic Underworld', the intellectual milieu of several Gnostic thinkers, as a legitimate subject for research. I have concentrated almost exclusively on Valentinus in my survey of Gnosticism, since he represents the Gnostic branch with the greatest concentration of Platonic elements.

In brief, the combination of thinkers analysed here represents the various traditions which attempted to make the *Timaeus* or the concepts expressed therein their own. Not only can one observe an attempt in subsequent thinkers to explain or to resolve the philosophical issues raised by the dialogue, which can occasionally sit uncomfortably with the desire to reconcile it with a particular tradition or allegiance; one also observes the emergence of certain trends throughout its progression. The separation of the demiurgic function from the role of the highest principle, beginning with Numenius (although it can be traced right back to the Young Gods of the *Timaeus*), leads to the emergence of an increasingly elaborate chain of entities insulating the highest principle from the Demiurge. In a sense, both the Christian tradition and Platonism bring this development to an end. For Christianity, multiple creators could easily be accommodated by the framework of the Trinity (although careless formulations can seem to undermine the role of the Father as final cause), while the Neoplatonist notion of automatic emanation by the One effectively broke away from the concept of the Demiurge as the primary agent of world-generation altogether.

The Nag Hammadi Library in English; third completely revised edition, ed. R. Smith and J. M. Robinson, San Francisco: Harper & Row and Leiden: E. J. Brill, 1988; and Nag Hammadi Codices XI, XII and XIII in *The Coptic Gnostic Library Edited with English Translation, Introduction and Notes;* ed. C. W. Hedrick, *Nag Hammadi Studies* 28, Leiden: E. J. Brill, 1990, reprinted in Vol. 5 of *The Coptic Gnostic Library: A Complete Edition of the Nag Hammadi Codices,* Leiden: E. J. Brill, 1981–90.

CHAPTER 2

Plato's Timaeus, *the original concept of the Demiurge and the exegesis of the dialogue*

The *Timaeus*

According to a malicious story which seems to have originated with the satirist Timon of Phlius (c. 325–235 BC), Plato was so desperate to learn Pythagorean metaphysics that he paid 'many pieces of silver' (apparently a hundred *minae*) for a book of little worth, which he then attempted to pass off as his own. This anecdote illustrates the regard in which the *Timaeus* was held in antiquity — although non-Platonists regarded it as 'worthless', they still saw it as important enough to attack). Even at the height of the Renaissance, Raphael could envisage Plato in *The School of Athens*, carrying the '*Timeo*' under his arm and pointing with his upraised index-finger to the sky, indicating his contribution to metaphysics.

To a certain extent, the *Timaeus* had a disproportionate influence upon subsequent Platonism, partly due to the perception that it was Plato's only 'physical' dialogue, but more importantly because in the medieval period (until the thirteenth century) the tenets of Plato were known, mainly from a Latin version of the first two-thirds of the dialogue by Calcidius and the *Consolatio* of Boethius, as well as an exegesis of Cicero's *Somnium Scipionis* by Macrobius, both of which drew heavily upon the *Timaeus*. The Neoplatonists regarded it as one of only two perfect dialogues:[1] perfect because it dealt with the highest aspects of metaphysics. Perhaps the only individual of note to dispute the authenticity of the work was the German philosopher Schelling, in *Philosophie und Religion* (*Werke v. 36*), because he disliked its dualism. However, Schelling later recanted his 'heresy' (*Werke vii 371*) in deference to Boeckh.[2] In spite of this, comparatively little was published on the *Timaeus* in the early twentieth century. The most notable exceptions were the commentaries by A. E. Taylor (1928) and F. M. Cornford (1937), although one might mention that the dialogue has returned to greater prominence in recent years.

---

[1] The other is the *Parmenides*.   [2] Taylor: 1928, 1

18

The *Timaeus* is, perhaps, most noted as the text which introduces the Demiurge. When the Demiurge finally appears, he is, to quote Dillon, 'a bizarre figure, introduced in a bizarre manner'.[3] The term *dêmiourgos* is itself surprising – one might expect such a character to be rather grandly titled *Nous* or *Logos*. At Athens, the craftsman was either a slave or if free, one who acquired a certain stigma as a result of his proximity to slaves. Plato himself excludes the *dêmiourgos* from political participation (*Republic*) and citizenship (*Laws*) as does Aristotle (*Politics*). Vlastos rightly calls this terminology the 'triumph of the philosophical imagination over ingrained social prejudice'.[4] He views the *dêmiourgos* as the stereotypical Platonic artist imposing pre-existing form on matter, not inventing new form.

The dialogue first uses the term *dêmiourgos* ('Craftsman') at 28a6, although there it seems to me that it does not signify 'the Demiurge' in a specialised sense, but rather a generic craftsman, or as Cornford so accurately translates 'the maker of anything'. Admittedly, Plato has previously used *dêmiourgos* to represent the God (*Rep.* VII.530a and *Soph.* 265b), but there the context was different. In the *Cratylus* (389a–b), the good *dêmiourgos* when constructing a new shuttle takes as his model not the broken shuttle, nor even an unbroken shuttle, but the Form of Shuttle. The *dêmiourgos* is then subsequently introduced as the cosmic Creator, by sleight of hand, in the Platonic tradition of converting illustrative analogy into fact without an intervening stage. A similar technique was employed at *Rep.* II.375a–376b when the guard dog analogy was suddenly adopted as the defining requirement for the Auxiliary class.

The Demiurge of the Platonic dialogues

The term *dêmiourgos* is not introduced for the first time at *Tim.* 28a6. At *Gorgias* 455a2, rhetoric is a πειθοῦς δημιουργός, while at *Sym.* 188d, it is prophecy (μαντική) that is considered to be a *dêmiourgos*. The *Republic* paves the way for the introduction of the Demiurge in the *Timaeus*. At *Rep.* VI.507c6–8, reference is made to the artificer of the eyes, while at *Rep.* VII.530a5–7, God is described as the artisan of heaven. At *Charm.* 174e, Temperance (σωφροσύνη) is said to be the producer (*dêmiourgos*) of health, while at *Euthyph.* 292d, the *dêmiourgos* is said to produce an effect neither good nor bad, though the word is clearly being used in a generic sense here and not to refer to the divine Craftsman. However, at

---

[3] Dillon: 1997, 27   [4] Vlastos: 1975, 26

Stat. 270a, we have a discussion of the role of the Demiurge in imposing order upon disorderly motion, and it seems that here, at least, Plato is beginning to move towards (or at the very least express openly) a concept approximating that of the Demiurge of the *Timaeus*.[5] Again at *Stat.* 273b, disorderly motion is presented as attempting to follow as closely as it can the instructions of its Demiurge and Father.

It is in the *Timaeus*, though, that the Demiurge is most comprehensively delineated. 27c–40d consists of a Prelude (27c–29d) and a discussion of basic metaphysical concepts, such as the Principles (29b–31b) and Body (31b–34c) of the World and Composition (34a–36c) and Functions (36e–40d) of the World-Soul. Other key components of the *Timaeus* which became important subsequently in delineating the concept of the Demiurge are the arrangement of the four elements in the cosmos by the Demiurge (32d), the guarantee of an everlasting world (41b), the Demiurge's delegation of responsibility to the Young Gods at 42d and the secondary production on the part of the Young Gods at 43a. Also important for subsequent Platonists is the discussion of Necessity (47e–53c), as well as the Platonic notion of space (the Receptacle) at 49b. The relevant section of the *Timaeus* ends at 57c–e with the generation of unmixed and primary bodies, while the dialogue then turns to deal with other physical matters, most notably the mechanisms by which the senses function.

There are two principal issues concerning any discussion of the Demiurge: the activity which is attributed to him by Plato on a literal reading and if the literal reading is denied, how the myth can be interpreted allegorically. Even a literal account of the Demiurge's activity is relatively complex. Faced with precosmic chaos, the Demiurge harmonises the four elements, using water and air as intermediate terms between fire and earth.[6] This harmonising by proportion (δι' ἀναλογίας ὁμολογῆσαν) is what brings the cosmos into existence, and the Demiurge shapes the cosmos into a sphere[7] and gives it circular motion.[8] To construct the soul (a prior activity, but recounted subsequently and with due apologies by Timaeus), the Demiurge produces three essences – Being, Sameness and Otherness.[9] The Demiurge cuts off

---

[5] 'But, as I said a little while ago, a single explanation remains, that the cosmos is conducted by an external and divine cause and obtaining life once again, it receives from the Demiurge (παρὰ τοῦ δημιουργοῦ) restored immortality and it remains by itself at another times and it moves by itself and during the period when it has been left to itself, it travels back again through a countless number of revolutions, because although it is extensive it revolves in a most balanced manner upon a very small axis.'

[6] *Tim.* 32c   [7] *Tim.* 33c   [8] *Tim.* 34c

[9] *Tim.* 35b. There are substances corresponding to the μέγιστα γένη of *Soph.* 244–5, allowing the soul to recognise the same, other and essence on the principle that like is known by like.

portions of this mixture in accordance with the mathematical series of 1, 2, 4, 8 and 1, 3, 9, 27, continuing to fill up the intervals until the mixture is used up. These portions are laid into two strips, the circles of the Same and the Different, which are bent into a cross, and then inserted or wrapped around the body of the world, woven throughout the entire heaven.[10] The Demiurge then organises the orbit of the planets and produces the Young Gods, to whom he delegates responsibility for the generation of the mortal *genera* and the lower soul. The mathematical aspect of the account, with its emphasis on intervals of 3:2; 4:3 and 9:8, which have to be filled with strips of soul-stuff, and its correspondence with a musical scale of four octaves and a major 'sixth' makes even a literal reading elaborate.

In contrast to the Empedoclean entities, Love and Strife, which are responsible for the production of the world, or the ordering, divine mind of Anaxagoras, Plato introduces a different type of cosmology. It is not as if the Demiurge can claim credit for all order, since even some sort of order (ἴχνη, traces) existed in the precosmos. The Demiurge only orders in a manner which furthers his objective: increased intelligibility, seen, for example, in his formation of the elements, ordered on geometric principles. The Demiurge's ordering activity is founded on a basis of rationality, which the sporadic traces of order in the precosmic state lacked.

At *Tim.* 48e, Plato turns to an examination of cosmology from below, and introduces Necessity (Plato's erratic cause, ἡ πλανωμένη αἰτία). He also introduces the Receptacle (ὑποδοχή) which he calls mother (μήτηρ) or nurse and additionally refers to it as space (χώρα) or place (τόπος). Plato's errant cause is a thorn in the side of the Demiurge; for example, he would prefer that humans could live longer and be intelligent, but when presented with a choice, he opts for intelligence over longevity.[11] This positing of Necessity helps to explain the imperfections of the cosmos and can be seen as an attempt to address the problem of evil, as well as a forerunner of the subsequent notion of the recalcitrance of matter. As for Plato's Receptacle, it becomes interpreted as ὕλη 'matter', with the beginning of a distinction between matter and space.

What is the precise nature of the relationship between the Demiurge and the Forms? Furthermore of what types of things do Forms exist? From the *Timaeus*, it would appear that the noetic realm contains (περιέχον 31a4,

---

[10] *Tim.* 36a–e

[11] At 75b, the Demiurge is forced to choose between giving man a head composed of dense bone or a lighter skull. The dense bone would enable him to enjoy a life several times longer than his current one. The speed of his perception, however, would be limited by the density of the bone (according to Timaeus).

περιλαβόν 30c8) biological Forms. Ostenfeld suggests that the Demiurge may be an all-embracing Form containing the various sub-Forms.[12] Is this sufficient to identify the Demiurge with the Form of the Good (as a Supreme Principle)?[13] I think not, although in defence of this position, one might cite *Tim.* 37a1: '(the Demiurge) is the best of the intelligible and eternal things' or *Tim.* 29e: 'He was good and . . . he wanted everything to be most like himself' or the reference to the Forms as gods at 37c6. Plato, though, is quite specific in referring to the Demiurge as good, but he does not call him 'the Good'. Furthermore, as Ostenfeld points out, Plato never mentions the Form of the Good in the *Timaeus*, although he acknowledges the possibility at 46c8.[14] In addition, the Good of the *Republic* is not a creative intelligence, so would it really be legitimate to equate the Demiurge with it?[15] In any case, if the Demiurge is to be regarded as an Intellect and the Forms are contemplated by Intellect, it would seem to be an unlikely conclusion.

Ostenfeld rejects the notion that the Forms in the *Timaeus* should be equated with the thoughts of God.[16] This to my mind is quite right, since this doctrine is most likely a Middle Platonist refinement. The Forms are not in anything else (*Tim.* 52a) and they are apart from sense-perception (*Crat.* 386e). This leads to the problem of how they can interact upon matter and suggests that they function as some sort of mathematical ratio. The introduction of the concept that the Forms were the thoughts of God not only resolved this problem, it reduced the number of principles from three to two. For Plato, the Form-sensible interaction is resolved by a 'model–copy' relationship, though he does acknowledge the difficulty when he states that sensibles 'partake' in some very puzzling way (ἀπορώτατα πῃ) of the intelligible and are very difficult to apprehend (*Tim.* 51a7–b1).

The alternative explanation is that the Demiurge is only an allegorical figure. Plato's account illustrates the importance of a rational element in the continual ordering of the universe and the myth can be deconstructed to produce a number of important philosophical insights: (1) The created realm is dependent upon a higher one, which it instantiates in a limited and approximate way. (2) The higher realm contains 'the beautiful model' according to which the world has been ordered. (3) The world is imperfect, not as the result of any malevolent, supernatural or divine being, but

---

[12] Ostenfeld: 1997, 170
[13] As was done by Wilamowitz and De Vogel. One might note here Aristotle's criticism of Plato for not making use of an efficient cause.
[14] Ostenfeld: 1997, 172
[15] *Rep.* ii.379b, vi.506, vii.517c rather muddy the waters, as do vi.507c and vii.530a, for which see my discussion above.
[16] Ostenfeld: 1997, 173

because an element of compromise is needed in the instantiation of the Forms in the material realm. (4) The sensible cosmos can never achieve a state of perfection. It does not even exist, but is always in a state of 'coming-to-be'. The changes and vicissitudes are due to the errant cause (Necessity), which has to be eternally ordered by Reason.

This leaves two main problems. Firstly, how are the Forms to be interpreted in this demythologised scheme? Secondly, there would then be no explanation for how the Forms come to affect matter. (One could argue that Plato does not achieve this on the metaphysical level, though he may do so on the mythological one.) Clearly, if there is no temporal creation, then there can never have been a stage when the Demiurge engaged in the activity envisaged in the *Timaeus*. The standard interpretation has been to assert that Plato is merely presenting an image of what the cosmos would be like if it were devoid of the influence of Reason. What is important is that it is not a mere mechanistic principle; Plato is reacting against earlier philosophers, whom he had criticised for not explaining the causality of the physical processes which they posited to explain world-generation (*Phaedo* 96a*ff.*).

How, then, can the Demiurge be interpreted? He is envisaged as the artificer of the World-Soul, but since this stage hardly took place and the functions which would be left for the Demiurge to engage in, if the generative process is discounted, are those of the World-Soul, one can envisage a situation where Plato's metaphysics could, in fact, have no requirement for a Demiurge and the task of functioning as a conduit between the suprasensible and material realms is effectively carried out by the World-Soul. In the *Phaedrus*, the soul is the source of all motion and in Book x of the *Laws*, regulation of the cosmos is carried out by the rational World-Soul, therefore this would appear to be a logical interpretation (if not *the* logical interpretation) of the *Timaeus* myth. The Demiurge is no more than the 'Cause of the Mixture' (*Phileb.* 23d*ff.*).

The dramatic setting of the dialogue the day after a discussion similar to that of the *Republic* took place, a discussion which dealt with the search for justice in the city and individual soul and which is summarised in the opening of the *Timaeus* (17a–20c) helps to reinforce the notion that the work deals with the continued regulation and governance of the cosmos, rather than with once-off generation. This political notion is enhanced by Plato's choice of the title 'Demiurge', which denotes not merely a Craftsman, but in certain Peloponnesian contexts means 'magistrate'.[17]

---

[17] As used at Thuc. 5.47, *Epist. Philipp. AP. Dem.* 18.157. Plato himself uses it in this context at *Rep.* 1.342 and Polybius uses it at 24.5, 16 to refer to magistrates of the Achaean League, The Doric

The Demiurge is usually regarded as ordering rather than creating. However at *Sym.* 205b8–c2, Plato blurs the distinction between a Demiurge and a Creator: 'You know that creation (ποίησις) is something multiple. For whatever passes from non-being into being, the entire cause is creation, so that what is manufactured by the arts is a kind of creation and their craftsmen (δημιουργοί) are all creators (ποιηταί).'[18] Again at *Soph.* 219b4–6, 'Whenever someone brings something into being which did not have being previously, we say that the one bringing it into being produces (ποιεῖν), and that brought into being is produced (ποιεῖσθαι).' Here it seems that Plato draws no distinction between merely ordering and actually creating.

Plato, I think, draws no distinction between the two because the idea of the Demiurge creating *ex nihilo* or even ordering according to his own whims (rather than according to the pre-existent Forms) would be for him unconscionable. The Greeks did not mention the idea of *creatio ex nihilo*, even satirically. The Demiurge moulds the world using geometric patterns; with the isosceles triangle he forms a cube, which becomes the atom of earth and out of the scalene triangle, he fashions the tetrahedron (fire), octahedron (air), icosahedron (water), and he also produces the dodecahedron used to adorn the universe (*Tim.* 55c4–6), which is later identified as *aether* by Xenocrates.[19] This positing of a fifth element may result from the non-interchangeability of the triangles used to form the dodecahedron with those which compose fire, water and air, and is just one of a number of problems which Plato, in the myth of the Demiurge, bequeaths to his successors.

Aristotle and the Old Academy

The bulk of Plato's immediate successors, whom we might imagine to be in a better position to know the views of the master, saw the myth as allegorical and as a feature of Plato's paideutic method. In fact, the principal philosopher in the generation after Plato to argue for a literal interpretation was Aristotle, and he does this primarily for the purposes of polemic, exploiting what he feels to be one of Plato's less readily defensible positions. Aristotle interprets the account of world-generation in time

forms δαμιωργός or δαμιοργός are also used, as at IG9 (1) 330 (Locr.) in the phrase δαμιοργέοντος Μίκκωνος and one finds the variant ἐπιδημιουργοί used to refer to the magistrates sent out annually by Doric states to their colonies at Thuc. 1.56 (Liddell and Scott).
[18] Sometimes this is translated as poetry and poets, rather than as creation and creators.
[19] Xenocrates, Fr. 53 (Heinze) = Simplicus, *Phys.* p 1165, 33–9

literally, since this allows him to attribute a weak argument to Plato,[20] but does not take the figure of the Demiurge seriously. Most notably in this regard, one may cite *De Caelo* 1.10.279b.17–31, where Aristotle, criticising Plato's position that the universe can be both 'generated' and everlasting, completely ignores the Demiurge. Aristotle also accuses Plato of not recognising the efficient cause, which would be one possible interpretation of the Demiurge.[21] Aristotle criticises Plato for suggesting that Forms (considered as Numbers) could be responsible for perceptible objects.[22] At *Metaphysics* 1091b, Aristotle criticises the view expressed throughout the *Timaeus*, that mathematical structure is necessary to make anything good.

Plato's other students do not seem to have much use for the Demiurge either. Philip of Opus (in the *Epinomis*) and Polemon seem to have interpreted him as a rational World-Soul. The second head of the Academy, Plato's nephew, Speusippus and his successor as scholarch, Xenocrates, proceeded to deconstruct the myth of the Demiurge, when faced with Aristotelian criticism. A good deal of Speusippus' doctrines can be gleaned from Aristotle's criticism of them as well as from (possible) fragments preserved by Iamblichus in *De Communi Mathematica Scientia*.[23] Speusippus regarded everything as the derivation of two principles: a One and an Indefinite Dyad (which he called multiplicity, *plêthos*).[24] He gets himself into considerable trouble, however, in his attempt to explain the existence of the variety of created being from only two principles. To counter this, he claims that the One imposes form on the Dyad in order to produce Number, which then, acting as a principle itself, imposes its own form on matter to produce the next level of being, and so on. Speusippus' situation was not helped by his decision to jettison or 'modify' the Theory of Forms.[25] The great difficulty with this theory lies in defining the sorts of things of which Forms exist. For Speusippus, Forms were only capable of manifesting themselves in the World-Soul, but not at any higher level.[26] Essentially, as a result of his attempts to break down this mythological framework, all

---

[20] The doctrine of temporal creation is notoriously difficult to defend within the context of Greek philosophy. The idea that God would suddenly create at a point in time raises the question of what he has been doing previously.

[21] At *Metaphysics* 1.6.988a8–16, Aristotle claims that Plato only recognises the formal and the material causes.

[22] E.g. at *Metaphysics I.9* (991b9ff.). Johansen: 2010 treats this issue in detail.

[23] This is based on a suggestion by Philip Merlan concerning the origin of chapter 4 of Iamblichus, though the view is opposed by Tarán: 1982.

[24] Dillon: 2003a, 40

[25] Aristotle testifies to this at *Met*. M9, 1085b36ff. (= Fr. 35 Tarán). For a full discussion, see Dillon: 2003a, 48

[26] Dillon: 2003a, 49

Speusippus is left with is a One which transcends the cosmos, Multiplicity, and a World-Soul.

Xenocrates attempted to systematise Platonic thought. He may have been reacting in response to Speusippus' innovations, as well as Aristotle's attacks, and attempting to return to what he viewed as the 'original' doctrine of Plato. Essentially, he too regarded the myth of the Demiurge as merely introduced 'for the purposes of exposition' and regarded the World-Soul as the product of his two principles: a Monad and Dyad. He also modified the Theory of Forms, equating them with Numbers. Unfortunately, the loss of all his works limits our knowledge of his doctrines, although information can be gleaned from Aristotle (particularly his *Metaphysics*), as well as from the *Metaphysics* of Theophrastus and the writings of Plutarch.

The need to demarcate more strongly the First Principle from the demiurgic one was influenced by the Aristotelian concept of an Intellect (*Nous*) as the First Principle, but characterised as a self-thinking unmoved mover, whose sole 'inner life' consists of contemplating itself, which prevents it from intervening in the world. Speusippus, to be sure, resisted this. However, Xenocrates did adopt such a conception and he, unlike Speusippus, had much greater influence upon the course of Middle Platonism. Aristotle criticised the description of the rotational movement of the heavens at *De Anima* 407a.22–34; since he interprets this revolution to be identical with Mind (407a.19–22) the same revolution reoccurring implies that Mind is continuously thinking the same thing (and thought has a purpose, so it should not be circular). Furthermore, thought is more similar to a state of coming to rest than movement (*cf. Physics* 247b.10–11).[27]

Since Xenocrates regarded the First Principle as an Intellect, this could be combined with the Aristotelian notion of a more 'passive' intellect.[28] Xenocrates envisages Intellect as actively concerned with the world as he regards it as containing the form-numbers. Evidence for this can be adduced from the comments of the Sicilian Alcimus: 'Each of the Forms is eternal and intelligible and not susceptible to change.'[29] This testimony can be taken as accurate; Alcimus was a contemporary and had no particular reason to distort the truth in this case. The only intellect which could think Forms in an unchanging and eternal manner is that of God. These Forms are then projected onto the World-Soul. One might cite in this context

---

[27] Cherniss: 1944, 394

[28] I mean *passive* here in the sense of not engaging in discursive thinking or becoming involved with the cosmos.

[29] ἔστι δὲ τῶν εἰδῶν ἓν ἕκαστον ἀίδιόν τε καὶ νόημα καὶ πρὸς τούτοις ἀπαθές, ap. DL, III.13. *Cf.* Dillon: 2003a, 121

Plutarch's *De An. Proc.* 1012e, according to which Xenocrates identified the 'indivisible being' of *Tim.* 35a with the Monad and the divisible with the Dyad. The third form, Number, (the total of the Form-numbers) with the addition of mobility and motivity (arising from the mixing in of Sameness and Otherness), results in Soul. This entity 'has the ontological capacity of creating individuals, of separating them from one another, and of grouping them in genera and species, as well as the epistemological capacity of identifying them and distinguishing between them.'[30]

Evidently, this is a deconstruction of the myth of the Demiurge, with the Monad and Dyad producing Number and Soul, and with Soul carrying out the Demiurge's activities with regard to the physical realm. By conceding (to some extent) to the Aristotelian conception of Intellect, Xenocrates can be viewed as beginning the trend observable in Middle Platonism to assign demiurgic functions to a sub-noetic level, a stance which led to the convergence in later Platonism of the First Principle with the Unmoved Mover of Aristotle's *Metaphysics* XII.

Interpretations of the *Timaeus*: first to third centuries AD

Perhaps surprisingly, despite the heated debate amongst Platonists in general concerning the status of the demiurgic myth, this does not seem to have been an issue with the philosophers and traditions investigated here from the first to third centuries AD. Plutarch, for example, was prepared to accept that a literal interpretation had been intended by Plato, a position he adopts principally for his own purposes. After all, he viewed the myths of other cultures as revealing the truths of Greek philosophy; an interest which prompted his *De Iside et Osiride*. Philo and Origen were less concerned with exposing the Demiurge as a myth than with drawing upon the imagery it presented as a means for expounding Biblical truth and reconciling it with Greek philosophy (or Greek philosophy with it, depending upon one's position). Gnosticism and Hermetism both regarded the Demiurge as a real figure and, given what we know of both these traditions, were unlikely to be perplexed by the mythological context in which he is introduced.

The same could be said for Numenius, for whom the Demiurge forms an important component of his metaphysics. Maximus of Tyre, for his part, seems to have seen no pressing need to investigate the matter in what was intended as an introductory series of lectures to Plato. If the status of the demiurgic myth could be shelved by Plato's less immediate interpreters,

---

[30] Dillon: 2003a, 122

the same did not apply for the status of the Demiurge himself. Though Jonas[31] has warned against the 'conveyor-belt' approach to Gnosticism, the Demiurge's status could be viewed as one of continual ontological decline (although to a certain degree such a view is rather naïve and simplistic: Philo, after all, did raise the status of the Creator by making him an architect, rather than a craftsman).

If the demiurgic myth was accepted as literal by thinkers from a wide range of traditions by the first century, the Demiurge himself took on an existence autonomous to that of the *Timaeus*, although several of the modifications envisaged subsequently can be traced to comments made by Plato in that dialogue. While the exact process used by the Demiurge does not seem to have been particularly important to some of Plato's heirs (Maximus of Tyre in particular springs to mind), two elements of this account were. Firstly, the notion that the world is generated along rational (i.e. mathematical) lines and secondly the Demiurge's delegation to the Young Gods of the production of the mortal elements and the lower soul leads to the development of various intermediary demiurgic figures in subsequent traditions, or even more strikingly the actual demotion of the Demiurge himself. The antagonism between the Demiurge and the First Principle in Gnosticism can be seen to result, in part, from Plato's distinction between the Form of Good and the Demiurge, or perhaps more accurately expressed, it was the possibility of using material from the *Timaeus* to expound (whether metaphysically or mythologically) dualistic tendencies that underpinned the widespread use of the demiurgic figure.

What in the *Timaeus*, if anything, suggests a hierarchy of levels of being? What is primarily suggested are two worlds, or metaphysical realms, that of Being and of Becoming. A hierarchy amongst suprasensible entities is suggested by the distinction between the Demiurge and the Young Gods; he is immortal, while they are merely everlasting at his pleasure. What he produces will not be dissolved, unlike the Young Gods, who produce the mortal component of man. This further suggests that world-generation is the result of collaboration between entities at various ontological levels, with very strictly delineated roles, an interpretation drawn upon by Gnosticism, but also by the Philonic *Logos*-Cutter. The distinction in the quality of the production of the Demiurge and the Young Gods stresses the hierarchy, as well as the ambivalent nature of man as an intermediary being containing elements with two ontological ranks (soul and body). Though Plato does not envisage it in these terms, it can be seen as the ancestor of

---

[31] Jonas: 1963 and 1967

the belief in a higher divine element in man, which has become entrapped in matter.

Another important passage for subsequent philosophers is 27d4–28b2, where Plato outlines the fundamental principles which underpin the *Timaeus*, while 28b2–29a3 applies them to the cosmos.[32] This results in three conclusions: (1) the cosmos has been produced, (2) it has a cause, the precise nature of which is difficult to explain and (3) the maker modelled it following an eternal model. The gaze of the Demiurge is fixed on the Eternal (29a4), but he himself does not appear to produce this model, leading to the ambiguity concerning his relationship to the Forms. Such ambiguity provided fertile ground for Middle Platonist speculations regarding God and the Forms. The Middle Platonist response, positing the Forms as the contents of the divine Mind is the most economical clarification of their relationship (as it reduces the number of Principles posited). Numenius also attempts to resolve this situation by effectively expanding the suprasensible realm, explaining the Demiurge's ancestry.

When Timaeus states at 28c that to find the father and maker of all men is difficult and, when he is found, that to reveal him to all is impossible, he is referring to the limits of human knowledge and Plato's awareness that this is just a 'likely story', to account for appearances, the most up-to-date scientific research of the day, though Plato himself knows that this will be superseded at some point in the future. This was adopted by Plutarch and Maximus of Tyre as a convenient response to evade a detailed discussion of certain (technical) aspects of demiurgy, when it no longer suited them. It is worth pointing out, in this context, the philosophical tradition of expressing an awareness of the limits of human knowledge; it suffices to cite Alcmaeon DK 24B1 (= DL VIII 83): 'Concerning what is unclear and concerning what is mortal, the gods have clarity, but it is necessary for humans to make educated guesses' and Metrodorus of Chios DK 70B1 (= Cic. *Acad.* 2.73): 'none of us knows anything, not even whether we know or do not know, nor even what it is not to know or to know, or indeed whether anything is or is not.'[33]

It is well known that Plato's myth regards the Demiurge as imposing order upon disorder, a position shared by Maximus and Plutarch, though disputed by the Gnostic and Hermetic traditions. But what exactly is this order and how might it be viewed as an improvement? The Demiurge's work can be seen in terms of an improvement of the world's intelligibility;

---

[32] Runia: 1997, 102

[33] nego, inquit, scire nos sciamusne aliquid an nihil sciamus, ne id ipsum quidem nescire (aut scire), scire nos, nec omnino sitne aliquid an nihil sit.

creating immanent standards (39e3–4) as a reflection of the standards of the phenomenal realm. This explains the Demiurge's replication of qualities possessed by his model which might seem to be irrelevant in his production. In order for the generated world to serve as a standard (Mohr suggests that it may be an immanent standard of animality),[34] he must invest it with permanence (through the introduction of the standard of time, 36e) and uniqueness (only one world generated). This is the real reason why (for Plato), the Demiurge improves matter, since it has heightened intelligibility (by being ordered as the sensible realm), rather than by imposing order. Reale counters the view that the Demiurge replicates irrelevant features of his model in his ordering of only one cosmos, and regards this as an actualisation of 'true measure'.[35] For Reale, producing only one universe and generating time as an image of the unit of eternity are both mechanisms by which the Demiurge unifies reality.

However, this is a feature not seized upon by the thinkers considered here – all of them tend to view creation or demiurgy in terms of this order/disorder framework. While Middle Platonists (including in this instance Philo under this label) tend to regard the Demiurge as responsible for order; the main objection that Gnostics tend to have against him is that he is responsible in some way for the breakdown of the natural ontological order by either entrapping Man (as a fragmented and enmattered part of the godhead) or through his ignorance of this order in his assumption that he is the highest principle.

Another hangover from Plato's *Timaeus* is the hierarchy of divinities. Is the Demiurge identical with the Idea of the Good? The Demiurge of the *Timaeus* never creates the Forms; rather the soul and the κόσμος αἰσθητός. In the *Republic*, for example, God is the creator (φυτουργός) of the Idea of the Bed, meaning that the Demiurge could in no way be identical with the principle of the One and the Good, although this *Republic* reference is not particularly helpful in determining the precise ontological status of the Demiurge, since the metaphysical value of the Idea of the Bed must surely differ from abstract ideas such as Justice or Beauty (or more importantly the Good).[36] Halfwassen points out that since the Demiurge is Mind at *Tim.* 36d8, and the highest principle must be beyond Mind (on account of its transcendence), this indicates that a Craftsman-god could not be identical with a First Principle, which is above both Being and Mind. Halfwassen also raises the point that the Demiurge could be identical with the totality of the Forms; if these are the thoughts of God in

---

[34] Mohr: 1989, 301   [35] Reale: 1997, 161   [36] Halfwassen: 2000, 49

Middle Platonism, then this would certainly be the case. This would make the Demiurge more than just the efficient cause, but also the *causa finalis et causa exemplaris*. Aristotle in his *Metaphysics* 988a7ff. asserts that Plato propounded two principles, the material principle (ἀνάγκη *Tim.* 47eff.) and the Form-principle (νοῦς). This perception forms the basis of the dualistic attitudes of Middle Platonism exemplified by Plutarch (especially with the disappearance of the Forms as a principle in their own right).

A further contribution of the *Timaeus* has been to our conceptualisation of Time. Plato regards Time as coming into being with the universe, although since he dismissed precosmic events, this indicates that he never envisaged a period when the generated world did not exist (although evidently Plato never claims that the Demiurge introduced temporal succession to the world). Time for Plato refers to the celestial motions by which we can measure time. I introduce this point here because it raises the question of why the Demiurge should choose to create at a particular point. Plato comments καὶ ὁ μὲν δὴ ἅπαντα ταῦτα διατάξας ἔμενεν ἐν τῷ ἑαυτοῦ κατὰ τρόπον ἤθει 'and having arranged all these things he duly remained in his habitual state' (*Tim.* 42e), which makes world-generation appear a little arbitrary. One can sidestep the issue if, like Proclus, one claims that for the Demiurge to always maintain a constant state in relation to the world, he must always generate.

This is precisely the position adopted by subsequent philosophers; exemplified equally by Philo and Origen's views concerning continual temporal creation and Origen's location of the Ideal realm of the Forms within the Son-*Logos*, as well as Plutarch's assertion that the Demiurge is continually engaged in geometry. In the Gnostic and Hermetic traditions, the situation is reversed. God is not involved in continual demiurgic activity, rather the generated world is spawned by the Demiurge (who is not immutable and so there is no metaphysical reason why he cannot create on an *ad hoc* basis) and man, who represents the pinnacle of creation, is a once-off production, generated inadvertently as the result of a flaw within the godhead itself. Indeed, there the divine is continually attempting to undo world-generation, rather than to further it. Numenius falls in between both extremes. The splitting of the Second and Third Gods by matter seems to be a non-recurrent event, but the contemplation of the Intelligibles by the First God, followed by a similar contemplation on the part of the Second God, which appears to fulfill some sort of demiurgic function, seems to be continuous.

Tim. 41a3ff. could be viewed as responsible for these divergent approaches concerning the continuity of the Demiurge's activity. However, Proclus' comment reveals more about subsequent interpretation than about Plato's own viewpoint. Although at *Rep.* II.381b–c, God is unchangeable, this refers to nature, but not activity. God could generate (or not) as seems good to Him, provided that this does not change his nature as God. However, this would not solve the problem of why God would allow precosmic chaos to exist before rectifying the situation (since it implies a change in God's ἦθος). (Again, this problem could be rectified by simply viewing the demiurgic myth as expository.)

Modern approaches to the *Timaeus*

The division between the literalists and those seeking to deconstruct the myth has persisted in modern scholarship, fuelled in part by the support which an allegorical interpretation of the *Timaeus* could have for the existence of 'unwritten doctrines' of Plato (such as the content of his lecture 'On the Good'). If the dispute has not been particularly acrimonious, then this is because the *Timaeus* was largely marginalised during the last century. The surge in recent publications on the *Timaeus*, though, indicates that the importance of the dialogue is being reassessed.[37]

The case for an allegorical interpretation has been persuasively argued by Tarán. Most forcible is Plato's own statement that the account which he presents is no more than a 'likely story'. Tarán mentions that the manner of telling the myth is systematic, rather than chronological, although I find this to be a particularly weak argument.[38] It seems to be rather like asserting that because a historian chooses to focus on events in relation to their significance, rather than chronologically, that these events could not have taken place.

The second argument advanced by Tarán appears more persuasive. He contends that the very structure of the myth is implausible. Plato chooses to dwell on the body of the universe, prior to dealing with the soul, even though soul is both ontologically superior and temporally prior. However, at *Tim.* 35a, Plato declares that soul is intermediate between Forms and body. If soul is an intermediary, this would imply that it must have been brought into existence later than the two extremes for which it functions as an intermediary. Conversely, if soul is prior to bodies, it cannot be composed of an element that is 'divided about bodies'.

For Tarán, it is legitimate for Plato to alter the presentation of the demiurgic myth in a temporal sense, provided that it is not used to mask

---

[37] For example, Af Hällström: 2009 and Mohr and Sattler: 2010   [38] Tarán : 1972, 373

contradictions which would occur if he was forced to follow the chrono-logical order. Otherwise, this would indicate that he never intended the myth of the Demiurge to be taken literally. *Tim.* 31b–35a indicates that soul and body are contemporaneous and that the use of the terms 'prior' and 'older' to refer to the relationship of soul to body is ontological and not chronological.[39] Against this could be advanced the view that Plato tends to be vague concerning the role of soul in administering the body. In the *Phaedo* (80a), where he discusses the rule of the body by the soul, or *Laws* x, where it is the source of all physical motion, he avoids explaining the underlying mechanism.[40] If soul is intermediate between the Forms and precosmic chaos, this would imply that the soul is the cause of the disorderly motion. If we take the myth literally, it implies that the Demi-urge must also be a soul, according to Tarán (why not a Mind?), since it is prior to body and intermediate between the Sensibles and the Forms. The Demiurge cannot also be 'prior' to the precosmic chaos, since this would imply that he had produced it.

Once again, the problem which arises here could be solved by drawing attention to Plato's view that the world, formed as it was, in his opinion, from a variety of triangles, does not constitute a 'solid' in the true sense of the word, and so there should be no problem in terms of the relation of soul upon body, although this does not really resolve the situation regarding why the Demiurge suddenly decided to order the precosmic chaos. To some extent, this could be viewed as a fallacious argument – according to Tarán's view, the contradictions are deliberately placed there by Plato, not because he found it difficult to reveal the father and maker of the universe to all men, but because he did not wish the concept of a temporal generation on the part of his mythical Demiurge to be taken literally. Tarán identifies a further problem with the view that the Demiurge generated the self-motion of soul (which seems to be contradictory, since souls are by their very nature self-moving). This leads to the problem of whether the Demiurge started the self-motion of the World-Soul or else attached it to the body of the cosmos, produced subsequently, and that after this insertion the soul commenced its self-motion. Tarán rejects Hackforth's argument that the mythology of *Tim.* 27d5–28c3 was deliberately arranged in order to deceive the reader; for Tarán, it is rather the case that Plato chose the form of a myth, rather than that of a causal analysis.

Tarán also points out that Plato does not openly claim in the *Timaeus* that soul is the cause of all motion (as self-motion) so there is no attempt

---

[39] Tarán: 1972, 375   [40] Dillon: 2009, 349

to contradict the reader in Plato's assertion of precosmic chaos; for Tarán, this precosmic chaos exemplifies the 'necessary cause', just as the Demiurge represents the intelligent cause; further evidence that the myth should not be taken literally.[41] Tarán bolsters his case by pointing to two indications that the *Timaeus* should be viewed as a myth; firstly Plato's statement that no account of the material world can ever be regarded as unchanging truth, and secondly his adoption of the form of a cosmology.[42] This locates Plato's myth of the Demiurge within the context of evolutionary cosmologies on the one hand and the mechanistic and haphazard explanation of the atomists. Plato, the argument goes, is attempting to propound the image of rational design; the precosmic chaos of the Receptacle is simply an account of what the universe would be like without the rational order represented by the Demiurge. Solmsen suggests that Plato himself warns us not to take the myth literally when he writes τὸν εἰκότα μῦθον ἀποδεχομένους πρέπει τούτου μηδὲν ἔτι πέρα ζητεῖν, 'it is fitting that we accept the likely story concerning these things and not inquire even further' (29d2–3).[43] Furthermore, Plato does not use any of the techniques which he employs in other works to indicate an expository nature, according to Vlastos.[44] The myth itself is preceded by another mythical narrative (the war between Athens and Atlantis), so one is already preconditioned to approach the myth of the Demiurge in an allegorical context.

Arguments in favour of a literal interpretation have been staunchly advanced by Vallejo. Against Tarán's position that soul must be the cause of motion in the precosmic chaos, he alludes to the role played by heterogeneity.[45] In the Receptacle, like is attracted to like and this accounts for precosmic motion (in addition to the winnowing motion of the Receptacle). Plato does not actually state in the *Timaeus* that either soul or demiurgic activity is the ultimate cause of motion and the explanation in terms of physical heterogeneity here seems to downplay any difficulty concerning soul's role in the motion of the universe; if it were the ἀρχή of motion, it would have to be coeval with the universe.[46]

A refutation of the argument that a literal generation of the world could not have taken place on account of the immutability of God is to be found in Timaeus' statement at 42e ἔμενεν ἐν τῷ ἑαυτοῦ κατὰ τρόπον ἤθει, 'he duly remained in his habitual state'. Plato is able to draw

---

[41] Tarán: 1972, 379   [42] Tarán: 1972, 396   [43] Tarán: 1972, 400, n. 41
[44] Vlastos: 1965, 380–3, discussed by Tarán: 1971, 390   [45] Vallejo: 1997, 151
[46] Such matters are treated in greater detail by Mohr: 1985, especially Chapter 2, 'Plato on Time and Eternity', and by Sedley: 2007.

a distinction between a change in God's actions and an alteration to his *morphê*. To a certain extent, the allegorical interpretation of the myth in modern scholarship has been influenced by the Hegelian view that myth is used to convey thought that is still underdeveloped. For Hegel, only once the conception was fully formed could it be stated without the support of a mythical framework.[47] Since such a charge could hardly be levelled at Plato, this has led to the assumption that he could surely not have expected or even wished to be taken literally, an interpretation that I would favour, but which, as we shall see in the following chapters, was not particularly fashionable in the first to third centuries AD.

[47] Vallejo: 1997, 151

CHAPTER 3

Logos *into Demiurge*
Philo of Alexandria as witness to developments in contemporary Platonism

Introduction

Much scholarly debate has raged over the issue of Philo's philosophical allegiances, if any. It is a matter of utmost concern as it can shed considerable light on his account of world-generation and his adoption of the myth of the Demiurge to delineate what is effectively a Judaeo–Christian form of *creation*. Philo can be referred to as a Middle Platonist, though this is somewhat misleading. Philo did not belong to a Middle Platonist institution or even owe his primary allegiance to Plato. It seems that he regarded the αἵρεσις to which he belonged as that of Mosaic philosophy (even if he does not express it in these terms with the same frequency as Josephus). To assert, however, as does Radice,[1] that Philo was the leading light in a Hellenistic–Jewish variant of Platonism, which subsequently merged with its mainstream counterpart, with Philo first positing the notion of the Forms as the thoughts of God, and therefore the most philosophically important component of Middle Platonism, is surely to go too far.

Philo can be considered a Platonising expositor, even if one has difficulties with considering him a Platonist. *De Opificio Mundi* can be read together with Plutarch's *De Iside et Osiride* as realisations on the part of intellectuals that philosophical truths could be found in other traditions. To paraphrase Sterling, if Moses offered a definitive statement concerning creation, this does not mean to say that it was an exclusive one.[2] It must be noted that Philo is operating within a different framework and with a different set of considerations in mind than the other Middle Platonists with which we are familiar. He does not seek to convert his readers to Platonism; rather he is using the structures of Greek philosophy to expound sacred Scripture.

---

[1] Radice: 1989, *passim*   [2] Sterling: 1993, 103

As will be seen and as would naturally be expected, Philo forms an important link between the later Christian Platonism of Origen and the Platonic tradition. He is an important contributor to the concept of the hypostasis, and therefore an important exemplar of the trend of increasing separation between the First Principle and the demiurgic one. His greatest contribution could possibly be the notion of the Forms as God's thoughts (though this is vehemently disputed). In any case, he does write extensively concerning the noetic cosmos. In this postulation of the *Logos* as a divine creational aid, he prefigures Origen's system, without its Christian modifications.

An important question to address regarding Philo is whether he can be regarded as working within the framework of the demiurgic concept, rather than just expounding *Genesis* in language that by this stage had become common currency. After all, while Philo may compare God to an architect, *Gen.* 2:4b*ff.* refers to God as a potter or builder. One response is to discern the obvious legacy of the *Timaeus* in Philo's account. The *Logos* is clearly the counterpart of the Young Gods in its role as a mediating entity (although when described allegorically as a sword, it also parallels the Demiurge's mixing-bowl in the original *Timaeus* 'myth', and in its assistance in God's continual governance of the cosmos, it fulfils the function of the World-Soul). The beautiful model of the *Timaeus* finds its counterpart in Philo's speculations on the noetic realm (though here a Jewish parallel may also exist). While 'creation' may take the Judaeo–Christian form of production by an omnipotent divine being, it is evidently an ordering process, like demiurgy, evinced by the continual division of the *Logos*. Furthermore, it seems unlikely that an exegete of Platonic leanings should remain completely uninfluenced by the *Timaeus*.

This does, however, underline the importance of paying attention to the influences under which Philo operated in order to understand the history of ideas of the period. There are a number of indisputable facts: Philo is one of our major sources for Middle Platonism, irrespective of how he is classified. Given his role in supplying a philosophical interpretation of *Genesis*, this means that he investigated thoroughly the nature of demiurgic causality, although he tends to obscure this with what can be termed 'creation'. In this respect, he could be hailed, as he sometimes is, as a proto-Gnostic.

Although certain modern scholars have cast doubt on whether Philo was a 'Middle Platonist' (due in part to the emergence of a more nuanced understanding of what this might mean), in antiquity his zeal for Plato was well-attested. Eusebius claims that he surpassed his contemporaries in his enthusiasm for κατὰ Πλατῶνα καὶ Πυθαγόραν ἀγῶγη ('the school of Plato and Pythagoras').[3] Jerome cites the proverb ἢ Πλατῶν φιλωνίζει ἢ Φιλῶν πλατωνίζει, ('either Plato philonises or Philo platonises').[4] One of the first modern scholars to recognise the debt that Philo owed to Plato, rather than just the Judaeo–Christian tradition, Johannes Albertus Fabricius, wrote in his important 1693 study *Exercitatio de Platonismo Philonis Iudaei* with reference to Philo's views on the κόσμος νοητός at *Conf.* 172: 'He who reads the *Timaeus* of Plato will not in the least doubt that at this point Philo goes back to and is influenced by Platonic doctrine. Philo himself in the book concerning the incorruptible world steals the words of Plato and let no one doubt it.'[5]

To a very great extent, Philo can be regarded as a bridge between the various traditions surveyed in this study. In his doctrine of the *Logos* as an intermediary creative entity, which effectively allowed him to jettison the more Platonic scheme involving a World-Soul, he can be viewed as a forerunner of Origen. He also certainly owes a great deal to the Stoicising Platonism of figures such as Antiochus of Ascalon and Eudorus of Alexandria. Stoic, Aristotelian and Neopythagorean terminology is acquired as a means of modernising Plato, as was common in Middle Platonism. As H. Dörrie puts it, Philo inherited his '*savoir s'exprimer*' from the Stoics, which helps in part to account for the Stoic elements found, particularly in his exposition of the *Logos*-Cutter.[6]

Philo has also been regarded by some scholars (notably Jonas and Harvey) as a Gnostic, although, at the 1966 Messina colloquium, Jonas pointed out that one cannot regard Gnosticism in terms of a factory conveyor-belt.[7] The reason for regarding Philo as the Cro-Magnon Man of Gnosticism is that by linking Biblical exegesis with Platonism, he created the intellectual conditions responsible for the rise of (Christian) Gnosticism. This is a fallacious assumption for a number of reasons. Firstly, the assistant demiurges of *Opif.* are not in opposition to the supreme God. Secondly, Philo uses the refrain of *Genesis* 'and God saw that it was good' to refer to the created world, whereas Gnosticism views the sensible realm in very negative terms.[8] Philo also refers to the cosmos as the younger Son of God (*Spec.* 1.96)[9] and at *Deus* 31–2 refers to the intelligible realm as God's older son.

---

[3] Runia: 1986, 27; *Hist. Eccl.* 2.4.2   [4] *De. Vir. Inl.* 1.11

[5] Qui Platonis legerit Timaeum, idem quoque minime dubitabit, hoc loco a Philone Platonicium referri spirarique doctrinam. Ipse Philo in libro de mundo incorruptibili Platonis verba, ne quis dubitet, in mediam affert. Fabricius, 155 (in *Opusculorum Sylloge* reprint, Hamburg, 1738). Cf. discussion at Runia: 1986, 28.

[6] Runia: 1986, 506   [7] Wilson: 1993, 85   [8] E.g. *Opif.* 21

[9] Cf. *Ebr.* 30: τὸν μόνον καὶ ἀγαπητὸν αἰσθητὸν υἱὸν ἀπεκύησε, τόνδε τὸν κόσμον, [Wisdom] 'bore her only son, beloved and sense-perceptible, this cosmos', or *Migr.* 220 : τὸν μέγιστον καὶ τελεώτατον ἄνθρωπον, τόνδε τὸν κόσμον, 'the greatest and most perfect man, this very cosmos'.

The Middle Platonist tradition, because it advocated studying a *Plato dimidiatus*, a few of the more celebrated dialogues in full and selections from lesser known works, rather than surveying the Platonic corpus in its entirety, gave a disproportionate amount of influence to the *Timaeus*. In fact most of the First Principles were drawn from this dialogue alone. David Runia's work *Philo of Alexandria and the Timaeus of Plato* reflects the many correspondences between the Philonic corpus and this particular dialogue. The *Timaeus* and the *Phaedrus* were the dialogues most often utilised by Philo. However, in the entire *corpus Philonicum*, Philo only quotes, paraphrases or refers directly to the *Timaeus* approximately twenty times, twelve in the philosophical treatises and seven in the exegetical group.[10] It might appear that these occurrences are relatively infrequent, but Philo quotes the *Timaeus* more often than the rest of Plato's other dialogues combined.

Rather than adopt Runia's method, which has been to analyse the correspondences between the *Timaeus* and the works of Philo and then synthesise the results, an undertaking which is clearly beyond the scope of this study, I wish to concentrate on the works most relevant for analysing Philo's views on the generation and (in)destructibility of the cosmos: *De Opificio Mundi* and *De Aeternitate Mundi*. In any case, Runia's research has found that *De Opificio Mundi* contains the greatest usage of the *Timaeus* (followed by the *Allegorical Commentary*).

Influence of the *Timaeus* is not uniform. Apart from use made of the travels of Solon and the Atlantis myth (17a–27d), which is irrelevant to the matter in hand, Philo draws mainly upon Timaeus' introductory speech (27d, 29d) and the section outlining the works of reason. In addition, Philo draws upon Plato's doctrines concerning Man's psychology (69a–72d) and the τέλος of Man (89d–92c). Even within these areas usage is not uniform. The most important sections are those outlining fundamental philosophical principles (27d–29d), the account of world-generation (29e–31b), Time (37c–38b), the Demiurge's address to the Young Gods (41a–d), the creation of human reason (41b–44c) and the theory of vision (47a–e).[11]

The Forms

There was some dispute in antiquity on the issue of whether Plato had posited two principles (as claimed by Theophrastus: matter and the source of movement; basically the One and the Indefinite Dyad being responsible

[10] Runia: 1986, 367, which also contains a complete list of these occurrences.
[11] Runia: 1986, 372

for the generation of Forms),[12] three principles: a Demiurge, the Forms and matter (as claimed by Alexander of Aphrodisias) or a sort of two and a half principle position, with the Forms regarded as the thoughts of God and therefore derivative, rather than an independent principle. (Simplicius' view that Plato posited six principles, three in a strict sense: the maker, the paradigm and the end and three auxiliary causes: matter, the form (in the sense of the Aristotelian immanent form) and the instrument, can be left aside for present purposes).[13] As Sharples notes, the Forms are the Demiurge's thoughts in the *Timaeus* in the sense that he is aware of them; the issue could be better phrased in terms of whether the Forms have an existence independent of the divine mind.[14] It has been suggested that the three principle theory developed from the theory of two and a half principles;[15] Tarrant demonstrates that it is characteristic of the second century AD; while Runia dates the three principle theory to the first century AD.[16]

In any case, Philo never refers to the Forms as ungenerated, since that would imply that they are independent of God. That does not automatically mean that they are generated in time.[17] The noetic realm, contained in the *Logos*, undergoes two phases. As the noetic realm, it exists eternally. As a physical instantiation, it becomes immanent in the world, but both of these phases occur simultaneously.

One issue dominating recent Platonist scholarship concerns the extent of Philo's contribution to the Middle Platonist theory of the Forms. According to Wolfson, Philo is the first to apply the term κόσμος νοητός ('intelligible world') to the ensemble of the Forms.[18] The notion of a 'noetic cosmos' may have been inspired by the opening of *Republic* X, where Socrates draws a distinction between three types of bed: a particular bed constructed by a carpenter, the image of a bed produced by a painter and the idea of the bed, produced by God. Plato had previously used the expression νοητὸς τόπος ('intelligible place', *Rep.* VI.504d, VII.517b) or ὑπερουράνιος τόπος ('supercelestial place') at *Phaedrus* 247c, to refer to the place of the Forms. Wolfson sees Philo as altering these terms to refer to a noetic cosmos which does not exist eternally in the mind of God, but which only comes into being when He decides to create.[19] I would not be as prepared as Wolfson to regard Philo as father of the term κόσμος νοητός. I think in any case that

[12] Sharples: 1995, 70   [13] Simplicius, *Commentary on Aristotles' Physics* 1.2
[14] Sharples: 1995, 74. Sharples also notes a passage in Varro (Varro ap. St. Augustine, *De civitate Dei* 7.28 = Varro *Ant. Rer. Div.* xv, fr. 206 in Cardauns: 1976, in which these three principles are identified with the Capitoline triad (Jupiter, Juno and Minerva), but since Minerva sprang from the head of Jupiter, it accommodates the two and a half principle theory also.
[15] Sharples: 1995, 75   [16] Tarrant: 1985, 116; Runia: 1993, 135   [17] Wolfson: 1968, 208
[18] Wolfson: 1968, 227   [19] Wolfson: 1968, 228

there is a distinction in Philo between an eternally existing *Logos* and the noetic realm which it contains, which emerges simultaneously when God turns to demiurgy. (This is apparent from the famous image of the architect designing a city in *Opif.*; see my discussion below. The envisaged city is only created when the architect considers what he wishes to construct; it does not exist otherwise.)

This notion that the noetic realm is the cosmos when God turns to create, means that it functions as the 'idea of ideas'.[20] A text from the Stoic philosopher Arius Didymus proves illuminating in this regard:

> Therefore the particular archetypes, as it were, precede the sense-perceptible bodies, so that the Form containing all the Forms itself, being the most beautiful and the most perfect, exists as the paradigm of this cosmos, for it has been made similar to it by the Demiurge and produced in accordance with divine Providence out of the whole essence.[21]

This passage is adapted by Alcinous at *Didasc.* 12.1, where he claims that God generates the cosmos by looking towards the idea of one.[22] This notion of the Forms as the contents of the divine mind may owe something to the Jewish tradition, where God is said to have used the Torah as a model, though this notion may in turn be derived from Platonic influence on Judaism.[23] This is instructive, since if God constructs the cosmos according to the Forms which are his thoughts, it leaves open the possibility that God has created according to (from our perspective) His own whims. However, since, in reality, the world is constructed on rational principles to allow it to attain the greatest degree of excellence of which it is capable, it is not that far removed from the production of the Platonic Demiurge.

It is true to state that the term κόσμος νοητός occurs in Philo for the first time in extant Greek literature. However, terms which express a similar concept are used elsewhere. Timaeus Locrus §30 mentions ὁ ἰδανικὸς κόσμος ('the ideal cosmos'), a phrase used also by Aëtius at *Ps.-Plutarch Plac.* 1.7 and 2.6.[24] Unfortunately, none of this proves that Philo could not have invented the doctrine. Plato himself, at times, comes close to

---

[20] *Opif.* 25   [21] Eusebius, *Praep. Ev.* XI.23.6   [22] Runia: 2001, 151

[23] This notion comes across in the exegesis of Rabbi Hoshai'a of Caesarea, a friend of Origen: 'The Torah declares: "I am the working tool of the Holy One, blessed be He." In human practice, when a mortal king builds a palace he builds it not with his own skill but with the skill of an architect. The architect moreover does not build it out of his head, but employs plans and diagrams to know how to arrange the chambers and the wicket doors. Thus God consulted the Torah, and created the world while the Torah declares "in the beginning God created (1:1) 'beginning' referring to the Torah . . . "' (Genesis *Rabbah* 1.1, Midrash Rabbah, trans. H. Freedman and M. Simon, The Socino Press, London, 1951). The Rabbi may owe this model to the Platonic tradition.

[24] Timaeus Locrus is generally dated to the mid-third century BC, while Aëtius (50–100 AD) was slightly later than Philo.

expressing doctrines which could be viewed as having given rise to such a belief. At *Rep.* vi.508c, he refers to 'noetic place', in the *Phaedrus* myth and at 247c1–2 to 'things outside the cosmos'.[25]

Radice goes further; for him Philo was the catalyst of the doctrine that the Forms are the thoughts of God. Clearly, the concept is not expressesed on a literal reading of the *Timaeus*, where the Demiurge is subordinate to the Forms, whereas for Philo, God produces the blueprint according to which he wishes to create the world. (If we accept a non-literal reading, it becomes rather a different matter. The Forms have to be interpreted in some way, and the view that they are the thoughts of God, or the rational World-Soul, would seem to be the most logical one.) For Radice, Philo considers God as the 'foundational' creator; that is the creator of the 'positive foundations' of the world.[26] This is because He only creates true being (the physical instantiation of the Forms) and not the negative components (matter and evil) which are non-existent and therefore could not be created. This is a break with the 'semi-creationalism' of Plato (what I refer to as true demiurgy; ordering matter in conformity with the Forms).

I agree that this distinction can be drawn regarding the function of the Demiurge in Plato and Philo. However, as Radice himself admits, attributing the origin of the doctrine that the Forms are the thoughts of God to Philo would create three main problems.[27] Firstly, Philo adopts this theory as part of his allegorical reading of the Bible, and no trace of this Biblical exegesis can be observed in Platonism subsequently. Secondly, it would imply that Philo was capable of exerting significant influence upon the subsequent Platonic tradition. Indeed, Radice even envisages a situation in which two co-existing Platonic traditions, the mainstream Greek one and a Hellenist–Jewish variant, merge after Philo, thereby explaining the means by which this Philonic theory could enter the mainstream tradition.[28] The third difficulty lies in Philonic interpretation; many scholars would view Philo as incapable of inventing a theory of this significance.

Radice adopts three responses. Philo never indicates a source for this doctrine in *De Opificio Mundi*. This is hardly reliable evidence, though, since he frequently avoids attributing specific doctrines even to Plato. Secondly, and more cogently, *De Opificio Mundi* presents a more original account of creation than *De Aeternitate Mundi* (a dual exegesis of the Bible and the *Timaeus*) and so can be seen as closer to Philo's own beliefs,

---

[25] Runia: 2001, 136   [26] Radice: 1991, 127
[27] Radice: 1991, 129   [28] Radice: 1991, 130

while *De Aeternitate Mundi* presents a more traditional Greek account. Additionally *De Natura Mundi* from Timaeus Locrus, which is regarded as a standard exegesis of the *Timaeus* at this period, is close to *De Aeternitate Mundi* and never claims that the Forms are the thoughts of God. I do not feel, however, that the evidence is sufficient to postulate both that Philo was the first to use the term κόσμος νοητός and that he invented (as opposed to developed) the notion of the Forms as God's thoughts. Given his position close to the beginnings of Middle Platonism, we must be careful not to foist originality upon Philo in our enthusiasm to arrive at a more detailed understanding of how this particular phase of Platonism began. That said, however, Philo probably displays originality in his utilisation of the *Logos* of God and in his location of the noetic realm in this *Logos*. The *Logos*-Cutter is, in all probability, a Philonic contribution, given the fact, that in the absence of these notions in his philosophical predecessors, such concepts could easily have commended themselves to him from Scripture.

The *Logos* and the *Logos*-Cutter

The image of the *Logos* as a tool is one of the predominant images presented by Philo in order to cast light on its functioning in the creation of the world. Additionally, the *Logos* can also be presented as a mediating entity.[29] A more obscure example has been noted by Dillon and does not seem to have received the attention which it deserves; the equation of the *Logos* with Ganymede.[30] Initially, this appears rather bizarre: Hermes normally represents the Stoic–Platonic *Logos* in later Platonism.[31] Philo usually prefers to use Athena, given the nature of her birth (sprung from the head of Zeus), as at *Leg. All.* 1.15 or *Opif.* 100. Obviously, Ganymede is not alluded to by name, though we could hardly expect Philo to do that, and indeed he avoids mentioning Athena by name in his equation of her with the *Logos*. On closer reflection, the equation of Ganymede need not

---

[29] 'To his chief and most honoured messenger, his *Logos*, the Father who engendered everything has bestowed a remarkable fiefdom, to stand on the frontier and separate the creator from his product. The *Logos* is both continuously the suppliant of stressed mortality to the immortal and the ruler's ambassador to his subject. He exults in his fiefdom and exalting it, he describes it in the following terms: "And I stood between the Lord and you" (*Deut.* 5:5), i.e. not being uncreated like God or created like you, but a mean term between both extremes, serving as a hostage to both sides, to the parent as a pledge that what has been generated should never refuse to obey the reins and revolt, choosing disorder instead of order and to the offspring as hopefulness that the merciful God will never look away from his own work' (*Her.* 205–6).

[30] Dillon: 1979, *passim*

[31] Dillon: 1979, 38 points out that for Philo, Hermes is merely the planet Mercury, as for example at *Dec.* 54.

appear so strange. As the wine-pourer (οἰνοχόος) of Zeus, he represents the flow of God's (ordering) grace to the rest of creation, precisely one of the activities carried out by the *Logos*. Dillon cites two passages in which this image is used: *Deus* 155–8 and *Spec.* 1.303.

οἷς δ᾽ ὁ θεὸς ἐπινίφει καὶ ἐπομβρεῖ τὰς ἀγαθῶν πηγὰς ἄνωθεν, ἐκ λάκκου πίνομεν καὶ βραχείας [καὶ] κατὰ γῆς λιβάδας ἀναζητοῦμεν, ὕοντος ἡμῖν ἀνεπισχέτως οὐρανοῦ τὴν νέκταρος καὶ ἀμβροσίας τῶν μεμυθευμένων ἀμείνω τροφήν; . . .

οὐκ ἂν οὖν ἐκ λάκκου πίοι, ᾧ δίδωσιν ὁ θεὸς τὰς ἀκράτους μεθύσματος πόσεις, τοτὲ μὲν διά τινος ὑπηρετοῦντος τῶν ἀγγέλων, ὃν οἰνοχοεῖν ἠξίωσε, τοτὲ δὲ καὶ δι᾽ ἑαυτοῦ, μηδένα τοῦ διδόντος καὶ τοῦ λαμβάνοντος μεταξὺ τιθείς.

Are we to drink from a tank and seek out small springs beneath the earth, we whom God snows and rains blessings upon from on high, when the heavens shower upon us without end food superior to the nectar and ambrosia recounted in myth . . . (*Deus* 155)

He, on whom God has bestowed unmixed draughts of intoxication, would not drink from a tank either from the hand of one of the angels that serve him, who is his designated wine-pourer or directly from his own hand, without anyone being placed between the one who gives and the one who receives. (*Deus* 158)

This image of God raining down his blessings upon mankind is instructive of Philo's view of the *Logos*. In the first place, it would appear that Philo is equating the *Logos* with an angel when he refers to one of the angels functioning as the winepourer of God. However, at *Her.* 205, Philo refers to the *Logos* as the chief messenger (ἀρχάγγελος). Philo elsewhere regards the *Logos* as an angel.[32] He is also the ἡνίοχος (charioteer) or ἔποχος (mount) of the powers (*Fug.* 16)[33] and their father and guide.[34] At *Conf.* 148, the *Logos* is said to be the oldest image of God. In the second instance, he contemplates the possibility that God dispenses benefits directly upon created matter without any mediation, without coming down in favour of one of his models of divine Providence. What is going on here?

The notion that benefits (as well as evils) are dispensed by angels, rather than by God directly, is found elsewhere in the Philonic corpus, as well as the understanding that God is capable of intervening directly upon the material world; He has no need of any entities to insulate Him from the phenomenal realm. In any case, it seems strange that Philo should attempt

---

[32] *Cher.* 3 and 35, *Mut.* 87, *Fug.* 5, *Deus* 182   [33] Billings: 1919, 45   [34] *Somn.* II.185–7

to portray the relationship between God and his *Logos* in (covert) homo-erotic terms. Dillon notes the lack of surviving testimony to this allegory elsewhere, although he notes the possibility that it was conceived some time previously and so was more acceptable by the stage that Philo came to use it.[35] A further indication of speculation in this regard is the identification of Ganymede with the Water-Carrier by Hellenistic times; leading one to believe that it was beginning to be regarded as a cosmic power.[36] In this context, Dillon mentions the demiurgic imagery of the Avestan tradition, in which Haoma, a spirit who inhabits alcohol, is responsible for the blessings of humanity. This is similar to the second equation of the *Logos* as Ganymede at *Spec.* 1.303, as the fountain from which God pours forth the virtues.

This reveals the complex nature of Philo's conception of the *Logos*. It is more than a mere tool or knife used by God during creation. It is a mediating entity, which functions as a co-Creator and plays an active role in the universe after genesis, although it does not compromise God's unity. The conceptions of the *Logos* as a knife and as the wine-pourer of God can be regarded as related. As wine-pourer, the *Logos* is responsible for conveying divine benefits upon mankind; as cutter, it provides the greatest of benefits in terms of the ordering division of the created realm.

The idea of the *Logos* as a continual outpouring from God evokes the later Plotinian notion of a creative flow from the One. Furthermore, it underpins the role which it plays in a continual creation. Philo uses the term *Logos* to refer to νοῦς, quite possibly because he wished to draw a distinction between the divine Intellect and the human mind. In this sense, it can be regarded as containing the Forms. It is also referred to as the oldest and the most generic of created things (*Leg. All.* III.175), as well as 'the first-born son of God' (*Agr.* 51). This seems to have paved the way for the later identification of the divine *Logos* with Christ in subsequent Christian thinking. Additionally, the *Logos* can resemble a proto-Gnostic Demiurge in so far as 'it is called a god by those with imperfect knowledge of the real god'.[37]

This positing of the *Logos* does not undermine the unity of the godhead, which remains indivisible for Philo:

ὁ γὰρ θεοῦ λόγος φιλέρημος καὶ μονωτικός, ἐν ὄχλῳ τῷ τῶν γεγονότων καὶ φθαρησομένων οὐχὶ φυρόμενος, ἀλλ' ἄνω φοιτᾶν εἰθισμένος ἀεὶ καὶ ἑνὶ

[35] Dillon: 1979, 39
[36] *Homiliae Clementis* 5.17, Ampelius 2.11, Ps.-Erathosthenes, *Catast.* 26, 30, as mentioned by Dillon: 1979, 39.
[37] *Leg. All.* III.207; *cf. Somn.* I.229–30; 238–39

ὁπαδὸς εἶναι μόνῳ μεμελετηκώς. ἄτμητοι μὲν οὖν αἱ δύο φύσεις, ἥ τε ἐν ἡμῖν τοῦ λογισμοῦ καὶ ἡ ὑπὲρ ἡμᾶς τοῦ θείου λόγου,ἄτμητοι δὲ οὖσαι μυρία ἄλλα τέμνουσιν.

For the Word of God is solitary and fond of solitude, never mixing with the throng of things that come into being and perish, but its accustomed station is always above and it has taken thought to be an attendant to One only. Therefore there are two indivisible natures, that of rationality within us and that of the divine reason above us and although indivisible themselves, they divide countless other things. (*Her.* 234)

This is reiterated at *Her.* 236, where Philo indicates that not only is the Father indivisible, but that this characteristic is possessed by the *Logos* also.[38] It is particularly interesting that Philo should attempt to preserve this sort of 'unity in the second degree', since it indicates that the *Logos* is not based on the Platonic Dyad. (Indeed, it is a masculine entity and has more in common with the World-Soul; it is Sophia that corresponds most closely with the Dyad.) One of the advantages in numerous metaphysical systems for postulating secondary gods is that it allows postulation of further hypostases, but Philo, as a monotheist, is very keen on preserving a united godhead, even as regards secondary divine entities. In spite of Philo's claim that the *Logos* is a second god, he does not use the phrase in the same manner as Numenius. Numenius' Second God, as we shall see, is divided by matter, whereas although the Philonic *Logos* is the sole cause of the division of matter, Philo is at pains to point out that it is not divided by it.

On two occasions, Philo refers to the *Logos* as an instrument used by God in the creation of the world. At *Leg. All.* III.96, we are told that God 'used it like an instrument when He was making the world (ἐκοσμοποίει)' and 'when He was fashioning the world (ἐκοσμόπλαστει), He used it as an instrument, so that the arrangement of all the things He was completing might be faultless' (*Migr.* 6). On three occasions, the role of the *Logos* as an instrument is implied. It is that 'through which' (δι' οὗ) the world was produced (ἐδημιουργεῖτο) at *Sacr.* 8, (and *Spec.* I.81) or that 'by which'

---

[38] τοῦτο δὲ συμβαίνει διὰ τὴν πρὸς τὸν ποιητὴν καὶ πατέρα τῶν ὅλων ἐμφέρειαν. τὸ γὰρ θεῖον ἀμιγές, ἄκρατον, ἀμερέστατον ὑπάρχον ἅπαντι τῷ κόσμῳ γέγονεν αἴτιον μίξεως, κράσεως, διαιρέσεως, πολυμερείας· ὥστε εἰκότως καὶ τὰ ὁμοιωθέντα, νοῦς τε ὁ ἐν ἡμῖν καὶ ὁ ὑπὲρ ἡμᾶς, ἀμερεῖς καὶ ἄτμητοι ὑπάρχοντες διαιρεῖν καὶ διακρίνειν ἕκαστα τῶν ὄντων ἐρρωμένως δυνήσονται.

'And this comes about as the result of its resemblance to the Maker and Father of all. For the godhead is pure, unmixed and without subordinate parts and has become for the entire cosmos the cause of mixture, blending, divisibility and multiplicity of parts. So that it is fitting that what is similar to God, the Intellect in us and the Intellect above us, should subsist as pure and indivisible and still be robust and capable of distinguishing everything that is.'

God made the world at *Cher.* 127. This is similar to the role played by Wisdom during creation. In *The Wisdom of Solomon*, the author treats Wisdom as equivalent to the *Logos* of God, although he refers to it as 'God's daughter'. Wisdom is equally that 'through which (δι' ἧς) the world came into existence'[39] or 'was brought to completion'.[40] Wisdom additionally is the title given to what seems to be the Philonic equivalent of the Receptacle at *Ebr.* 31, where it is called the 'mother and nurse (τιθήνη) of the all'.

The *Logos* functions in the typical role of a divine mediator, insulating God from the disorder (in Philo's case, evil might be a little too strong) inherent in matter:

ἐξ ἐκείνης γὰρ πάντ᾽ ἐγέννησεν ὁ θεός, οὐκ ἐφαπτόμενος αὐτός – οὐ γὰρ ἦν θέμις ἀπείρου καὶ πεφυρμένης ὕλης ψαύειν τὸν εὐδαίμονα καὶ μακάριον – ἀλλὰ ταῖς ἀσωμάτοις δυνάμεσιν, ὧν ἔτυμον ὄνομα αἱ ἰδέαι, κατεχρήσατο πρὸς τὸ γένος ἕκαστον τὴν ἁρμόττουσαν λαβεῖν μορφήν.

For God generated everything out of that [matter] without touching it himself – for it was not right for his happy and blessed nature to touch unlimited and jumbled matter – but he employed incorporeal powers, aptly called Forms, so that each genus might be able to take its appropriate shape. (*Spec.* 1.329)

This mode of creation is echoed when God calls upon his powers to aid Him in the forming of man. These incorporeal powers which allow matter to take a shape do not themselves become enmattered (unlike the man of the *Poimandres*: see below). Although it may not be 'lawful' for God to act directly upon matter, this does not prevent Him from dispensing benefits directly to mortals (*Leg. All.* III.178). While Philo compares these incorporeal powers which assist in creation to the [Platonic] Forms, they also reflect the influence of the Stoic doctrine of efficient causes.

The image of the *Logos* as a cutter might well have suggested itself to Philo from the flaming sword of the Cherubim at *Gen.* 3:24, once Philo had equated this with the *Logos*.[41] Among the Nag Hammadi texts, according to *The Testimony of Truth* 9.3, it is the Word (*logos*) which separates us from the error of the angels, where it is associated with the incarnate Son of Man.[42] In *The Teaching of Silvanus*, the *Logos* is also regarded as a cutting-agent, and an identification with the incarnate Christ is made

---

[39] *Fug.* 10　　[40] *Det.* 54

[41] This is suggested by Harl: 1966 – *Quis rerum divinarum heres sit* (PM 15).

[42] 'But the saw is the Word of the Son of Man which separates us from the error of the angels. But no one knows the God of the truth except the man alone, this one who will forsake all the things of the world since he has renounced the whole place having grasped the fringe of his garment' (trans. Birger Pearson, as furnished by Hay: 1973, 18).

explicit.[43] *The Gospel of Truth* compares the *Logos* to a drawn sword.[44] However, just as in *The Teaching of Silvanus*, this cutting-action has a *soteriological*, rather than a *demiurgic* significance, evoking the Johannine conception of Incarnation, with the Word condemning some and saving others. The three Nag Hammadi texts quoted above date from the second century AD.

This portrayal of the *Logos* as a saw or sword may either be influenced in some way (directly or indirectly) by Philo, or indicate a current in Judaeo–Christian philosophical thought, which Philo himself adopted. Philo may have drawn upon the Jewish tradition's view of the divine word as a sword used for protection of the faithful and punishment of the wicked,[45] and conflated this with the cosmological elements of the Stoic *Logos*. The *Logos*-Cutter can be viewed as a Jewish response within the current of Greek philosophy, which attempted to explain the imposition of order upon a disordered universe using figures such as Hermes or Osiris as a personification of divine wisdom. As a divine mediator, the *Logos* appears at *Poimandres* 10–11 and at Plutarch's *De Iside et Osiride* (53–4, 372e–373c). Eudorus (of Alexandria) may also have expressed the combination of the Monad and Dyad as the thought or λόγος of a supreme One.[46] Tobin suggests that the *Logos* in Philo may reflect an element from the early stages of Alexandrian Middle Platonism, ignored by subsequent thinkers.[47]

A useful source for Philo's doctrine of the *Logos-Tomeus* is his commentary *Quis Rerum Divinarum Heres Sit* ('Who is the Heir of Divine Things?'), an exegesis of *Gen.* 15:2–18, concerning Abraham's sacrifice of the heifer, ram and birds. Although the concept of the *Logos*-Cutter is only fully developed in *Her.*, at *Fug.* 194–6, it is mentioned as a Divider. In an interesting philosophical insight, Philo portrays Yahweh as the inventor of Platonic *diairesis* by which he differentiates the various levels of the created realm. At *Her.* 132, Philo refers to Abraham's division of his sacrifice as symbolic of the *Logos'* division of our consciousness into rational and irrational soul, true and false speech and cognitive and non-cognitive impressions. Philo has no qualms here about adopting a twofold division of the soul, despite the more Platonic tripartite division, in favour of Stoic tendencies. At *Her.*

---

[43] 'Knock on yourself that the Word (*Logos*) may open for you. For he is the Ruler of Faith and the Sharp Sword, having become all for everyone because he wishes to have mercy on everyone' (trans. Peel and Zandee, quoted by Hay: 1973, 19). Teach. Silv. 117, 5–10

[44] '... for this is the judgment that came forth from Heaven, having judged everyone, being a drawn sword of two edges cutting this way and that, when came into the midst the Word who is in the heart of those who speak it, it was not mere sound, but it became a *soma.*' GT 25.25–26.15 (trans. Grobel). The original Greek text does not survive; *The Gospel of Truth* has been preserved in a Coptic translation.

[45] Hay: 1973, 19   [46] Tobin: 1993, 149   [47] Tobin: 1993, 149

133, Philo again signals the link between *diairesis* and demiurgy. The Artificer (ὁ τεχνίτης) creates by dividing our soul and limbs in the middle, the technique he uses for creation of the world itself, which is equated with division into equal parts and the division of opposites.

This notion of the *Logos* engaged in division is central to Philo's notion of world-creation. It is hardly surprising that it is the *Logos* which is engaged in this sort of activity, as the human mind, which Philo also describes as a *Logos*, is occupied with much the same function on a smaller scale, when it is engaged in *diairesis*.[48] *Her.* 134 continues this concept of a creative division on the part of the *Logos*, based around the four main elements.

> λαβὼν γὰρ αὐτὴν ἤρξατο διαιρεῖν ὧδε· δύο τὸ πρῶτον ἐποίει τμήματα, τό τε βαρὺ καὶ κοῦφον, τὸ παχυμερὲς ἀπὸ τοῦ λεπτομεροῦς διακρίνων· εἶθ’ ἑκάτερον πάλιν διαιρεῖ, τὸ μὲν λεπτομερὲς εἰς ἀέρα καὶ πῦρ, τὸ δὲ παχυμερὲς εἰς ὕδωρ καὶ γῆν, ἃ καὶ στοιχεῖα αἰσθητὰ αἰσθητοῦ κόσμου, ὡσανεὶ θεμελίους, προκατεβάλετο.

> For taking this, he began to divide it in the following manner. First he made two sections, one heavy and the other light, distinguishing the coarse particles from the fine ones. And then he divides each of these again, the rare particles into air and fire and the dense ones into water and earth, which as the sensible elements of the sensible realm, he established as the foundations.

The first task of the *Logos*-Cutter is division based on the elements. The activity of the *Logos* here parallels very closely the ordering through differentiation engaged in by the Demiurge of the *Timaeus*.[49] It is interesting that in spite of a certain adoption of Stoic elements, a great deal of Philo's exposition of the *Logos*-Cutter is expressed in terms generic to all the schools. Certainly Stoic, however, is the division of fire into two kinds at §136; the useful variety and what amounts to the Stoic *pyr technikon*, set aside to preserve the heavens.[50]

---

[48] This parallel is made more explicit at *Her.* 235: ὅ τε γὰρ θεῖος λόγος τὰ ἐν τῇ φύσει διεῖλε καὶ διένειμε πάντα, ὅ τε ἡμέτερος νοῦς, ἅττ’ ἂν παραλάβῃ νοητῶς πράγματά τε καὶ σώματα, εἰς ἀπειράκις ἄπειρα διαιρεῖ μέρη καὶ τέμνων οὐδέποτε λήγει.

'The divine *Logos* separated and distributed everything that is in nature, and our mind dealing with the material and immaterial things grasped by intellection, divides them into an infinity of infinities and *at no point does it stop cutting them.*'

[49] This notion is developed at *Her.* 135: πάλιν δὲ τὸ βαρὺ καὶ κοῦφον καθ’ ἑτέρας ἔτεμεν ἰδέας, τὸ μὲν κοῦφον εἰς ψυχρόν τε καὶ θερμόν – ἐπεφήμισε δὲ τὸ μὲν ψυχρὸν ἀέρα, τὸ δὲ θερμὸν φύσει πῦρ –, τὸ δὲ βαρὺ εἰς ὑγρόν τε αὖ καὶ ξηρόν· ἐκάλεσε δὲ τὸ μὲν ξηρὸν γῆν, τὸ δὲ ὑγρὸν ὕδωρ.

'Once again he divided heavy from light according to a different method of classification. He divided the light into cold and hot and he called the cold "air", and that which is hot by nature, "fire", and the heavy into wet and dry; and he called the dry "earth" and the wet "water".'

[50] *Cf. SVF* I.120

At *Her.* 140, Philo makes it quite clear that God is the true Demiurge and the *Logos* is merely the means or tool by which He creates, rather than some kind of independently-operating agent.

οὕτως ὁ θεὸς ἀκονησάμενος τὸν τομέα τῶν συμπάντων αὐτοῦ λόγον διῄρει τήν τε ἄμορφον καὶ ἄποιον τῶν ὅλων οὐσίαν καὶ τὰ ἐξ αὐτῆς ἀποκριθέντα τέτταρα τοῦ κόσμου στοιχεῖα καὶ τὰ διὰ τούτων παγέντα ζῷά τε αὖ καὶ φυτά.

And so God sharpened the blade of his all-cutting *Logos* and he divided universal being, previously formless and without quality and the four elements of the cosmos set apart from it and the animals and plants solidified from them.

The Being which God divides here is *ousia* or the Stoic conception of matter, although God is envisaged as ordering, rather than creating. The continual division of matter by the *Logos* can be viewed as Philo's version of the continual geometry engaged in by the Demiurge at *Quaest. Conviv.* 1002e., stressed at *Her.* 235 (quoted at n 48), where the *Logos* is said to never cease to cleave matter. The passage describes the *Logos* as dividing matter into an infinity of infinities; for Philo, there was no such thing as an atom in the philosophical sense – it was always possible, even if only for the *Logos*, to subdivide matter eternally. The οὐδέποτε here, I would suggest, could be taken as 'at no point' as well as 'never'; the *Logos* never ceases to divide matter in the temporal sense, but equally in its continual care for the phenomenal realm, it is capable of infinite division, or at least to a point beyond that which can be comprehended by the human mind.

This notion of the *Logos* as a tool is echoed in a similar passage at §167: 'these tables too were cut by the Divine Legislator and by Him only'. This notion of cutting suggests that the thought of God can be equated with the τομεύς. The passage helps to reinforce the notion of the *Logos*-Cutter as an instrument of the Demiurge, since the identification of a legislator with a Demiurge is an old one, etymologically and conceptually, as both can be regarded as imposing order upon disorder. Although Philo's image of the *Logos*-Cutter appears to be a unique contribution, *Her.* 146 reveals how much he owes to the Demiurge of the *Timaeus*:

τούτων προϋποτυπωθέντων ἴδε πῶς μέσα διελὼν ἴσα διεῖλε κατὰ πάσας τὰς ἰσότητος ἰδέας ἐν τῇ τοῦ παντὸς οὐρανοῦ γενέσει. ἀριθμῷ μὲν οὖν ἴσα τὰ βαρέα τοῖς κούφοις ἔτεμνε, δύο δυσί, γῆν καὶ ὕδωρ, τὰ βάρος ἔχοντα, τοῖς φύσει κούφοις, ἀέρι καὶ πυρί, καὶ πάλιν ἓν ἑνί, τὸ μὲν ξηρότατον τῷ ὑγροτάτῳ, γῆν ὕδατι, τὸ δὲ ψυχρότατον τῷ θερμοτάτῳ, πυρὶ ἀέρα, τὸν αὐτὸν δὲ τρόπον καὶ σκότος φωτὶ καὶ ἡμέραν νυκτὶ καὶ χειμῶνι θέρος καὶ ἔαρι μετόπωρον καὶ ὅσα τούτων συγγενῆ.

Having sketched this in outline, note how God in 'dividing in the middle' when creating the universe divided according to all principles of equality. For with respect to equality of number, he cut heavy parts equal in number to the light parts, two parts corresponding to two parts, earth and water, being heavy, corresponding to air and fire, the parts which are light by nature. And in this way again one corresponds to one, the driest to the wettest, earth to water and the coldest to the hottest, fire to air, and in the same way darkness corresponds to light and day to night and summer to winter and spring to autumn and there are many other examples of the same kind.

This activity is similar to the separating action of the Receptacle (under the guidance of the Demiurge). The stress on division based on equality (i.e. rational principles) echoes the mixing together of the Same and the Different; Philo points to the rationality visible in the cosmos, as evidence that it must have been created by a rational principle.

This is echoed in the description of the equitable construction of the heavens at *Her.* 147, which is very similar to the construction of the heavens and the insertion of the World-Soul at *Tim.* 35. The Demiurge creates parallel circles in heaven: the spring and autumn equinoxes and the summer and winter solstices. He further observes equality in his creation of two uninhabited zones adjoining the poles and two habitable and temperate zones. The description here is very similar to the construction of the heavens and the insertion of the World-Soul at *Tim.* 35. Although Philo dispenses with the World-Soul, which becomes largely replaced by the *Logos*, he is prepared to adopt the imagery of the *Timaeus* for his own purposes.[51] Dillon suggests that Philo may be using a Stoic handbook in delineating his concept of the *Logos*. In this context, he cites the presentation of Antiochus of Ascalon in Cicero's *Academica Posteriora*, where mention is made of an infinite 'cutting' and 'dividing' of matter.[52] However, Cicero does not go into details of how this division contributes to the organisation of matter, or indeed any details at all.

---

[51] *Her.* 153 develops the notion that man is a compound generated by an equitable mixture of his components by the *Logos*: . . . καὶ τὰ περὶ ἡμᾶς μέντοι τέτταρα, ξηρόν, ὑγρόν, ψυχρόν τε αὖ καὶ θερμόν, τὴν δι' ἀναλογίας ἰσότητα κερασαμένην ἁρμόσασθαι, καὶ μηδὲν ἄλλο <ἡμᾶς> ἢ κρᾶσιν εἶναι τῶν τεσσάρων δυνάμεων ἀναλογίας ἰσότητι κραθεισῶν.

'. . . and they tell us that the four components: dry, wet, cold and hot have been mixed and harmonised according to equal mathematical proportion and we are nothing other than the mixture of the four constituents blended together on the basis of mathematical proportion.'

[52] 'infinite secari atque dividi', ap. Cicero, *Acad. Post.* 27.

Just like his Platonic predecessor, the Philonic Demiurge constructs the world based on significant numbers, which reveals the perfection of the cosmos (*Her.* 156).[53] It is this that allows Philo to explain in philosophical terms creation in six/seven days; obviously there is no reason why an omnipotent deity should require a week to create the cosmos, since he would be capable, as Philo asserts, of creating it simultaneously. However, the importance of six and seven underline the perfection of what was created. This perfection of the created world is evoked by the menorah.[54] This importance of six and seven is stressed subsequently at *Her.* 215.[55]

It is evident that the cosmos as a whole is good. God 'judged equally about the little and the great, according to Moses' (*Her.* 157). There can be no question of the recalcitrance of matter as an explanation of the existence of evil in the created realm: God, like the Platonic Demiurge, made the best kind of world possible, but unlike him, was in no way limited by the materials which He used.[56] The prejudicial Platonic view of matter does come across at *Her.* 158, although not as a limitation on God's bounty. Rather, matter is not responsible for the beauty of the cosmos, which must be attributed to the superior science of the Demiurge.[57] For Philo, in spite

[53] ταῦτα δ' οὐκ ἀπὸ σκοποῦ διδάσκουσιν, ἀλλ' ἔγνωσαν ὅτι ἡ τοῦ θεοῦ τέχνη, καθ' ἣν ἐδημιούργει τὰ σύμπαντα, οὔτε ἐπίτασιν οὔτε ἄνεσιν δεχομένη, μένουσα δὲ ἡ αὐτὴ κατὰ τὴν ἐν ὑπερβολαῖς ἀκρότητα τελείως ἕκαστον τῶν ὄντων δεδημιούργηκε, πᾶσιν ἀριθμοῖς καὶ πάσαις ταῖς πρὸς τελειότητα ἰδέαις καταχρησαμένου τοῦ πεποιηκότος.

'And in teaching this they are not short of the mark, but they know that the art of God, according to which He produced everything, does not accept either tightening and slackening, but remains the same and through its transcendent superiority it has perfectly framed all things that are, all numbers and all forms that orient towards perfection are fully employed by the Maker.'

[54] *Her.* 225: ἐπίγειον οὖν βουληθεὶς ἀρχετύπου τῆς κατ' οὐρανὸν σφαίρας ἑπταφεγγοῦς μίμημα παρ' ἡμῖν ὁ τεχνίτης γενέσθαι πάγκαλον ἔργον προσέταξε, τὴν λυχνίαν, δημιουργηθῆναι. δέδεικται δὲ καὶ ἡ πρὸς ψυχὴν ἐμφέρεια αὐτῆς·

'Therefore the Craftsman wishing that we might possess an imitation of the archetypal heavenly sphere with its seven lights ordered this most beautiful work, the candlestick, to be made. Its similarity to the soul has been demonstrated.'

[55] ... τὰ γὰρ λεγόμενα διχοτομήματα τριῶν ζῴων δίχα διαιρεθέντων ἓξ ἐγένετο, ὡς ἕβδομον τὸν τομέα εἶναι λόγον, διαστέλλοντα τὰς τριάδας, μέσον αὐτὸν ἱδρυμένον.

'... therefore what are referred to as the half-portions of the three animals cloven in two made six and the *Logos*-Cutter, separating both sets of three, and stationing himself in the centre, was the seventh.' *Cf. Her.* 219.

[56] This non-recalcitrance of matter also seems to appear at the Ciceronian passage *Ac. Post.* 27, as pointed out by Sedley; a Stoic position.

[57] *Her.* 158: ... ἐπεὶ καὶ ὅσοι τῶν τεχνιτῶν εἰσι δόκιμοι, ἃς ἂν παραλάβωσιν ὕλας, εἴτε πολυτελεῖς εἶεν εἴτε καὶ εὐτελέσταται, δημιουργεῖν ἐθέλουσιν ἐπαινετῶς. ἤδη δέ τινες καὶ προσφιλοκαλοῦντες τὰ ἐν ταῖς εὐτελεστέραις οὐσίαις τεχνικώτερα τῶν ἐν ταῖς πολυτελέσιν εἰργάσαντο βουληθέντες προσθήκῃ τοῦ ἐπιστημονικοῦ τὸ κατὰ τὴν ὕλην ἐνδέον ἐπανισῶσαι.

'... for all noted craftsmen, whether they use expensive materials or those easily paid for, wish to employ them in a manner worthy of praise and indeed some have wrought better work with the

of what humans might think, there is no dichotomy between an inferior or superior part of creation (*Her.* 159):

τίμιον δ' οὐδὲν τῶν ἐν ὕλαις παρὰ θεῷ· διὸ τῆς αὐτῆς μετέδωκε πᾶσι τέχνης ἐξ ἴσου. παρὸ καὶ ἐν ἱεραῖς γραφαῖς λέγεται· ʼεἶδεν ὁ θεὸς τὰ πάντα ὅσα ἐποίησεν, καὶ ἰδοὺ καλὰ λίανʼ (*Gen.* 1:31), τὰ δὲ τοῦ αὐτοῦ τυγχάνοντα ἐπαίνου παρὰ τῷ ἐπαινοῦντι πάντως ἐστὶν ἰσότιμα.

But no honour is bestowed to any type of material by God. And on account of this he endowed them all with the same art and in equal proportion. And so in the holy Scriptures it says 'God saw all things that He had made and behold they were good' (*Gen.* 1:31) and those things which receive the same praise are equal in honour according to the one who praises.

This passage seems to indicate the existence of different types of matter. But Philo perhaps uses ὕλη to refer to material in general, rather than 'matter' in the technical sense. I think that Philo is influenced here by the *Genesis* account, in which man is created from a mixture of materials, such as mud and *pneuma*. The account finds an echo in Plotinus' comment at *Enn.* III 2 [47] 11.6 that a craftsman could not make an animal only with eyes, even if these are its finest feature. The beauty of the cosmos lies in its instantiation of all possibilities, and even though some of these possibilities may appear better than others, God has applied the same skill in making everything.

This point is picked up at *De Prov.* 2.59 when Philo states that the creation of reptiles has not come into being by a direct act of Providence (κατὰ πρόνοιαν), but as an attendant circumstance (κατʼ ἐπακολούθησιν) Philo adopts the response also favoured by the Christians in explaining why God has created wild animals (they encourage bravery) at *De Prov.* 2.56–8. Philo's response is more systematic, however. Worms and lice cannot be blamed on the Demiurge, but occur for scientific reasons (putrefaction in food and perspiration).[58] Just as Plato asserts that only what is good can be attributed to God, Providence is only responsible for that which is created 'from its proper material by a generative and foremost process of nature' (ἐξ οἰκείας ὕλης κατὰ φύσιν σπερματικὴν καὶ προηγουμένην ἔχει γένεσιν).[59] Philo also adopts the Stoic approach that apparent evils, upon closer inspection, turn out to be beneficial, when he points out the utility of many venomous animals in medicinal processes at *De Prov.* 2.60f.

The *Logos* goes on to allocate various portions to humanity at *Her.* 180. There are two distinct categories of good: a superior kind marked by a

cheaper than the expensive substances: for they had an even greater love of beauty and by relying upon additional technique, they wished to make deficient material equal.'

[58] *De Prov.* 2.59   [59] *De Prov.* 2.59

stamp (ἐπίσημα) is given to the lover of learning and a formless version (τὰ ἀτύπωτα καὶ ἄσημα) is bestowed upon the ignorant. Once again Philo can be regarded as a proto-Gnostic here, in his view of a Demiurge who distributes two different qualities of goods to two different classes of humanity, although this is also a a very Platonic distinction. The image of the stamp is similar to his use of the seal at *Opif.*, and refers to those elements of the phenomenal realm which are made after the image of the *Logos* (in Platonic terms, an instantiation of a Form). Therefore it seems that the *Logos* distributes to men of ignorance that which is purely material.

Philo has a Stoicised reading of the *Timaeus* in mind at *Her.* 187–9, where he refers to the *Logos* as a bond holding together creation, though he uses the terms κόλλα and δεσμός, rather than the more Stoic ἕξις:

> ... μονὰς δὲ οὔτε προσθήκην οὔτε ἀφαίρεσιν δέχεσθαι πέφυκεν, εἰκὼν οὖσα τοῦ μόνου πλήρους θεοῦ. χαῦνα γὰρ τά γε ἄλλα ἐξ ἑαυτῶν, εἰ δέ που καὶ πυκνωθείη, λόγῳ σφίγγεται θείῳ. κόλλα γὰρ καὶ δεσμὸς οὗτος πάντα τῆς οὐσίας ἐκπεπληρωκώς· ὁ δ᾽ εἴρας καὶ συνυφήνας ἕκαστα πλήρης αὐτὸς ἑαυτοῦ κυρίως ἐστίν, οὐ δεηθεὶς ἑτέρου τὸ παράπαν.

> ... and a unit does not accept either addition or subtraction, being the image of the sole God, who also has plenitude. For other things are porous in themselves and if the pores are closed, it is because they are bound tight by the divine *Logos*. For the *Logos* is a glue and a bond and fills up all things with His essence. But He, fasting and weaving together each individual thing, is in a true sense filled with Himself and He requires absolutely nothing else.

This echoes the portrayal of the *Logos* at *De Plantatione* 7–10, as a bond holding together opposites. There is an interesting parallel in the pseudo-Aristotelian *De Mundo*, where Nature is regarded as responsible for the harmony of opposites. As in Philo, Heraclitus is regarded as the originator of this concept. Although no exact parallel of the Philonic *Logos*-Cutter (in a demiurgic sense) prior to Philo can be found, Heraclitus does mention a spiritual principle which he calls *logos* (the origin of the Stoic doctrine), and which contributes to world-order by combining opposites rather like Philo's *Logos* does at *Her.* 199–200:[60]

> τὴν δὲ τούτων ἐμμελῆ σύνθεσίν τε καὶ κρᾶσιν τὸ πρεσβύτατον καὶ τελειό-τατον ἔργον ἅγιον ὡς ἀληθῶς εἶναι συμβέβηκε, τὸν κόσμον, ὃν διὰ συμ-βόλου τοῦ θυμιάματος οἴεται δεῖν εὐχαριστεῖν τῷ πεποιηκότι, ἵνα λόγῳ μὲν ἡ μυρεψικὴ τέχνη κατασκευασθεῖσα σύνθεσις ἐκθυμιᾶται, ἔργῳ δὲ ὁ θείᾳ σοφίᾳ δημιουργηθεὶς κόσμος ἅπας ἀναφέρηται πρωὶ καὶ δειλινῆς ὁλοκαυτούμενος.

[60] Fr. 1 ap. Sextus *adv. math.* VII.132; Fr. 2 ap. Sextus *adv. math.* VII.133; Fr. 50 ap. Pseudo-Hippolytus *Ref.* IX.9, 1; Fr. 67 ap. Pseudo-Hippolytus *Ref.* IX.10, 8. See interpretation in Kirk, Raven, and Schofield: 1983.

And the harmoniously-concocted mixture, that most honoured and most polished work; which is truly sacred, the cosmos, which he holds under the token of incense, thanks its Maker, so that in speech it has been put together by the art of the *parfumier*, burnt up as incense, but in fact the cosmos, having been crafted by divine wisdom, is offered up and is a burnt offering morning and evening.

This image of a cosmic mixture produced by the Demiurge could easily be inspired by Plato. However, Philo stresses that this mixture is harmonious, which is clearly not the case in the *Timaeus*, compounded as it is of the passive and the recalcitrant (Sameness and Difference). Indeed, at *Her.* 214 and QG. III.5, Philo points out that Heraclitus' cosmology shares similarities with that of Moses. In the Hermetic tradition there is also a *Logos*-Cutter of sorts; Poimandres, who produces the cosmos through differentiation, and Hermes who is a combined Truth and *Logos* figure. Philo's mention of Heraclitus does not indicate that he was father of a doctrine involving the *Logos*-Cutter. One can only conclude that the *Logos*-Cutter is an original contribution of Philo's or he acquired it from a Hellenistic Jewish source. One can seen how he could have arrived at the idea, through considering the creative activity of the Demiurge in terms of the Platonic procedure of *diairesis* and stimulated by the division of the animals at *Gen.* 15:10.

The division of the *Logos*-Cutter should not be viewed as a crude creational mechanism. As Radice has shown, the *Logos* engages in a very complex process.[61] (1) It engages in actual division (*Her.* 133–40). (2) It engages in a secondary, equalising division (*Her.* 141–200). (3) Mediation (*Her.* 201–6) is followed by (4) the placing of the divided components (*Her.* 207–29) and finally (5) the non-division of noetic reality (*Her.* 230–6). This creation is part of a whole sequence of the ordered and proportional construction of subordinate structures. For example, the heavy cosmic substance becomes separated into earth (dry) and water (wet), while the light forms air (cold) and fire (hot). Earth is divided into continents and islands, while water is drinkable and undrinkable. This reveals not just a continual division of cosmic substance, but a logical division that itself is responsible for cosmic structure.[62]

In this sense, the *Logos* is a mediator, not just between the First Principle and the rest of creation, but an equaliser in terms of size (§§147–50; night and day, the equinoxes, both poles etc.) as well as in terms of proportion (§§152*f.*; between the four elements in the cosmos or between the four

---

[61] Radice: 1989, 67
[62] Radice: 1989, 70 presents a schema detailing the symmetrical structure inherent in this division by the *Logos*.

constituent factors, dry, wet, cold and hot, in Man). This can, naturally, be viewed as a development of the notion of creation as a transition from disorder to order expressed at *Tim.* 30a (*cf. Her.* 133) and unity based upon the harmony of proportions reflected at *Tim.* 31a–32a. To a great extent this notion of division is also echoed at *Soph.* 253d–e, in the distinction of different classes of things through the practice of dialectic.

This structured approach to creation by division is a metaphysical necessity in Philo's scheme. Although Philo does not recognise an atom, in the sense of a particle which cannot be further divided, he does recognise the absurdity of an infinite division on the part of the *Logos*. For this reason intellects and noetic reality are not divided by the *Logos*.[63] Philo finds Biblical justification for this approach in the comment on Abraham's sacrifice at *Gen.* 15:10: 'but the birds he did not divide'. I think that this is what Philo means when he states that the *Logos* 'never ceases to divide, for when it has gone through all sensible objects down to the atoms and what are called indivisibles, it begins from them again to divide those things contemplated by reason into inexpressible and indescribable parts' (*Her.* 26). By things contemplated by reason, Philo is not referring to the noetic realm, rather particles which although they may not be humanly divisible can still be reduced by the *Logos*.

This system of creation is complemented by agricultural imagery at *De Plantatione*.[64] This is drawn from the notion of God as a cultivator at *Rep.* x.597c–d8. The cosmos can be considered like a living creature or farm which requires continual tending on the part of God. However, this image is not a model for an alternative type of creation, but only an alternative explanation of creation: it is still essentially an account detailing transition from disorder to order (εἰς τάξιν ἐξ ἀταξίας, *Plant.* 3). If the earth is composed of the heavier elements (water and earth) at the centre, and the lighter ones (water and fire) at the exterior, this leads to the question of how these elements do not neutralise one another through their close proximity.[65] This is the effect of the mediating presence of the *Logos*.[66]

[63] Radice: 1989, 75

[64] *Plant.* 2–3: ὁ μὲν τοίνυν τῶν φυτουργῶν μέγιστος καὶ τὴν τέχνην τελειότατος ὁ τῶν ὅλων ἡγεμών ἐστι, φυτὸν δὲ αὖ περιέχον ἐν ἑαυτῷ τὰ ἐν μέρει φυτὰ ἅμα παμμυρία καθάπερ κληματίδας ἐκ μιᾶς ἀναβλαστάνοντα ῥίζης ὅδε ὁ κόσμος...

'The greatest of all cultivators and the most perfect in his craftsmanship is the ruler of the universe and his plant does not only consist within itself of individual plants, but rather myriads of them, shooting forth like vine-shoots from a single root, that is the cosmos'.

[65] *Plant.* 4–9

[66] *Plant.* 8:...λόγος δὲ ὁ ἀίδιος θεοῦ τοῦ αἰωνίου τὸ ὀχυρώτατον καὶ βεβαιότατον ἔρεισμα τῶν ὅλων ἐστίν.

'...and it is the eternal *Logos* of the eternal God, the most solid and the firmest support of the whole'.

De Opificio Mundi

The *De Opificio Mundi* is Philo's most detailed account of creation. Essentially, this treatise can be viewed as attempting to rewrite the *Timaeus* in terms of the cosmology of *Genesis*. Philo attempts to show how the original great cosmological account was compiled by Moses, superior to that of the philosophers, not only on account of its antiquity,[67] but also because it was based upon divine revelation. Runia suggests that the philosophical (as opposed to thematic) influence of the *Timaeus* is weaker than that of other dialogues (such as the *Republic*, the *Symposium* and the *Phaedrus*).[68] This is evident from the system expounded here which does not envisage any role for the Platonic World-Soul. Part of this eclipse of the *Timaeus* may stem from Philo's aversion to the use of myth when discussing God, which he shares with other Hellenistic–Jewish writers.[69] Philo is also opposed to what he regards as a Chaldean view of the cosmos (cosmos-worship), which is also to be found in Platonists such as Numenius.[70]

The main problem which Philo faces is trying to reconcile temporal *creatio ex nihilo* with Greek philosophy which could not countenance such a position. At *Gen.* 3:9, it does not seem that Man has come into being from nothing: 'for dust thou art, and into dust shalt thou return' and again at *Gen.* 2: 'And the Lord God formed man of the dust of the ground and breathed into his nostrils the breath of life.' However, at *2Macc.* 7:3 and 7:8 *creatio ex nihilo* is envisaged; the majority of modern scholars interpret *Gen.* 1 as referring to *creatio ex nihilo* also.[71] O'Neill argues that Philo believed in *creatio ex nihilo* based upon his comments at *De Deo* 7–8, where it is clear that God produces matter, all of which he transforms into the various elements.[72]

---

[67] It is a well-known observation that in antiquity the older a belief, the greater the authority which it commanded. *Cf.* Boys-Stones: 2001.

[68] Runia: 1986, 33

[69] *Spec.* 1.28–31 where Philo rejects the gods whom the makers of myth have deceived people with. *Cf.* Aristobulus frg. 2, (10.2), Josephus *Ant.* 1.14.

[70] *Abr.* 69–70 Χαλδαῖοι γὰρ . . . τὴν ὁρατὴν οὐσίαν ἐσέμνυνον τῆς ἀοράτου καὶ νοητῆς οὐ λαβόντες ἔννοιαν, ἀλλὰ τὴν ἐν ἐκείνοις τάξιν διερευνώμενοι . . . καὶ κατὰ τὴν τῶν οὐρανίων πρὸς τὰ ἐπίγεια συμπάθειαν τὸν κόσμον αὐτὸν ὑπέλαβον εἶναι θεόν, οὐκ εὐαγῶς τὸ γενόμενον ἐξομοιώσαντες τῷ πεποιηκότι.

'the Chaldeans magnified visible being and they did not consider what is unseen and intelligible, but in investigating the arrangement of numbers . . . and the sympathy between heaven and earth, they assumed that the cosmos was a god and impiously assimilated what had been generated to the one who generated.'

[71] O'Neill: 2002, 453

[72] O' Neill: 2002, 462, goes on to argue that *creatio ex nihilo* had already been established as a credal statement by the time of the New Testament. e.g. *John* 1:3 'All things were made by [the *Logos*] and without him was not even one of the things that exist made.'

Philo resolves this tension between *creatio ex nihilo* and Greek philosophy by putting forward a defence akin to that initially advanced by Speusippus and Xenocrates, that God generated (from eternity) the intelligible archetypes,[73] which are the contents of His Intellect (*Logos*), which are then projected onto matter. This is atemporal 'for we must think of God as doing all things simultaneously'.[74] The sequence is a logical one, with heaven listed first because it ranks first in degree of excellence. Philo claims that on the first day the κόσμος νοητός was created. Being allotted an entire day merely to create the intelligible world helps to stress a degree of separation from the visible cosmos (it seems that this is the underlying reason behind the semantic debate concerning the first day and day one). To a great extent, Philo is absolved from the necessity of presenting the mechanism of God's creative activity; merely His Will suffices (which cannot be understood by man). However, this does not prevent Philo from providing a detailed analysis in order to render this creative activity comprehensible to the faithful.

It is no coincidence, however, that God should be said to have created the cosmos in six days.

> ἓξ δὲ ἡμέραις δημιουργηθῆναί φησι τὸν κόσμον, οὐκ ἐπειδὴ προσεδεῖτο χρόνων μήκους ὁ ποιῶν – ἅμα γὰρ πάντα δρᾶν εἰκὸς θεόν, οὐ προστάττοντα μόνον ἀλλὰ καὶ διανοούμενον –, ἀλλ' ἐπειδὴ τοῖς γινομένοις ἔδει τάξεως. τάξει δὲ ἀριθμὸς οἰκεῖον, ἀριθμῶν δὲ φύσεως νόμοις γεννητικώτατος ὁ ἕξ·

> He says that the cosmos was generated in six days, not because the maker required a duration of time – for it is reasonable that God did everything simultaneously, not only in commanding but also in intelligising, – but because order was necessary for the things being generated. Number is native to order and according to the laws of nature, six is the most generative number. (*Opif.* 13).

Moses' indication that the cosmos was created in six days underpins the rational structure which underlies it. Philo draws upon Pythagorean numerology to illustrate that it is the first perfect number, since it is the product of its factors ($1 \times 2 \times 3 = 6$), as well as their sum ($1 + 2 + 3 = 6$). It is also the sum of its half, its third and its sixth ($3 + 2 + 1 = 6$).[75] It is a combination of the odd (3 was considered the first odd number) and the even (2), as well as of male (3) and female (2). In this way 6 indicates the bountiful nature of the cosmos, since the male and the female are necessary for its perpetuation. The fact that the world was created in six days

---

[73] Dillon: 2003a, 10   [74] *Opif.* 13   [75] *Opif.* 13

indicates its perfection and that it consists of all possibilities. Just as Plato does, Philo views the cosmos as a wondrous production emanating from God's goodness.[76] It is worth noting that the Judaic cosmogony is the only one in the ancient world which envisaged creation as taking place in six days. In this context, it is possible that comments such as that expressed at *Theol. Arith.* 50.8–10: 'Because the perfection of the cosmos falls under the six, the excellence of the demiurgic god is rightly thought to be hexadic', or indeed the Pseudo-Iamblichean tradition concerning the six may owe something to Philo.

While the creation in six days is Judaic, the work processes of Philo's divine creator are Platonic:

προλαβὼν γὰρ ὁ θεὸς ἅτε θεὸς ὅτι μίμημα καλὸν οὐκ ἄν ποτε γένοιτο δίχα καλοῦ παραδείγματος οὐδέ τι τῶν αἰσθητῶν ἀνυπαίτιον, ὃ μὴ πρὸς ἀρχέτυπον καὶ νοητὴν ἰδέαν ἀπεικονίσθη, βουληθεὶς τὸν ὁρατὸν κόσμον τουτονὶ δημιουργῆσαι προεξετύπου τὸν νοητόν, ἵνα χρώμενος ἀσωμάτῳ καὶ θεοειδεστάτῳ παραδείγματι τὸν σωματικὸν ἀπεργάσηται, πρεσβυτέρου νεώτερον ἀπεικόνισμα, τοσαῦτα περιέξοντα αἰσθητὰ γένη ὅσαπερ ἐν ἐκείνῳ νοητά.

For God, since he is God, anticipated that a beautiful copy would not come about without a beautiful model and that none of the sense-perceptible things would be blameless, if it was not modelled upon the archetypal and intelligible form and having decided to fabricate the invisible cosmos beforehand, in order that he might employ it as an incorporeal paradigm, most similar to God, and bring to perfection the corporeal world, a younger representation of an older exemplar, which encompasses as many sense-perceptible kinds as there are intelligible kinds in the other cosmos. (*Opif.* 16).

Even though it is a central tenet of Platonic philosophy that a noetic realm exists, Philo here regards it as something which his all-powerful creator cannot do without.[77] Of course, the Demiurge's dependence upon

---

[76] σπείρει μὲν οὖν οὗτος, τὸ δὲ γέννημα τὸ ἴδιον, ὃ ἔσπειρε, δωρεῖται· γεννᾷ γὰρ ὁ θεὸς οὐδὲν αὑτῷ, χρεῖος ἅτε ὢν οὐδενός, πάντα δὲ τῷ λαβεῖν δεομένῳ.

'Therefore God sows, but what is generated, He gives as a gift, for God does not generate anything on his own account, for He does not require anything, but everything is for the sake of the one needing to receive it.' *Cher.* 44 (*cf. Leg. All.* III.14; *Post.* 4)

[77] *Cf. Opif.* 19: τὰ παραπλήσια δὴ καὶ περὶ θεοῦ δοξαστέον, ὡς ἄρα τὴν μεγαλόπολιν κτίζειν διανοηθεὶς ἐνενόησε πρότερον τοὺς τύπους αὐτῆς, ἐξ ὧν κόσμον νοητὸν συστησάμενος ἀπετέλει καὶ τὸν αἰσθητὸν παραδείγματι χρώμενος ἐκείνῳ.

'The opinion which we have concerning God must be of this kind, that is, having decided to found a great city, he first considered its general character, and having framed the noetic cosmos from this, he completed the sensible cosmos, using this outline as a model.' This closely parallels the relationship of the Living Creature to the cosmos at *Tim.* 30a–d.

the noetic realm (as a model for the production of the world) is a feature commonly found within Platonism. It is noteworthy that Philo, as a Jewish philosopher, adopts this notion, since such a model is not found in *Genesis* (though the Torah in the rabbinic tradition is sometimes portrayed as God's model). This illustrates that we really are discussing demiurgy here, as opposed to merely parallel speculations regarding the origin of the world. Furthermore, Philo does break away from the imagery frequently found in Platonism which assigns a specific location (supra- and sublunar) to each of the two realms. This leads Philo to introduce his famous comparison of the Demiurge with a king founding a city at *Opif.* 17. Once the king has decided upon construction, the architect mentally draws up the plans. The means by which he replicates this mental conception in the material realm echoes what the Demiurge accomplishes.[78] The *Logos*, then, contains the noetic realm, as the mind of the Demiurge, but it is not true to state that it has a physical place.[79] This is the world of Forms as God is actually engaged in creation, but as Philo considers God as continually engaging in the process of creation, no fine distinction need be made concerning this point.[80]

Philo blurs the distinction between the king and the architect. This may be an attempt to preserve God's transcendence. Another reason may be that he did not wish to open speculation concerning an ontological chain of demiurgic intermediaries. It indicates that the function of Demiurge does not exhaust God's being; it is only one of his roles. Philo drew a distinction between God as θεός and as κύριος.[81] Secondly, Philo presents the architect as envisaging the future city mentally, when in point of fact he

---

[78] *Opif.* 18: εἶθ' ὥσπερ ἐν κηρῷ τῇ ἑαυτοῦ ψυχῇ τοὺς ἑκάστων δεξάμενος τύπους ἀγαλματοφορεῖ νοητὴν πόλιν, ἧς ἀνακινήσας τὰ εἴδωλα μνήμῃ τῇ συμφύτῳ καὶ τοὺς χαρακτῆρας ἔτι μᾶλλον ἐνσφραγισάμενος, οἷα δημιουργὸς ἀγαθός, ἀποβλέπων εἰς τὸ παράδειγμα τὴν ἐκ λίθων καὶ ξύλων ἄρχεται κατασκευάζειν, ἑκάστῃ τῶν ἀσωμάτων ἰδεῶν τὰς σωματικὰς ἐξομοιῶν οὐσίας.

'Then taking up in his own soul the impressions of each object, just as if in wax, he carries the noetic city as an image. Stirring up the images by means of his ingrained memory and stamping their features (in his soul) to a still greater extent, just like a good craftsman Demiurge, looking at the model, he begins to build from stone and wood, making sure that the corporeal substances correspond to each of the incorporeal Forms.'

[79] *Opif.* 20

[80] *Opif.* 24: . . . τὸν νοητὸν κόσμον εἶναι ἢ θεοῦ λόγον ἤδη κοσμοποιοῦντος· οὐδὲ γὰρ ἡ νοητὴ πόλις ἕτερόν τί ἐστιν ἢ ὁ τοῦ ἀρχιτέκτονος λογισμὸς ἤδη τὴν [νοητὴν] πόλιν κτίζειν διανοουμένου.

'. . . the noetic cosmos is simply the *Logos* of God as he is engaged in the process of making the cosmos; for the noetic city is nothing other than the architect's calculation, as he is contemplating the foundation of the [noetic] city.'

[81] Runia: 1986 discusses Philo's notion of κατάχρησις – misuse of language, usually applied in relation to God. Even though God is nameless, his powers may be used to address him. *Cf. Mut.* 11–14; *Mut.* 27–8; *Post.* 168; *Somn.* 1.229 and *Abr.* 120. Runia: 1986, 438 n. 165 supplies a full list of examples of Philo's use of the concept of κατάχρησις.

would use written plans. However, this would not suit Philo's contention that the noetic realm does not occupy physical space. Philo's Demiurge is upwardly mobile with this promotion to architect, perhaps in response to sniping comments passed by other philosophical groups.[82]

The reason for creation is God's beneficence. The explanation for the apparently uneven distribution of goods is that God confers them in proportion to the capacity of the recipient.[83] Knowledge of God's essence was not even granted to Moses: 'You shall see what is behind me but my face you shall not see' (*Ex.* 33:18–23). To know the οὐσία of God would place man on a par with God.

> ἀλλ' οὐ πρὸς τὸ μέγεθος εὐεργετεῖ τῶν ἑαυτοῦ χαρίτων – ἀπερίγραφοι γὰρ αὗταί γε καὶ ἀτελεύτητοι –, πρὸς δὲ τὰς τῶν εὐεργετουμένων δυνάμεις· οὐ γὰρ ὡς πέφυκεν ὁ θεὸς εὖ ποιεῖν, οὕτως καὶ τὸ γινόμενον εὖ πάσχειν, ἐπεὶ τοῦ μὲν αἱ δυνάμεις ὑπερβάλλουσι, τὸ δ' ἀσθενέστερον ὂν ἢ ὥστε δέξασθαι τὸ μέγεθος αὐτῶν, ἀπεῖπεν ἄν, εἰ μὴ διεμετρήσατο σταθμησάμενος εὐαρμόστως ἑκάστῳ τὸ ἐπιβάλλον.

> But He does not bestow good things in accordance with His own power of grace; for these are uncircumscribed and unlimited, but rather according to the capacities of those receiving the benefits; for what has been generated cannot receive benefits in proportion to God's ability to bestow them, since His powers overflow and the one who receives is weaker and would fall short of their magnitude, if it were not that God measures them appropriately and harmoniously assigns to each its share. (*Opif.* 23)

This is similar to the situation regarding matter, which has to partake of God's goodness in order to sustain the weight of creation. Philo uses Plato's argument that the cosmos can only be beautiful if the Demiurge follows an immutable model. There is an important distinction, however, between Philo's 'noetic cosmos' and Plato's Forms. Plato's model seems only to consist of *genera* and *species* (but not the totality of creation, which appears to be the case with Philo). Although the question of the Forms has already been dealt with above, here I wish to revisit the relationship between the ideal world and the Demiurge. It is clear, given the image of the architect, that Philo's Demiurge is actually involved in the design of the cosmos, though it is unclear whether this is the case with the Demiurge in the *Timaeus* (most probably not, since the model is pre-existent). The

---

[82] For example the Epicurean at Cicero *ND.* 19 mockingly states 'By what insight of the soul was your Plato able to imagine such a great process of craftsmanship, by means of which God constructed the world? What contrivances, what iron implements, what levers and cranes and what attendants were used for such great walls?'

[83] *Opif.* 23

image of the seal imprinting itself upon matter as upon wax introduced at §16 reinforces the image of matter as a passive recipient of the Forms, rather than as a principle in its own right.

The theme of the inexhaustibility of God suggests that Philo envisaged divine infinitude. This is clearly not the case with the limited but well-intentioned Demiurge of the *Timaeus* or the god of Aristotle. Divine infinitude first emerges in developed form in Gregory of Nyssa, who was heavily influenced by Philo (though Plotinus would recognise the infinitude of divine potency).[84] This is related to the 'overdose of being' suggested at *Spec.* 1.43–4 in relation to Moses' desire to see God.[85]

The mechanism of creation

Philo reserves the right to interpret the Biblical account of creation in a non-literal fashion. 'Beginning' does not have a temporal sense. His views at *Opif.* 26 are compatible with both *creatio simultanea* and *creatio aeterna*.[86] In favour of *creatio simultanea*, one can point to §§7–12 which makes much better sense in terms of a simultaneous temporal beginning of the cosmos and of time itself. Secondly, at *Aet.* 14, Philo is opposed to a non-literal interpretive tradition of the *Timaeus*. As Radice comments, this type of creation is a necessary postulate in order to remove anthropomorphism from the image of God, as well as quashing the possibility of an idle

---

[84] For divine infinitude in Gregory of Nyssa, see *CE* 1.167–71. Kees-Geijon: 2005, 152 points out that in the Greek philosophical tradition infinity (which by its very nature is undetermined and therefore imperfect) is not predicated of the highest being. For further discussion on this topic, *cf.* Mühlenberg: 1966.

[85] χαρίζομαι δ' ἐγὼ τὰ οἰκεῖα τῷ ληψομένῳ· οὐ γὰρ ὅσα μοι δοῦναι ῥᾴδιον καὶ ἀνθρώπῳ λαβεῖν δυνατόν· ὅθεν ὀρέγω τῷ χάριτος ἀξίῳ πάσας ὅσας ἂν οἷός τε ᾖ δέξασθαι δωρεάς. τὴν δ' ἐμὴν κατάληψιν οὐχ οἷον ἀνθρώπου φύσις ἀλλ' οὐδ' ὁ σύμπας οὐρανός τε καὶ κόσμος δυνήσεται χωρῆσαι.

'I graciously give what is in accordance with the one who receives. For not everything which I can give can be easily received by humanity. For this reason, I stretch forth my hand to the one worthy of grace with the gifts which he is able to receive. But neither the nature of mankind, not the whole heaven or cosmos is able to sustain the apprehension of me.'

[86] *Opif.* 26: φησὶ δ' ὡς 'ἐν ἀρχῇ ἐποίησεν ὁ θεὸς τὸν οὐρανὸν καὶ τὴν γῆν', τὴν ἀρχὴν παραλαμβάνων· οὐχ ὡς οἴονταί τινες, τὴν κατὰ χρόνον· χρόνος γὰρ οὐκ ἦν πρὸ κόσμου, ἀλλ' ἢ σὺν αὐτῷ γέγονεν ἢ μετ' αὐτόν· ἐπεὶ γὰρ διάστημα τῆς τοῦ κόσμου κινήσεώς ἐστιν ὁ χρόνος, προτέρα δὲ τοῦ κινουμένου κίνησις οὐκ ἂν γένοιτο, ἀλλ' ἀναγκαῖον αὐτὴν ἢ ὕστερον ἢ ἅμα συνίστασθαι, ἀναγκαῖον ἄρα καὶ τὸν χρόνον ἢ ἰσήλικα κόσμου γεγονέναι ἢ νεώτερον ἐκείνου· πρεσβύτερον δ' ἀποφαίνεσθαι τολμᾶν ἀφιλόσοφον.

'When he says "in the beginning God made the heaven and the earth", He does not take "beginning", as some people think, temporally. For before the cosmos there was no time, but it came into being either along with the cosmos or after it. For time is an extension of the cosmos' movement, and no movement could come about before what moves but it must necessarily come about later or at the same time, and therefore it is necessary that time is either coeval with the cosmos or younger than it. To dare to state that it is older is contrary to philosophy.'

Demiurge.[87] The whole reason for claiming that the world is actually created is largely to stress its complete dependence upon God (rather than determining a particular point of time at which it came to be).[88] Temporal creation would be unacceptable to Philo, since it would go against the immutability of God's nature, so Philo resorts to the Platonic notion of the simultaneous commencement of time and the cosmos. God might continually have a demiurgic role to fulfil, but creation is also simultaneous 'for we must think of God as doing all things simultaneously'.[89]

The creation which God engages in throughout *Opif.* evokes the division of the *Logos*-Cutter delineated in *Her.* The primary division is between heaven and earth, followed by air and void and then water, spirit and light.[90] A subsequent division between light and darkness produces day and night.[91] Light and darkness appear to be physically confined to particular regions of the cosmos. By void here, Philo implies (following Plato and Aristotle) that the cosmos occupies all available physical space.[92] Philo opposes the Stoic notion of extra-cosmic void (to accommodate for fluctuations in the size of the cosmos) at *Her.* 228. The seven items listed in the initial creation include the four elements (heaven = fire). Void is the Platonic Receptacle; Philo clarifies that it is created by God, unlike Plato who leaves this point vague. Since the Forms and the void into which these Forms are instantiated are both created by God, matter must also be a product of God. Philo, however, does not actually explicitly identify the Receptacle with the void.

God then creates the firmament, a situation which proves problematic for Philo since he is unable to reconcile his Hellenised cosmology with the Mosaic version. At *Her.* 283–4, Philo considers the nature of the material which forms the heavens:

τὰ μὲν σωματικὰ ταῦτα, τὸ δὲ νοερὸν καὶ οὐράνιον τῆς ψυχῆς γένος πρὸς αἰθέρα τὸν καθαρώτατον ὡς πατέρα ἀφίξεται. πέμπτη γάρ, ὡς ὁ τῶν ἀρχαίων λόγος, ἔστω τις οὐσία κυκλοφορητική, τῶν τεττάρων κατὰ τὸ κρεῖττον διαφέρουσα, ἐξ ἧς οἵ τε ἀστέρες καὶ ὁ σύμπας οὐρανὸς ἔδοξε γεγενῆσθαι, ἧς κατ' ἀκόλουθον θετέον καὶ τὴν ἀνθρωπίνην ψυχὴν ἀπόσπασμα.[93]

These belong to the body, but the nature of the soul, which is noetic and celestial, will seek a father in the purest aether. For according to the account of the Ancients, there is a fifth substance, moving around in a circle, and

[87] Radice: 1989, 116   [88] Runia: 1993, 134
[89] *Opif.* 13: ἅμα γὰρ πάντα δρᾶν εἰκὸς θεόν, οὐ προστάττοντα μόνον ἀλλὰ καὶ διανοούμενον . . .
[90] *Opif.* 29   [91] *Opif.* 33   [92] *Cf. Plant.* 6–8, *QE* 2.68
[93] ἀπόσπασμα appears to be a Stoic term, occurring in Zeno (x3), Chrysippus and Epictetus, although it also occurs in Plutarch and Philo seven times (TLG).

differing on account of its superiority from the four, and they supposed that out of this, stars and the entire heaven had been generated and following on from this, it was concluded that the human soul was a piece torn off from it.

Origen claimed that at the end of the world human souls would become aether; his position appears to be a more refined version of the one that Philo expresses here.[94] Philo adopts the Aristotelian fifth element and asserts that it is the substance of which the heavens are composed. More interesting is his assertion that the soul is a fragment of heaven; this is a rather weaker form of the Gnostic view that the soul was a trapped fragment of the godhead.

Again at *Opif.* 36, Philo runs into difficulties in trying to make the Mosaic account compatible with a hellenised cosmology.[95] Philo cannot fit waters above and below the firmament into a hellenised version and so simply ignores this aspect of the Biblical account. There is no place for supracosmic waters, since this region is already occupied by the heavenly bodies. However, Philo mentions water subsequently (at *Opif.* 38) portraying it as a sort of cosmic 'glue' (κόλλα), which is able to bind together opposed elements. This is the nearest that Philo gets to positing moisture that lies beneath the cosmos.

The Demiurge creates by apportioning everything in due measure. Philo's description of the sweet water here, which has been separated from its salty counterpart and which goes on to form the sea, echoes this division of water into sweet and salty elsewhere (e.g. at *Her.* 136 or *Somn.* 1.18). The notion of the moisture retained by earth as a binding element was common in Greek philosophy e.g. Aristotle, *Meteor.* 4.4. 382b (citing Empedocles) or Plotinus, *Enn.* II 1 [40] 6. It is, however, missing from *Genesis*. Philo draws upon Greek philosophy as a means of 'modernising' the Mosaic account. A similar parallel can be found at *Deus* 35–6, where cohesion (ἕξις, the most basic kind of Stoic cohesion) is only one mechanism by which God holds

---

[94] None of this is particularly original. Heraclides of Pontus in the Old Academy had declared souls to be composed of aether, the substance of the stars, while Xenocrates also accepted aether as a fifth substance.

[95] ὁ μὲν οὖν ἀσώματος κόσμος ἤδη πέρας εἶχεν ἱδρυθεὶς ἐν τῷ θείῳ λόγῳ, ὁ δ' αἰσθητὸς πρὸς παράδειγμα τούτου ἐτελειογονεῖτο. καὶ πρῶτον αὐτοῦ τῶν μερῶν, ὃ δὴ καὶ πάντων ἄριστον, ἐποίει τὸν οὐρανὸν ὁ δημιουργός, ὃν ἐτύμως στερέωμα προσηγόρευσεν ἅτε σωματικὸν ὄντα· τὸ γὰρ σῶμα φύσει στερεόν, ὅπιπερ καὶ τριχῇ διαστατόν·

'For the incorporeal cosmos had been formed and settled in the divine *Logos*, but the perceptible cosmos was being perfected according to the incorporeal model. And the Demiurge made the heaven, as the first of its parts, and the best of all, which He truly called the firmament, since it is a body. For body is solid by nature, since it is three-dimensional.'

together the world.[96] At *Opif.* 131, this moisture is vital for holding the earth together in the preliminary stages of creation, but becomes supplemented by the 'unificatory spirit'. This could be the *Logos*, since Philo refers to it as 'the glue and the bond' (*Her.* 188) or the 'unbreakable bond of the universe' (*Plant.* 9).

The creation of plants and animals is treated at *Opif.* 42–3. God creates these merely by ordering it. Philo, in keeping with the *Genesis* account, posits the creation of animals prior to that of Man, rather than viewing it as a secondary creation to provide Man with what is necessary for survival. This later forces him to justify the location of the creation of Man in his account.

> ὁ μὲν δὴ προστάττει τῇ γῇ ταῦτα γεννῆσαι· ἡ δ᾽ ὥσπερ ἐκ πολλοῦ κυο-
> φοροῦσα καὶ ὠδίνουσα, τίκτει πάσας μὲν τὰς σπαρτῶν, πάσας δὲ τὰς
> δένδρων, ἔτι δὲ καρπῶν ἀμυθήτους ἰδέας. ἀλλ᾽ οὐ μόνον ἦσαν οἱ καρποὶ
> τροφαὶ ζῴοις, ἀλλὰ καὶ παρασκευαὶ πρὸς τὴν τῶν ὁμοίων ἀεὶ γένεσιν, τὰς
> σπερματικὰς οὐσίας περιέχοντες, ἐν αἷς ἄδηλοι καὶ ἀφανεῖς οἱ λόγοι τῶν
> ὅλων εἰσί, δῆλοι καὶ φανεροὶ γινόμενοι καιρῶν περιόδοις.

> He commanded the earth to generate these things and just as if it had been pregnant for a long time and was in labour, it gave birth to all sown plants, and to every sort of tree and to unspeakable types of fruit. But the fruit was not only food for living animals, but it was prepared for the continuous generation of its kind and it contained substances in the form of a seed, in which the invisible and unseen ordering principles of the whole living thing is found, and they become visible and manifest as the seasons progress.

The earth appears to be like a machine which can just keep functioning once it has been installed without too much direct intervention by God. The *spermatikoi logoi* mentioned by Philo are a Stoic innovation. They regarded the seed as containing the generic pattern necessary for the continued reproduction of the organism, although it could not be seen and had to be logically inferred. Philo mentions this theory elsewhere at *Leg. All.* III.150 and *De Animalibus* 20 and 96.

[96] τῶν γὰρ σωμάτων τὰ μὲν ἐνεδήσατο ἕξει, τὰ δὲ φύσει, τὰ δὲ ψυχῇ, τὰ δὲ λογικῇ ψυχῇ. λίθων μὲν οὖν καὶ ξύλων, ἃ δὴ τῆς συμφυΐας ἀπέσπασται, δεσμὸν κραταιότατον ἕξιν εἰργάζετο· ἡ δέ ἐστι πνεῦμα ἀναστρέφον ἐφ᾽ ἑαυτό· ἄρχεται μὲν γὰρ ἀπὸ τῶν μέσων ἐπὶ τὰ πέρατα τείνεσθαι, ψαῦσαν δὲ ἄκρας ἐπιφανείας ἀνακάμπτει πάλιν, ἄχρις ἂν ἐπὶ τὸν αὐτὸν ἀφίκηται τόπον, ἀφ᾽ οὗ τὸ πρῶτον ὡρμήθη·

'For He bound some of the bodies by means of cohesion, and others by the principle of growth, and still others by soul or rational soul. For in stones and in timber, which has been removed from its innate growth, he made cohesion an extremely powerful bond. For it is a spirit which returns to itself, since it begins to stretch from its centre to its boundaries and having touched the furthermost visible surface, it bends back again until it arrives back once more at the same place from which it first departed.'

Philo invests a great deal of energy in attempting to expound the level of rational design which underpins the created world. The creation of heaven on the fourth day has considerable metaphysical significance, especially since it can be equated with the nature of the solid (*Opif.* 49). It is this order which reveals the beauty inherent in creation. The importance of four in the Greek philosophical tradition is illustrated by the comment of Alexander of Aphrodisias (*Comm. in. Met.* 38.10–16) that δικαιοσύνη (usually 'justice', but here probably 'fairness') could be found in numbers, and four was the first number equal to the multiplication of itself.[97] Therefore, four can be identified with equality (as it was by the Pythagoreans) and, by extension, it indicates the fair distribution God engaged in during creation. Philo mentions the mathematical properties of the four at *Opif.* 51, and although he does not explicitly identify it with δικαιοσύνη, the tradition seems to have been too well known for him not to have been conscious of it when he introduced it in this context. At §89–128, this numerical symbolism is expanded further, when Philo begins to discuss the merits of the number seven. At §97, he comments that it represents the right-angled triangle that is the ἀρχή ('starting-point') of the (Timaean) universe. The significance of the number seven is stressed by the fact that it 'neither begets nor is begotten' (§100). Philo means that seven is a prime number which is incapable of generating any philosophically important number.

There are seven zones of heaven (§112). The Ἄρκτος the most important constellation for navigation, is composed of seven stars (§114). Like six, seven contains the universe because it is composed of three (irregularity) and four (disorder) (§97). There are seven parts of the visible body and seven viscera (§118). There are seven parts of the head and seven entrances and exits from the body (§119; an allusion to *Tim.* 75d). This is somewhat expedient, though, since the mouth is the source of three: entrance for food and drink and the exit for words. Following the *Timaeus*, there are seven motions. The Latin word for seven, *septem*, is etymologised by Philo as a derivation of σεμνός (reverend) and σεβασμός (reverence).

This is a combination of Philo's attempt to illustrate rational design in the cosmos, along with the importance of the number seven in Jewish culture. Plato glimpsed the truth in assessing numerical importance, but Philo utilises Judaic 'wisdom-figures' in addition to Plato's Pythagorean ones. Seven is important because it symbolises the *Logos* of God.[98] As Runia notes, although Philo introduces the τόπος of the rational order of creation, this remains subordinate to the theme of God's beneficence.[99] For

---

[97] Runia: 1986, 194   [98] Dillon: 1977, 160   [99] Runia: 1986, 199

example, at *Opif.* 53, he introduces the Timaean motif of the creation of the heavenly bodies in order to encourage mankind to engage in the study of philosophy.

On day five, Philo alters the Biblical version of the creation of land animals, ignoring the division into two days. He prefers to allocate day six to the creation of the cosmos in its entirety, rather than to completion of the creation of land animals. It is not immediately apparent what would remain for God to create on day six, since everything by this stage would appear to have already approached completion. Runia regards Philo's anthropocentric emphasis as responsible for this alteration, since it allows him to set the human creation apart from that of other land animals.[100] It is worth noting that Philo regards animals as having been designed to fit the environment in which they live and the first generation enters the world at the period of reproductive maturity.

His creational sequence has a different structure to Plato's, which is one of continual ontological descent (Young Gods, humans, creatures of the sky, land and finally sea). Philo is very vague concerning the actual beings created on the fifth and sixth days. At *QG* 1.19, he responds to the difficulty concerning the double creation of days five and six. He is unwilling to commit himself (his response begins with 'perhaps'), but proposes that during the preceding six days, only incorporeal, generic images (ἰδέαι) of animals were created, and on the final day, the sensible likeness is produced.

The creation of man

Man, as he is physically created, is inferior to the blueprint from which he has been made. Man is made not 'in the image of God', but after this image. The similarity which man shares with God is not one of the body, since God should not be envisaged as adopting a physical form.[101] Rather, the notion that man is made in the 'image of God' means that he is modelled on the mind or intellect of God.[102] It is unclear what sort of creation Philo regards as taking place. Is man created in one fell swoop, or is only the intellect created and then inserted from outside (similar to the insertion of the soul into the heavenly bodies posited later by Origen)? This double creation would parallel that posited by Philo in the case of animals. Most probably, the difficulty in understanding Philo's account stems from the source text, with the double account of creation at *Gen.* 1:26–7 and again at 2:7.

---

[100] Runia: 1986, 211   [101] *Opif.* 69   [102] *Her.* 231

Philo considers the question of why God did not make man on his own at
Opif. 72. The problem is introduced by the Septuagint passage 'Let us make
man (ποιήσωμεν ἄνθρωπον)'.[103] Evidently, God does not actually require
help to create man. He has, after all, already single-handedly constructed
the entire cosmos. Philo solves this problem by pointing out that there are
three categories of created beings (§73): plants and animals which partake
neither of goodness or evil, other creatures, such as the heavenly beings,
which are good only, and humanity, which possesses a mixed nature. On
account of this, it is not completely appropriate that God should make
man.

This differs from the generation of man in the *Timaeus*. There is some
similarity with *Tim.* 42d where the Demiurge does not produce man
single-handedly because otherwise man would be immortal, and because
the Demiurge does not wish to be responsible for man's immorality. However, the Platonic Demiurge profits from the opportunity to announce his
retirement (*Tim.* 42e5–6). God, on the other hand, calls upon unnamed
assistants, but does not sub-contract the task. Plato's Demiurge is only
responsible for the rational soul, while the irrational soul and the body are
produced by the Young Gods. In Philo, there is no clear division of labour.
Indeed, God could conceivably play a role in the creation of the human
body, though Winston argues that God is not responsible for anything
corporeal.[104]

Yet God (through the agency of his *Logos*) still creates the mortal genera
of the fifth and sixth days and he is responsible for the human body at
Gen. 2:7. If it is not beneath God's dignity to create animals, then there
is no reason why He might not create the human body. (Philo's statement
concerning morality appears unsatisfactory, since God can claim complete
credit for a lower order of life, but only partial praise for a higher one,
although this is a highly 'speciesist' argument.) Philo does not go into
graphic detail of which body part was created by which entity, as can be
found in certain Gnostic texts. From the context, though, it would not be
forcing the issue to conclude that the element in man which is capable of
engaging in evil activities cannot be the product of God. The assistants of
the *Timaeus* are the planetary gods; in Philo they are unnamed. There is
no reason for assuming that Philo is following Plato here. I think it more

---

[103] ἀπορήσειε δ᾽ ἄν τις οὐκ ἀπὸ σκοποῦ, τί δήποτε τὴν ἀνθρώπου μόνου γένεσιν οὐχ ἑνὶ δημιουργῷ
καθάπερ τἆλλα ἀνέθηκεν, ἀλλ᾽ ὡσανεὶ πλείοσιν·

   'It would not fall short of the target to consider the problem of why he only assigned Man's
   generation not to a single Demiurge, as for the other creatures, but as if to a multitude of creators.'

[104] Cf. *Spec.* I.329. Winston: 1973 and 1974–5.

likely that Philo envisages the angels as helpers, in keeping with rabbinic teaching.[105]

This part of Philo's account of the creation of man has encouraged many scholars to read proto-Gnostic tendencies into Philo's work. For example, Fossum thought that attributing a portion of the creation of the human body to angels indicates that they are a source of evil.[106] It is true that the actual human co-created by God and the angels is inferior to the archetypal one envisaged by God himself, but it is important to note that this is a part of the divine plan, not the result of some sort of conspiracy on the part of the angels. Unfortunately, God's reason for not realising the superior design (the provision of something which can be blamed for the morally incorrect choices which humans engage in) does not seem to be particularly praiseworthy.[107]

Philo provides a detailed outline of the creation of earthly man:

μετὰ δὲ ταῦτά φησιν ὅτι 'ἔπλασεν ὁ θεὸς τὸν ἄνθρωπον χοῦν λαβὼν ἀπὸ τῆς γῆς, καὶ ἐνεφύσησεν εἰς τὸ πρόσωπον αὐτοῦ πνοὴν ζωῆς' (*Gen.* 2:7). ἐναργέστατα καὶ διὰ τούτου παρίστησιν ὅτι διαφορὰ παμμεγέθης ἐστὶ τοῦ τε νῦν πλασθέντος ἀνθρώπου καὶ τοῦ κατὰ τὴν εἰκόνα θεοῦ γεγονότος πρότερον· ὁ μὲν γὰρ διαπλασθεὶς αἰσθητὸς ἤδη μετέχων ποιότητος, ἐκ σώματος καὶ ψυχῆς συνεστώς, ἀνὴρ ἢ γυνή, φύσει θνητός. ὁ δὲ κατὰ τὴν εἰκόνα ἰδέα τις ἢ γένος ἢ σφραγίς, νοητός, ἀσώματος, οὔτ' ἄρρεν οὔτε θῆλυ, ἄφθαρτος φύσει.

He says that after this 'God moulded a human taking mud from the earth and He breathed the breath of life into his face' (*Gen.* 2: 7). By this, he illustrates most clearly that there is an immense difference between the human moulded at this stage and the one previously generated in the image of God. For the one who has been moulded as sense-perceptible, shares in quality and has been composed of body and soul, is man or woman, and is mortal by nature. But the one produced according to the image is a sort of idea or genus or seal; it is apprehended by intellect and is without body, neither male or female, by nature immortal. (*Opif.* 134).

---

[105] There is a Judaeo–Christian association of the angels with the planets, seen in the belief in seven archangels, a view related to the fact that there were seven known planets at the time.

[106] Runia: 1986, 238. *Cf.* Fossum: 1982.

[107] *Opif.* 75: . . . ἵνα ταῖς μὲν ἀνεπιλήπτοις βουλαῖς τε καὶ πράξεσιν ἀνθρώπου κατορθοῦντος ἐπι-γράφηται θεὸς ὁ πάντων ἡγεμών, ταῖς δ' ἐναντίαις ἕτεροι τῶν ὑπηκόων· ἔδει γὰρ ἀναίτιον εἶναι κακοῦ τὸν πατέρα τοῖς ἐκγόνοις· κακὸν δ' ἡ κακία καὶ αἱ κατὰ κακίαν ἐνέργειαι.

' . . . whenever a person acts correctly and in an irreproachable manner in judgements and in actions, this can be ascribed to God, the director of all, but opposite acts result from others subordinate to him. For the Father is necessarily blameless for the evil in his offspring, and viciousness and acts accomplished in accordance with unrighteousness are evil . . . '

God is portrayed as the one actually doing the moulding, while no mention is made of the extent of the angelic contribution. The distinction here is not between a rational and irrational component in man, but rather between the archetype and the prototype. At *Conf.* 179, Philo avoids interpreting this collaboration in terms of the production of parts of the soul, although at *Fug.* 69, he regards God as responsible for creating the rational part, while the powers make the (presumably irrational) subordinate part. *Conf.* 171–4 also mentions three possible collaborators with God; his powers, the heavenly bodies or the angels.

Philo lists four possible explanations for mankind's late creation. The first is that all the necessities of life might already be available (*Opif.* 76–8). Secondly, an ethical lesson is provided, since when Man is in a state of innocence, there is an abundance of food. It is only once he falls from this state that he has to engage in agriculture (*Opif.* 79–81). The third reason is that creation is framed by the construction of heaven and of the human being, who can be viewed as a miniature heaven. The final reason is that Man is the king of creation and his sudden appearance at the final moment might overawe the beasts. For Philo, the entire cosmos has been created principally for the benefit of humanity (for example, he even suggests that the heavenly bodies were created earlier than mankind, so that they would be available for mankind to contemplate when it was created). In this respect, he resembles Origen. Even though they accept the Hellenic superiority of the heavenly beings, Philo refers to the heavenly gods as God's ἔκγονοι, although here he is only following Plato's lead at *Tim.* 41a–42d, but they still both regard the heavenly bodies as being created primarily in order to serve humanity.

Philo digresses into an excursus on the hebdomad at *Opif.* 89–128, provided with this opportunity by his account of the seventh day of creation. In fact, here again Philo diverges from the Biblical account. God does not create the world in seven days, but in six (and rests on the seventh, *Gen.* 2:2–3), a situation ignored by Philo here (though not at *Leg. All.* 1.5–7, 16).[108] Instead, Philo posits the peculiar notion of the birthday of the cosmos, which is inspired by *Gen.* 2:3 (God blesses the cosmos) and which may be unique to him.[109] The Hebrew Bible differs from the *Septuagint*, since at *Gen.* 2:2, it indicates that God only finished creating on the seventh day. As Runia notes, the Samaritan Pentateuch, *Jubilees* 2.16, *Vetus Latina*

---

[108] Runia: 1986, 257
[109] The concept of a seven day week was unique to Judaism at this period and was only officially instituted by the Emperor Constantine in 321 AD, though the third-century writer Censorinus composed a text concerning time entitled *On the Birthday*.

and the *Peshitta* have the same reading as the *Septuagint*.[110] This passage is parallel to the Demiurge's retirement at *Tim.* 42e when he appears to abdicate responsibility to the Young Gods. At *Leg. All.* 1.5–7, Philo comments that Moses does not use ἔπαυσατο (middle voice) which would imply that God is the one who rests, but κατέπαυσεν ᾧ ἤρξατο (active voice): 'He caused to rest those (creatures) which He had begun.'[111] The seventh day was given as a day of rest by God to His creatures, not something that He required Himself. Philo is influenced by the Aristotelian view that God can engage in endless activity and complete his tasks effortlessly. It is this ceaseless but effortless ἐνέργεια that is God's rest. Philo believes that while God's creatorship does not exhaust His being, it is continuous.

At *Opif.* 135, there is no mention of the anonymous collaborators assisting in the creation of the soul:

> τοῦ δ' αἰσθητοῦ καὶ ἐπὶ μέρους ἀνθρώπου τὴν κατασκευὴν σύνθετον εἶναί φησιν ἔκ τε γεώδους οὐσίας καὶ πνεύματος θείου· γεγενῆσθαι γὰρ τὸ μὲν σῶμα, χοῦν τοῦ τεχνίτου λαβόντος καὶ μορφὴν ἀνθρωπίνην ἐξ αὐτοῦ διαπλάσαντος, τὴν δὲ ψυχὴν ἀπ' οὐδενὸς γενητοῦ τὸ παράπαν, ἀλλ' ἐκ τοῦ πατρὸς καὶ ἡγεμόνος τῶν πάντων· ὃ γὰρ ἐνεφύσησεν, οὐδὲν ἦν ἕτερον ἢ πνεῦμα θεῖον ἀπὸ τῆς μακαρίας καὶ εὐδαίμονος φύσεως ἐκείνης ἀποικίαν τὴν ἐνθάδε στειλάμενον ἐπ' ὠφελείᾳ τοῦ γένους ἡμῶν, ἵν' εἰ καὶ θνητόν ἐστι κατὰ τὴν ὁρατὴν μερίδα, κατὰ γοῦν τὴν ἀόρατον ἀθανατίζηται.

> He says that the sense-perceptible and differentiated human is constructed out of earthly substance and divine spirit; for the body was generated when the Craftsman took mud and shaped the human form from it, but the soul was formed not from something that had been generated, but from the Father and leader of all things. For he breathed in nothing other than the divine breath, having moved its abode from that happy and prosperous nature in order to benefit our species, so that if its visible part is mortal, at least the part which is unseen might be made immortal.

Here again Philo is vague concerning the details of distribution of labour between God and his powers in the creation of the soul. Philo also breaks with Plato's account, since it is evident that God plays a role in the creation of the human body, unlike the Demiurge of the *Timaeus*. Philo posits a dual creation; rather like the situation he envisages with the universe as a whole; hardly surprising given his Platonic conviction that Man is a miniature cosmos. This 'double creation' had a long career in the Platonic 'underworld'.[112] For example, the Hermetic *Poimandres* (12–15) recounts the creation first of Essential Man, before that of ordinary man. There

---

[110] Runia: 1986, 267   [111] trans. Runia: 1986, 257   [112] Dillon: 1977, 176

are five main differences between the human created at this point and the one created earlier. One is created after the image of God (*Gen.* 1:27), the other is moulded (*Gen.* 2:7). The archetypal human is an object of thought while the other is an object of sense-perception. The first evidently is an archetype as one of the Forms, while the second is an instantiation of the Form. The archetypal human is without sexual differentiation. Obviously, this is not the case for its younger counterpart. The archetype is immortal, while the later human, as a compound of body and soul, has only been allotted a certain lifespan.[113] Whatever significance this set of contrasts may have meant to Philo, he does not elaborate.

Another difficulty with interpreting this passage is identifying how many humans Philo envisages here. Some scholars posit a distinction between a 'plasmatic' human at 134 and a 'pneumatic' one at 135. For example, Baer posited three separate entities: generic heavenly man (the man after the image), generic earthly man (the man moulded at 134) and the first empirical man (emerges at 135).[114] Radice identifies only two figures; 'plasmatic' man who is the sense-perceptible counterpart of the heavenly archetype and 'pneumatic' man, who is the individualisation of the generic Form.[115] Philo addresses this issue at *QG* 4, where he draws a distinction between sense-perceptible ('moulded') man and incorporeal man, made after the image and a copy of the original seal, which he identifies with the *Logos*.

God is said to have inbreathed πνεῦμα (135). The word πνεῦμα which Philo uses is a more scientific term than πνοή. In Stoicism, πνεῦμα was the active divine principle which played a role in the structuring of matter and for Aristotle, it was a substance which allowed the soul to act upon the body. It really is not a technical Platonic term at all. (When it is used in Platonic circles, it is usually as a result of external influence.) Origen picked up on this distinction at *Hom. Gen.* 1.13, where he claims that the human made after the image is not corporeal, since the shape of the body does not

---

[113] This comes out in the context of man's composite nature at *Her.* 282–3: καθάπερ γὰρ ὀνόματα καὶ ῥήματα καὶ τὰ λόγου μέρη πάντα συνέστηκε μὲν ἐκ τῶν τῆς γραμματικῆς στοιχείων, ἀναλύεται δὲ πάλιν εἰς ἔσχατα ἐκεῖνα, τὸν αὐτὸν τρόπον ἕκαστος ἡμῶν συγκριθεὶς ἐκ τῶν τεττάρων καὶ δανεισάμενος ἀφ' ἑκάστης οὐσίας μικρὰ μόρια, καθ' ὡρισμένας περιόδους καιρῶν ἐκτίνει τὸ δάνειον, εἰ μέν τι ξηρὸν εἴη, ἀποδιδοὺς γῇ, εἰ δέ τι ὑγρόν, ὕδατι, εἰ δὲ ψυχρόν, ἀέρι, εἰ δ' ἔνθερμον, πυρί.

'For in the same way that nouns and verbs and all parts of speech composed of the grammatical element once again are dissolved into the most primary of these, in the same way each of us is compounded of the four primary elements and borrows a small portion of the substance from each one, and he pays this debt back in full at the end of the revolutions of time, that part of him that is dry, he returns to earth, what is wet to water, what is cold to air and what is warm to fire.'

[114] Baer: 1970, especially Ch. 2   [115] Radice: 1989

contain the image of God, and the human is described as moulded, not made.

The soul enters man as a result of this inbreathing. However, at *Gig.* 6–18, in the case of subsequent generations, souls (which Philo identifies with the angels of Moses and the *daimones* of the philosophers) can chose to either remain in heaven, become sanctified and assist God in his governing of men, or to descend. Of these, the philosophers finally learn to release themselves from bodily concerns.[116]

The original human being was superior to subsequent generations.[117] Philo supplies three reasons: (1) materialistic: since the earth had just been newly separated from the sea, the material used to create man was the purest possible. (2) teleological (*Opif.* 137): God would not have taken the first piece of earth that came to hand, but would have located the best part 'taking from pure matter the purest and utmost refined part which was especially suited for the construction'.[118] (3) theological (*Opif.* 138): Philo regards this reason as being the most important. God constructed the first man with the most perfect proportions, so that everything should form a symmetrical and harmonious whole. The soul is also excellent, since it is modelled on the divine *Logos* (*Opif.* 139). Subsequent generations are inferior, not in the Gnostic sense of having become corrupted by the Archons, but rather because a copy of a copy will always be inferior.

Philo makes this point explicitly at *QG* 2.62. The Father of the universe does not serve as the model for anything mortal; it is the Second God, whom Philo equates with the *Logos*. Philo's mention of a Second God, of course, evokes the Numenian Second God, since the First God in both cases remains absolutely transcendent. Furthermore, the Second God Philo mentions here seems to have a demiurgic function, since it is the creator of the rational element in the human soul. It is quite rare in Philo to find an explicit declaration of which particular component of humankind was created by which power, but it seems that the rational part of the soul must have been created by a power, rather than the Father. When God says 'let us make man', the exhortation would be most obviously addressed to the *Logos*.

---

[116] This certainly has connotations of a fall: ἐκεῖναι δ' ὥσπερ εἰς ποταμὸν τὸ σῶμα καταβᾶσαι ποτὲ μὲν ὑπὸ συρμοῦ δίνης βιαιοτάτης ἁρπασθεῖσαι κατεπόθησαν, ποτὲ δὲ πρὸς τὴν φορὰν ἀντισχεῖν δυνηθεῖσαι τὸ μὲν πρῶτον ἀνενήξαντο, εἶτα ὅθεν ὥρμησαν, ἐκεῖσε πάλιν ἀνέπτησαν.

'Those who descend, into the body, just as if into a river, are snatched away at times and gulped down by the suction of an extremely violent eddy, but when they are able to resist the stream, at first they swim upwards, and then they fly back up to that place from which they set out.'(*Gig.* 13–14).

[117] *Opif.* 136   [118] trans. Runia

Philo proceeds to describe the creation of women. Following the Mosaic account leads to a more logical sequence than that of the *Timaeus*, since both sexes are present in the first generation. At *Opif.* 151, Philo points out that man would have resembled God more closely, if it had not been for the subsequent 'moulding' of woman. However, at *Opif.* 152, Philo, using the imagery of Aristophanes' speech at *Sym.* 191a–193, adopts a more balanced stance, recognising the value of procreation for the perpetuation of the species.[119]

Philo differs from most of the other traditions studied, which tend to view mankind as capable of living an immoral life without the help of women, as must have been the case with some members of the first generation of Plato's *Timaeus*. Woman is not responsible for the fall of souls in Origen, although the fall of Man in the *Poimandres* or the error of Sophia in the Gnostic tradition would seem to be caused by female error. The female responsibility for the fall of man in Philo appears disproportionate in view of the Mosaic account he is following, where it is the serpent who is the cause of all the trouble (§157). For Philo, the serpent represents pleasure: he is sunk prone on his belly, consumes earth with his food and by nature he destroys those whom he has bitten.

The creation of woman is based on *Gen* 2:21–5, but from this point on, Philo strays away from the Biblical account of creation. In fact, he engages in an excursus upon the moral decline of mankind. Interestingly, he makes no attempt to explain the creation of woman from Adam's rib (he never actually mentions Adam by name in *Opif.*), although he allegorises the serpent. Philo believes that the creation of woman from the side of man is an indication that she is inferior in both age and in honour to him.[120] He also views it as a sign that man is bound to protect woman since she is a necessary part of him, but that she is bound to serve him as a whole.

Philo's main problem regarding the creation of woman appears to be that once she is created, man can no longer imitate God's solitary existence.[121] Clearly, this is not a particularly persuasive argument, but it does recall the

---

[119] ... ἔρως δ' ἐπιγενόμενος καθάπερ ἑνὸς ζῴου διττὰ τμήματα διεστηκότα συναγαγὼν εἰς ταὐτὸν ἁρμόττεται, πόθον ἐνιδρυσάμενος ἑκατέρῳ τῆς πρὸς θάτερον κοινωνίας εἰς τὴν τοῦ ὁμοίου γένεσιν· ὁ δὲ πόθος οὗτος καὶ τὴν τῶν σωμάτων ἡδονὴν ἐγέννησεν, ἥτις ἐστὶν ἀδικημάτων καὶ παρανομημάτων ἀρχή, δι' ἣν ὑπαλλάττονται τὸν θνητὸν καὶ κακοδαίμονα βίον ἀντ' ἀθανάτου καὶ εὐδαίμονος.

'And the love which results is exactly like drawing together two separate parts of a living being and joining them together, and in this way sets in place in each desire for sexual intercourse for the other with the aim of generating what is similar to them. This desire, however, resulted in bodily pleasure, which is the origin of unjust and illegal behavior and for this reason they trade a life of immortal bliss for a mortal and miserable one.'

[120] *QG* 27   [121] *Opif.* 143–4

stress Plato lays on the importance of a single cosmos, which can therefore imitate its model more closely at *Tim.* 30c–31b. Philo is so hostile to woman since he views her as particularly liable to temptation, and through her, man is also tempted to yield to pleasure.[122] He propounds this view because he regards mind as corresponding to man and the senses to woman, and it is the senses which are first to succumb to pleasure. Philo regards this schema as applying to all of humanity; in the context of his moral allegory, Adam and Eve represent respectively archetypal male and female characteristics. Soul, as a female element, is influenced to a greater extent by the physical than the male element (mind). In concluding his account, Philo compares demiurgy to a political system, attacking polytheism, since he views it as a form of divine ochlocracy.[123] At *Opif.* 171, he argues that since God would only create something like himself, He must have only created one cosmos. Clearly, in light of Philo's comments concerning the creation of man, this would seem to be a particularly weak argument, since despite the similarity between man and God, God still created multiple humans. In keeping with the *Timaeus*, Philo argues that God's beneficence is adequate guarantee that he would never allow the cosmos to be destroyed.

Reproduction occurs at *Tim.* 91a–d, but Philo does not deal with this aspect subsequent to the creation of man at *Opif.* Parents are the mortal counterparts of the Young Gods of *Tim.* 41c, e4 and 42d4. They imitate God by creating something new. Like the Young Gods, they receive the immortal part 'from outside' (*Opif.* 6, *Her.* 184) and only 'mimic God in framing life' (ἐν τῷ ζωοπλαστεῖν, *Decal.* 120). The Demiurge's speech is equated to God's exhortation on reproduction at *Gen.* 1:11–13, 20–3, 28–30. Parents as 'visible Gods' (*Decal.*120) are accessory causes of creation, while God is the true cause.

Matter

The question of Philo's views on the status of matter is an interesting one; according to Philo it cannot be regarded as a principle in its own right.[124]

---

[122] *Opif.* 165   [123] *Opif.* 171

[124] *Cf. Opif.* 8 : Μωυσῆς δὲ ... ἔγνω δή, ὅτι ἀναγκαιότατόν ἐστιν ἐν τοῖς οὖσι τὸ μὲν εἶναι δραστήρ ιον αἴτιον, τὸ δὲ παθητόν, καὶ ὅτι τὸ μὲν δραστήριον ὁ τῶν ὅλων νοῦς ἐστιν εἰλικρινέστατος καὶ ἀκραιφνέστατος, κρείττων ἢ ἀρετὴ καὶ κρείττων ἢ ἐπιστήμη καὶ κρείττων ἢ αὐτὸ τὸ ἀγαθὸν καὶ αὐτὸ τὸ καλόν· τὸ δὲ παθητὸν ἄψυχον καὶ ἀκίνητον ἐξ ἑαυτοῦ ...

'Moses ... realised that it was most necessary amongst the things that exist that there is an active cause and a passive counterpart and that the active cause is the mind of the all, most pure and unmixed, beyond excellence and knowledge and the Good and Beautiful itself, but that which is passive is without soul and has no motion from itself ... '

Philo is not influenced solely by Platonism; *Opif.* 8–9 is important in terms of illustrating Philo's debt to the Stoa, which attributes everything to God (though naturally Philo as a pious Jew would subscribe to this view). Philo also uses Stoic terminology, even referring to matter as τὸ παθητόν, emphasising its lack of causality.[125] He tends to use terms which emphasise matter's passivity: ἄμορφος (shapeless),[126] though at the same time mentioning its disorder; it is ἀνείδεος (formless) at *Mut.* 135, and ἀσχημάτιστος (figureless) at *Somn.* II.45.[127]

Matter is defined negatively through the use of alpha-privatives (ἄτακτος, ἄποιος, ἄψυχος, *Opif.* 22). It lacks the positive characteristics of the Platonic Receptacle (οὐχ ἡσυχίαν ἄγον ἀλλὰ κινούμενον πλημμελῶς, *Tim.* 30a). Philo's characterisation of matter as ἄψυχος contrasts with the Middle Platonist tradition which based its view on *Tim.* 30a.[128] Philonic matter lacks disorderly motion, although it does contain potentiality, an Aristotelian feature (δυναμένη δὲ πάντα γίνεσθαι). Matter is capable of 'changing for the best', though this is due to God allowing it to share in his nature.[129] At *Opif.* 8–9, Moses recognises that reality consists both of τὸ δραστήριον αἴτιον (*Nous*) and τὸ παθητόν. Philo adopts the Timaean account, but he is not in favour of the level of dualism often found in Platonism, since this would place God and matter on the same level.

One problem here is whether Philo regarded God as creating matter. Philo does not explicitly say that God made the world out of nothing. Since this would be a new concept to Greek philosophy, one might be forgiven for expecting him to. Philo faces two problems if he is going to suggest that God created matter. Firstly, if God is the source of order, He would hardly create matter that is disorderly and then order it.[130] Secondly, it would imply that God is responsible for evil, explained by Philo's predecessors as due to the recalcitrance of matter. Philo emphasises the material (ἐξ οὗ) aspect of the Timaean Receptacle, without really accounting for the spatial (ἐν ᾧ) aspect, and that seems to be responsible for some of the difficulty in the interpretation. The Receptacle in which creation takes place is not identical to the matter 'out of which' creation takes place At *Somn.* 1.76, the implication is that matter is created (οὐ δημιουργὸς μόνον ἀλλὰ καὶ κτιστής, not only the Demiurge [of matter] but its maker), a view strengthened by the declaration that matter is a 'perfect substance', but this is contradicted by other passages (*Opif.* 9, *QG* 1.55, *Somn.* II.45, *Spec.* I.329).

---

[125] *Opif.* 8–9   [126] *Her.* 140, *Spec.* 1.328   [127] Wolfson: 1968, 309
[128] Runia: 1986, 143   [129] *Opif.* 22   [130] Runia: 1986, 289

Philo explains that God calculated the precise quantity of matter required for creation, since even a human craftsman is able to work out the amount of material which he requires for a given task.[131] This draws upon Plato's assertion that all matter was used up in the act of creation.

Περὶ δὲ τοῦ ποσοῦ τῆς οὐσίας, εἰ δὴ γέγονεν ὄντως, ἐκεῖνο λεκτέον. ἐστο- χάσατο πρὸς τὴν τοῦ κόσμου γένεσιν ὁ Θεὸς αὐταρκεστάτης ὕλης ὡς μήτ' ἐνδέοι μήθ' ὑπερβάλλοι. καὶ γὰρ ἄτοπον ἦν τοῖς μὲν κατὰ μέρος τεχνίταις, ὁπότε τι δημιουργοῖεν, καὶ μάλιστα τῶν πολυτελῶν, τὸ ἐν ὕλαις αὔταρκες σταθμήσασθαι, τὸν δ' ἀριθμοὺς καὶ μέτρα καὶ τὰς ἐν τούτοις ἰσότητας ἀνευρηκότα μὴ φροντίσαι τοῦ ἱκανοῦ. λέξω δὴ μετὰ παρρησίας, ὅτι οὔτ' ἐλάττονος οὔτε πλείονος οὐσίας ἔδει τῷ κόσμῳ πρὸς κατασκευήν, ἐπεὶ οὐκ ἂν ἐγένετο τέλειος, οὐδ' ἐν πᾶσι τοῖς μέρεσιν ὁλόκληρος· εὖ δὲ δεδημιουργη- μένος ἐκ τελείας οὐσίας ἀπετελέσθη· πανσόφου γὰρ τὴν τέχνην ἴδιον, πρὶν ἄρξασθαί τινος κατασκευῆς, τὴν ἱκανὴν ἰδεῖν ὕλην.

It is necessary to say the following concerning the quantity of substance, if this was really created: God had regard for the adequate amount of matter for the creation of the world so that the quantity should neither be lacking nor excessive. For it would be out of place that craftsmen, when they are constructing something and most especially something expensive, allow for a sufficient amount of material, but that the one who invented numbers and measures and the equality in them did not consider what was sufficient. I will say openly that there was no need of either more or less substance for the construction of the world, since otherwise it would not have been perfect or complete with regard to all of its parts. But it was brought to completion, having been well-constructed from a perfect substance. For it is proper for one who is most clever to see that the material is sufficient, before he begins to construct anything. (*Prov.* 1.1–15)

Philo here is responding to the argument that if God created the world, why did He use a given quantity of matter and only four elements. Perhaps Philo is here conceding for the purposes of argument that God may not have created matter, but that this would not prevent it from being ruled or ordered by divine Providence.[132] (This would of course differ from the approach of Origen who regards matter as unsuitable to be ordered by divine Providence, if it has not been created by divine wisdom.)

The term that Philo uses for matter here is οὐσία, rather than ὕλη. Zeller views this as indicative that Philo has adopted a more Stoic view of matter, regarding it as identical to body.[133] This does not really help matters, since Plato did believe in a material substratum; it is just that he did not use the term οὐσία to refer to matter. For Plato, phenomena cling to οὐσία, rather

---

[131] *Prov.* 1.625–6   [132] Colson: 1941, (= vol. IX), 454   [133] Zeller: 1919–23

than that they are composed of οὐσία. I do not think that Philo's adoption of this term can be interpreted as a Stoicising move.

De Aeternitate Mundi

One must proceed with caution when using *De Aeternitate Mundi* as a core text for analysing some of Philo's views. There has been some dispute as to its authenticity. It is not mentioned in Eusebius' list of Philo's works, although it has always been included in the *corpus Philonicum*. It expresses viewpoints that would prove problematic if attributed to Philo. He is usually hostile to the view that the world is uncreated and indestructible: a thesis that this work appears to propound. It contains other curiosities, such as breaking away from Philo's usual practice of citing the doctrines of Greek philosophers anonymously. Here the author mentions them by name. The second half of the *De Aeternitate Mundi* contradicts Philo's belief in God's creation of the cosmos. The treatise also appears incomplete or at least seems to require a sequel.

Scholars have been divided over the work's authenticity. Bernays (1863, 1876, 1882) viewed the work as unPhilonic, while Cumont (1891) asserted that linguistically the treatise was unmistakably Philonic.[134] He concluded that the *De Aeternitate Mundi* was an early work, while Bousset (1915) claimed that it was a school exercise.[135] The treatise may, in fact, have other parallels. *De Plantatione*, an adaption of a Greek philosophical treatise, dealing with the drunkenness of Noah at *Gen.* 9:20–1, has a similar structure. It consists of an introduction recounting the main opinions held on the issue, a section containing arguments in favour of the proposition and the third section arguing against the proposition. Another parallel is *Concerning which is more Useful: Water or Fire* from the corpus of Plutarch's *Moralia*, which exhibits this structure also.

Runia argues that *De Aeternitate Mundi*, like these other two works, is a θέσις/ *quaestio infinita*.[136] What makes *Aet.* difficult to interpret is that it discusses the merits of three viewpoints, not two (§7). The cosmos is either ungenerated and indestructible, generated and destructible or generated and indestructible. The second position was propounded by Democritus and Epicurus and by the Stoics (§8–9). For Philo, the Stoic doctrine is on a higher level than that of the mechanistic atomists. They, at least, regard God as the creator of the cosmos. Their *ekpyrosis* is followed by

---

[134] Runia: 1981, 107   [135] Runia: 1981, 108   [136] Runia: 1981, 116

rebirth, which indicates belief in Divine Providence, although Philo does not suggest that God is responsible for *ekpyrosis*.

At §§83–4, Philo, like Boethus of Sidon, asks what God is doing during the period of *ekpyrosis*, when it is the Stoics themselves who claim that he is in perpetual activity. Philo regards *ekpyrosis* as illogical. If the universe is resolved into fire, nothing will remain from which to reconstruct the universe (§§85–8). Earlier Stoics may have regarded God as the fire destroying the universe at *ekpyrosis*, but for Philo this would be blasphemous. *Ekpyrosis* is contrary to belief in equality of reciprocation of the elements (§§107–12).[137]

For Philo, Aristotle is superior to the Stoics since he appreciated the order of the cosmos. In advocating the second proposal, that the cosmos is γένητος καὶ ἄφθαρτος, Philo draws heavily upon *Tim.* 41a7–b6. Plato reached a higher level of truth than Aristotle, since he recognised that the cosmos is not autonomous, but was created due to God's goodness. Plato also recognised that the cosmos is not eternal in an absolute sense, but it gains its eternity from God's will. At §14, Philo expresses his preference for the literal interpretation of the *Timaeus*. §17 even goes so far as to assert that Hesiod is the father of Plato's doctrine. This is not because Philo wishes to denigrate Plato; rather, in antiquity, the older a belief, the more reputable it was.[138] Plato's doctrine is therefore portrayed not as a radical innovation, but rather as an aspect of the truth which was imbued with the authority of even older thinkers.

At §19, Philo ascends to the highest level by dealing with the views of Moses. This introduces the motif of the 'theft of the philosophers', a common Jewish apologetic device. The doctrine that the cosmos is generated and indestructible ultimately came from Moses and this in turn ensures its accuracy. This also helps to explain why it appears that part of the θέσις is missing. Philo, instead of developing two positions as is standard in a θέσις, expounds three, refuting the first with the second and the second with the third.[139]

Philo makes the debt he owes to the *Timaeus* clear at the outset of *De Aeternitate Mundi*. He invokes God in a manner reminiscent of *Tim.* 27c, where Timaeus invokes the gods before speaking on such a great matter as whether the cosmos is created or uncreated. At §25 Philo quotes *Tim.* 32c and §38 quotes *Tim.* 33c concerning the autarchy of the earth. But not all of Philo's use of the *Timaeus* is to be commended. His version at §74 of the description of the intestinal tract at *Tim.* 73a is particularly unfortunate.

[137] Colson: 1941, 181   [138] Runia: 1981, 127   [139] Runia: 1981, 138

His use at *Aet.* 146–50 of the myth of the periodic destructions of human populations, described at *Laws* III.676 and *Tim.* 22a, is merely superficial, although this may be composed under the influence of Stoic *ekpyrosis* and the Jewish *dies irae*. Overall, *De Aeternitate Mundi* reveals more about the intellectual environment in which the author was working than it does about Philo's conception of the Demiurge.

Conclusion

Philo's vision of the Demiurge is undoubtedly a complex one, leading him to adopt nuanced or highly-qualified positions on a number of issues. His independence of mind (to a large extent due to his Jewish background, which would render some of the assumptions of Greek philosophy unpalatable to him) has led to difficulties in attempting to classify him. On the creation of the world, his view is, in general terms, that of *Genesis*, though a *Genesis* illuminated more by the Demiurge of Plato's *Timaeus* and the questions of Middle Platonism than those of Jewish wisdom.

This is illustrated by his investigation into the origin of the world. He mentions three possibilities: the Aristotelian position (the world is uncreated and indestructible),[140] the Stoic (the world is created and destructible, but this world is only one of a series)[141] and the 'Platonic' one (created and not destructible).[142] The Aristotelian notion of uncreatedness is rejected (what does it leave for God to do?),[143] although Philo only challenges the grounds for Aristotelian cosmic indestructibility (a corollary of its uncreatedness).[144] Philo rejects the Stoic position (*Aet.* 20–51) in favour of the Platonic one (*Aet.* 19).

Although Philo follows the Biblical account of creation, he draws heavily upon demiurgic imagery. He most frequently refers to God as δημιουργός, τεχνίτης, ποιητής, κοσμοπλάστης, or uses a compound with πλάσσω. God is frequently portrayed as engaged in demiurgic activity: he divides (*Her.* 133–43), shapes and sculpts (*Her.* 156, *Prov.* 2.48–50) and builds (*Cher.* 126–7).[145] Philo upgrades the demiurgic imagery by portraying God as an architect. This is related to his social upgrading of the term δημιουργός, referring to its meaning as a magistrate in certain Greek states (*Somn.* II.187). More importantly, this alteration of God from craftsman to

---

[140] *Aet.* 7, 10–12; *Opif.* 2–7, *Conf.* 23, 114; *Somn.* II.283   [141] *Aet.* 8–9
[142] *Aet.* 13–16. Clearly, though, this position is not that held by the majority of Platonists and whether Plato himself held it depends on whether we read the *Timaeus* literally or not.
[143] *Opif.* 7–14   [144] Wolfson: 1968, 295   [145] Runia: 1986, 421

architect is related to the difference between the Philonic and Platonic conceptions of the Demiurge. Since for Philo, the Forms are the thoughts of God, He designs the pattern that He brings to creation, rather than following independently existing Forms, like the Platonic Demiurge. However, although Philo refers to God as both a Demiurge and a Creator (κτίστης), this does not seem to necessarily imply that God created matter, rather that He created the noetic realm.

However, the notion of a Demiurge is only one model of creation and Philo regards others as compatible. This is chiefly due to his notion that his exegesis or indeed any particular exegesis cannot do justice to the richness of Scripture or explain it fully. God is also a planter (φυτουργός, *Conf.* 196). Indeed, so important is this model of creation in Philo that Radice in *Platonismo e Creationismo* devotes a whole chapter to it. This agricultural model of creation is related to the creation of plants and trees in the *De Opificio Mundi*. They are created at the period of sexual maturity, not just that everything might be ready in advance of the coming of Man, but more importantly as a visible symbol that all fertility is attributable to God as primary cause. The biological image of creation is also drawn upon. God is the Parent (γεννητής, *Spec.* 1.209), Father (πατήρ, *Opif.* 74) and also Cause (αἴτιος, *Somn.* 1.147). This paternal notion enters Philo from Scripture.[146] God's intercourse with Sophia (His Wisdom and daughter, rather than the youngest Aeon) produces His younger son; the visible cosmos.[147]

The co-existence of these various creational mechanisms is complementary; there is no contradiction between a demiurgic God and one who is actually the parent of what He creates. Indeed, Wolfson notes that one cannot draw a distinction between Philo's use of the terms 'Creator' or 'Craftsman', pointing out that certain medieval Jewish philosophers see no contradiction between the Biblical account of creation and a pre-existent, uncreated matter.[148] This makes a definitive statement on Philo's views on a *creatio ex nihilo* difficult. Still, it would seem that Philo does envisage God as a 'creator', rather than a Demiurge, since He does create the noetic realm, rather than merely using a pre-existent model.

Finally, the concept of the *Logos*-Cutter is Philo's major contribution to metaphysical speculations concerning creation. The *Logos* that Philo envisages appears to incorporate numerous functions, from being a tool used by God to produce the world to His cup-bearer (figuratively speaking). These multitudinous functions might seem at first glance to indicate the

---

[146] *Deut.* 32:6: πατὴρ ἐποίησε σε'; *Gen.* 2.8: 'ἐφύτευσεν ὁ θεὸς', but *cf. Tim.* 25.
[147] Runia: 1986, 422. This allegory is found at *Ebr.* 30.
[148] Wolfson: 1968, 302

lack of a coherent concept. However, this can be viewed as a direct corollary, both of the multiple models of creational and demiurgic activity to be found in Philo, as well as the breadth of functions attributed to the *Logos* by Scripture, where it is viewed as a mechanism for creating or governing the world as well as facilitating prophecy. This allowed Philo to use it in order to refer to the demiurgic mind, rather than using the term νοῦς. Philo possesses an elaborate concept of demiurgy, in spite of, or perhaps because of, being a Platonising expositor rather than a Platonist, due to his self-appointed mission to do justice to the richness of scriptural thought. It is this very complexity which not only makes it difficult to categorise him in terms of philosophical allegiance, but coupled with his chronological position at the advent of Middle Platonism, can make him appear as the protogenitor of multiple intellectual traditions.

CHAPTER 4

Plutarch and the Demiurge of Egyptian mythology

Introduction

Even if Plutarch cannot be regarded as a significant original philosopher, he merits consideration for the evidence he provides on the development of Middle Platonism.[1] Plutarch's philosophical œuvre is essentially Platonist, even if influenced by Peripateticism and by (a reaction against) Stoicism. Unfortunately for our purposes, No. 66 in the *Catalogue of Lamprias*, Περὶ τοῦ γεγονέναι κατὰ Πλάτωνα τὸν κόσμον, has not survived. This leaves *De Animae Procreatione in Timaeo*, and *Quaestiones Platonicae* as the only extant exegetical works of Plutarch. In his surviving corpus, Plutarch quotes or refers to Plato in 650 passages, most frequently the *Timaeus*. In *Quaestiones Platonicae*, Questions II, IV, VII and VIII deal with sections of the *Timaeus*, with the interpretations of Questions II and IV being expanded in *De Animae Procreatione*.[2] It is the loss of many of Plutarch's technical treatises that leads Kenny to warn against attempts to extrapolate a theological system from the surviving sections of the *Moralia*.[3] (Kenny laments in particular the loss of No. 67 in the *Catalogue of Lamprias*, 'Where are the Forms?')

Another work of relevance is *De Iside et Osiride*, in which Plutarch represents the Isis and Osiris myth as a *demiurgic* account. In this sense, it is related both to the myth of the Demiurge in the *Timaeus* and the Valentinan myth of Sophia. In recounting the myth of Isis and Osiris, the philosophical doctrines are expounded, at times, in a confusing manner, as various details of the myth have to be included. One might compare Plutarch's situation to that of Philo, who also has to deal with a creative religious myth (that of the *Pentateuch*). There is, however, an important distinction between the cases. Plutarch was under no compulsion to use this myth in order to expound philosophy; he does so, because it evidently interests him, and he

---

[1] Dillon: 1977, 185   [2] Hershbell: 1992, 235   [3] Kenny: 1991, 44

presumably viewed it as containing philosophical truth (to some degree). Philo attempts to expound another generational account, the *Pentateuch*, in philosophical language; as a pious Jew, it represents the core of his belief and he could not simply ignore it, as Plutarch could with the Isis myth. Plutarch's work fits within the context of an increasing interest in cross-cultural projects amongst first and second century philosophers; Cornutus' *Theologia Graeca* also investigated the philosophical truth behind the Isis and Osiris myth.[4]

It is important to remember that Plutarch as an exegete works on the assumption that Plato's works express parts of the same system (as opposed to a 'developmental' theory) and that passages and specific phraseology in Plato should be taken literally.[5] Therefore, his attempts to manipulate the text, an allegation made by Cherniss,[6] can also be regarded as rendering certain passages in terms consistent with what Plato states elsewhere. Plutarch takes the demiurgic myth literally, as opposed to attempts by others within Platonism (such as Xenocrates) to deconstruct the myth to its constituent activities. Certain aspects of the myth are particularly important, especially the concept that the Demiurge is not in any way responsible for evil. Plutarch draws distinctions between the Demiurge and the First Principle in the *De Iside et Osiride*, where immanent Osiris can be seen as approximating a *Logos*-type figure (ironic in terms of Plutarch's opposition to the Stoics). In the history of the demiurgic concept, Plutarch represents (unlike the other philosophers I consider) less an attempt to develop it, than to resolve some of the problems bequeathed by Plato.

Plutarch's religious development

Plutarch is typical of the Middle Platonist movement, according to which the goal of life is assimilation to God, rather than to nature. For Antiochus of Ascalon, the Supreme Good was represented not just by virtue, but also the primary needs of nature, in the absence of which (he felt) virtue itself could not exist. By the time of Eudorus, the τέλος has come to mean assimilation to God, with virtue alone considered important.[7] This is the justification for Plutarch's attempts to understand the essence of God and becomes apparent from *De Sera* 550d*ff.*, where the greatest blessing which Man can derive is to imitate God's goodness, which he can observe in the order of the cosmos. Plutarch's later works were

---

[4] Schott: 2008, 21   [5] Opsomer: 2004, 138   [6] Cherniss: 1976, XIII.1, 999c–1032f, 137–8
[7] See Dillon: 1977, 71 and 122 for discussion of this topic.

viewed by nineteenth-century German academics as a return to his youth-ful scepticism.[8] Plutarch's religious ideas are also characterised by his reaction against Stoicism, by his dualism and by his Pythagorean leanings. His Neopythagoreanism is apparent from *De Esu Carnium* where he proposes the doctrine that animals contain reincarnated human souls as a deterrent against eating flesh. In *De Sollertia Animalium*, his father, Autobulus, speaks in defence of Pythagoreanism, and from *Quaestiones Convivales* 1.2 (615d–619d), concerning a family dispute, it appears that Plutarch was ideologically closer to his father than to his brothers. *De E apud Delphos* attests to Plutarch's early interest in Pythagorean number theory. Ziegler proposed that his Pythagorean sympathies were inherited from his father, while Dillon argues that he was influenced by a Pythagoreanised Platonism imported by his teacher, Ammonius, from Alexandria.

For Dillon, Plutarch is 'orthodox', as exhibited by Ammonius' speech (*De E* 391e–394c), *De Iside and Osiris* and *De Genio Socratis*, whereby Plutarch's view that the τέλος of life was assimilation to God can be viewed as the culmination of Middle Platonic thought, post-Eudorus.[9] Certain scholars (such as Dörrie) viewed Plutarch's doctrines as a departure from their own conception of *Schulplatonismus*; specifically the idea that God created the soul as part of himself and out of himself (*Quaestiones Platonicae* 1009b–c), which vitiates the role of three principles (God, Forms, Matter), though the *Dreiprinzipienlehre* is more a popular doxographical doctrine than a litmus test of Platonic orthodoxy.[10] Dörrie further objects to Plutarch's positing of God as *paradeigma* (*De Sera* 550d), to his placing of God among the Intelligibles (*Quaestiones Platonicae* 1002b) and the posthumous ascent of the soul, which separates the psyche and the *nous* (*De Facie* 944e).

In reaction to Dörrie's view, *De Sera* 550d only serves to strengthen Dillon's position, since it emphasises the τέλος as assimilation to God. Furthermore, God is the *paradigm* of πάντα καλά in Plato's *Theaet.* 176e. At *Rep.* x.613a–b, human *arete* is described as assimilation (ἐξομοίωσις) to God. Plutarch also avoids use of the terms τὸ καλόν and τὸ ἀγαθόν, which would explicitly locate Plato's main Forms in God. Instead he prefers to use plurals. He does, however, identify God with the Form of the Good and Beautiful (*De Facie* 944e), an identification which emerges very early on in Platonism. In fact, on a literal level, Plutarch maintained the distinction between the Forms, νοῦς and the Demiurge and resisted the prevailing

[8] Brenk: 1987, 256
[9] 'Orthodoxy' obviously does not have an absolute sense in a Platonist context, in the absence of any 'certifying' body.
[10] Brenk: 1987, 258

intellectual trend to unite these elements. Admittedly, at certain times, Plutarch fuses God and the Forms.[11] In this sense, it seems that Plutarch may be closer to the true Platonic interpretation than many other 'orthodox' Platonists.

The Demiurge and the Forms

As R. M. Jones commented 'Plutarch usually treats the Forms and God as independent entities and never calls the Forms the thoughts of God.'[12] Jones points out that this misinterpretation of Plato's thought already existed by the time of the *Didaskalikos* of Alcinous (Ch. 9.1):[13]

> Form considered in reference to God is his intellection, in reference to us the first object of thought, in reference to matter, the measure, in relation to the sensible cosmos, the model, and with reference to itself, essence... For if God is a mind (νοῦς) or has a mind (νοέρον), he has thoughts and these are eternal and unchanging.

However, the notion can certainly be found in Philo of Alexandria, although he was probably not the inventor, but may have borrowed the concept from Eudorus of Alexandria, and the original idea may go back to Plato's pupils, in particular Xenocrates. It seems that this interpretation may have crept into Platonic thought under the influence of the Aristotelian concept that God only engages in thought and he himself is the object of his own thought along with the νοητόν.

The same can also be posited for one of Plutarch's other great 'heresies' against 'orthodox' Platonism; his positing of temporal world-generation. Some scholars, such as Whittaker, have suggested that Plato, in fact, believed in a literal creation of the world in the *Timaeus*, but that, influenced by Aristotle's criticisms, Platonists such as Xenocrates reinterpreted the more embarrassing passages in favour of atemporal creation.[14] In this case, it would seem that Plutarch is closer to Plato's original thought, although he is frequently criticised for attempting to distort Plato's words in order to enlist the philosopher's support for his own ideas. In *De Facie*, it is apparent that the Demiurge and the Forms are not identical. The Forms are the *paradigm* which he imitates (1023d). At 1026e–f, Plutarch adapts the *Statesman* myth, postulating that at certain periods the world is rolled backward by the World-Soul and that by contemplating the intelligible

---

[11] Jones: 1926, 325. This occurs in *Quaestiones Platonicae* and *De Iside and Osiride*.
[12] Jones: 1926, 325   [13] Jones: 1926, 322   [14] Whittaker: 1969

principles, it reapprehends them. The Intelligibles are therefore not just abstract concepts, but the principles which underpin visible reality.

Plutarch's response to Stoic physics

Amongst the Middle Platonists, Plutarch in particular displays a heightened level of bitter hostility to the Stoics, although at the same time his metaphysical views are influenced by his reaction against this philosophical school. One might expect Plutarch to adopt an open-minded attitude towards the Stoa. He is, after all, an 'intellectual magpie', to borrow Dillon's phrase. His *De Iside et Osiride* can be seen as a cross-cultural project, reading the Egyptian myth of Isis and Osiris in terms of Plato's *Timaeus*. Although Plutarch feels that Platonic philosophy attained greater clarity than Egyptian wisdom, this does not mean that the Platonists have a monopoly on the truth. Such tolerant pluralism is absent from Plutarch's attitude to the Stoics, however. Unfortunately, in this regard, six out of the nine polemics against the Stoics mentioned by the Lamprias Catalogue are no longer extant: *Against Chrysippus on Justice, Against the Stoics on Common Experience, Selections and Refutations of Stoics and Epicureans, Reasons Why the Stoics Vacillate, Against Chrysippus on the First Consequent* and *Against the Stoics on What is in our Control*. This leaves just *On Stoic Self-Contradictions, Against the Stoics on Common Conceptions* and a σύνοψις of *That the Stoics Talk More Paradoxically than the Poets*.

As Hershbell notes, since the nineteenth century, Plutarch's interaction with the Stoics has been read in three different ways: as a determined opponent, as an eclectic borrowing from both the Stoa and the Academy, or as a Stoic despite his own better judgement.[15] To understand Plutarch's relationship with the Stoa, it is necessary to consider the influence of Stoic concepts of world-generation upon Platonism. Although the initial interpretative controversy regarding the *Timaeus* had been between the Platonists and the Aristotelians, by the first to third centuries, however, Platonist speculations on the issue were heavily influenced by Stoic physics. For example, the Stoics identify two principles: God and matter, as opposed to the original Platonic three of God or the Demiurge, matter and Forms.[16]

---

[15] Hershbell: 1992, 3342
[16] This is illustrated by Diogenes Laertius' exposition of their position: 'According to them there are two principles of everything: that which acts and that which is acted upon. The passive one is matter, the essence which is without qualitiy, and the active is the divine *logos*. For being eternal, it fabricates each individual through all of the matter. This position is advanced by Zeno of Citium in *On Substance*, by Cleanthes in *On the Atoms*, by Chrysippus towards the end of the first book of

The Middle Platonists also argue for two principles, using the same terms, God and matter, to denote them, creating this reduction in the original three elements through using the claim that the Forms are the thoughts of God. These principles are represented differently in the more dualistic of the Middle Platonists than amongst their Stoic counterparts. Whereas the Stoics regard matter as completely passive, the Middle Platonists see it as recalcitrant. It might appear that the Middle Platonists are modifying their position under Stoic influence. However, it is possible to see a trace of a two-principle theory in the *Timaeus*. David Sedley has suggested this doctrine goes back to the fashion in the Old Academy for regarding the Monad and the Indefinite Dyad as the original two principles of Plato's unwritten teaching, although perhaps the notion of the world as the result of the collaboration of two principles is more forcefully expressed in the *Timaeus* as a result of the tension between Reason and Necessity.

The Stoic conception of God differs in a very important respect from the Platonic one. The Stoic active principle or god is all-pervasive and is therefore present in all matter. Zeno and Chrysippus identified the substance of god with 'the whole cosmos and the heaven' (DL 7.148 = F 20 E–K), a position in which they were followed by the first century BC Stoic, Posidonius.[17] A second passage from Aëtius elaborates this concept of god with a triple identification of god with productive fire, *pneuma* and the cosmos:

> The Stoics declare that god is (1) crafting fire, which proceeds methodically to the generation of the cosmos and encompasses all the *logoi spermatikoi*, according to which everything happens in accordance with fate and (2) pneuma, pervading the whole cosmos, taking names as it partakes in alternation throughout all of the matter in which it is divided and (3) the cosmos and the stars and the earth are gods and the mind is the highest of all in the aether. [Aëtius 1.7.33 (Stob. 1.129b, Euseb. *Praep. Ev.* 14.16.19)]

Stoic theology, then, as is the case with the Platonists, is intrinsically bound up with their cosmology which, despite divergences from Platonism on major metaphysical issues, exhibits the influences of the *Timaeus*, in so far as both regard God as a benevolent Demiurge, both envision the

---

the *Physics*, Archedemus in *On the Elements* and Poseidonius in the second book of *Physical Theory*. They say that principles differ from elements: for principles are ungenerated and indestructible, and the elements perish during *ekpyrosis*, but principles are incorporeal and shapeless, while the elements have form.' [DL 7.134 = F 5 E–K]

[17] 'Poseidonius [said that God is] an intelligent and fiery spirit; it does not have a form, but transforms into what it wishes and joins itself to all things.' [Aëtius plac.1.7.19 p. 301 sq. Diels (Stob. 1.1.29b) = F 101E–K]

cosmos as a living entity comprising soul and body, and both have a notion of two metaphysical principles, though this latter point is more evident in interpretations of the *Timaeus* than in the dialogue itself, even if Plato draws an active–passive distinction at *Theaet.*157a–b, *Soph.* 247d–e and *Phil.* 26b–27b.[18] While the Epicureans are traditionally considered the marginalised group amongst the ancient philosophical schools with their atheistic viewpoints, attracting the united opposition of the Stoics, Peripatetics and the Platonists, this masks the fact that Stoic theology could in certain respects be considered every bit as reprehensible and could, and did, serve as the target of combined attacks from the other philosophical groups, as the following text from the late second/third-century AD Peripatetic commentator, Alexander of Aphrodisias, makes clear:

> How is it not unworthy of divinity to state that god pervades the entirety of the matter which underlies all things and stays in it, whatever sort of nature it has, and has as his chief duty the continuous generation and forming of anything that can be generated from it and to make god the Demiurge of worms and mosquitos, just like some modeller of small figures, who devotes himself to mud and makes all things which can be produced from it? (Alexander, *De Mixtione* p. 226, 24–9 = *SVF* 2.1048)

Alexander outlines several of the challenges typically levelled at the Stoics. There are two grounds on which the Stoic conception of God is typically criticised. The first is the notion of his industriousness: the idea that he is continually concerned with even the most minor matters, the idea that he was a craftsman of grubs and gnats: a position which was especially attacked by the Epicureans and the Platonists.[19]

However, the Stoics are particularly attacked by the Platonists on another major issue. The Stoic account of world-generation, like the version of the *Timaeus*, posits a temporal production on the part of God: 'and being by himself in the beginning, [God] transformed all substance through air into water' (*SVF* 1.102 = DL 7.136) and again 'the cosmos is generated when substance is transformed from fire through air into moisture' (*SVF* 1.102 = DL 7.142). The Stoics use the language and imagery of Plato's *Timaeus* in referring to God in his capacity as generator of the sensible realm as a Demiurge: God produces 'everything throughout all matter like a craftsman (δημιουργεῖν)' (*SVF* 493 = DL 7.134). However, in contrast to the transcendent Demiurge of Platonism, the Stoic god is immanent

---

[18] Salles: 2009, 3   [19] Cf. Maximus of Tyre's attitude at *Orat.* 13.2.43–7, quoted below.

(as discussed in Chapter 1), and works on matter from within, a major point of divergence with the Platonists.

The Stoics reject material monism, but they are not quite dualists either. The Stoics justify this claim of an immanent generating god through the appeal to biological imagery. Though the most famous image of the *Timaeus* associated with world-generation is the technological one, that of God as a craftsman, the dialogue also relies on a biological image. The world at 30b is, after all, a living being and the Receptacle, the space in which world-generation takes place and which, under Aristotelian influence, becomes equated with matter, is described as a 'mother'.

Although the Stoics draw on this technological language, their usage of it is no more than metaphorical. The Stoics reject the technological image of Plato's *Timaeus*. They reject too crude a comparison between God and a craftsman. Artistic products, they claim, do not come to be in the same way as the things of nature. The image which they prefer to use is the biological one. God's working on the cosmos could be more accurately compared to the activity of semen. Just as the semen can work from within an organism to influence its development in accordance with the information it contains, so too god works from inside matter.

This influence of the *Timaeus* should not come as a surprise. Zeno studied at the Academy where the *Timaeus* played a prominent role in a Platonic education. Stoicism can be viewed originally as an attempt to modernise Socratic thought and early Stoics even went by the title 'Socratics'.[20] This allows us to consider the Stoic rejection of the technological image, the rejection of the use of the Forms as a paradigm and the avoidance of mathematical terms to express the rational underpinning of the cosmos as a rejection of the Pythagorean elements of Plato's cosmology in favour of its Socratic features.[21]

The Stoics, like the Platonists and Aristotelians, draw a distinction between the heavens and the sublunar world. The following distinction between a world of order and one of chaos, expressed by the Stoic, Balbus, would not appear out of character if expressed by a Platonist:

> Therefore in the heavens there is neither chance nor accidence nor error nor absence of purpose, but on the contrary the order of everything, truth, reason and immutability and whatever lacks these and is false, erroneous and full of error, belongs to the area around the earth and below the moon, which is the last of all (the celestial bodies) and to the earth. (Cicero, *ND* II.56)

---

[20] Dorandi: 1982.   [21] *Cf.* Sedley: 2007, 209

Such comments make perfect sense in a Platonist context, though on the surface appear rather more difficult to justify when placed in the mouth of a Stoic. The Stoics after all, regard god as active in all matter. Possibly this could be read as a defence of Stoic theology composed as a reaction to Platonism, accepting the Platonic hierarchy of the universe. This is indicated also by DL 7.138–9, which points out that god is active throughout the universe, but has a greater presence in the aether or heaven, which functions as the command centre of the universe. God regulates the universe from heaven, acting on matter just as soul on body. Once again the technological image of the *Timaeus*, God acting on matter like a craftsman, is rejected in favour of the biological one.

In his anti-Stoic writings, Plutarch's strong dualistic tendencies may be observed coming into conflict with the monistic causality of the Stoics. In *De Stoicorum Repugnantiis*, Plutarch sets out to undermine Stoic thinkers, particularly Chrysippus, his main method of attack being, as the title suggests, to point out what he perceives as the gross inconsistencies in their philosophy. Plutarch tries to show that Chrysippus was the sort of man 'who says absolutely anything that may come into his head' (1047b). The reason for Plutarch's concentrated attack on Chrysippus is no doubt the status which he held within the Stoic school; he was one of the principal authorities amongst the Stoics and, according to Epictetus, education meant knowledge of the older Stoics.[22]

At §30, Plutarch attacks Chrysippus on his doctrine of 'promoted indifferents', items such as health, status and material possessions which are beneath virtue to concern itself with. These 'promoted indifferents' are shown not to be good, since they can be put to evil use. Virtue alone is beneficial, though it is bestowed not by god, but is the object of free choice. This means that god cannot benefit man in the only matter that counts (1048d). For Plutarch, this has the effect of making the Stoic god essentially powerless. While this criticism appears to be in the realm of ethics, the Stoics intrinsically link ethics and metaphysics, due to their equation of God and Providence. Chrysippus also argues for the notion of the divine choice of the best (§ 31); a position also advocated in Platonism, but then, as Plutarch points out, this divine choice from the Stoic point of view was not particularly fortunate, since they view humanity as in a wretched and miserable state.

Plutarch is opposed to the view that God can be responsible for evil and attacks what he views as the lack of sophistication in Chrysippus' stance

---

[22] Epictetus, *Discourses*. I.iv.28–32

on this matter: 'you've made the easiest plea, to blame the gods'.[23] Plutarch is hostile to the idea that the Demiurge could be responsible for evil, in contrast to the Chrysippean position that evils are dispersed according to the will of Zeus, either for the purpose of punishment, or in the course of other arrangements, as is the case in cities (*De Stoic. Repug.* 1051). In the same passage, he attacks Chrysippus' insensitivity for comparing the evil things which happen to the virtuous man to a few husks which get lost in a well-run household. Plutarch here favours a more inclusive form of divine Providence. Chrysippus' reasoning is based on the role of Necessity in the sensible world. Even Plato (*Tim.* 47e5–48a2) and the author of *De Placitis* at 885a recognise the limits placed on the Demiurge by Necessity. However, for Plutarch, if Necessity controls events to such a large degree, than many events lie beyond the control of the Demiurge and the world is not completely ordered in conformity with his reason. This would absolve him from guilt for the existence of evil in the world, although, as Plutarch illustrates, Chrysippus vitiates this by claiming that even vice is the creation of the Demiurge, 'since nothing, neither small nor great, is contrary to the reason of Zeus or his law or justice or Providence'.[24] At *De Stoic. Repug.* 1050e–1051a, Plutarch attacks this statement and responds with a spirited defence of the Demiurge. Zeus, according to Plutarch's polemical interpretation of Chrysippus, is to be blamed if he is responsible for the creation of useless vice (ἄχρηστον . . . τὴν κακίαν) or having created (πεποίηκεν) it, attempts to punish it.

Plutarch also attacks the Chrysippean notion that God is cruel and responsible in some way for the sufferings of man. If even humans kill unwanted puppies when they are just born, it seems unlikely that Zeus would have produced men and allowed them to attain maturity, before he starts contriving ways to torture them. It would have been more logical to simply prevent human generation. Zeus, in Greek mythology, despite his title as father of gods and men, is not actually responsible for their generation, so it is quite clear that Plutarch is treating Zeus as something of a philosophical principle here.

Of course, Plutarch is being polemical. It is clear, though, that part of Plutarch's hostility to Stoicism stems from its view that everything in the universe takes place in accordance with universal reason; i.e. God. The result is to make God responsible for the existence of evil. Plutarch at *De Stoic. Rep.* 1051d continues his opposition to this line of thought and notes that declaring that the Demiurge is responsible for the appointment

---

[23] *De Stoic. Repugn.* 1049f   [24] *De Stoic. Repugn.* 1050d

of evil men to positions of power is tantamount to accusing a king of having appointed evil officials and turning a blind eye to the abuse of his virtuous subjects. Given this context, it seems apparent that a dualistic philosophy was the obvious means for Plutarch to extract himself from the difficulty created by the problem of evil. In defence of the Stoics, their comparison of the suffering virtuous to a few husks of grain is not a callous statement. Rather God, for Chrysippus and also the Stoic Balbus in Cicero's account, is justified in ignoring minor matters to concentrate on greater cosmic problems. That is essentially the position which Plato adopts in the *Timaeus*,[25] in his view of the Demiurge who concerns himself with the ordering of the whole and is never depicted as being especially concerned with the welfare of the individual. Indeed, his obligation to comply with the dictates of Necessity would seem to be incompatible with a theodicy of this sort.

Certain aspects of the problem of evil are touched upon in *De Communibus Notitiis adversus Stoicos*. But first, the use of this text perhaps requires a brief justification. Its Plutarchean pedigree has been challenged, but the arguments against its authenticity have long been refuted. In any case, many of the arguments overlap with those used in *De Stoicorum Repugnantiis*. At 1065e–1066a, Plutarch again levels at the Stoics the charge of making the Demiurge responsible for evil:

> And the paternal and supreme and righteous Zeus, the best of artificers according to Pindar, did not craft the cosmos as a great, embroidered and manifold play, but as a town shared by gods and men, who should be associates in accordance with justice and virtue, blissfully in agreement and for this most beautiful and most holy goal, he did not need pirates and slayers of men and parricides and tyrants. For what is bad has not been generated as an intermezzo that is pleasurable to the divinity, and it is not for the sake of liveliness and laughter and as a joke that injustice has come into contact with concrete matters, so that is not possible to glimpse even the phantom of the harmony which they celebrate.

Here again, Plutarch views the Demiurge as essentially good, having generated the world with the best aim in mind. He even goes further, regarding vice as unessential to the Demiurge's plan (in contrast to the Stoics, as they are presented in *De Stoic. Repugn.*, who regard vice as necessary for the existence of evil): 'For matter has not of itself brought forth what is evil' (1076c). Plutarch then goes on to argue here that matter is ἄποιος ('without quality'), its motions coming directly from the moving principle. This is

---

[25] Plato adopts a similar position at *Laws* x.903–5.

not very far from the view of matter outlined in Plato's *Timaeus*, but it is a long way from the attempts to insulate God from matter exhibited by Philo.

However at 1085b–c, he does touch on the relationship of this Demiurge to matter.[26] Plutarch's problem here is with the Stoic concept of the Demiurge, as rationality permeating matter. For Plutarch, the Demiurge, as a principle, should be pure (καθαρός) and incomposite (ἀσύνθετος). If matter is without quality and incomposite, it fulfils the criteria to be regarded as a principle. According to Plutarch's reading of the Stoic position, however, the assumptions which the Stoics make concerning God are inappropriate for a principle. For example, at 1085c Plutarch points out that since, according to the Stoic position, the Demiurge is not pure Reason, but only has reason on deposit as a kind of trustee (ταμίας), he would then be neither Reason nor matter. He becomes, according to Plutarch's polemic reading of the Stoic account, not a principle, but a participant in two opposed principles, and hence a compound. This would make the Demiurge or God a second-order construct. Compounds are, of course, less perfect than principles, since they always run the risk of being reduced to their constituent elements. Worst of all, Plutarch claims that the Stoics have attributed corporeality to God.

Plutarch here presents a serious criticism of the Stoic position, and though he is engaged in polemics, the passage can be viewed within the broader context of the Platonist preoccupation with insulating the Demiurge from matter, but simultaneously attempting to explain his interaction

---

[26] Στοιχείου γε μὴν ἀρχῆς καὶ ἔννοια κοινὴ πᾶσιν ὡς ἔπος εἰπεῖν ἀνθρώποις ἐμπέφυκεν, ὡς ἁπλοῦν καὶ ἄκρατον εἶναι καὶ ἀσύνθετον· οὐ γὰρ στοιχεῖον οὐδ' ἀρχὴ τὸ μεμιγμένον ἀλλ' ἐξ ὧν μέμικται. καὶ μὴν οὗτοι τὸν θεὸν ἀρχὴν ὄντα σῶμα νοερὸν καὶ νοῦν ἐν ὕλῃ ποιοῦντες οὐ καθαρὸν οὐδὲ ἁπλοῦν οὐδ' ἀσύνθετον ἀλλ' ἐξ ἑτέρου καὶ δι' ἕτερον ἀποφαίνουσιν· ἡ δ' ὕλη καθ' αὑτὴν ἄλογος οὖσα καὶ ἄποιος τὸ ἁπλοῦν ἔχει καὶ τὸ ἀρχοειδές· ὁ θεὸς δέ, εἴπερ οὐκ ἔστιν ἀσώματος οὐδ' ἄυλος, ὡς ἀρχῆς μετέσχηκε τῆς ὕλης. εἰ μὲν γὰρ ἓν καὶ ταὐτὸν ἡ ὕλη καὶ ὁ λόγος, οὐκ εὖ τὴν ὕλην ἄλογον ἀποδεδώκασιν· εἰ δ' ἕτερα, καὶ ἀμφοτέρων ταμίας ἄν τις ὁ θεὸς εἴη καὶ οὐχ ἁπλοῦν ἀλλὰ σύνθετον πρᾶγμα τῷ νοερῷ τὸ σωματικὸν ἐκ τῆς ὕλης προσειληφώς.

'But a common conception of what an element or principle is, is innate in all men, as it were; it is simple and unmixed and uncompounded. For the element or principle is not what has been mixed but that out of which it is mixed, but these people [the Stoics], by making God, who is a principle, an intellectual body and enmattered mind, proclaim that He is neither pure nor simple, nor uncompounded, but from something else and on account of something else. But matter, being itself irrational and without quality, has simplicity and is of the nature of a principle, but God, if He really is not incorporeal and not immaterial, partakes in matter as one sharing in a principle. For if matter and reason are one and the same thing, they have not done well in conceding that matter is irrational and if they are different, God has both as a kind of trustee and is not simple but a composite thing with material corporeality added to intellectuality.' (*De Communibus Notitiis*, 1085b–c)

on it. Polemics aside, the Stoics actually have a major problem. They typically identify God with one of the elements, either fire or air, or with a
compound (*pneuma* or breath). Once God is regarded as a compound,
he becomes ontologically inferior to the elements, since a compound can
always be dissolved into its constituent parts and indeed presupposes their
existence. The Stoics must therefore face the charge of being both materialists and of circular argumentation, if they derive everything including
God from matter and then argue that God is responsible for the ordering
of the material realm.

Plutarch's writings against the Stoics also contain some interesting
insights on the longevity of the Demiurge. Chrysippus argues that only
Zeus and the universe are not subject to destruction, but the other gods
are, also denying the other gods self-sufficiency. Cherniss regards the name
'Zeus' at *De Stoic. Rep.* 1052b–c to be a synonym for the universe, though
strictly speaking it is probably really the divine reason active within it:[27]

> τροφῇ τε οἱ μὲν ἄλλοι θεοὶ χρῶνται παραπλησίως, συνεχόμενοι δι᾿ αὐτήν·
> ὁ δὲ Ζεὺς καὶ ὁ κόσμος καθ᾿ ἕτερον τρόπον *** ἀναλισκομένων καὶ ἐκ πυρὸς
> γινομένων.

> The other gods use nourishment similarly and they are held together by it.
> But Zeus and the cosmos 'maintain themselves' in a different manner 'from
> those who' perish and come into existence from fire.

At *De Stoic. Rep.* 1052c, Plutarch quotes from the first book of Chrysippus'
On Providence, pointing out that Zeus continues growing until everything
has been consumed in his growth. This is a reference, of course, to *ekpyrosis*, the periodic conflagration during which the universe is consumed
by fire. Sambursky claims that 'here the Stoics hit upon an important
physical law which applies to closed systems that are not subject to any
interference'.[28] Perhaps Sambursky was unaware that Chrysippus' was imi-
tating *Tim.* 33c8–d3.[29] The destructibility of the 'lesser gods' is, in fact,
justifiable in Platonic terms, although Plutarch here expresses opposition
to it (possibly for the purposes of polemic). After all, the Young Gods of
the *Timaeus* are not immortal, merely everlasting at the pleasure of the
Demiurge. The Stoics, though, only believe in one God: the 'lesser gods'
are to be regarded as examples of specific powers of Zeus. In this respect,
they diverge from the ontological systems advanced by Platonism (and
also by Gnosticism, though they did not engage with this tradition) and

---

[27] Cherniss: 1976, 392   [28] Sambursky: 1959 quoted by Cherniss: 1976, 567.
[29] Cherniss argues that Sambursky was unaware of Bréhier's discovery of this imitation.

are not able to attribute evil or the imperfection of the universe to lesser intermediaries.

At 1052d, Plutarch counters the Stoic doctrine of the self-sufficiency of the universe, justified on the basis that nourishment is provided by the interchange of different parts with each other.[30] Plutarch is not as impressed as Sambursky, arguing that since the universe is nourished by its own decay, while the gods are nourished by the universe, they expand while the universe contracts. This is interesting; Plutarch refutes a Stoicised Platonic theory by using an argument from *Tim.* 33c7–8, the passage immediately preceding that utilised by Chrysippus. The *Timaeus* passage runs 'αὐτὸ γὰρ ἑαυτῷ τροφὴν τὴν ἑαυτοῦ φθίσιν παρέχον' ('for it [the cosmos] supplied nourishment for itself from its own decay') and Plutarch's argument is 'μόνον μὴ αὔξεσθαι τὴν αὐτοῦ φθίσιν ἔχοντα τροφήν' ('only it does not grow, having its decay as its nourishment'). It seems here that demiurgic activity is not solely noetic action to regulate pre-existent matter, but, in fact, the energy required by this activity eventually uses up the available store of matter, as if only a limited supply is available and the Demiurge is incapable of producing any more.

Essentially, Plutarch's objection to the Stoic conception of divinity can be reduced, as has been done by Babut, to three main problems.[31] Firstly, the Stoic divinity is perishable as he is constrained by the destiny of the cosmos. In the second place, he is confused with material realities. Finally, he is deprived of all power of initiative, whereas for Plutarch, as a Platonist, these problems can be solved if the Demiurge is located in the suprasensible world and separated from matter. The Stoics, because of their notion of inert and insensible matter, are forced to posit that a benevolent divinity is the sole cause of evil.[32] Plutarch saw that the Stoics needed to posit a third term between God and matter to justify their position and his denial of divine responsibility for evil is clearly a major factor in his dualism.[33]

De Iside et Osiride

In the *De Iside et Osiride*, Plutarch attempts to resolve this problem and outlines his conception of demiurgic causality under the guise of an exegesis of Egyptian mythology, with Osiris representing the Demiurge. The Isis myth is well-known: Isis' husband, Osiris, is killed and dismembered

---

[30] As expressed at *SVF* 2.604.   [31] Babut: 1969, 454   [32] *De. Stoic. Repug.* 1048
[33] *Cf. De Iside* 369d: 'If, as is the case, it is impossible that something comes to be without cause and if the good is not able to give birth to evil, it is necessary that there is in nature a separate origin and principle for evil as there is for good.'

by Seth-Typhon and Isis assembles the scattered pieces in order to resurrect him, subsequently bearing him Horus. Plutarch's treatise is a cross-cultural product; he sees this foreign myth as containing the same sort of metaphysical truth which had been discovered by the Greeks. To this extent, Plutarch's exposition resembles Philo's and Origen's exegeses of *Genesis*. The important difference is that Plutarch is examining a foreign tradition; he has much greater freedom in his interpretation than is possible for a Jew or Christian examining his own tradition. The difficulty in examining such a text in order to understand Plutarch's conception of demiurgy is that it is recounted not directly, but as an exegesis of two separate 'origin' myths: the Isis myth as well as that of the *Timaeus*.

The work reveals a belief in a universal providence, within the context of which the conflict between good (represented by Isis, Osiris in various guises and Horus) and evil (represented by Seth-Typhon) takes place; a conflict in which the Demiurge himself adopts a rather passive role. The third term that Plutarch requires between matter and the Demiurge here are *daimones*. Isis and Osiris are themselves great *daimones*, but perfectly good, by virtue of which they become gods. Thus, the dualism of Plutarch is a conflict between two principles, not between two gods. At 369d, Plutarch excludes the idea of a god of evil:

> καὶ δοκεῖ τοῦτο τοῖς πλείστοις καὶ σοφωτάτοις· νομίζουσι γὰρ οἱ μὲν θεοὺς εἶναι δύο καθάπερ ἀντιτέχνους, τὸν μὲν ἀγαθῶν, τὸν δὲ φαύλων δημιουργόν· οἱ δὲ τὸν μὲν ἀμείνονα θεόν, τὸν δ' ἕτερον δαίμονα καλοῦσιν . . .

> And this seems to be the case to the greatest and wisest (thinkers). For some believe that there are two antagonistic gods, one the Demiurge of Good and the other the *Demiurge* of what is bad. And they call the better one God and the other one the *daimon*.

In practice, Plutarch links the concept of a god of evil with Iranian thought (369d), while he himself prefers to shun this idea. At 369c–d, strong Zoroastrian echoes can be observed:

> Life and the cosmos, if not all of the cosmos at least the sublunar part which is diverse, and variegated and subject to all kinds of change are formed from two antagonistic causes, and if the good does not furnish the cause of evil, it is necessary that Nature has the source and principle of evil, as well as of good.

Interestingly here, Plutarch considers the possibility that the evil principle only has jurisdiction 'below the moon', rather like the sublunar Valentinian Demiurge. It seems here that the positive δύναμις is also like a benevolent sublunar Demiurge, but I think that possibly he has jurisdiction over the cosmos as a whole, but only in the sublunar region is he forced to enter into conflict with the evil principle, hence the reason for 'all manner of changes'.

Typhon is an evil *daimon* in conflict with the Demiurge and even he appears to be the only *daimon* entirely evil, while the others are 'more or less good' (360e). The great *daimones* serve as intermediaries between the supreme *Logos* and the 'Powers' or between the 'Powers' and men.[34] These 'Powers' are lesser entities, which, on the ontological scale, rank just above men. This positing of *daimones*, rather like Plato's positing of the Young Gods, helps to free the Demiurge from bearing any responsibility for the existence of evil. However, in *De Defectu*, the *daimones* assist the Demiurge by preserving cosmic order as an additional regulatory power.[35]

However, the problem with this aspect of the demonology is vitiated by the active role of Isis, who also regulates the disorder of the sublunar world and attempts to preserve it. The role played by Isis is essential in Plutarch's understanding of the Demiurge, since she plays a much more active part in the preservation of the world than her husband. As Frankfort comments: 'Isis, the devoted, but subservient consort of Osiris, became the vehicle of Plutarch's philosophy, his peculiar amalgam of Platonic and Stoic views' (though Frankfort's study is not the most nuanced).[36] Additionally, the demonology helps to regulate theological problems, such as the existence of cults. However, these are relatively minor matters when compared to the attempt to solve the problem of evil and need not concern us here.

Incomplete matter brings forth the first creation (a product not yet ordered by the *Logos* or divine reason). This first creation is merely the 'wraith and phantasm' of the created world that is generated later. As Dillon comments, it seems indicative of Isis' desire for the order of the world, rather than a production of Seth-Typhon, whom Plutarch uses to represent Plato's 'errant cause', Necessity.[37] Read in terms of Plato's *Timaeus*, we seem to have an equivalent here of the limited attempt at order that took place due to the winnowing-motion of the Receptacle. Since it is produced by matter, it indicates that while Plutarchean matter may be, in itself, inert before the creation of the world, a (maleficent) soul already exists; perhaps illustrated here by the conception of the elder Horus in the womb.

---

[34] Illustrated also in the *De Defectu Oraculorum*, where *daimones* convey oracles from the gods to men.
[35] Cherniss: 1976, 100   [36] Frankfort: 1951, 22   [37] Dillon: 1977, 204

Isis is a highly symbolic figure for Plutarch's account of demiurgy: 'Isis is the female principle of nature, τὸ τῆς φύσεως θῆλυ, that which receives all generation, from which arise the names '*nurse*' (τιθήνη) and '*universal receptacle*' (πανδεχής), which Plato gives here and also '*myrionym*' ('with a thousand names'), because under the influence of reason she undergoes change and adopts every sort of form and appearance' (*De Iside* 372e).

As is evident here, Isis is the equivalent of the Receptacle of the *Timaeus*, although she also adopts the role of matter to some extent, as can be seen from 372e*ff.*, where she is explicitly identified with matter. This is a rather radical shift from *Tim.* 49a–b and 51a, where the Receptacle is defined as the place *in which* creation occurs, rather than the material *out of which* it occurs. However, Plutarch is not the first Platonist to equate the Platonic Receptacle with Aristotelian matter.[38] While the Receptacle is more usually regarded as place or space, support can be found for Plutarch's perception of it as matter. Plato uses terms such as ἐκμαγεῖον (impression), κινούμενον (moving), διασχηματιζόμενον (shaping), τυπωθέντα (being struck), which are difficult to reconcile with the notion of space and seem to allude to a feature such as plasticity.

Another problem is that Isis is neither passive receptacle nor inert matter, but she is capable of choosing between good and evil, though naturally inclining to what is best. Far from being recalcitrant, she actively seeks ordering by the Demiurge (evidently Osiris), although she also assists in demiurgy by sowing effluxes in herself. All this suggests an active receptacle; perhaps overactive, since it is difficult to see what remains for the Demiurge to do, other than perhaps communicating the *paradeigma* to Isis, who then plays a role in ordering herself (not actually a question of creation, similar to the situation in the *Timaeus*).

In a more implicit manner, Isis serves a role somewhat similar to Philo's *Logos*-Cutter. As Plutarch comments at 352d 'it is not lawful, as Plato says,

---

[38] For example compare Alcinous' *Handbook of Platonism*, where in Chapter 8.2 on matter, Alcinous misreads the *Timaeus*: 'Plato calls this [matter] a "mould" (*Tim.* 50c), "receiver of everything" (51a), "nurse" (49a, 52d, 88d), "mother" (50d, 51a) and "space" (52a–d) and a substrate "tangible by non-sensation" and apprehensible only "by a sort of bastard reasoning" and he states that it has this characteristic, that it receives all of generation and plays the role of a nurse in sustaining it and receiving the Forms, but it remains shapeless and qualityless and formless itself. For nothing would be easily adapted for receiving a variety of imprints and shapes, unless it itself was qualityless and did not participate in those forms which it necessarily receives itself' (trans. after Dillon). Although Alcinous himself is later than Plutarch, it is probable that he is preserving earlier doctrines, for example from Arius.

for the pure to touch the impure'.[39] This would help to elucidate the
passivity of the Demiurge, as part of an increasing tendency after Plato to
move to a more transcendent First Principle. This tendency is motivated
by a variety of factors including the desire to insulate the First Principle
from matter/responsibility for the existence of evil or attempts to clarify
the nature of the relationship between the First Principle, the demiurgic
one and the Forms. Another explanation is the attempt to explain the
movement from unity to multiplicity by positing an increasing number of
intermediary stages.

Isis also contains elements shared by Philonic/Gnostic Sophia. At 351e,
Plutarch refers to her as divine wisdom, although the words he chooses
are *eidêsis* and *phronêsis*, not Sophia.[40] Dillon views her as a fusion of
the positive aspect of matter with the World-Soul, connected with the
Pythagorean/Old Academic Dyad and the Philonian Sophia.[41] I think that
the origin of Plutarchean Isis can be found somewhere in this syncretistic
mix.

Isis certainly comes across as an imperfect (irrational) entity requiring
completion by the divine *Logos*, and in this context Isis and the Younger
Horus neatly parallel the Gnostic pairing of Sophia and the Demiurge.
Froidefond argues that Isis is not actually the incomplete Gnostic entity,
but rather the Aristotelian *être en puissance*.[42] He further claims that Isis
cannot be identified with a disorderly World-Soul. It seems to me that Isis'
search for Osiris indicates the World-Soul's awareness of its own imperfect
nature and its desire to be guided by God towards the model of the Good,
even if, in fact, it is difficult to see any justification within the framework of
the myth for Isis' portrayal as a fallen entity. The identification of World-
Soul/active Receptacle seems most plausible, given Isis' management of
matter. Isis' search for Osiris can also be read in terms of the *Statesman*
myth, in which God periodically rolls back the world to a vision of the
Good.

At 372e–f, Plutarch explains how his view of demiurgic causality
works:

ἔχει δὲ σύμφυτον ἔρωτα τοῦ πρώτου καὶ κυριωτάτου πάντων, ὃ τἀγαθῷ
ταὐτόν ἐστι, κἀκεῖνο ποθεῖ καὶ διώκει· τὴν δ' ἐκ τοῦ κακοῦ φεύγει καὶ
διωθεῖται μοῖραν, ἀμφοῖν μὲν οὖσα χώρα καὶ ὕλη, ῥέπουσα δ' ἀεὶ πρὸς
τὸ βέλτιον ἐξ ἑαυτῆς καὶ παρέχουσα γεννᾶν ἐκείνῳ καὶ κατασπείρειν εἰς

[39] καθαροῦ γάρ' ᾗ φησιν ὁ Πλάτων (*Phaedo* 67b) οὐ θεμιτὸν ἅπτεσθαι μὴ καθαρῷ· (*Cf. Phaedo* 67b).
    Admittedly, there Plutarch is discussing the rationale behind the abstinence of Egyptian priests, but
    given its location, I feel that it sheds some light on the situation here.
[40] Dillon: 1977, 204   [41] Dillon: 1977, 204   [42] Froidefond: 1987, 119

ἑαυτὴν ἀπορροάας καὶ ὁμοιότητς, αἷς χαίρει καὶ γέγηθε κυισκομένη καὶ ὑποπιμπλαμένη τῶν γενέσεων· εἰκὼν γάρ ἐστιν οὐσίας <ἡ> ἐν ὕλῃ γένεσις καὶ μίμημα τοῦ ὄντος τὸ γινόμενον.

And she [Isis] has an innate love of the First Principle and the lord of all, who is the Good itself, and she desires and pursues him, but she flees and pushes away from evil and being the receptacle and matter of both she continuously inclines towards the Good and hands herself over to him so that he might generate from her and sow in her emanations in his own likeness, she rejoices and is glad that she is impregnated with these and filled with generation. For this generation in matter is an image of the essence and a copy of that which really is.

This text seems to posit generation from below. Matter desires form and so the Demiurge obliges, rather than the Forms becoming enmattered or order being imposed on matter from above. Matter or Isis desires to be ordered according to the Forms, so that she herself can participate in the Intelligible.[43] Although Isis' functions are in part identical to those of Timaeus' Receptacle as an active recipient, her role goes beyond that: she not only receives and nourishes the seeds of generation, but she strengthens them (συνίστησι 375c). She divides this seminal reason (διανέμουσαν 377b) and rehabilitates cosmic harmony (συναρμόττειν πάλιν 373a), whenever it is threatened by disorder and destruction (φθορά).[44]

Isis, in this context, differs from Aristotelian matter. As 373b–c makes clear, sensible matter to every degree is penetrated and ordered by the Forms; this development of the '*matérialisme de l'idée*' is hailed by Froidefond as the '*phase ultime de l'évolution de la pensée de Platon*'.[45] In spite of this management of the sensible world, Froidefond is unhappy with identifying Isis with the World-Soul of the *Timaeus*, because by relaying to the sensible λόγοι σπερματικοί ('generative principles') in a sort of continuous action, she takes over the role of the Demiurge. However, I think that while Isis cannot be exclusively identified with the Timaean World-Soul, she does act as its replacement in Plutarch, as he regards the World-Soul as present in matter. Froidefond outlines the mediating powers that exist between transcendent *Logos* and the σπερματικός: immanent *Logos*, the

---

[43] *Cf.* the description at *De Iside* 373b–c: γένεσις Ἀπόλλωνος αἰνίττεται τὸ πρὶν ἐκφανῆ γενέσθαι τόνδε τὸν κόσμον καὶ συντελεσθῆναι τῷ λόγῳ τὴν ὕλην φύσει ἐλεγχομένην ἀφ' αὑτῆς ἀτελῆ τὴν πρώτην γένεσιν ἐξενεγκεῖν·

'The birth of Apollo (from Isis and Osiris) hints that before the cosmos appeared and was brought about by reason, matter, striving to produce, imperfectly brought forth from itself this first generation.'

[44] Froidefond: 1987, 116   [45] Froidefond: 1987, 116

demiurgic World-Soul and the regulatory World-Soul.[46] Part of the problem in interpreting Isis' role is that she combines elements of all three.

The description at 373b–c, quoted above, describes the ordering of Isis in terms of physical insemination. In reality, the imagery is contradicted by passages of the *De Iside et Osiride* which reveal the weakness and passivity of the Osirian Demiurge. This emerges in the description of Osiris' dead body, in the loss of his phallus (358b) and in the weakness of Harpocrates (358e).

At 373a, Plutarch elaborates on the role played by the Good in the ordering of matter:

τὸ γὰρ ὂν καὶ νοητὸν καὶ ἀγαθὸν φθορᾶς καὶ μεταβολῆς κρεῖττόν ἐστιν· ἃς δ᾿ ἀπ᾿ αὐτοῦ τὸ αἰσθητὸν καὶ σωματικὸν εἰκόνας ἐκμάττεται καὶ λόγους καὶ εἴδη καὶ ὁμοιότητας ἀναλαμβάνει, καθάπερ ἐν κηρῷ σφραγῖδες οὐκ ἀεὶ διαμένουσιν, ἀλλὰ καταλαμβάνει τὸ ἄτακτον αὐτὰς καὶ ταραχῶδες ἐνταῦθα τῆς ἄνω χώρας ἀπεληλαμένον καὶ μαχόμενον πρὸς τὸν Ὧρον...

For Being and the Intelligible and the Good are superior to decay and change; but the images moulded under its impression in the sensible and corporeal, the ordering-principles, the Forms and the likenesses which matter takes up just like a seal in wax, do not persist forever, but are overtaken by disorder and disturbances which the Good, fighting agains Horus, has expelled here from the places above.

Here the same dualistic attitude is expressed. But the Demiurge is given a much more active role than is frequently the case in Plutarch; he is involved in the continual creation of the world of Becoming, which would soon collapse under the power of the forces of disorder were it not for his benevolence and continual care. Isis also adopts a much more passive role, since she is compared to wax which is merely stamped with an impression: no mention is made of her capacity to respond to the Good in a manner that prompts creation. The dualism is weaker too; there is no question of the Demiurge being overcome by disorder, although in the myth, Osiris is overcome by Seth-Typhon and indeed would have no prospect of triumphing were it not for Isis.

In this passage, Osiris is beyond the reach of disorder; it is only his productions which can be subjected to it. One possible explanation for the change in focus is that Plutarch here ceases to use myth and explains Isis and Osiris in philosophical terms. However, I think that what Plutarch is describing is the becoming world in a state of flux and the reason that the

[46] Froidefond: 1987, 11

Demiurge has a more active role is because he must continually transmit images from the intelligible world to matter (the Plutarchean version of world-generation) in order to prevent cosmic collapse in the face of the Principle of Disorder.

The Demiurge and the Receptacle-matter give birth to the sensible world (373a–b):

> . . . τὸν Ὧρον, ὃν ἡ Ἶσις εἰκόνα τοῦ νοητοῦ κόσμου αἰσθητὸν ὄντα γεννᾷ· διὸ καὶ δίκην φεύγειν λέγεται νοθείας ὑπὸ Τυφῶνος, ὡς οὐκ ὢν καθαρὸς οὐδ᾽ εἰλικρινὴς οἷος ὁ πατήρ, λόγος αὐτὸς καθ᾽ ἑαυτὸν ἀμιγὴς καὶ ἀπαθής, ἀλλὰ νενοθευμένος τῇ ὕλῃ διὰ τὸ σωματικόν. περιγίγνεται δὲ καὶ νικᾷ τοῦ Ἑρμοῦ, τουτέστι τοῦ λόγου, μαρτυροῦντος καὶ δεικνύοντος ὅτι πρὸς τὸ νοητὸν ἡ φύσις μετασχηματιζομένη τὸν κόσμον ἀποδίδωσιν.

> Horus is the sensible world, which Isis has borne as an image of the noetic cosmos. It is for this reason that it is said that he is indicted because of his illegitimacy by Typhon, since he does not have the purity or unmixed nature of his father, Reason itself which is unmixed and impassible, but he is bastardised by matter on account of his corporeality. And he gets the upper hand and obtains his victory since Hermes, that is to say Reason, comes forward as a witness and demonstrates that nature, having been altered in form in accordance with the Intelligible, produces the cosmos.

From Plutarch's interpretation here, it seems that he does not regard the sensible world as produced by the Demiurge out of matter in the Receptacle, but as a co-production between the Demiurge and Receptacle-matter, existing as an independent entity. Also confusing is the double mention of Λόγος, but presumably the distinction here is between transcendent Λόγος represented by Osiris and immanent reason (Hermes). Plutarch, at this point, also has recourse to the Platonic conception of the inherent evil of matter.

Horus is then forced to engage in combat with Typhon (Disorder) in a battle for survival. This, in fact, has been previously revealed by Plutarch at 373a (quoted above), without the aid of an allegory. This battle between Horus and Seth-Typhon is Plutarch's mechanism for harmonising his dualism. Typhon is revealed as essential for cosmic order at 367a, where it is claimed that a perfect world would be impossible without the igneous element, and at 371a:

> μεμιγμένη γὰρ ἡ τοῦδε τοῦ κόσμου γένεσις καὶ σύστασις ἐξ ἐναντίων οὐ μὴν ἰσοσθενῶν δυνάμεων, ἀλλὰ τῆς βελτίονος τὸ κράτος ἐστίν· ἀπολέσ-θαι δὲ τὴν φαύλην παντάπασιν ἀδύνατον, πολλὴν μὲν ἐμπεφυκυῖαν τῷ

σώματι, πολλὴν δὲ τῇ ψυχῇ τοῦ παντὸς καὶ πρὸς τὴν βελτίονα ἀεὶ δυσ-
μαχοῦσαν.

For the generation and composition of this cosmos comes about from the
mixture of opposing, but inequal, powers; the superior force is that of good,
but it is impossible that the evil power would altogether disappear, since it
is firmly implanted in the body, and particularly in the soul of the universe
and it is continuously fighting in vain against the good.

This idea echoes Hesiod's description of the 'mixed' life of the human
race.[47] Here Plutarch assigns Typhon a role, not merely in ensuring cosmic
order, but actually a part in demiurgy. Typhon at 371b is an errant cause:

... Τυφὼν δὲ τῆς ψυχῆς τὸ παθητικὸν καὶ τιτανικὸν καὶ ἄλογον καὶ
ἔμπληκτον, τοῦ δὲ σωματικοῦ τὸ ἐπίκηρον καὶ νοσῶδες καὶ ταρακτικὸν
ἀωρίαις καὶ δυσκρασίαις, καὶ κρύψεσιν ἡλίου καὶ ἀφανισμοῖς σελήνης, οἷον
ἐκδρομαὶ καὶ ἀφηνιασμοὶ [καὶ] Τυφῶνος·

And Typhon is the receptive, titanic, irrational and impulsive component of
the [World] Soul and in the [World] body that which is subject to death and
ailing and disturbed and seasonal disorder and bad temperament, and solar
eclipses and lunar occultations, all of these are the skirmishes and seditions
of Typhon.

At 373c–d, Plutarch outlines another myth to explain Typhon's role in
cosmic harmony, in which Hermes uses the nerves of Typhon to make the
cords of the lyre:

... διδάσκοντες ὡς τὸ πᾶν ὁ λόγος διαρμοσάμενος σύμφωνον ἐξ ἀσυμ-
φώνων μερῶν ἐποίησε καὶ τὴν φθαρτικὴν οὐκ ἀπώλεσεν ἀλλ' ἀνεπήρωσε
δύναμιν. ὅθεν ἐκείνη μὲν ἀσθενὴς καὶ ἀδρανὴς ἐνταῦθα φυρομένη καὶ προσ-
πλεκομένη τοῖς παθητικοῖς καὶ μεταβολικοῖς μέρεσι.

... teaching that Reason regulated the universe and generated harmony
from dissonant components and it did not destroy them utterly but only
incapacitated their destructive power, so that they are here weak and without
strength, and they jumble together and attack those parts which are receptive
and subject to change.

It is for this reason that, although Horus acts as a check on Typhon, he is
not permitted by Isis to kill him because she did not wish that the element
opposed to humidity should completely disappear, but she preferred that
the mixture should subsist (367a). In any case, the existence of an 'errant
cause', Necessity, in the *Timaeus* opens the way for this sort of dualistic

---

[47] Froidefond: 1987, 117

opposition. Bianchi views this as radical dualism, with a split between Being and Becoming existing prior to the beginning of the world.[48]

Bianchi also sees Seth as combining destructive aggressivity with unavoidable sterility. However, I feel that perhaps one more naturally associates sterility with the Plutarchean Demiurge, symbolised by loss of the phallus. This stresses that Osiris cannot create, but merely regulate, though taken in conjunction with the attitude expressed in the *Quaestiones Convivales*, it may be a rejection of the biological image of the *Timaeus*, which was developed by the Stoics, in favour of the technological one. A comparison with biology is inevitable given Isis' representation as nurse and universal receptacle, while her husband Osiris is presented as the *Logos* and together they have a son. This grotesque detail concerning the missing phallus seems to be provided in case we might be tempted to interpret Plutarch's Isis allegory as a reference to *Logos* working inside matter in a manner similar to procreation. Bianchi also characterises Isis in terms of 'passive receptivity' and Seth as 'violent reactivity'. This distorts the picture; Isis as Receptacle-matter is much more active than her counterparts in other mythological systems and characterising Seth in terms of 'reactivity' masks the fact that he is ultimately regulated to some extent by demiurgic reasoning and owes his very existence to Isis; perhaps a Plutarchean echo of the recalcitrance of matter, which is essentially responsible for the errant cause. Bianchi also raises the interesting point that in Seth we have a typical example of the Demiurge-trickster found in the Gnostic systems. However, Bianchi links this identification with his view of the sterility of Seth, whereas I feel that this is a trait more associated with Osiris (given the loss of his phallus).

Plutarch is playing a complicated game here in his account of the Isis myth since it is a dual exegesis of an aspect of Egyptian mythology, as well as of the *Timaeus*. Plutarch's interpretation of the *Timaeus* shapes his reaction to the Isis myth. Despite the fluidity of the allegory, Plutarch distinguishes the Platonic triad of First Principles: Matter (Isis), Forms (transcendent Osiris) and a sort of World-Soul (immanent Osiris).[49]

Quaestiones Convivales

Quaestiones Convivales is a work that has curiously been largely ignored in terms of the background which it can provide on demiurgic causality

---

[48] Bianchi: 1987b, 354
[49] This same distinction is drawn also at *Quaestiones Convivales* 720b, quoted below, where Plutarch refers to the three principles which Plato posits in the *Timaeus*.

(though it has been analysed by Ferrari).[50] Admittedly, the *Quaestiones* are records of dinner conversations, rather than technical, philosophical discussions, and are not actually cited in the *Catalogue of Lamprias*, but they contain interesting insights on certain specific details of world-generation. Book I, 615f–616a, contains an allusion to *Tim.* 30a–b. Plutarch stresses the fact that the Demiurge orders rather than produces: 'by a general arrangement that the great God substituted order for disorder'. He arranges, rather than creates, for it is 'without taking away anything from that which existed and without adding anything and that it is in placing each thing in the most suitable location that he generated from extreme confusion the most beautiful form for nature'.

In Book II, Plutarch raises the question of which existed first; the chicken or the egg. Though this might appear frivolous, the discussion is related to Aristotle's problem, concerning the priority of the actual or the potential. Matter is initially slow to submit itself to the weak impulsions of nature and so can only produce 'shapeless and indefinite images' (τύπους ἀμόρφους καὶ ἀορίστους) such as eggs which then produce (ἔνδημιουργρεῖσθαι) living creatures.[51] Here we have an echo of the *De Iside*'s 'phantom' of the world, spontaneously produced by matter, with the interesting use of the verb δημιουργέω to describe this action.[52] This is rationalised at 636c–d; in every transformation the original form must precede the resultant one. At 636d, Plutarch draws an allusion to the Orphic myth which claims that the egg must precede all generation, because, as 636e makes clear, the egg represents the being who generated the universe (i.e. the Demiurge) and who contains it in himself.

So far these points only add some further details to the tenets expounded in *De Iside*. The second question of Book VIII is more enlightening. It asks why the Demiurge continually engages in geometry. Plutarch, like his Stoic opponents, believes in the continual activity of God (even if Plutarch envisages God as less industrious than the Stoic version). The first exegesis proposed by Tyndarus is that it underlines the role played by geometry in the intellectual ascent towards the Forms. Florus proposes that humans, rather than the Demiurge, have need of geometry. Lycurgus raises an interesting point on arithmetical proportion (719b): 'For he teaches that justice is equal (for all) but it is not necessary to consider equality justice.'[53] For Lycurgus, the Demiurge preserves a sort of meritocracy by determining the principle of law by the principle of proportion (γεωμετρικῶς, 719c).

---

[50] Ferrari: 1995b   [51] *Quaestiones Convivales* 636c   [52] *De Iside* 373c
[53] This is a further way in which the activity of the Demiurge is comparable with the activity of a legislator.

Autobulus' response is the most valuable, as he claims that without geome-try the Demiurge would have no other means of regulating the universe (a point touched on above within the context of the sexual sterility of Osiris.)

The Stoics, of course, do not posit recalcitrant matter, regarding it as completely passive. Their God, though, operates from within matter continuously; both the comparison of Zeus' activity on the world to that of soul and body expounded by Cotta at Cicero, *ND* 3.92, and the image of his activity within matter being similar to that of semen, imply that his responsibility for the world is not limited solely to the generation of the cosmos. While Plutarch conceives demiurgic activity in geometrical terms, the Stoics, in defending themselves against the Epicurean charges of an over-industrious God, claim that this interaction is effortless, like soul's influence over the limbs. The most vivid image to illustrate this effortless activity comes from the Platonist Galen of a bird which does not appear to move in air, but, in fact, is engaged in activity to preserve its position.[54] The Stoics regard God as engaged in such continuous activity to preserve the cosmos.

There is a major difference between both accounts of regulatory activ-ity: in Plutarch's case, the Demiurge is continuously combating matter's natural tendency towards disorder. In the case of the Stoics, the world is continuously in decline: in a passage quoted by Plutarch we learn that 'Zeus continues to grow until he has used up everything on himself.'[55] Despite God's interaction within matter, the Stoic position is that the cosmos is in continual decline. This leaves the Stoics with the problem of divine inactivity: what is God actually doing during the conflagration? If God is to be identified with fire, we might suggest that he is still active and involved in cosmic dissolution. Such a claim would be unthinkable from a Platonic position: the Demiurge does not allow the dissolution of what has been well put together. Seneca, however, claims that divine activity is suspended during *ekpyrosis*.[56] According to Philo of Alexandria, Boethus and Panaetius abandoned belief in *ekpyrosis* on such grounds and attributes the following argument to 'Boethus and his school':

> And if, as they say, everything will be burnt up, what will God do during this period? Will he do absolutely nothing? That is the most likely conclusion. For now he supervises each thing and governs all things, just like a father, and if it is necessary to speak the truth, he guides and steers the universe in the manner of a charioteer and helmsman, the defender of the sun and

---

[54] Galen, *Mus. Mot.* 4.462–463.10 = *SVF* 2.450 + LS 47k
[55] Plut. *De Stoic. Repug.* 1052c–d = *SVF* 2.604   [56] Bénatouïl: 2009, 29

moon and the planets and the fixed stars, as well as the air and the other parts
of the cosmos and helps in so far as concerns the permanence of the whole
and its blameless internal administration in accordance with correct reason.
But if all things are destroyed, lack of employment and terrible inactivity
will make his life lifeless and what can be more unnatural than this? (Philo,
Aet. 83)

Plato's account of the Demiurge's geometry is not just a comment on
his continuous activity, but a reaffirmation of the technological image of
the *Timaeus* in opposition to the Stoics' preference for the biological one,
suggested by Autoboulus' comment that geometry is God's only mechanism for regulating the universe. Plutarch rejects the biological image of
world-generation elsewhere. At 718a, just preceding Autoboulus' comment,
Plutarch, while outlining his opposition to the notion of divine filiation,
refers explicitly to the generative account of the *Timaeus*:

> ἀναθαρρῶ δὲ πάλιν αὐτοῦ Πλάτωνος (*Tim.* 28c) ἀκούων πατέρα καὶ ποι-
> ητὴν τοῦ τε κόσμου καὶ τῶν ἄλλων γεννητῶν τὸν ἀγέννητον καὶ ἀίδιον
> θεὸν ὀνομάζοντος, οὐ διὰ σπέρματος δήπου γενομένων, ἄλλη δὲ δυνάμει
> τοῦ θεοῦ τῇ ὕλῃ γόνιμον ἀρχήν, ὑφ᾽ ἧς ἔπαθεν καὶ μετέβαλεν, ἐντεκόν-
> τος . . . καὶ οὐδὲν οἴομαι δεινόν, εἰ μὴ πλησιάζων ὁ θεὸς ὥσπερ ἄνθρωπος,
> ἀλλ᾽ ἑτέραις τισὶν ἁφαῖς δι᾽ ἑτέρων καὶ ψαύσεσι τρέπει καὶ ὑποπίμπλησι
> θειοτέρας γονῆς τὸ θνητόν.

> And once again I find this confirmed by Plato himself, hearing him call the
> ungenerated and eternal God the father and maker of the cosmos and of all
> other generated things, not at all being generated through insemination, but
> the generative principle was inserted into matter by means of *another power*,
> rendering it passible and changeable . . . and I do not think it strange if God
> does not have sexual intercourse like a man but employs *other contacts and
> attachments*, so that he might alter mortal nature in a different manner and
> engender more divine offspring.

At the *Life of Numa* iv.3, Plutarch points out that the link between man
and God is not physical (one of substance), but intellectual (man is related
to God by his desire to pursue the Good). There he rejects the notion of a
human–divine union that is even partly physical, although here he seems
prepared to consider the strange idea that a god can impregnate a woman,
although a man cannot impregnate a goddess.[57] However, this is expressed
as an Egyptian belief, not as the view of Plutarch's spokesman, Tyndarus.
For Plutarch only the soul can be regarded as ὅμοιος θεῷ. This seems

---

[57] At the *Life of Numa* iv.4, Plutarch denies that man can respond to the ordering force of divinity in
a similar manner: ἀγνοοῦσι δὲ ὅτι τὸ μιγνύμενον ᾧ μίγνυται τὴν ἴσην ἀνταποδίδωσι κοινωνίαν.
('But they do not perceive that both parties involved in intercourse react in an equal communion.')

to be underlined by the loss of Osiris' phallus in *De Iside*: it seems that demiurgy exists only as a noetic activity and not as a physical insemination, as the imagery of *De Iside* 373 would lead one to believe. Indeed, in his discussion of the nature of divine filiation at 717e–f (*Quaestiones Convivales* VIII, question 1), Plutarch does not regard incorruptibility as compatible with physical insemination.

This raises the question of what exactly the other contacts and attachments are, by which the Demiurge regulates the phenomenal realm. From *Quaestiones Convivales* VIII.2 it would appear that by engaging in geometry, the Demiurge inculcates the generative principle in matter, but should he ever cease from geometric activity, matter would return to disorder. In the *De Iside*, the quasi-material principle represented in the person of Isis by its orientation towards the Good, appears to play a role in regulating itself. At *Quaestiones Convivales* 718a–b, Plutarch claims that Apis was created by the contact of the moon.[58] From these divergent comments, it is possible that Plutarch uses the phrase 'other contacts and attachments' as a sort of escape route, but is himself not very clear on the exact nature of the demiurgic image which he is propounding.

However, perhaps it is not stretching the bounds of possibility to suggest that Plutarch is here questioning the entire demiurgic imagery, aware of its value for exposition, but equally aware that God does not toil at creation like a craftsman. If Plutarch regards the Demiurge's geometry as these 'other contacts and attachments', he is again rejecting the biological image adopted by the Stoics in favour of a technological one (though representing God as a geometrician may be more acceptable than God as an artisan). This would be a neater solution, as it would take into consideration Plutarch's rejection of a biological model of world-generation elsewhere (illustrated most graphically in the stress he lays on the loss of Osiris' phallus). It is as if Plutarch is drawing attention to both models, technological and biological, with the ambiguous phrase εἰ μὴ πλησιάζων ὁ θεὸς ὥσπερ ἄνθρωπος, which might be interpreted more loosely as 'God does not fabricate like a man', although of course πλησιάζω is used of sexual relations.

Autobulus' Demiurge sets to work in a manner similar to Timaeus'; he first introduces numbers and proportions, then lines and contours, followed by surfaces and volumes (octahedrons, icosahedrons, pyramids

---

[58] . . . ἀλλ' Αἰγύπτιοι τόν τ' Ἆπιν οὕτως λοχεύεσθαί φασιν ἐπαφῇ τῆς σελήνης, ' . . . But the Egyptians say that Apis is born by contact of the moon'. However, this is explicitly stated to be an Egyptian position, and it is unclear what, if any, philosophical sense can be read into engendering by the contact of the moon.

and cubes) in order to produce the first elements (719c–d). Autoboulos then makes an interesting point:

> . . . τῆς μὲν ὕλης ἀεὶ βιαζομένης εἰς τὸ ἀόριστον ἀναδῦναι καὶ φευγούσης τὸ γεωμετρεῖσθαι, τοῦ δὲ λόγου καταλαμβάνοντος αὐτὴν καὶ περιγράφοντος καὶ διανέμοντος εἰς ἰδέας καὶ διαφοράς, ἐξ ὧν τὰ φυόμενα πάντα τὴν γένεσιν ἔσχεν καὶ σύστασιν.(719e)

> If matter always struggles forcefully to shrink back to indeterminacy and escape from being arranged in a geometrical order, Reason constrains it and circumscribes it and apportions it in forms and species, out of which everything which is produced has its birth and its composition.

Here the Demiurge is shown as continually engaging in the process of generating and structuring, something one would expect more from Philo than Plutarch, who posits a temporal creation. This could perhaps be explained as Osiris' continual conflict with Typhon, but this cannot mask the shift in the portrayal of the quasi-material principle (Isis) here. In the *De Iside* it is attracted to the good, but here it has a predisposition towards evil, or at least disorder. I think that the answer to this problem can be found in the response of Plutarch which follows (720b):

> . . . ἡ μὲν οὖν ὕλη τῶν ὑποκειμένων ἀτακτότατόν ἐστιν, ἡ δ᾽ ἰδέα τῶν παραδειγμάτων κάλλιστον, ὁ δὲ θεὸς τῶν αἰτίων ἄριστον. ἐβούλετ᾽ οὖν μηθέν, ὡς ἀνυστὸν ἦν, ὑπολιπεῖν ἄχρηστον καὶ ἀόριστον, ἀλλὰ κοσμῆσαι λόγῳ καὶ μέτρῳ καὶ ἀριθμῷ τὴν φύσιν, ἕν τι ποιῶν ἐκ πάντων ὁμοῦ τῶν ὑποκειμένων, οἷον <ἡ> ἰδέα καὶ ὅσον ἡ ὕλη γενόμενον. διὸ τοῦτο πρόβλημα δοὺς αὐτῷ, δυεῖν ὄντων τρίτον ἐποίησε καὶ ποιεῖ καὶ φυλάττει διὰ παντὸς τὸ ἴσον τῇ ὕλῃ καὶ ὅμοιον τῇ ἰδέᾳ τὸν κόσμον·

> Therefore matter is the most disorderly substrate, Form is the most beautiful paradigm and God is the best cause. Consequently, he wished, as far as was practicable, to leave nothing unlimited and indeterminate, but to order nature according to Reason and proportion and number, making out of all substances a single substrate, which contained qualities of both Form and matter. Having been given this problem, from these two, he made, and he makes a third, the cosmos, and he continually preserves it and it is equal to matter and it approximates to the Form.

Here the Demiurge is ordering, but by virtue of doing that, it appears that he is creating a new product. The three principles Plutarch elucidates here: Demiurge (active cause), matter and form are those of *Tim.* 27b–29d.

Book IX deals with the aspect of destiny treated at greater length in *De Fato*, sometimes attributed to Plutarch. The problem with using *De Fato* is that it certainly is not genuine, as its author claims to have written little else, but given the overlap between this work and *Quaestiones* IX, I feel that it is legitimate to draw attention to some of the interesting points which it raises here. (In any case, it expresses a Middle Platonist viewpoint). Destiny is the action of the World-Soul, divided into three parts, corresponding to the three Moirai – the highest is Clotho, followed by Atropos and Lachesis, who receives the more celestial activities of her sisters and transmits them to men.[59] They can be viewed either as a stable element, an errant element and a terrestrial/sublunar element or a Supreme Providence (volition of the first God), a second Providence (that of the heavenly Gods) and the third that of the *daimones* (573a). The cosmos is governed by divine law, which has an existence outside the Demiurge, not existing as his thoughts; in the same way that he regulates the world by mathematical principles that he does not produce. This destiny still preserves independence of action (through *Tyche* and Free-Will), but has the advantage of not making the Demiurge responsible for the existence of evil.

Other texts

The *Quaestiones Convivales* yield more information on demiurgy than the more technical *Quaestiones Platonicae*. Here, the most relevant point raised is at 1002e–3a:

> τί δήποτε, τὴν ψυχὴν ἀεὶ πρεσβυτέραν ἀποφαίνων τοῦ σώματος αἰτίαν τε τῆς ἐκείνου γενέσεως καὶ ἀρχήν, πάλιν φησὶν (*Tim.* 30b) οὐκ ἂν γενέσθαι ψυχὴν ἄνευ σώματος οὐδὲ νοῦν ἄνευ ψυχῆς ἀλλὰ ψυχὴν μὲν ἐν σώματι νοῦν δ᾽ ἐν τῇ ψυχῇ; δόξει γὰρ τὸ σῶμα καὶ εἶναι καὶ μὴ εἶναι, συνυπάρχον ἅμα τῇ ψυχῇ καὶ γεννώμενον ὑπὸ τῆς ψυχῆς.

> Why then does he announce that the soul is always older than the body and the cause and starting-point of its generation and again he says (*Tim.* 30b) that the soul could not have been generated without body, nor mind without soul, but soul in body and mind in soul? For it seems that the body both is and is not, if it is coexistent with soul and generated by soul.

This passage is modelled upon *Tim.* 30b3–5.[60] Plutarch answers the question at 1003, pointing out that the soul does not fabricate (ἐδημιούργει)

[59] Echoing Plato's *Laws* 960c, Arist., *De Mundo* 40b14.
[60] ... νοῦν δ᾽ αὖ χωρὶς ψυχῆς ἀδύνατον παραγενέσθαι τῳ. διὰ δὴ τὸν λογισμὸν τόνδε νοῦν μὲν ἐν ψυχῇ, ψυχὴν δ᾽ ἐν σώματι συνιστὰς τὸ πᾶν συνετεκταίνετο, ὅπως ὅτι κάλλιστον εἴη κατὰ φύσιν ἄριστόν τε ἔργον ἀπειργασμένος.

'...and it is not possible that mind belongs to anything except soul. For on account of this reasoning, He put together mind in soul and soul in body, as he was fabricating the world, in order that work he was accomplishing might be in its nature the fairest and best.'

the nature of body out of itself or out of what is non-existent, but converts a disorderly body into an orderly one. For Plutarch, this helps to explain how amorphous and indefinite matter (ἡ ἄμορφος ὕλη καὶ ἀόριστος, 1003b) acquires form and a specific disposition (διάθεσις) through the interaction of soul upon it. Plutarch may infer this from the description of the Demiurge putting the soul into the body of the cosmos.

Some further light can be thrown on the issue of demiurgic causality by turning to *De E*. Of the seven possible interpretations of the symbolism behind the E at Delphi, only the response of Ammonius, since it deals with the most elevated issues, need concern us here (*De E* 392a–b):

> ἡμῖν μὲν γὰρ ὄντως τοῦ εἶναι μέτεστιν οὐδέν, ἀλλὰ πᾶσα θνητὴ φύσις ἐν μέσῳ γενέσεως καὶ φθορᾶς γενομένη φάσμα παρέχει καὶ δόκησιν ἀμυδρὰν καὶ ἀβέβαιον αὐτῆς·

> We do not participate in Real Being, but all mortal nature, being ranked between generation and destruction, supplies itself an obscure and inconstant appearance and apparition.

Ammonius draws the Platonic distinction between Being and Becoming, before going on to expound the continual temporal generation at 392d.[61] This, like *Quaestiones Convivales* 719d, posits a continually active Demiurge, similar to Plato, and at odds with the passivity of Osiris. Ammonius describes Real Being at 392e:

> τί οὖν ὄντως ὄν ἐστι; τὸ ἀΐδιον καὶ ἀγένητον καὶ ἄφθαρτον, ᾧ χρόνος μεταβολὴν οὐδὲ εἷς ἐπάγει. κινητὸν γάρ τι καὶ κινουμένη συμφανταζόμενον ὕλη καὶ ῥέον ἀεὶ καὶ μὴ στέγον, ὥσπερ ἀγγεῖον φθορᾶς καὶ γενέσεως, ὁ χρόνος·

> What is Real Being? The eternal and ungenerated and indestructible, which do not undergo change in time. For time is in motion and is to be imagined along with matter and it is in constant flux and unrestrained, so that it is like the vessel of generation and destruction.

Plutarch here places the Demiurge beyond the reach of the evil principle. As has previously been illustrated, the evil principle is not equal in power to the Demiurge. By Real Being, Plutarch must be referring to the transcendent *Logos* represented in the *De Iside* by the soul of Osiris, rather than the immanent Λόγος represented by his body, which is subject to Time.

---

[61] μένει δ᾽ οὐδεὶς οὐδ᾽ ἔστιν εἷς, ἀλλὰ γιγνόμεθα πολλοί, περὶ ἕν τι φάντασμα καὶ κοινὸν ἐκμαγεῖον ὕλης περιελαυνομένης καὶ ὀλισθανούσης.

'No one continues or stays the same, but we are many beings, and around us is a common appearance and an impression of matter moves around and glides along.'

De Animae Procreatione in Timaeo

Some interesting points can be gleaned from *De Animae Procreatione*, which along with *Quaestiones Platonicae*, is the only surviving exegetical treatise of Plutarch. However, as Cherniss comments on Plutarch's supposedly literal interpretation of the *Timaeus*: 'his motive was not strict fidelity to Plato's words, but concern to enlist Plato's authority for the proposition that the universe was brought into being by God'.[62] As Cherniss also points out, there is little in the treatise that is original and it is interesting mainly due to information which it provides on earlier treatments of the *Timaeus*.[63] Although *De. An. Proc.* is an ἀναγραφή Plutarch composed in response to his son's request that he synthesise what he had said frequently on the soul (and therefore can be taken as evidence of his carefully considered position on the matter), it only deals with *Tim.* 35a1–36b5. *De Iside*, by contrast, displays greater breadth and scope in dealing with the metaphysical matters addressed by the *Timaeus*.

Extensive lists of the distortions of Plato's thought created by Plutarch have been compiled by both Cherniss[64] and Hershbell.[65] For example, Plutarch's quotations tend to be inaccurate (but this is probably due to the fact that he reproduced a text that differs from ours). At 1012b–c, Plutarch adapts *Stat.* 273b4–6, but omits the preceding τὸ σωματοειδὲς τῆς συγκράσεως which would undermine his interpretation.[66] At 1024c Plutarch equates χώρα (Receptacle) with ὕλη (matter). At 1014b–c and 1016d–1017a, he identifies χώρα with 'precosmic' chaos. At 1015d–e, Plutarch inverts the situation, equating ὕλη with χώρα: ὁ γὰρ Πλάτων μητέρα μὲν καὶ τιθήνην καλεῖ τὴν ὕλην, αἰτίαν δὲ κακοῦ τὴν κινητικὴν τῆς ὕλης. ('For Plato calls matter the mother and nurse and he calls the motion of matter the cause of evil'), ignoring the fact that Plato actually calls the Receptacle Mother and Nurse. Cherniss and Hershbell both censure Plutarch for this wilful distortion of Plato's thought. Yet Plutarch synthesised ὕλη and χώρα into the Receptacle-matter represented by Isis and so for him they both represent the same thing (as they did for other Platonists, as a result of Aristotelian influence). Indeed, identification between the two is justifiable in terms of the *Timaeus* text, as has been noted above.

Plutarch has been severely criticised for his reading of the *Timaeus* at *De An. Proc.* 1012b–c. Plutarch, quoting from *Tim.* 35a–b states: τῆς τε ταὐτοῦ φύσεως αὖ πέρι καὶ τῆς τοῦ ἑτέρου καὶ κατὰ ταὐτὰ συνέστησεν

---

[62] Cherniss: 1976, 146   [63] Cherniss: 1976, 135   [64] Cherniss: 1976   [65] Hershbell: 1992
[66] I.e. Plutarch omits 'on account of the corporeal element in its composition' in a passage outlining the reason for the disorder in the cosmos.

ἐν μέσῳ τοῦ τ'ἀμεροῦς αὐτὴν καὶ τοῦ κατὰ τὰ σώματα μεριστοῦ. There are several variations here between Plutarch's text and the standard reading of the *Timaeus*, the most problematic of which is αὐτὴν for αὐτῶν. αὐτὴν is incompatible with the standard interpretation of 'in the case of the nature of the same and the different, according to the same principle he made a compound intermediate between that which is indivisible and that which is divisible in bodies'. This implies that for sameness and for difference, the divisible and indivisible kinds are mixed together. Plutarch's reading is 'and as far as concerns the nature of sameness and that of difference, he compounded it in this manner, in the middle, out of the indivisible and what is divisible among bodies'.

Opsomer provides an extensive analysis of the matter, which I shall just trace over briefly.[67] Essentially, Plutarch interprets the soul as the mixture of sameness, difference and the blend of divisible and indivisible being. As indivisible being for Plutarch represents the intelligible, the realm of the Demiurge, this is how Plutarch is led to claim that something of the Demiurge is imparted to soul (*cf. Quaest. Plat.* II.1001c). At 1014–17, it is clear that Plutarch's idea of world-generation is different from that of *creatio ex nihilo*. The Demiurge creates the cosmos from ἀρχαί (precosmic principles consisting of disorganised corporeality (τὸ σωματικόν) and irrational motivity (τὸ κινητικόν)). This principle combines the 'infinitude' (ἀπειρία) of the *Philebus*, the 'Necessity' (ἀνάγκη) of *Tim.* 52d, with the disorderly soul of *Laws* x. Although the Demiurge of the *Timaeus* creates soul (even though he regulates matter), and Plutarch is generally thought of as favouring a literal reading of the *Timaeus*, Plutarch's Demiurge only regulates soul by combining it with νοῦς.

At 1014d–e and 1015e, Plutarch disregards the fact that in the *Laws*, Plato does not refer to the evil aspect of soul as precosmic to beneficial soul, but describes it as coeval with good souls. Given Plutarch's marked dualistic tendencies, this might appear to be an acceptable manoeuvre. But at 1023c, Plutarch argues that the Demiurge's relationship to soul is that of producer to product. Since the Demiurge introduces νοῦς, which is a part of the Demiurge, the soul is akin to God, rather than his finished product. This makes the indivisible being of the *Timaeus* practically identical to the Demiurge.[68] If the ungenerated universe is coeval with soul (1013e–f), this neither provides strong evidence that God exists or any reason for his existence, when the Demiurge's existence requires that the soul of the

[67] Opsomer: 2004, *passim*   [68] Cherniss: 1976, 142

universe has its beginning prior to that of the corporeal cosmos.[69] He does also refer, at *Quaest. Plat.*, 1001c, to the soul as not just the product, but a part of God (οὐκ ἔργον ἐστὶ τοῦ θεοῦ μόνον ἀλλὰ καὶ μέρος).

This is all in accordance with Plutarch's views that soul exists and is capable of causing motion, prior to the addition of harmony and order by the Demiurge (clearly an attitude taken directly from the pages of the *Timaeus*), but the motion that it caused was disorderly. To this extent it is a cause of evil (*cf.* 1027a). The Demiurge's great contribution is to bind sameness and difference by means of the intermediate terms of indivisible and divisible and to use this ordered soul to transmit harmony lower down the ontological scale.

Conclusion

Plutarch's most distinctive doctrines, his dualism and his belief in temporal world-generation contrary to the majority of Platonic interpreters, such as Speusippus, Xenocrates and Crantor, shapes his understanding of the mechanics of demiurgy, as can be seen from *De Iside et Osiride*. While some other passages of Plutarch indicate less originality, the fact that the *De Iside* contains his essential thoughts on this matter is illustrated by the confirmation provided by certain other texts.

Plutarch's demiurgic system owes a great deal to his attempts to extricate himself from many of the problems he saw encountered by Stoicism: a procedure which has earned him censure as an eclectic. As Dillon comments: 'In fact there is nothing at all wrong with being "eclectic" if that means simply that one is prepared to adopt a good formulation, or a valid line of argument, from a rival school or individual and adjust one's philosophical position accordingly. In this sense, most of the great philosophers are eclectics, and eclecticism is a mark of acuteness and originality as opposed to narrow-minded sectarianism.'[70] Plutarch should be viewed as an original 'thinker' (although perhaps 'philosopher' would be stretching the point), who adapted ideas from rival schools and was even prepared to distort Plato's thought to produce a modified version of demiurgic causality, which resolved the problem of evil. His skill in doing this, as well as the open-mindedness he displayed in his cross-cultural project, *De Iside*, which investigated two traditions, Egyptian and Greek, in order to identify a universal truth, has not perhaps been adequately appreciated.

---

[69] Cherniss: 1976, 148   [70] Dillon: 1988b, 103

Plutarch was very much in the vanguard of attempts to use the *Timaeus* as the philosophical subtext which could unlock the meaning of the generational/creational accounts of other religious/intellectual traditions, such as can be observed in Philo, as well as the Gnostic, Hermetic and Christian traditions.

Plutarch's opposition to the Stoics appears to be not just philosophical, but also religious. He is typical of the objection to Stoic theological belief found amongst the Platonists and Peripatetics. The Stoics degrade God, from Plutarch's point of view, in their representation of him as immanent. They lay themselves open to the charge of failing to distinguish between both of their metaphysical principles: if God is active within matter, where does God end and matter begin? The Stoics are frequently represented as materialists. This is not entirely accurate. If God works on matter in a manner similar to semen than the Stoics are vitalists, not materialists. While this biological image can claim a Timaean pedigree, Plutarch rejects it in favour of the technological image of demiurgy. From a Platonic perspective, their logic also appears weak and attacking it is one of Plutarch's favoured polemical techniques. Much of his opposition to his Stoic opponents concentrates on what he views as their attribution of the origin of evil to God, and for a pious dualist of the Platonist persuasion, like Plutarch, that is just a step too far.

CHAPTER 5

A simplified understanding of God
Maximus of Tyre

Introduction

Maximus of Tyre, usually rather disparagingly termed a *Halbphilosoph* or a 'sophist' rather than a philosopher, still deserves closer attention than is generally paid to him. It is his lack of originality which renders him useful in trying to form an impression of the current of second-century philosophical thought. Maximus' forty-one orations tend to focus on practical morality, although some have a bearing on theology. Unfortunately, Maximus treats the problem of demiurgy (and indeed practically every other philosophical problem that he encounters) in a superficial way. Modern scholarship on Maximus has tended to focus on emendation of the text (notably by Trapp and Renehan), or on attempts to locate Maximus within the current of Middle Platonism. Puiggali's magisterial study provides a comprehensive survey of Maximus' orations themselves and reveals how fruitful a detailed investigation of the writings of this *Halbphilosoph* can be.

As a result of the nature of his philosophical *oeuvre* (introductory lectures to students of philosophy), he does not provide a detailed analysis of the problems of the *Timaeus*, but only some standardised interpretations of certain points of Platonist metaphysics. His influence upon the development of the Demiurge does not appear to have been particularly great, though he does present some noteworthy imagery (such as the comparison of causality to machinery). He was interested in factors limiting the influence of the Demiurge (such as Fortune), but his main stance is a moralising and antisectarian one. Once God receives his appropriate honours, fine theological distinctions pale in comparison.

Maximus propounds the standard conception of a Demiurge who engages in noetic activity in order to stabilise the universe and considers the origin of evil, where he adopts formulations that appear close to Stoic

The titles of works referred to in this chapter do not originate with Maximus himself and are therefore sometimes misleading.

thought. Maximus also concerns himself equally with how the Demiurge continually cares for or administers the cosmos, as well as the generative act itself. Perhaps because of his personal religious views, he stresses divine transcendence (through his articulation of the power of Zeus' 'nod' or divine assent). Maximus, in general, does not consider how the mechanics of demiurgy function, although he does consider how a continuous ontological link can be formed from the Demiurge to mankind through the *daimones*. One of his most interesting insights is the deeply-allusive reference to Anaximander's philosophy through the medium of the marriage of Zeus and Chthonie as a metaphor for the principle of harmony. (The story itself, as it appears in Maximus, derives from Pherecydes.) For Maximus, the Demiurge is the supreme god, though he stresses the unity of the divine, regarding various deities as functioning in association with one another, while they may have their own alloted spheres. Though Maximus speculates regarding the limits which Necessity imposes upon the Demiurge during world-generation, as well as during his continual governance of the cosmos, he mainly expounds the metaphysics of the *Timaeus* in an engaging literary fashion, rather than developing the philosophical issues involved.

Oration 11

Oration 11: τίς ὁ θεὸς κατὰ Πλάτωνα, 'What is God according to Plato?' is an account of the opinions which Maximus believed that Plato held concerning the divinity. God is portrayed as a supreme, transcendent intellect. One cannot really hope for a critical analysis of the Platonic Demiurge from Maximus' opening statement, where he asserts that only a fool would advance an opinion when even Plato, despite his eloquence, was unable to compose a convincing account of God. §5 expresses a belief in a demiurgic God who rules assisted by subordinates. The only noteworthy point here is at 11.5.89–90 that everything is the handiwork of God (though this comment is represented as an exclamation of the soul as it longs for the craftsman). Interestingly, Maximus does not refer to his Craftsman-god as the Demiurge at this point, but as τεχνίτης (artisan).

Maximus' aim here is not a detailed explanation of the divine nature, but rather an attack on agnostic or atheistic philosophical theories. Like Plato in the *Timaeus*, Maximus opposes the mechanistic view of the atomists, and claims that they still speak of God even without wanting to; although Leucippus removed his goodness and Democritus added the notion of 'community of sensation'. The same is true for Strato, with his attempts to alter God's nature, Epicurus who allows his god (or really gods) to feel pleasure and it is the case even for the agnostic Protagoras or Diagoras who denied God's very existence.

It is typical of Maximus to adopt a moralising stance, perhaps less in order to avoid engaging in serious philosophical inquiry than from his conviction that belief in God is what matters, rather than the refinements of various metaphysical schemes. However, at §8, he tries to locate God's position in the cosmos, placing him in the suprasensible world, before discussing the activities of actualised and potential Intellects. Here there is a textual complication:

> ... ἀλλὰ καὶ ἐνταῦθα διαφυὴν (Shorey διαφῇ R) ὁρῶ· τοῦ γὰρ νοῦ ὁ μὲν νοεῖν πέφυκεν, καὶ μὴ νοῶν, ὁ δὲ καὶ νοεῖ· ἀλλὰ καὶ οὗτος οὔπω τέλειος, ἂν μὴ προσθῇς αὐτῷ τὸ καὶ νοεῖν ἀεὶ καὶ πάντα νοεῖν καὶ μὴ ἄλλοτε ἄλλα· ὥστε εἴη ἂν ἐντελέστατος ὁ νοῶν ἀεὶ καὶ πάντα καὶ ἅμα.

> ... but I see that there is a distinction here, for there is one kind of mind that by its nature is capable of thinking, although it does not think, and another kind which thinks. But this mind is not perfect, unless you attribute to it thinking eternally and thinking all things and not thinking in a different manner at different times, so that the most complete mind thinks all things, both eternally and simultaneously. (11.8.186–91)

I have opted for Trapp's reading ὁ δὲ καὶ νοεῖ ('and another kind (of mind) which thinks'), rather than the manuscript reading of ὁ δὲ καὶ πέφυκεν ('and has the natural capacity'). Both Heinsius and the corrector of Harl (possibly Janus Lascarius) observed a problem here with the readings καὶ <νοεῖ καὶ> πέφυκεν (Heinsius, 'both actually thinks and has the natural capacity') and καὶ πέφυκεν <καὶ νοεῖ> (Harl. 5760) *post corr.* ('both has the natural capacity and actually thinks').

Trapp observed that light can be shed on the problem by a similar passage, Chapter 10 of the *Didaskalikos* of Alcinous (itself probably deriving from the doxographic work of Arius Didymus: ἐπεὶ δὲ ψυχῆς νοῦς ἀμείνων, νοῦ δὲ τοῦ ἐν δυνάμει ὁ κατ᾽ ἐνέργειαν πάντα νοῶν καὶ ἅμα καὶ ἀεί: 'Since intellect is superior to soul and superior to potential intellect there is actualised Intellect which cognises everything simultaneously and eternally' (*Didasc.* 10.2, trans. Dillon). The distinction between a potential and actualised Intellect was ultimately Aristotelian, but is a standard part of Middle Platonist theology, which Trapp observes is likely to be found here, as the passage evinces a 'more than usual dependance upon scholastic material'.[1] As Trapp's reading actually develops a pointed statement, it is the one which I follow here. The passage highlights the Platonic perception of demiurgy as noetic activity. Maximus draws a further distinction: 'Yet

---

[1] Trapp: 1991, 569

even this latter does not yet rank as perfect intellect, unless you add to it the further properties of thinking eternally and thinking all things and not thinking differently at different times. Thus the most perfect form of intellect is that which thinks all things for ever and at the same time.'

Maximus here seems to be close to Berkeley's view that all objects have a continuous existence in the mind of God. God thinking eternally the same things seems to posit a continual noetic creation. This may be seen as straining the text, but in the introduction to this section, Maximus questions 'For what being can be stable, if God does not touch it lightly?' (11.8.165–7), which seems to indicate his belief in the Demiurge's ordering of the cosmos in this manner.

Conflicting concepts of the Demiurge in Maximus

A much more promising oration for present purposes is *Oration* 41: τοῦ θεοῦ τὰ ἀγαθὰ ποιοῦντος, πόθεν τὰ κακά, 'Good being the work of God, from where does evil come?' In this attempt to solve the problem of evil, Maximus expresses certain interesting comments concerning the mechanics of demiurgy. He adopts a Stoicising attitude – after absolving the gods from responsibility for evil, he claims that evil either results from alterations to matter or from human freedom of choice. This echoes his stance at *Oration* 2, in which he elegantly expresses a platitude concerning the manner in which the demiurgic intellect pervades the universe. The demiurgic intellect is like the sun's light simultaneously embracing all parts of the earth and ordering it. Human intelligence, by contrast, resembles the daily passage of the sun; it gradually passes over each individual point of the earth in turn.

In *Oration* 41, Maximus then draws the commonplace Platonic distinction between the suprasensible and sublunar realms. In an argument familiar from the *Timaeus*, Maximus states that the suprasensible realm is insulated from evil, while the sublunar realm possesses good, which flows down to it from above, although it also possesses evils as a result of its own inherent imperfections (ἐξ αὐτοφυοῦς μοχθηρίας).[2] Maximus distinguishes between two kinds of imperfections: the modification of physical matter (ὕλης πάθος) and the freedom of the soul (ψυχῆς ἐξουσία). Maximus combines both of the traditional explanations for the existence of evil: the inherent evil of matter and human free will.

---

[2] *Oration* 41.4.109–13

There appears to be a process of emanation by which the lower realm receives necessary goods, indicating that the Demiurge continues to care for the sublunar realm, though it is not stated expressly here.[3] The notion that the earth is a blend of good and evil echoes Plato's portrayal of the cosmos as a blend of Reason and Necessity. Maximus' view of the inherent imperfections of the cosmos still parallels Plato's view that the cosmos is the best type that can exist. But what is particularly noteworthy is Maximus' explanation of physical evil: ὕλης πάθος. It was common for second-century Platonists to oppose God, the source of Good, and recalcitrant matter, the source of evil. As Simone Pétrement comments '*Au second siècle après Jésus-Christ, les platoniciens sont nettement dualistes: Plutarque, Maxime de Tyr, Atticus, Hermogène, Celse, Numénius d' Apamée, Cronius, Harpocration opposent profondément Dieu à la matière au point que la plupart d'entre eux font de celle-ci le principe du mal.*'[4]

The problem is that Maximus here does not speak of matter as being responsible for evil, but rather the modifications which matter undergoes to create the cosmos; a Stoic turn of phrase. Maximus is not dualist in the same sense as certain other Platonists, who view world-generation as an ongoing conflict between the Demiurge and matter; or indeed in the manner of Plutarch and Numenius, who posit an evil or an irrational soul as a third principle. Maximus is only dualist in the sense that like all Platonists, he draws a sharp distinction between the intelligible world and the realm of phenomena.[5]

The difficulty with Maximus' Stoic formulation here is that he is still preserving the Platonic transcendent divinity, while the Stoic explanation of evil operates in the context of a monistic system, with God and matter perpetually united. Admittedly, other Platonists during this period also adopted the Stoic formulation. Regarding the existence of evil as a by-product of the creation of the cosmos still makes the Demiurge responsible for evil, although Maximus does not seem to think that this is the case. After all, an industrialist is still responsible for harmful by-products, even though the end product of the process may be valuable:

ὕλην ὁρᾷς ὑποβεβλημένην δημιουργῷ ἀγαθῷ, ἧς τὸ μὲν κοσμηθὲν ἥκει παρὰ τῆς τέχνης, εἰ δέ τι ἀκρατῶς ἑαυτῶν τὰ ἐν γῇ ἔχοντα πάσχει πλημμελές, ἀναίτιόν μοι τὴν τέχνην τίθει· βούλησις γὰρ οὐδεμία τεχνίτου ἄτεχνος, οὐδὲ γὰρ νομοθέτου ἄδικος· ὁ δὲ θεῖος νοῦς ἀνθρωπίνης

---

[3] ἢ τὰ μὲν ἀγαθὰ ἐπίρρυτα ἐκ τῆς ἑτέρας. ('the goods flow down to it from the other' [realm = heaven]).

[4] Pétrement: 1947, 11   [5] Puiggali: 1983, 315

τέχνης εὐστοχώτερος. καθάπερ οὖν ἐν ταῖς τῶν τεχνῶν χειρουργίαις τὰ
μὲν ἡ τέχνη προηγουμένως δρᾷ, στοχαζομένη τοῦ τέλους, τὰ δὲ ἕπεται
τῇ χειρουργίᾳ, οὐ τέχνης ἔργα ἀλλ᾽ ὕλης πάθη, σπινθῆρές τε ἐξ ἄκμονος
καὶ ἐκ βαύνου αἰθαλώσεις, καὶ ἄλλο ἐξ ἄλλης πάθος, ἀναγκαῖον μὲν τῇ
ἐργασίᾳ, οὐ προηγούμενον δὲ τῷ τεχνίτῃ· οὕτως ἀμέλει καὶ ὅσα περὶ γῆν
πάθη γίνεται, ἃς καλοῦμεν κακῶν ἀνθρωπίνων ἐμβολάς, ἐνταῦθα ἡγητέον
ἀναίτιον {καὶ} τὴν τέχνην, εἶναι δὲ ταῦτα τῆς τοῦ ὅλου δημιουργίας ὥσπερ
τινὰς ἀναγκαίας καὶ ἑπομένας φύσεις. ἃ δὲ ἡμεῖς καλοῦμεν κακὰ καὶ φθοράς,
καὶ ἐφ᾽ οἷς ὀδυρόμεθα, ταῦτα ὁ τεχνίτης καλεῖ σωτηρίαν τοῦ ὅλου·

You see matter which has been subjected to a good Demiurge, and it has
been ordered in accordance with his craftsmanship, but if there is anything
disorderly and disharmonious upon the earth, I suppose that the craft is
blameless. For no craftsman has a desire that is contrary to his craft, for a
lawgiver does not desire what is unjust, and the divine mind has a steadier
aim than the art of man. Just as in practising the crafts, the craft produces
some things directly, striving after its goals and other things follow its
practice, not as the word of the craft, but as affectations of matter, just
like sparks from an anvil or clouds of sooty smoke from the furnace and
other affectations from other things, which necessarily arise from the work,
but which the craftsman does not directly produce. No different are the
affectations on the earth, which we call attacks of human evil. Here it is
necessary that we suppose that the craft is without blame and are natural
and necessary consequences of the demiurgy of the whole. What we call evil
and destruction and what we cry over, the craftsman calls the conservation
of the whole. (41.4.114–31)

I have quoted this passage at length as it is one of Maximus' most detailed
discussions of demiurgic causality. Maximus is evidently alluding to the
Aristotelian concept of accidental causation.[6] Here the demiurgic image
is developed at the expense of philosophical coherence; if the Demiurge
really creates the cosmos in the same manner as a blacksmith works, he
would cease to be a transcendent divinity. The comparison of the Demiurge
with the lawmaker is perhaps more apt, placing him in the position of a
regulator, rather than a creator, although it is a Platonic commonplace.
Maximus indicates that there are restrictions on the Demiurge when he
creates the universe, although unlike many other philosophers, he is reticent
as to what exactly these are.

Fortunately, Maximus elaborates on why exactly the Demiurge is not to
be blamed for the production (albeit indirect) of evil (§4) by regarding it
as preservation of the whole: 'for he is concerned for the whole and it is
necessary that the part suffers for the benefit of the whole'. For Maximus,

---

[6] Cf. ps.-Alex., *Mantissa* p. 17ff.

evil does not exist on the physical plane; its existence is merely a human perception. In fact, these so-called evils are useful, necessary as they are for the preservation of the cosmos as a whole. This is a typically Platonist stance; God orders on a macrocosmic level, but there is no real belief in theodicy for the individual (though see the discussion below). Physical evil is a human conception, because men are unable to comprehend the intentions of the divinity. This idea of minor unpleasantness resulting from generative activity had been previously adopted by other Platonists[7] and can be justified by reference to Plato (*Laws* x.903b), but it is ultimately Stoic.[8]

The demiurgic image above contrasts sharply with a parallel account of demiurgic causality, which exists in the same sermon, in which the universe takes form in response to Zeus' νεῦμα (nod or divine assent).[9] For Maximus, the Demiurge's νεῦμα is a sign of his power. World-generation takes place merely by his assenting to it. This also helps to preserve his status as a transcendent deity and to insulate him from matter. Incidentally, matter in Maximus' conception here must be inert or actually desire to be ordered. Here also, no mention is made of any force opposing the Demiurge during the act of world-generation. Unfortunately, one cannot avoid reading this passage without the same feeling of disappointment that one experienced upon encountering Plutarch's view that the Demiurge generates the universe 'by other contacts and attachments'. In both cases it seems to provide an escape route that is a little too convenient. Maximus' description of Zeus' nod allows him to preserve the dignity of his chief divinity, but it also absolves him from having to engage in any serious philosophical enquiry on how the Demiurge operates on matter or orders it.

Apart from seeming to abandon the (Stoicising) Platonist conception of matter as an independent or quasi-independent principle here, Maximus also makes no mention of the World-Soul or how he perceives that it should operate within his system; it seems that the divine intelligence of Zeus' νεῦμα is enough to pervade the cosmos.[10]

This image of Zeus' νεῦμα is used also in *Oration 4*, when Maximus is considering the accounts of the gods produced by poets and philosophers.

---

[7] Phil., *Prov.* (Armenian tr.) 100, 102,104, Aurelius, 6.36, 7.75

[8] E.g. *SVF* 2. 1170   [9] *Oration* 41.2.51–4

[10] The importance of the divine νεῦμα as an illustration of the authority of Zeus is exhibited also by Atticus at Eusebius, *Pr. Ev.* xv.4.9: οὐ παλινάγρετον, ὅττι κεν οὗτος τῇ κεφαλῇ ἐπινεύσῃ: '(Zeus' promise) will not be taken back, if he has confirmed it with a nod of his head', Ps.-Justin, *Ch.* 23 and Stobaeus *Flor*, III.11.2 (= III.430.1–2H). Puiggali: 1983, 185, quoting from Homer, *Il.* 1.526–7.

Zeus nodding his assent is responsible for regulating the cosmos: earth, sea, air and fire all remain within their assigned bounds as a result of it, rather like the demiurgic activity of the *Timaeus*. The revolution of the heavens, the birth of the animals and the growth of trees are likewise aspects of world-generation examined in the *Timaeus*. Zeus' νεῦμα also regulates human interaction: 'human virtue and human happiness are likewise products of Zeus' nod of assent'.

Here again, though the Demiurge is not really involved in creating or indeed in ordering; all he has to do is assent to world-generation and matters, or rather matter, takes care of itself. This is underlined by the reference to human virtue as equally the product of Zeus' nod of assent. At *Oration* 5.8.193–5, Maximus considers Socrates prayer to the gods in the context of human virtue as a divine gift. Socrates' virtue and blameless life might be τὰ θαυμαστὰ δῶρα, τὰ θεοῖς δοτά, 'amazing divine gifts', but he receives them from the gods, not on account of his prayer, but on his own account (παρ' ἑαυτοῦ). It is as if Socrates appeals to God to allow him to be virtuous, but promises himself to take care of it. In Maximus' view, everything appears to regulate itself to some degree, although perhaps the νεῦμα of Zeus is more than just an assent, but rather the initial impetus required to start the process of world-generation, followed by a less active role where the Demiurge engages in continual production 'by thinking the same things'.

Limits imposed upon the Demiurge

Maximus frequently alludes to the limits placed upon demiurgy by external factors. For example at *Oration* 13 (8.163–7), he considers the principle of Necessity. Maximus finds it difficult to define (or name: ὀνομάσαι) this principle and considers whether it should be equated with destiny, although this does not help to clarify its nature (φύσις) or essence (οὐσία). Unfortunately, Maximus shies away from any attempt to investigate the principle of Necessity and indulges instead in Homeric quotation and moralising. People, like Elpenor, who claim to have been led astray by the gods are simply trying to evade their moral responsibility.[11]

Maximus does, however, engage in a somewhat more 'scientific' study of other factors that affect the Demiurge's relationship with the world in *Oration* 5: εἰ δεῖ εὔχεσθαι, 'Whether One Ought to Pray'. Maximus here considers God's relationship with the world. Four factors, other than the

---

[11]   *Oration* 13.8.167–79

Demiurge, play a role in causality: Providence, Destiny, Fortune/Chance and Science. A demarcation dispute exists between these factors and it is unclear what distinction Maximus intends between them. Like *Oration* 41, this provides another opportunity to absolve the Demiurge from responsibility for the existence of evil, although in that sermon also Maximus tends to rely more on moralising assertion than upon reasoned philosophical argument. 'God does not distribute evils; they are rather the gift of chance coming blindly from their unreasoning source like the cheery greetings of drunkards.'[12] Here, though, Maximus gives a brief outline of the role played by each of these factors:

> καὶ ἡ μὲν πρόνοια θεοῦ ἔργον, ἡ δὲ εἱμαρμένη ἀνάγκης, ἡ δὲ τέχνη ἀνθρώπου, ἡ δὲ τύχη τοῦ αὐτομάτου· διακεκλήρωνται δὲ τούτων ἑκάστῳ αἱ ὗλαι τοῦ βίου· ἃ τοίνυν εὐχόμεθα, ἢ εἰς πρόνοιαν συντελεῖ θεοῦ ἢ εἰς εἱμαρμένης ἀνάγκην ἢ εἰς ἀνθρώπου τέχνην ἢ εἰς τύχης φοράν.

> Providence is the work of God, Destiny that of Necessity, craftsmanship the work of man and Fortune the work of random spontaneity and the material of life is allocated to one of these. What we pray for must be completed by the Providence of God or by fated Necessity or by the craft of man or by the act of Fortune. (5.4.83–7)

Maximus adheres to the Platonist opposition to Destiny as the sole factor in causality, as opposed to the Stoic unification of Providence and Destiny and their denial of the existence of Chance.[13] Platonist accounts can be found at *De Fato*, *Didasc.* 26 and *De Plat.* 1.12. Trapp states 'Quite what distinction Maximus himself intends here and in §§4–5 between Providence and Destiny remains obscure'.[14] However at §4, Maximus refers to Providence as that exercised by God on behalf of the generated world as a whole; so I believe that it represents demiurgic Reason. This fits with the general Platonic view that nature or Providence is only secondary to the causality of the Demiurge, caused as it is by the agents which he has created.[15]

Since Destiny is explicitly said to be the work of ἀνάγκη, it must be Maximus' equivalent of the Necessity which Plato's Demiurge has to confront in the *Timaeus*, despite his hesitance to equate the two at 13.8.163–71. Perhaps, the real problem here is not the distinction between Providence and Destiny, but rather how Fortune and Science play a role in the act of

---

[12] *Oration* 5.1.22–5; *Cf. Tim.* 30a. [13] Trapp: 1997, 45 [14] Trapp: 1997, 45
[15] For example, the Young Gods of the *Timaeus* play a role in cosmic order and might all be referred to under the general heading of Providence. They are, obviously, in no way a limitation on the activity of the Demiurge, since they owe their existence to him. For Platonist views on Providence and their relationship with Stoic doctrines, see Boys-Stones: 2007.

world-generation, along with the two original factors (Reason and Necessity) found in the *Timaeus*. Maximus' lack of interest in the more technical aspects of metaphysics appears in the statement that the raw material (αἱ ὗλαι could equally be applied to matter, although the use of the plural creates a certain degree of ambivalence) is allocated to one of the four factors, but Maximus is not overly interested in which one. Furthermore, who or what exactly does the allocating? Another problem exists concerning the precise nature of εἱμαρμένης ἀνάγκη. How exactly is Necessity destined? Presumably in the same sense as in Plato's *Timaeus*; certain features cannot of necessity be combined by the Demiurge in the production of the phenomenal realm and so in this manner ἀνάγκη is preordained.

Maximus, like Plato, stresses that the Demiurge, not just in the act of world-generation, but even in his theodicy, is bound by Necessity, discussing the famous example of Zeus being forced to consent to the death of his son, Sarpedon, at the hands of Patroclus (*Il.* 16.433–4). In fact, in the parallel that Maximus uses, Zeus was capable of overruling Fate, but chose not to do so, as the other gods would have disapproved. I think that Maximus' suppression of this aspect is deliberate, not an oversight, since introducing this point would vitiate the efficacy of this allegory; the Demiurge cannot go against the dictates of Necessity. In Maximus' second example, from *Il.* 18.54, when Thetis laments the impending death of her son, she is suffering as the result of Achilles' free choice (to die a glorious death). Admittedly, in both cases Maximus is discussing Providence within the context of its influence over human lives, rather than any role it may play in world-generation. However, the example of Zeus is indicative of how Maximus conceptualises the interrelation between God/the Demiurge and factors which limit his activity.

Maximus goes on to describe Fortune, but in a manner that is particularly vague and so it is difficult to work out what kind of restriction this could impose upon the Demiurge:

ἀλλ᾽ οὐδὲ ἐν τοῖς κατὰ τὴν τύχην εὐκτέον, καὶ πολὺ μᾶλλον ἐνταῦθα οὐκ εὐκτέον· οὐδὲ γὰρ ἀνοήτῳ δυνάστῃ διαλεκτέον, ἔνθα οὐ βούλευμα οὐδὲ κρίσις οὐδὲ ὁρμὴ σώφρων οἰκονομεῖ τὴν ἀρχήν, ἀλλὰ ὀργὴ καὶ φορὰ καὶ ἄλογοι ὀρέξεις καὶ ἔμπληκτοι ὁρμαὶ καὶ ἐπιθυμιῶν διαδοχαί. τοιοῦτον ἡ τύχη, ἄλογον, ἔμπληκτον, ἀπροόρατον, ἀνήκοον, ἀμάντευτον, Εὐρίπου δίκην μεταρρέον, περιφερόμενον, καὶ οὐδεμιᾶς ἀνεχόμενον κυβερνήτου τέχνης. τί ἂν οὖν τις εὔξαιτο ἀστάτῳ χρήματι καὶ ἀνοήτῳ καὶ ἀσταθμήτῳ καὶ ἀμίκτῳ;

But it is not possible to pray about matters governed by Fortune and it is no more possible to pray in this case (than in other cases). For it is not possible to talk to an irrational tyrant, where there is no planning or judgement or temperate impulses and where power is wielded by anger and rapid motion and irrational impulses and capricious drives and successions of desire. This is what Fortune is: irrational, capricious, without precedent, incapable of hearing, unforeseeable, eddying and whirling round like the current of the Euripus and not submitting to any art of the helmsman. Therefore what prayer might one make to something so unstable and irrational and unsteady and disharmonious? (5.6.135–44)

This description is very loosely modelled on the description of the tyrant at *Rep.* 571a*ff.*, but it is difficult to read this passage as anything more than an elaborate literary flourish. It also seems that in a world produced by a rational Demiurge, admittedly under the constraints of Necessity, there is no room for an additional irrational force. Necessity already accounts for the irrational substratum that persists in the sublunar realm. The situation becomes even more confusing in the subsequent passage:

λοιπὸν δὴ μετὰ τὴν τύχην ἡ τέχνη. καὶ τίς τέκτων εὔξεται περὶ κάλλους ἀρότρου, τὴν τέχνην ἔχων; ἢ τίς ὑφάντης περὶ κάλλους χλανίδος, τὴν τέχνην ἔχων; ἢ τίς χαλκεὺς περὶ κάλλους ἀσπίδος, τὴν τέχνην ἔχων; ἢ τίς ἀριστεὺς περὶ εὐτολμίας, τὴν ἀνδρείαν ἔχων; ἢ τίς ἀγαθὸς περὶ εὐδιαμονίας, τὴν ἀρετὴν ἔχων;

And after Fortune, craftsmanship remains and what carpenter, when he possesses craftsmanship, prays for a good plough? What weaver, when he possesses craftsmanship, prays for a good cloak? What coppersmith, when he possesses craftsmanship, prays for a good shield? What brave man prays for courage, when he possesses daring? What virtuous man prays for happiness, when he possesses virtue? (5.6.145–50)

Trapp states that this passage underlines 'the proper provinces of human enterprise and divine assistance'.[16] What is unclear is how human science can be regarded as a causal factor (in our lives) comparable to the Demiurge, Necessity and Fortune. Perhaps Maximus envisages that in some sense humanity is capable of becoming a co-producer with the Demiurge in a manner akin to the Christian notion of procreation. However, in the absence of any detailed comment from Maximus, who breaks his promise, by claiming that it only remains to speak of science and then failing to expound the topic, it is idle to speculate.

Evidently, here Maximus is dealing with two separate problems: the limitations imposed upon the Demiurge during the actual process of world-generation, and the limitations that emerge in relation to his governance of

---

[16] Trapp: 1997, 48

the world in order to allow room for human free will. Even though it is clear that at *Oration* 5 Maximus intends to deal with the latter problem, once he starts to investigate the limits imposed on the Demiurge by Necessity, he immediately opens up the related question of the limits to the Demiurge's powers during world-generation. Both problems were related by the Stoics in their theory that humans should become artisans of their lives, and I think that this is what Maximus is getting at here.

Maximus seems to be aware that all four factors play a role in demiurgic causality, but he does not appear to have worked out a coherent system and he avoids elaborating on the manner of their interaction during the process of world-generation. Πρόνοια, often translated as 'Providence', is perhaps something more akin to 'forethought', and is possibly intended to play a role similar to Ἔννοια in Philo's system; an emanation of the transcendental God, which engages in demiurgic activity and helps to insulate Him from matter. At *Oration* 5, Maximus again points out that apparent evils only appear to be so: 'You may call such breakings-up "destruction" but the true doctor knows their cause; he disregards the prayers of the parts and preserves the universe for his concern is of the whole' (trans. after Trapp, modified).[17] Maximus here adopts the Stoic formulation of God's concern for the good of the whole. He does acknowledge some theodicy on a more individual level (κατὰ μέρος, on the level of particulars). Maximus reiterates the points made concerning Socrates' prayer: '. . . God's Providence does in fact extend to particulars as well. But prayer is out of place there too, being like a patient asking his doctor for food or medicine on his own initiative: if it is efficacious, the doctor will give it unasked; if it is dangerous, he will withhold it, even when asked.' It is unclear what restrictions Fortune and Necessity could possibly place upon the Demiurge, since these 'breakings-up' are in fact not evil at all and here they are even attributed to his πρόνοια.

Oration 13: εἰ μαντικῆς οὔσης, ἔστιν τι ἐφ᾽ ἡμῖν, 'Whether given the reality of prophecy, there is free will', also investigates the nature of causality, demiurgic and otherwise, although Maximus concentrates more on the compatibility of prophecy with human intelligence, rather than with free will. This is linked with the ideas expressed in *Oration* 5, since here also Maximus regards events in the cosmos as caused by (and therefore predictable by) multiple factors. Maximus expresses some rather interesting comments on the nature of divine intellect:

---

[17] *Oration* 5.103–9

τὸ δὲ θεῖον δοκεῖ σοι γινώσκειν πάντα ἑξῆς, καὶ τὰ καλὰ καὶ τὰ αἰσχρά, καὶ τὰ τίμια καὶ τὰ ἄτιμα; φείδομαι τῶν ῥημάτων καὶ αἰδώς με τοῦ θείου ἔχει· σεμνὸν γάρ τι τὸ πάντα εἰδέναι, καὶ ἀριθμὸν ψάμμων καὶ θαλάττης μέτρα, καὶ ξυνιέναι ἀτόπου λέβητος ἑψομένου ἐν Λυδοῖς·

Does it seem to you that the divine knows everything in order, both the beautiful and the ugly, both the honourable and the shameful? I am sparing of words and have awe of the divine. It is venerable to know everything, both the number of the sands and the measure of the sea and to be aware of a strange cauldron boiling in Lydia. (13.3.43–7)

Evidently, Maximus is being rather sarcastic here. I think that what underlines this statement is the Stoicised notion that God or Providence focuses on the entire cosmos, only considering smaller parts insofar as they contribute to the whole. Yet here, Maximus appears to contradict his own comments at *Oration* 11 that the divine intellect thinks all things simultaneously and eternally. It is, however, in keeping with his conception of the demiurgic νεῦμα as responsible for world-generation. If the Demiurge actively generated or ordered, he should have some idea of the number of grains of sand. It is as if by giving his νεῦμα, he stands back and allows matter to order itself, rather than adopting a more active role. However, this stance allows Maximus to preserve the transcendent nature of the deity, highlighting God's separation from the world. God is not 'a terribly meddlesome busybody'.[18] He cares for the world as a whole, rather than being excessively concerned with its parts.

There then follows a description of demiurgic causality, which is effectively a summary of the *Timaeus*. God's craftsmanship is to cause harmony to spread from himself through the cosmos, like the harmony of a musical activity. Maximus compares his activity to that of the leader of a choir bringing an end to the discord that exists amongst the choristers.[19] The harmony mentioned alludes to the harmonic ratios according to which the soul is divided in the *Timaeus*. The notion of a direct descent of the divine is to be found at *De Mund.* 399b15 and 400b8, although Maximus develops it in a Platonic direction by hinting at world-generation through ordering.

Maximus then provides a more explicit statement concerning the mechanics of divine causality:

τίς δὲ ὁ τρόπος τῆς θείας τέχνης, ὀνόματι μὲν εἰπεῖν οὐκ ἔχω, εἴσῃ δὲ αὐτῆς τὴν δύναμιν ἐξ εἰκόνος † ἢ οἵα δήποτε † ἐθεάσω νεῶν ἐρύσεις ἐκ θαλάττης ἄνω καὶ λίθων ἀγωγὰς ὑπερφυῶν κατὰ μέγεθος παντοδαποῖς ἑλιγμοῖς καὶ ἀναστροφαῖς ὀργάνων· ὧν ἕκαστον πρὸς τὸ πλησίον τὴν

---

[18] *Oration* 13.3.50–3; trans. Trapp   [19] *Oration* 13.3.64–71

ῥώμην νειμάμενον, ἕτερον ἐξ ἑτέρου διαδεχόμενον τὴν ἀγωγήν, κινεῖ τὸ πᾶν· καὶ τὸ μὲν ὅλον ἔχει τὴν αἰτίαν τοῦ ἔργου, συνεπιλαμβάνει δέ τι αὐτῷ καὶ τὰ μέρη.

And what the nature of this divine craft is, I am unable to say in detail, but you can understand its force from this image: you have seen ships being dragged up out of the sea and and enormous stones being moved by the convolutions and whirling of machinery of all kinds. Each part dispenses force to the next and one part receives the impetus from another and the whole (machine) moves. The whole has responsibility for the task, but the individual parts partake in it. (13.4.71–9)

Finally, it appears that Maximus is ready to explain the manner in which the Demiurge collaborates with Necessity and Fortune in the generation of the cosmos. These separate elements are co-responsible with the Demiurge for the generation of the sublunar realm. This image is similar to that of *De Mund.* 398b11–17, but here Maximus is straying away from the question that he had previously set out to discuss, exploring how the Demiurge causes events, rather than the manner in which God foresees them. Unfortunately, as is so frequently the case with Maximus, he appears to be on the point of providing a detailed account of demiurgic causality, before dealing with the matter in a superficial manner. The Demiurge is merely a part of the machine involved in world-generation. The image of the machine is similar to Aristotle's view of causality in terms of contact between bodies; the efficient cause has to touch bodies lower down the chain in order to operate on them. This is what is going on here, although Maximus never elaborates on the sort of twistings or rotations that he imagines to be necessary for a component to transmit its impetus to the next.

A more detailed account of how the Demiurge interacts with Fate then follows:

κάλει τοίνυν τεχνίτην μὲν τὸν θεόν, ὄργανα δὲ τοὺς λογισμοὺς τοὺς ἀνθρωπίνους, τέχνην δὲ τὴν μαντικὴν σπῶσαν ἡμᾶς ἐπὶ τὴν ἀγωγὴν τῆς εἱμαρμένης. εἰ δέ σοι καὶ σαφεστέρας εἰκόνος δεῖ, νόει μοι στρατηγὸν μὲν τὸν θεόν, στρατείαν δὲ τὴν ζωήν, ὁπλίτην δὲ τὸν ἄνθρωπον, σύνθημα δὲ τὴν εἱμαρμένην, ὅπλα δὲ τὰς εὐπορίας, πολεμίους δὲ τὰς συμφοράς, σύμμαχον δὲ τὸν λογισμόν ἀριστείαν δὲ τὴν ἀρετήν, ἥτταν δὲ τὴν μοχθηρίαν, μαντικὴν δὲ τὴν τέχνην αὐτὴν τὴν ἐκ τῆς παρασκευῆς ἐπισταμένην τὸ μέλλον. καὶ γὰρ κυβερνήτης ναῦν ἔχων καὶ εἰδὼς τὰ ὄργανα καὶ τὴν θάλατταν ὁρῶν καὶ αἰσθανόμενος τῶν πνευμάτων, οἶδεν τὸ ἀποβησόμενον·

Call the craftsman God, and the machinery human reasoning, and craftsmanship the prophetic art which draws us towards the necessity of Destiny.

And if a clearer image is necessary for you, envisage God as the general, life as an expedition, man as a hoplite, Destiny as the cipher, supplies as weapons, Reason as an ally, virtue as the prize of valour, depravity as a defeat and the prophetic art as that which can predict future events from armaments. For a helmsman too, in command of his ship and familiar with his equipment and with an eye on the sea, and observing the winds, knows what will happen. (13.4.79–90)

The Demiurge is also compared to a doctor, who, relying on his art, can foresee the probable result of an illness. Here again, Necessity or Fate is portrayed as an external factor, which is not subject to the authority of the Demiurge, but his knowledge of the art of demiurgy allows him to predict the probable result of the dictates of Necessity. Maximus then moves away from the topic of demiurgic causality to consider whether there is any place for human free will or autonomy, concluding that it is inextricably bound up with Necessity/Fate (§4), but the regular operations of Fate make it predictable, even by human intellect (§5).

The wording here is particularly ambivalent. Maximus tries to demonstrate that human free will is ultimately autonomous, but expresses himself in such a way as to make it appear that it is actually one aspect of an overarching 'Stoic' Fate; although Maximus exhibits a classic Middle Platonist difficulty in trying to combine universal divine control with human autonomy; exhibited also at *Didasc.* 26 and *De Fato* 569*ff.*, where use is made of a comparison between Fate and law.[20] Alcinous' theory, which seems to be the basic Platonic one during this period, is as follows:

(1) All things are within the sphere of Fate, but not all things are fated.

(2) Fate has the status of a law, but it does not make specific statements, since that would result in an infinity of possibilities.

(3) If all things are fated, the concept of what is in our power (τὸ ἐφ' ἡμῖν) would disappear.

(4) The soul is autonomous; it is not compelled to act, but once it makes a specific choice, a particular chain of causality results, which is fulfilled according to Fate. (*Didasc.* 26.1–2)

---

[20] Ps-Plut., *De Fato* 569d*ff.*: σχεδὸν μὲν οὖν καὶ τοῦτο δηλοῖ, ὁποῖόν τι τυγχάνει ἡ εἱμαρμένη, πλὴν οὐχ ἥ γε κατὰ μέρος οὐδ' ἡ καθ' ἕκαστα. ποία τις οὖν καὶ ἥδε κατ' αὐτὸ δὴ τὸ εἶδος τοῦ λόγου; ἔστι τοίνυν, ὡς ἄν τις εἰκάσαι, οἷος ὁ πολιτικὸς νόμος, <ὃς> πρῶτον μὲν τὰ πλεῖστα, εἰ καὶ μὴ πάντα, ἐξ ὑποθέσεως προστάττει, ἔπειτα μὴν καθόλου τὰ πόλει προσήκοντα εἰς δύναμιν περιλαμβάνει. πάλιν δὴ τούτων ἑκάτερον ὁποῖόν τί ἐστι, σκεπτέον.

'Then it is quite clear from this what Destiny is, although not what particular or individual Destiny is. Under this form of the argument what, then, is Destiny? It can be explained in terms of civil law, which first of all subordinates the majority, if not everybody, to itself and it universally embraces, as far as it can, the affairs of the city. And now it is necessary to examine each of these items and what sort of nature they have.'

This is in accordance with Maximus' speculations on Fate and human free will. (This is illustrated by the example which he provides of Laius: it was fated that Laius would be killed by his son, although Laius could always have abstained from sexual activity. Once he sired Oedipus, the causal chain which resulted in his death commenced. The Laius/Oedipus example was a popular one in Middle Platonist discussions of Fate). However, another Middle Platonist, Apuleius of Madaura, attempted to work out more specifically the interaction between Fate and the actions of the Demiurge, with a triadic division of Providence (which recalls the three spheres administered by the Moirai in pseudo-Plutarch). At *De Plat.* 1.12, he distinguishes between a primary providence – that of the supreme god (Demiurge), a secondary providence entrusted to secondary gods (the Young Gods of the *Timaeus*) and a tertiary providence, (although he does not refer to it as such), which is administered by the *daimones*.[21] A similar system can be found in *De Fato* 572f., Calcidius (ch. 155) and Nemesius (ch. 34 p. 287 Matthaei).[22]

In general, these theories seem to be part of a Middle Platonist attempt to work out how demiurgic Providence can enclose Fate which then encloses Free Will and to place all elements in a coherent system. The comparison with other Middle Platonists is instructive, since it illustrates the lack of refinements and subtleties inherent in Maximus' account, where very little attempt is made to define the four elements of causality, which he identifies, in anything approaching a coherent system.

Maximus then quotes Plato's *Laws* 709b–c to summarise the Platonic view concerning the manner in which Fate, Science, Chance and the Demiurge all contribute to causality:

> ... ὡς θεὸς μὲν πάντα, καὶ μετὰ θεοῦ τύχη καὶ καιρὸς τὰ ἀνθρώπινα κυβερνῶσιν τὰ ξύμπαντα· ἡμερώτερόν γε μὴν τρίτον ἐπὶ τούτοις προσθεῖναι δεῖν ἕπεσθαι τὴν τέχνην. καιρῷ γὰρ χειμῶνος συλλαβέσθαι κυβερνητικὴν ἢ μή, μέγα πλεονέκτημα ἔγωγ' ἂν θείην.

> ... so God directs all human affairs and Fortune and opportunity along with God. More benignly it is necessary for a third factor to follow these, craftsmanship. For during a storm, the helmsman might seize a favourable opportunity or not, but it would be advantageous, I would say, if he did so. (13.7.151–5)

From the echo of this text at Plut., *Quaest. Conv.* 740c, it seems to have been used as a proof text in Middle Platonist discussions of the topic.[23] The oration closes with a Stoicising comment that humanity confronted

---

[21] Dillon: 1977, 325   [22] Dillon: 1977, 323   [23] Trapp: 1997, 122

by Necessity has the autonomy of a man in chains who follows his captors of his own free will (a variant of Zeno's example of a small dog tied to a cart) and an assertion that nothing that is evil can be the work of the Demiurge.[24]

An alternative explanation of the functioning of demiurgic causality can be found in *Oration* 4: τίνες ἄμεινον περὶ θεῶν διέλαβον· ποιηταὶ ἢ φιλόσοφοι; 'Who produced the better account of the gods, poets or philosophers?'. In the course of the sermon, Maximus makes allusion to the work of the Presocratic, Pherecydes of Syros, entitled, according to the *Suda*, ἑπτάμυχος ἤτοι θεοκρασία ἢ θεογονία (The Seven Sanctuaries or Divine Mingling or Genealogy of the Gods). This work begins with the lines Ζὰς μὲν καὶ Χρόνος ἦσαν ἀεὶ καὶ Χθονίη. Χθονίη δὲ ὄνομα ἐγενέτο Γῆ, ἐπειδὴ αὐτῇ Ζὰς γῆν γέρας διδοῖ ('There was always Zeus and Chronos and Chthonie. And the name earth was given to Chthonie since Zeus, on the occasion of his marriage with Chthonie, offered her the earth as a present').[25]

Fr. 7B3 elaborates: Zeus 'μέλλοντα δημιουργεῖν' (Zeus 'being about to order the world'), transformed himself into Eros and τὸν κόσμον ἐκ τῶν ἐναντίων συνιστὰς εἰς ὁμολογίαν καὶ φιλίαν ἤγαγε ('bringing together the cosmos out of opposites he led it to order and attraction'). Chronos produces the various elements, but Zeus, having transformed himself into Eros (the principle of harmony) orders in this manner the unified world. Zeus is clearly similar to the Platonic Demiurge, ordering pre-existent and recalcitrant matter. Chronos, I think, is not pre-cosmic chaos, but rather something akin to the winnowing motion of the *Timaeus*, which is responsible for the initial creative impulse.

Further light is shed on this matter by Proclus' *Commentary on the Timaeus* (II.54 Diehl): τὴν γὰρ Ἀφροδίτην παρήγαγεν ὁ δημιουργός... Ἔχει δὲ καὶ αὐτὸς ἐν ἑαυτῷ τὴν τοῦ Ἔρωτος αἰτίαν, 'For the Demiurge leads Aphrodite along... And he contains within himself the cause of Eros'. The Demiurge harmonises the cosmos through the introduction of the Principle of Love and attraction. Maximus' allusion to this seems to have largely gone unnoticed by commentators, with the exception of Puiggali:

> ἀλλὰ καὶ τοῦ Συρίου τὴν ποίησιν σκόπει, τὸν Ζῆνα καὶ τὴν Χθονίην καὶ τὸν ἐν τούτοις ἔρωτα καὶ τὴν Ὀφιονέως γένεσιν καὶ τὴν θεῶν μάχην καὶ τὸ

---

[24] This reminds us of the strong interaction between Stoicism and Platonism in the second century AD.

[25] Fr. 7B1 – *Vorsokr.* Diels-Kranz

δένδρον καὶ τὸν πέπλον· σκόπει καὶ τὸ Ἡρακλείτου, θεοὶ θνητοί, ἄνθρωποι ἀθάνατοι.

But examine the poetry of the man from Syros and his Zeus and Chthonie and their love and the birth of Ophioneus and the battle of the gods and the tree and the dress; and examine this remark of Heraclitus 'mortal gods, immortal men'. (4.4.77–81)

Puiggali interprets τὸν Ζῆνα καὶ τὴν Χθονιήν καὶ τὸν ἐν τούτοις Ἔρωτα (rather than Trapp's ἔρωτα somewhat differently: 'Zeus, Chthonie and *the Eros which is in them*').[26] Maximus is not recounting a simple love story, but how the Demiurge and his spouse both transformed themselves into the principle of harmony at the moment of world-generation in order to allow this generation to occur.

Ophioneus is Maximus' name for Ophion, a name for which there are two candidates: (1) the first master of the world and the adversary of Chronos and (2) a giant in conflict with Zeus and who was defeated by him. Wüst's opinion was that Maximus confounds the two,[27] while Puiggali feels that Maximus only refers to Ophion (1). If Ophion (1) is referred to, Maximus is alluding to an additional ordering principle (the adversary of Chronos) or if (2) is referred to, he is alluding to Necessity or an evil World-Soul, a disordered principle, which is in conflict with the Demiurge.

The πέπλος (robe) is the φάρος (dowry) which Zeus offers Chthonie as a wedding present: τότε Ζὰς ποιεῖ φάρος μέγα τε καὶ καλὸν καὶ ἐν αὐτῷ ποικίλλει τὴν καὶ Ὠγηνου δώματα ('Then Zeus made a great and beautiful dowry and enrobed in itself the house of Ogenos', Fr. B2). As for the tree, it is alluded to by Clement of Alexandria (*Strom.* VI.53. 5: ὑπόπτερος δρῦς καὶ τὸ ἐπ' αὐτῇ πεποικιλμένον φάρος, 'a winged oak and gift wrought upon itself'.) Diels explains the allusion to the tree by referring to Anaximander's representation of the earth. Anaximander compared the earth to the trunk of a tree and the sky which surrounds it to bark.[28] The garment which Zeus offers Chthonie must therefore be the surface of the earth. Taken together, then, the Demiurge offers Chthonie (the generative female principle) the earth at the moment of world-generation, when both engage in the demiurgic act by simultaneously transforming themselves into the principle of harmony.

Here we have an allegory of demiurgic causality far removed from Maximus' usual superficial treatment of this (and practically every other) matter.

---

[26] Puiggali: 1981   [27] Wüst: 1939a, 1939b and 1939c   [28] Puiggali: 1983, 79

In the passage immediately following, Maximus expresses his approval of the use of myth to expound philosophical truth (although as a sophist he does not really have views on such matters and just presents variations on a theme):

πάντα μεστὰ αἰνιγμάτων καὶ παρὰ ποιηταῖς καὶ παρὰ φιλοσόφοις, ὧν ἐγὼ τὴν πρὸς τὸ ἀληθὲς αἰδῶ ἀγαπῶ μᾶλλον ἢ τὴν παρρησίαν τῶν νεωτέρων· πραγμάτων γὰρ ὑπ' ἀνθρωπίνης ἀσθενείας οὐ καθορωμένων σαφῶς εὐσχημονέστερος ἑρμηνεὺς ὁ μῦθος... τί γὰρ ἂν ἄλλο εἴη μύθου χρεία <ἢ> λόγος περισκεπὴς ἑτέρῳ κόσμῳ, καθάπερ τὰ ἱδρύματα οἷς περιέβαλλον οἱ τελεσταὶ χρυσὸν καὶ ἄργυρον καὶ πέπλους, {τὰ} ἀποσεμνύνοντες αὐτῶν τὴν προσδοκίαν;

Among poets and philosophers allegory is common, so that I have greater admiration for these writers' love of the truth, more than the outspokenness of the younger writers. For myth is the most appropriate interpreter for things which we cannot clearly see on account of human weakness... for what other need of a myth is there, but reason concealed by a different order, just like the statues which priests clothe in gold and silver and robes, so that their appearance is more worthy of respect. (4.5.82–94)

Since this passage is delivered immediately after the allusion to the Zeus and Chthonie myth, it seems probable that Maximus was aware of the philosophical insight contained therein, and was prepared to accept it.

Unity of the divine

Maximus, like many educated Greeks of his time, moves away from the polytheistic tendencies of Greek religion, believing instead that the traditional gods are merely aspects of the Demiurge (who, for him is presumably the supreme God, as he appears to be equated with Zeus). At *Oration* 2.1, Maximus points out that all gods assist all men, but humanity has been led to assign spheres of responsibility to individual gods. At §10, he then describes the Demiurge:

ὁ μὲν γὰρ θεός, ὁ τῶν ὄντων πατὴρ καὶ δημιουργός, {ὁ} πρεσβύτερος μὲν ἡλίου, πρεσβύτερος δὲ οὐρανοῦ, κρείττων δὲ χρόνου καὶ αἰῶνος καὶ πάσης ῥεούσης φύσεως, ἀνώνυμος νομοθέταις καὶ ἄρρητος φωνῇ καὶ ἀόρατος ὀφθαλμοῖς·

For God, the Father and the Demiurge of Being is older than the sun, older than the heavens and mightier than time and eternity and the entire flux of nature; he is unnameable for lawgivers, and unspeakable in sound and invisible to eyes. (2.10.183–7)

This echoes numerous Platonising descriptions of the divine, owing their inspiration to *Tim.* 41a. Apart from the usual commonplace ideas concerning the ineffability of the divine,[29] what is interesting is that the Demiurge is here regarded as greater than Eternity and the flux of Nature, which would seem to indicate that he is not under any constraint in the generation of the sensible world, but given the fact that this conflicts sharply with the opinion which Maximus expresses elsewhere, I think that we must regard this more as rhetorical flourish than reasoned philosophical argument.

Unity of the divine is also stressed at *Oration* 39.5. There Maximus claims that the gods share customs, life and character. All rule, all are of the same age and are the saviours of mankind. They only have one nature, although they have many names and it is through ignorance that the gifts which they bestow collectively are attributed to individual divine names. This concept of the unity of the divine is essentially Stoic, rather than Platonic, although Maximus tends to develop it in a Platonising direction.[30]

For example in *Oration* 4, Maximus refers to Zeus as 'the supreme and venerable Mind' (νοῦν πρεσβύτατον καὶ ἀρχικώτατον), Athena as Intelligence (φρόνησις) and Poseidon as the cosmic breath (πνεῦμα) pervading land and sea.[31] Maximus portrays the traditional Olympian pantheon as merely aspects and extensions of the Demiurge and his activity. All things follow and obey Zeus; this seems to place the Demiurge above the dictates of Necessity. Maximus has located him in the suprasensible realm, providing contact with the sublunar realm by means of the πνεῦμα represented by Poseidon. This is an interesting development, as in Stoic accounts, Poseidon pervades the seas, not both land and sea as here.[32]

For Maximus, πνεῦμα has become an immanent World-Soul, the counterpart of the Philonic *Logos*, allowing the Demiurge to interact with the sensible realm. Maximus further elaborates on the Demiurge's interaction with the cosmos in *Orations* 8 and 9 – τί τὸ δαιμόνιον Σωκράτους, 'What was Socrates' divine sign?', which points out that *daimones* are necessary in the hierarchy of entities in order to prevent the cosmos splitting in two between the suprasensible and sublunar realms. The *daimones* are similar to the Young Gods of the *Timaeus* as assistants of the Demiurge, although here they seem to be involved more in administration than in the act of world-production:

---

[29] Found also at Alcin., *Didasc.* 10.164–5 and Apul., *De Plat.* 15.
[30] Cf. *SVF* 2.1021, Cic., *ND* 2.63ff.   [31] *Oration* 4.8.165–72
[32] Chrysippus – ap. Cic., *ND* 1.40 and Diogenes of Babylon Fr. 33

Θεὸς μὲν οὖν αὐτὸς κατὰ χώραν ἱδρυμένος οἰκονομεῖ τὸν οὐρανὸν καὶ τὴν ἐν οὐρανῷ τάξιν· εἰσὶ δ' αὐτῷ φύσεις ἀθάνατοι δεύτεραι, οἱ καλούμενοι δαίμονες, ἐν μεθορίᾳ γῆς καὶ οὐρανοῦ τεταγμένοι·

God himself, being settled and fixed, regulates heaven and the arrangement in heaven. And there is a second sort of immortals, who are called *daimones*, stationed inbetween earth and heaven. (*Oration* 8.8.180–3)

This parallels the description of the Demiurge at *Oration* 11.12, where he is compared to the Great King sitting motionless, but governing through a hierarchy of entities, who are compared to courtiers. At *Oration* 8.8.186–9, the *daimones* play a role in demiurgy as a result of the harmonising effect which they have on the cosmos as a whole.

In *Oration* 9, Maximus goes on to argue that the existence of *daimones* is necessary in providing a link between the Demiurge and man, due to the dependence of continuity upon shared terms, a concept owing its origin to Arist., *Met.* 10.1069a5*ff.*, but first applied to the intermediate status of *daimones* by Xenocrates.

Interestingly, unlike Plutarch, Maximus never uses his daimonology as a mechanism for resolving the problem of evil. For him, the *daimones* are the assistants of the Demiurge in the act of world-generation and in the administration of the cosmos. Even in their terrifying aspect (8.8.207), they are beneficial, since they punish the wicked, although Maximus merely says ὁ μὲν φοβερός and does not elaborate on this point. However, Maximus probably avoids making *daimones* responsible for the existence of evil, not just because such a notion was unpalatable to him, but because he had no need for such an explanation, as he attempts to regulate the problem by means of the Stoic formulation that evils only appear to be such, but in fact occur for the good of the whole.

Conclusion

Maximus never really elaborates on the causality of the Demiurge – for him the world is created merely by the νεῦμα of Zeus. Yet in spite of this, his orations are rich in imagery and insights on this topic, which due to his lack of originality reveal the preoccupations of Middle Platonist speculations concerning world-generation. Maximus himself tends to steer clear of attempts to resolve any of these, although at points he can avoid difficulties experienced by other Platonists, because of his acceptance of Stoic formulations; which in itself indicates that these concepts had by the second century become common philosophical property.

Maximus fails to perceive that there is a major metaphysical difficulty in explaining how a transcendent First Principle is able to act upon matter. Indeed, he frequently uses two contrasting images of the Demiurge: the transcendence of Zeus' νεῦμα and the more active artisan or blacksmith who has to physically toil to produce the world. He has no concept of a division between a first principle and a secondary, mediating divinity. There is no suggestion of an entity above the Demiurge, corresponding to the One or Good. Furthermore, he does not investigate how the Demiurge actually operates on matter or his relationship with Necessity and the other causal factors. This is possibly because such intricacies, which would naturally have a sectarian nature, hold no interest for him. All that is important for him is that the world was ordered by a benevolent Demiurge, who continues to care for it and who is only responsible for good, not evil. What is important is that God generated the world; how is irrelevant. This point is expressed forcefully at *Oration* 2.10: 'What point is there in inquiring further . . . I do not not oppose such inconsistency. They must only know God, love him and be mindful of him.'

CHAPTER 6

Numenius and his doctrine of three gods

Introduction

Surveying Numenius of Apamea's views concerning demiurgy is a task fraught with difficulty, given the fragmentary remains of his work. Numenius forms a bridge between Philo and the Gnostic and Hermetic traditions, as well as ranking as an important predecessor of Plotinus, to such an extent that the latter philosopher was actually accused of plagiarising him. Numenius composed a treatise *On the Unfaithfulness of the Academy to Plato* and one *On The Good* in (at least) six books. Many of the fragments have been gleaned from Eusebius' *Praeparatio Evangelica*, with some supplementary material from Calcidius' *Commentary on the Timaeus*, Origen and certain Neoplatonic sources. There is a great difference in the quality of the fragments which we possess from Eusebius (actual quotations) and those obtained from other sources (Numenian texts altered by the writer) and one of the drawbacks of Des Places' 1973 edition is that it tends to treat both sets of fragments with an unjustified level of equality.[1] My practice here has been to use the actual fragments, taken from Eusebius, to build up my case for each sub-topic and then to turn to the *testimonia*, using them for evidence that might help to confirm or deny my theses, but not giving them excessive weight and also noting very clearly the original source-text.

This discrepancy in the quality of fragments is not the only reason why the study of Numenius is problematic. Another is the unjustified prejudice with which he has been viewed on account of his syncretistic tendencies. This is exemplified by Dodds: 'The main fabric of Numenius' thought is no doubt derived from Neopythagorean tradition... But because he was, as Macrobius says, *occultiorum curiosior* (F39), he welcomed the superstitions of his time, whatever their origin and thereby contributed to the eventual

---

[1] Despite this criticism, I am indebted to him for his edition and have found his French translation invaluable in preparing my own English version.

degradation of Greek philosophical thought.'² A more accurate observation (on account of its greater balance) is that of Dillon, which illustrates
an alternative approach to the fragments: 'In Numenius, we have a fascinating figure about whom we know all too little but who plainly combines
in his doctrine various strands; Platonic and Neopythagorean, Hermetic
and Gnostic, Zoroastrian and Jewish. In his person, the "underworld" of
Platonic-influenced theorizing... attains some modicum of philosophical
respectability.'³

In the ancient philosophical tradition, there was tension between the
Platonic–Pythagorean perception of the First Principle as Unity (the
One/Monad) and the Anaxagorean/Aristotelian view of it as an intellect
which thought itself. While both perceptions are not actually mutually
incompatible, a tension between these opposing views can be observed in
Middle Platonism,⁴ exemplified by the views of Numenius (and indeed
in his subsequent influence upon Plotinus). While the Platonic supreme
principle is the Good of *Republic* VI–VII, it is less clear how this principle is
actually responsible for demiurgic causality. While some Platonic philosophers stripped away the mythology of the Timaean Demiurge, equating
him to the Stoic *Logos*, Numenius adopted the alternative approach of
positing the Demiurge as a second intermediate god between the Supreme
Principle and the World-Soul, who creates the sublunar world from pre-
existent Matter.⁵

Numenius, in many ways, appears as an important precursor of Gnosticism (although it is difficult to prove conclusively in which direction the
influence was travelling), with his sharp distinction between three divine
entities, and explicitly according the Demiurge only second rank. To this
extent, he can be regarded as intermediate between the *Timaeus* and Gnosticism: for him, the Demiurge is clearly less than entirely good. The First
God remains relatively inert and transcendent. The continuity of the ontological descent posited by Numenius is stressed through the familial lineage
of Grandfather, Father and Grandson, as well as the assertion of the sameness of the Second and Third Gods. Numenius prefigures the ignorant
Demiurge of Gnosticism by stressing his divisibility and negligence of the
upper-tending part of his own nature. In this sense too, he is part of the
intellectual current which led to the supposition of decreased unity (and
therefore less perfect entities) as one descends the ontological scale.

A further point of interest is the role of the Third God, who takes on
the functions of the World-Soul, an entity without a very great level of

---

² Dodds: 1960, 11   ³ Dillon: 1977, 379   ⁴ Dillon: 1992b, 192   ⁵ Dillon: 1992b, 195

activity in the Numenian system. Numenius also details very clearly the mechanics of the interaction between the First Principle and the Demiurge. As a result of the cooperation he posits between both entities, he is, in this regard, more reminiscent of Judaeo–Christian thinkers, such as Philo and Origen. However, while they both regard God as a Demiurge by extension, Numenius stresses that the First God should not be regarded as a Demiurge, though he does appear to be a conduit, ensuring that the Forms are communicated to the Demiurge. As a result of the cooperation between both entities he is an interesting pagan comparison to the model of world-generation assumed in the Judaeo–Christian tradition.

Numenius also represents an important attempt to reconcile two aspects of the divine: the immanent and the transcendent. While the First God contemplates the Intelligibles, there is no suggestion (in the extant fragments) that they are actually his thoughts. The Second God is not to be completely identified with demiurgic activity, as he also has a separate 'inner life' comprising contemplation of the Forms; in this sense he could be said to 'retire', like his counterpart in the *Timaeus*. While Numenius follows the *Timaeus* quite closely in certain respects, explaining demiurgy in terms of Intellect's attempt to smooth out the recalcitrance of matter, he extends the concept, examining the origin of the Demiurge himself. All this renders all the more regrettable the fragmentary remains of his work, as he played a central role in the demiurgic debate.

The First Principle

Being (τὸ ὄν) resembles Plato's realm of the same name. It is perfectly stable.[6] It never existed (οὔτε ποτὲ ἦν), it never has the chance to be (οὔτε ποτὲ μὴ γένηται), but it is constantly in a fixed time (in) the present only (ἀλλ᾽ ἔστιν ἀεὶ ἐν χρόνῳ ὁρισμένῳ τῷ ἐνεστῶτι μόνῳ). It is eternal (ἀΐδιον), constantly stable (βέβαιόν), immutable and identical (τέ ἐστιν ἀεὶ κατὰ ταὐτὸν καὶ ταὐτόν). It does not increase or decrease and it does not move (οὐδὲ γὰρ θέμις αὐτῷ κινηθῆναι).

This is a fairly standard Platonic division between the realms of Being and Becoming. The lack of motion of Being evokes Plato's description of the motion of the cosmos in the *Timaeus*. Numenius even goes one step further. He not only denies Being all irrational movement, but also the only rational movement: rotation around a fixed point. It seems evident here that Being is not actually described in terms appropriate to a realm;

---

[6] Fr. 5 (14L.) = Eus., *Praep. Ev.* XI.9.8–10, 5

it seems more akin to an entity. I would contend that Being is, in fact, equivalent to the Numenian First God, as is indicated at Fr. 17.[7] This is not indisputable, however, as Numenius struggles with the idea that his First God is beyond Being: 'it rides upon Being' (Fr. 2) and Numenius is almost forced into this position because of his Second God being equated with true Being and Intellect.[8] However, he never breaks with the traditional Greek philosophical identification of God with Being and Intellect.[9] This is in spite of the postulation of his Pythagorean predecessor, Moderatus of Gades, of a 'One above Being and all essence'.[10]

In Fragment 11 (20 L. = Eus., *Praep. Ev.* XI.17, 11–18, 5), the investigation of divinity is formally introduced. Numenius opens his account of divinity with a prayer to the God, just like Timaeus, before investigating the nature of the relationship between the First and Second Gods. From this fragment, it would seem that he was rather more interested in demiurgic causality than in the nature of his First Principle, which he glosses over very rapidly. The First God here seems rather inert; since he is alive he must have motion of some sort, but Numenius seems to be caught in a bind, since to attribute motion to him would be to deny his stability.

Fr. 8 (17L. = Eus., *Praep. Ev.* XI.10, 12–14) elaborates further:

εἰ μὲν δὴ τὸ ὂν πάντως πάντῃ ἀΐδιόν τέ ἐστι καὶ ἄτρεπτον καὶ οὐδαμῶς οὐδαμῇ ἐξιστάμενον ἐξ ἑαυτοῦ, μένει δὲ κατὰ τὰ αὐτὰ καὶ ὡσαύτως ἔστηκε, τοῦτο δήπου ἂν εἴη τὸ τῇ 'νοήσει μετὰ λόγου περιληπτόν'. Εἰ δὲ τὸ σῶμα ῥεῖ καὶ φέρεται ὑπὸ τῆς εὐθὺ μεταβολῆς, ἀποδιδράσκει καὶ οὐκ ἔστιν. Ὅθεν οὐ πολλὴ μανία μὴ οὐ τοῦτο εἶναι ἀόριστον, δόξῃ δὲ μόνῃ δοξαστὸν καί, ὥς φησι Πλάτων, 'γιγνόμενον καὶ ἀπολλύμενον, ὄντως δὲ οὐδέποτε ὄν';

If then Being is absolutely and everywhere eternal, immutable, if in no manner and in no place it does not issue forth from itself, but stays within the same parameters and maintains itself completely stable, then it is without doubt what is graspable by intellection with the help of reason. And if body is fluid, if it is removed by an immediate change, it runs away and has no stable existence. In consequence, is it not great folly not to call it indeterminate, the object of opinion only, and which, as Plato says, 'comes to be and perishes, but never really exists'?

Again, Numenius stresses the stability of Being. It cannot issue forth from itself, which underlines the (limited) role which it is capable of playing in

---

[7] ... πρῶτον νοῦν, ὅστις καλεῖται αὐτοόν..., 'the First Intellect which bears the name of Being in itself', see discussion below.

[8] For a detailed treatment of these matters, see Dillon: 2007, 397*ff.*

[9] Dillon: 2007, 398, cites several examples where he comes close to doing this.

[10] Dillon: 2007, 398

world-generation; it requires another conduit by which it can inform the sensible world, since it is confined to certain defined parameters. Being is characterised by eternal identity in essence (ἀεὶ κατὰ ταὐτὸν).[11] Numenius' First God resembles the Pythagorean Monad, which in multiplication cannot bring about self-change or alter another number. This situation creates a need for the Second God who can actually engage in the motion involved in world-generation.

This Second God is not in any way evil, but as he does not possess the unity of the First (since he is divisible, though this is a once-off occurence) it is true to say that he is less good. As Plotinus points out, the ontologically prior entity must be superior: 'For being perfect it was necessary for it to generate, and not be without a product since it was such a great power. But what it produced could not be better than it (this is not the case here either), but it was necessary for it to be a lesser image, and in a like manner, indefinite, but defined by what generated it and provided with a form, as it were.'[12]

Admittedly, this text comes from Plotinus, but since it outlines his response to a problem similar to that which confronted Numenius, it is valid to cite it here. However, Plotinus' One is not Intellect and does not intentionally generate anything: the question here is whether this is true of Numenius' First God. I think not. Since Numenius' First Principle has a kind of demiurgic role, in terms of the production of soul, it is not equivalent to Plotinus' One. Since it continually contemplates the Intelligibles, then it can also be regarded as Intellect. Though Plotinus' One engages in this activity, it can best be regarded as a sort of super-Intellect or beyond Intellect, while for Numenius it is not actually clear whether it can be considered in the same way. However, since the Numenian Demiurge can be regarded also as an Intellect, to which the First God transmits aspects of the Forms which it contemplates, it must contain an intellective element.

It is clear that as a dualist, Numenius did not regard the First God as responsible for the production of matter. It must always have been there as part of a duality of causes. One can compare the explanation of Proclus regarding the relationship between Monad and Dyad: 'for the One precedes all opposition, as the Pythagoreans say. But when the second cause appears (ἡ δυὰς τῶν ἀρχῶν ἀνεφάνη), after the first cause, among these too the Monad is superior to the Dyad.'[13] Numenius attributes the same doctrine

---

[11] O'Meara: 1976, 120–9

[12] Plotinus, *Enn.* v i [10] 7.37–42. Plotins is referring here to Intellect's generation of soul.

[13] Proclus, *Commentary on the Timaeus*, 1.176.9 Diehl

to various Neopythagoreans, as does Calcidius.[14] He was certainly opposed to Pythagorean claims that the One retired from its own nature and put on the guise of duality.[15] It is important to note this, as Numenius is often classed as a Neopythagorean, but his dualistic views mean that his version of demiurgic causality owes more to Plato.

The Demiurge and his relationship with the First God

The Numenian First God is not involved in the business of world-generation; his main purpose is to produce the Demiurge (Fr.11):

ὁ θεὸς ὁ μὲν πρῶτος ἐν ἑαυτοῦ ὤν ἐστιν ἁπλοῦς, διὰ τὸ ἑαυτῷ συγγιγνό-
μενος διόλου μή ποτε εἶναι διαιρετός· ὁ θεὸς μέντοι ὁ δεύτερος καὶ τρίτος
ἐστὶν εἷς· συμφερόμενος δὲ τῇ ὕλῃ δυάδι οὔσῃ ἑνοῖ μὲν αὐτήν, σχίζεται
δὲ ὑπ᾽ αὐτῆς, ἐπιθυμητικὸν ἦθος ἐχούσης καὶ ῥεούσης. Τῷ οὖν μὴ εἶναι
πρὸς τῷ νοητῷ (ἦν γὰρ ἂν πρὸς ἑαυτῷ) διὰ τὸ τὴν ὕλην βλέπειν, ταύτης
ἐπιμελούμενος ἀπερίοπτος ἑαυτοῦ γίγνεται. Καὶ ἅπτεται τοῦ αἰσθητοῦ
καὶ περιέπει ἀνάγει τε ἔτι εἰς τὸ ἴδιον ἦθος ἐπορεξάμενος τῆς ὕλης.

The First God, who remains inside himself, is unified, due to the fact that, entirely concentrated within himself, he is in no way divisible. However, the Second and Third Gods are in fact one, but coming into contact with matter, which is the Dyad, even though he unifies it, he is divided by it, having a character that is without concupiscence and that is fluid. Not being attached to the intelligible (for in this case he would be concentrated upon himself), because he is looking at matter he is preoccupied with it and he is forgetful of himself; he enters into contact with the sensible and raises it up to his own proper character, because he has directed his desire towards matter.

Here it seems that the Demiurge is turned in two directions during the act of world-generation, contemplating the Forms, while he transmits the Intelligibles to the sensible realm. Part of the problem is why exactly the Demiurge should be split in two by the Dyad. I do not think it is the case that the upper-tending part of the divinity returns to contemplate the Forms, while the lower part engages in the production and continual generation of the sensible world. It is possible that the Third God is merely

---

[14] 'Sed non nullos Pythagoreos vim sententiae non recte adsecutos putasse dici etiam indeterminatum et immensam divinitatem ad unica singularitate institutam, recedente a natura sua singularitate et in divinitatis habitum migrante', 'But some Pythagoreans, who have not correctly understood this theory, thought that this indeterminate and unlimited Dyad was also produced by this single Monad, when this Monad withdraws from its nature and adopts the aspect of a Dyad.' Calcidius, *In Timaeum*, 295 Waszink.

[15] Rist: 1965, 337

a lower aspect of the Second. Clearly the Demiurge creates as the result of an act of lust or *orexis*, which is not particularly praiseworthy, since it prevents him from contemplating the Intelligibles and even leads him to become forgetful of his own nature. This guilty element could be regarded as being expelled from the Second God, in the same manner that a lower Sophia is expelled from the Pleroma in the Gnostic systems.

However, I do not feel that it is necessary to posit a lower aspect of the Second God. The *orexis* of the Demiurge can be viewed in a more favourable light, as part of a natural desire to produce, observable also in Plotinus' One, and which is presumably the reason why the First God produced the Second God (if that is in fact what he did). It is quite possible that the First God merely split a pre-existent entity into the Second and Third Gods, who then share the functions of the Demiurge. However, this would make it difficult to explain the terminology of Grandfather, Son and Grandson, relayed by Proclus, and would also deny the evidence of Fr. 12 (which is reliable, since it comes from Eusebius). The Second God can only produce something less perfect than himself (since to replicate himself would be to accomplish nothing), and so he produces the World-Soul which is less perfect, since it is further removed from the First God, although the World-Soul is an entity downplayed by Numenius. In the act of world-generation, the Demiurge is forced to give something of himself to matter in order to regulate it and to produce the sensible world.

This giving of himself to produce the World-Soul is the Demiurge's mechanism for generating the phenomenal realm. I think that this is the meaning of the expression that the Demiurge raises matter to his own character, but because he has to provide his substance to generate, he becomes divided by matter. It would also neatly explain why the Second and Third Gods are in fact one, since they share the same substance. The Third God, as World-Soul, has actually become enmattered, and is in a sense, dragged down by matter, which prevents him from fully contemplating the Intelligibles, while after the process of world-generation, presumably the Demiurge is capable of doing this.

The Second and Third Gods must then be substantially the same, while the First God is of a different substance (because he does not know how to be divisible, for if he was, it would compromise his unity, a necessary trait in the Numenian First Principle). This elucidates why Numenius posited a god whose sole *raison d'être* is to produce another Demiurge. In fact, the Second and Third Gods appear to differ principally in their interaction to the Intelligibles and matter.

This relationship between the First and Second Gods is clarified at Fr. 12 (21L. = Eus., *Praep. Ev.* XI.18.6–10), but not greatly: 'In fact, it is necessary that the First does not generate, but it is necessary to regard the First God as the father of the demiurgic god'. Some additional details are provided:

> ... τὸν μὲν πρῶτον θεὸν ἀργὸν εἶναι ἔργων συμπάντων καὶ βασιλέα, τὸν δημιουργικὸν δὲ θεὸν ἡγεμονεῖν δι' οὐρανοῦ ἰόντα. Διὰ δὲ τούτου καὶ ὁ στόλος ἡμῖν ἐστι, κάτω τοῦ νοῦ πεμπομένου ἐν διεξόδῳ πᾶσι τοῖς κοινωνῆσαι συντεταγμένοις. Βλέποντος μὲν οὖν καὶ ἐπεστραμμένου πρὸς ἡμῶν ἕκαστον τοῦ θεοῦ συμβαίνει ζῆν τε καὶ βιώσκεσθαι τότε τὰ σώματα κηδεύοντα τοῦ θεοῦ τοῖς ἀκροβολισμοῖς· μεταστρέφοντος δὲ εἰς τὴν ἑαυτοῦ περιωπὴν τοῦ θεοῦ ταῦτα μὲν ἀποσβέννυσθαι, τὸν δὲ νοῦν ζῆν βίου ἐπαυρόμενον εὐδαίμονος.

> ... the First God remains inactive during the whole process of generation, he is the King, while the Demiurge-god is the overseer, who circulates in the heavens. It is the Demiurge who sends us on our voyage, when Mind is sent below, crossing the sphere, to those who are destined to participate in it. And so while the God watches and is oriented towards each of us, the bodies participate in life and are animated by the radiations of the God to which they unite, but if the God returns to his own contemplation, these are extinguished, while Mind partakes of a happy existence.

I think that these radiations by which the Second God animates are comparable to the manner in which he is said to be split by matter.

Fr. 13 (22L. = Eus., *Praep. Ev.* XI.18.13–14), though short, outlines a view of demiurgic causality which has been the source of much difficulty:

> Ὥσπερ δὲ πάλιν λόγος ἐστὶ γεωργῷ πρὸς τὸν φυτεύοντα, ἀνὰ τὸν αὐτὸν λόγον μάλιστά ἐστιν ὁ πρῶτος θεὸς πρὸς τὸν δημιουργόν. Ὁ μέν γε ὢν σπέρμα πάσης ψυχῆς σπείρει εἰς τὰ μεταλαγχάνοντα αὐτοῦ χρήματα σύμπαντα· ὁ νομοθέτης δὲ φυτεύει καὶ διανέμει καὶ μεταφυτεύει εἰς ἡμᾶς ἑκάστους τὰ ἐκεῖθεν προκαταβεβλημένα.

> And even as is the relation between the farmer and the planter; such is that which relates the First God to the Demiurge. *The one who is sows the seeds of every soul* into the things which partake of it, while the Lawgiver plants and distributes and transplants what has been sown from that source into each one of us.[16]

This notion of sowing again evokes the *Timaeus*. Much speculation has been expended on the precise use of the word γεωργός, who is generally felt to be the proprietor of a garden or or a farmer who directs operations from a distance, while the φυτεύων is regarded as a labourer who works under

---

[16] trans. Dillon: 1977, 368 with modifications by Andron.

his direction.[17] The head-gardener sows a single seed of each type of plant, while the gardener distributes the seeds and cultivates them individually. All souls come from the First God, who produces one mass of soul-stuff, while the Second God, the Demiurge, distributes the seeds, implants them in individual human bodies and transfers impure souls into a new human body for reincarnation.[18]

Part of the reason behind this speculation is the supposed textual corruption of the fragment. The phrase Ὁ μέν γε ὤν is interpreted variously as a biblism or Hebraism, which is felt to be out of place in Numenius. Scott reads Ὁ μέν [γὰρ ἕν] σπέρμα πάσης ψυχῆς σπείρει εἰς τὰ μεταλαγχάνοντα [αὐτῆς] χρήματα σύμπαντα. ['The First God sows one seed (or one sowing) of all soul (or life) to serve for all things that together partake of soul.'] This avoids the problem of ὁ ὤν, but is not convincing palaeographically and, as Andron points out, posits a change for two passages instead of just one, as in other approaches.[19] Dillon's response is 'I read with hesitation, *georgon*, for the *ge on* of the MSS. . . . I agree that Numenius is probably not using *ho on* here in the Philonic sense of He Who Is'.[20]

Andron favours this reading over all other proposals for changing the text, but prefers that the text should remain in its original state. He contends that to read ὁ γεωργῶν damages the balance, since there does not appear to be any obvious relationship between a lawgiver and a farmer.[21] He interprets this fragment to refer to two different kinds of occupation, and the rapport or *logos* between them. For him there is no problem with the phrase ὁ ὤν to refer to ὁ πρῶτος θεός, and ὁ νομοθέτης to refer to the Second, since he views the first as pure existent and the second as the Demiurge is obviously an ordering force. Andron further states that The One Who Is, given the Jewish influence on Apamea, is not a particularly problematic phrase, citing two passages of Philo which help to elucidate our fragment:

ὁ μὲν τοίνυν τῶν φυτουργῶν μέγιστος καὶ τὴν τέχνην τελειότατος ὁ τῶν ὅλων ἡγεμών ἐστι, φυτὸν δὲ αὖ περιέχον ἐν ἑαυτῷ τὰ ἐν μέρει φυτὰ ἅμα παμμυρία καθάπερ κληματίδας ἐκ μιᾶς ἀναβλαστάνοντα ῥίζης ὅδε ὁ κόσμος. ἐπειδὴ γὰρ τὴν οὐσίαν ἄτακτον καὶ συγκεχυμένην οὖσαν ἐξ αὐτῆς εἰς τάξιν ἐξ ἀταξίας καὶ ἐκ συγχύσεως εἰς διάκρισιν ἄγων ὁ κοσμοπλάστης μορφοῦν ἤρξατο, γῆν μὲν καὶ ὕδωρ ἐπὶ τὸ μέσον ἐρρίζου, τὰ δὲ ἀέρος καὶ πυρὸς δένδρα πρὸς τὴν μετάρσιον ἀνεῖλκεν ἀπὸ τοῦ μέσου χώραν, τὸν δὲ

---

[17] *Cf.* e.g. Scott: 1968, vol. III, 79 n.5 or Festugière: 1972.   [18] Des Places: 1973, 109
[19] Andron: 2001, 6*ff.*   [20] Dillon: 1977, 368   [21] Andron: 2001, 7

αἰθέριον ἐν κύκλῳ τόπον ὠχυροῦτο τῶν ἐντὸς ὅρον τε καὶ φυλακτήριον
αὐτὸν τιθείς...

The guide of all things is the greatest planter and the most perfect in his craft. And this cosmos is the plant which contains in itself the particular plants in their myriads, just like vine-branches shooting forth from a single root. For when the world-maker, finding a disorderly substance which of itself was in a state of confusion, began to give it shape, he brought it to order out of disorder and out of its state of confusion into resolved form and he caused earth and water to be roots at the centre and he dragged air and fire as the trees from the midmost space to upon high and he established the aetherial space in a circle, placing it as the boundary and guardpost of what is within... (*De Plantatione* 2–3)

Here the First Principle is explicitly defined as a φυτουργός. The same is true of the following fragment from *De Agricultura* 1–4:

οἱ μὲν πολλοὶ τῶν ἀνθρώπων τὰς φύσεις τῶν πραγμάτων οὐκ εἰδότες
καὶ περὶ τὴν τῶν ὀνομάτων θέσιν ἐξ ἀνάγκης ἁμαρτάνουσι... τίνι γὰρ
τῶν προχειροτέρων οὐκ ἂν δόξειε τὰ αὐτὰ εἶναι γεωργία τε καὶ γῆς
ἐργασία, καίτοι πρὸς ἀλήθειαν οὐ μόνον οὐκ ὄντα τὰ αὐτά, ἀλλὰ καὶ
λίαν ἀπηρτημένα, ὡς ἀντιστατεῖν καὶ διαμάχεσθαι; δύναται μὲν γάρ τις
καὶ ἄνευ ἐπιστήμης περὶ τὴν γῆς ἐπιμέλειαν πονεῖσθαι, γεωργὸς δὲ τὸ
μὴ ἰδιώτης ἀλλ᾿ ἔμπειρος εἶναι καὶ τῷ ὀνόματι πεπίστωται, ὅπερ ἐκ τῆς
γεωργικῆς τέχνης, ἧς φερώνυμός ἐστιν, εὕρηται.

Many men, not knowing the nature of things, of necessity make mistakes in naming them ... for would not anyone suppose off-hand that husbandry (γεωργία) and toiling on the land (γῆς ἐργασία) were the same, although in truth they not only are not the same things but are also extremely disharmonious, so that they are in opposition and in contention? For someone even without experience might care for the land, but the farmer is not a lay person but one with experience and he is trusted on account of his name, which is derived from the craft of farming, which he is named after.

This term γεωργός is not to be found in the *Timaeus* (although the image of cultivation as part of the process of world-generation already exists there), but it was used to refer to divinities during the imperial age.[22] Philo draws a distinction between the farmer and the labourer, which results from

[22] In this context, one might cite the cult of Ζεὺς γεωργός. This element can further be traced in popular Stoicism: 'Deus ad homines venit immo quod est proprius in homines venit; nulla sine deo mens bona est. semina in corporibus humanis divina dispersa sunt, quae si bonus cultor excipit similia origini prodeant et paria iis, ex quibus orta sunt, surgunt.' etc. 'God comes to men, in fact he comes more closely, he comes into men. No mind without God is good. Divine seeds are distributed in human bodies, which if they are received by a good cultivator, they come forth similar to their origin and arise equal to that from which they arose'. Seneca *Ep.* 73.16. Andron: 2001 13 n. 31.

his attempt to combine the Book of *Genesis* with the *Timaeus*. Numenius observes this same distinction, but brings it into sharper focus by positing two separate Gods. It is probable that Numenius had read Philo, but difficult to prove. For Andron, ὁ ὤν or Being is the name of the First God, taken from *Exodus* 3:14, just as the Second God is called the Demiurge.[23]

The supposed Hebraism is not the only difficulty:[24] the fragment can be taken to mean that the First God is the seed of all souls, a position resisted by the majority of interpreters, since the First God is also the one doing the sowing and 'a sower does not sow himself'.[25] Edwards prefers to read 'the one who is the seed of all souls sows into those who partake of it all things together'. There is the question of what 'all things together' means. Edwards explains this by citing Fr. 41 (Des Places, preserved in Iamblichus' *De Anima*) where Iamblichus claims that Numenius located the entire intelligible universe (gods, *daimones* and the Good) in the soul.[26] However, this interpretation is problematic since it leads Edwards to identify Numenius' First God with the Demiurge and the Second God with the Younger Gods. (From a careful reading of Numenius' fragments, however, it is clear that the Demiurge can rank no higher than the Second God.)[27] Furthermore, it seems that Iamblichus' comment here is really a reference to *monopsychism* (individual souls, when removed from the sensible world, share an identity with the World-Soul) rather than a description of how souls are composed.[28]

The Platonist Alcinous outlined a method of soul construction from indivisible and divisible substance, allowing the soul to perceive both of these substances; either on the principle that like is known by like (the Pythagorean position) or that unlike is known by unlike (Heraclitus' position). He cites an alternative means of constructing soul.[29] As a Pythagorean, one would expect Numenius to subscribe to the doctrine that like is known by like. This would suggest that the soul and the First God share some properties. This is suggested by the text following Fr. 42 (Iamblichus, Περὶ Ψυχῆς ap. Stob., *Anth.* 1.49.67), where there is some support for the opinion that the soul is an emanation from the First God:

ἕνωσιν μὲν οὖν καὶ ταὐτότητα ἀδιάκριτον τῆς ψυχῆς πρὸς τὰς ἑαυτῆς ἀρχὰς πρεσβεύειν φαίνεται Νουμήνιος, σύμφυσιν δὲ καθ' ἑτέραν οὐσίαν οἱ πρεσβύτεροι διασῴζουσι. καὶ ἀναλύσει μὲν ἐκεῖνοι, συντάξει δὲ οὗτοι προσεικάζουσι· καὶ οἳ μὲν ἀδιορίστῳ συναφῇ, οἳ δὲ διωρισμένῃ χρῶνται.

[23] Andron: 2001, 20
[24] In actual fact, this need only imply familiarity with the Septuagint: Edwards: 1989b, 479
[25] Scott: 1925, vol. II, 79, n.3   [26] Edwards: 1989b, 481   [27] Edwards: 1989b, 481
[28] Andron: 2001, 34   [29] *Didaskalikos* XIV

Οἱ μέντοι κρατεῖται ὁ διορισμὸς αὐτῶν ὑπὸ τοῦ κόσμου ἢ κατέχετα ὑπὸ
τῆς φύσεως, ὥσπερ τινὲς τῶν Πλατωνικῶν ὑπειλήφασιν· ἀνεῖται δὲ πάντη
ἀφ' ὅλων, ὥσπερ ἐπὶ τῶν χωριστῶν οὐσιῶν τουτὶ νοοῦμεν.

Numenius appears to prefer a unity and undiffentiated sameness of the soul
with its principles, whereas the ancients maintain a natural junction with a
different substance. Numenius compares it to a dissolution, but the ancients
to an ordering, and Numenius treats it as a union without individuation,
the ancients as one with individuation. However, their individuation is not
governed by the cosmos or controlled by nature, as has been supposed by
some of the Platonists, but has been completely released from the universe,
just as we conceive to be the case with separated substances. (trans. after
Finamore-Dillon ed. §50, p. 72–3)

Part of the problem with using this fragment is that it may not refer to
the generation of soul, but rather to the rewards given to good souls after
their death, since this is the subject-matter of the text preceding, Fr. 42.[30]
Furthermore, Fr. 42 comes from Iamblichus and, as such, it provides us
only with very weak evidence for Numenius' thought.[31]

Here the Demiurge is regarded as responsible for the construction of soul,
which is not necessarily a contradiction of Fr.13; there too the Demiurge
distributes soul, even though he does not actually produce it. Here also, the
Demiurge is not said to produce either essence, he merely mixes them like a
bartender making a cocktail. Numenius then goes on to expound the view
that even if the Demiurge has to provide some of his own substance to initiate world-generation and even if he is split by matter, he is not weakened
by this process. The divine gift of knowledge differs from material gifts:
just like a lamp which lights up a second one without being extinguished,
God is not impoverished as a result of this divine benefaction.

This image of a lamp transmitting its flame without being diminished
probably goes back to Posidonius.[32] The idea that the Demiurge illumi-
nates us by the transmission of knowledge is noteworthy. I think that for
Numenius it emphasises the notion that the basic principle of cosmic order
is number, which is transmitted by the self-contemplating intellect to the
Demiurge. It is possible for humanity to possess the number-principle
(possibly soul) in a manner that is identical with the God who supplied
it, because the Numenian Demiurge is only the producer of Becoming,
not the producer of true Being. In this way, the difference between the
Demiurge and the First God is more than just one of an intellect at rest
and one in motion. They must be substantially different, since it is not

[30] Finamore and Dillon: 2002, §50 72–3   [31] Finamore and Dillon: 2002, §50 72–3
[32] Witt: 1931, 200 n. 8

possible that the generator of Being can exist in the same sense as generated Being. Clearly the Second and Third Gods are in fact one, but soul must be of a different order, since it is supposed to come from the First God. In this case, the Numenian Demiurge also takes over the role of the Young Gods of the *Timaeus*. This is hardly surprising and is part of the tendency to assign less important activities to the Demiurge, accompanying his declining ontological rank.

At Fr. 15 (24L. = Eus., *Praep. Ev.* XI.18.20–1) Numenius reiterates the position of the Second God as the generator of the world of Becoming:

> εἰσὶ δ' οὗτοι βίοι ὁ μὲν πρώτου, ὁ δὲ δευτέρου θεοῦ. Δηλονότι ὁ μὲν πρῶτος θεὸς ἔσται ἑστώς, ὁ δὲ δεύτερος ἔμπαλίν ἐστι κινούμενος· ὁ μὲν οὖν πρῶτος περὶ τὰ νοητά, ὁ δὲ δεύτερος περὶ τὰ νοητὰ καὶ αἰσθητά. Μὴ θαυμάσῃς δ' εἰ τοῦτ' ἔφην· πολὺ γὰρ ἔτι θαυμαστότερον ἀκούσῃ. Ἀντὶ γὰρ τῆς προσούσης τῷ δευτέρῳ κινήσεως τὴν προσοῦσαν τῷ πρώτῳ στάσιν φημὶ εἶναι κίνησιν σύμφυτον, ἀφ' ἧς ἥ τε τάξις τοῦ κόσμου καὶ ἡ μονὴ ἡ ἀΐδιος καὶ ἡ σωτηρία ἀναχεῖται εἰς τὰ ὅλα.

> Such are the lives of the First and Second Gods. The First God remains stable, the second remains in motion, while the First God occupies himself with intelligibles, the Second occupies himself with intelligibles and sensibles. And do not be surprised if I have spoken in this manner; because you will hear something that is even more surprising. Corresponding to the inherent movement of the Second God, I declare that the inherent stability of the First God is an innate movement from which proceeds the order of the world and its eternal stability, and from which salvation spreads out over all beings.

Here the Second God seems to play a role akin to God's *Logos* in the Philonic and Christian traditions, going into those parts of the cosmos where it would be beneath God's dignity to go.

It is worth considering this inherent motion at rest of the First God. Since he is a living being, he needs to have a motion of some sort. This is provided by his contemplation of the Intelligibles. At the same time, the First God here appears to play a role in demiurgic causality, beyond merely spawning the Demiurge. He is responsible for world-order and its stability. Des Places interpreted the situation as follows: the First God appears to contemplate the Intelligibles with the assistance of the Second, so that the Second God also corresponds to intellect and states that the Second produces in his turn using the Third God, so that the Third God also corresponds to an intellect which uses discursive intelligence.[33] I think it

---

[33] Des Places: 1973, 109

is justifiable to cast an eye on Plotinus at this point; the Neoplatonist was heavily influenced by Numenius and there are certain issues concerning Numenius that he can help to illuminate. As Dillon points out, the Platonist concept of 'the First God as intellect was under strain when Plotinus came to examine it'.[34]

The First God is required to think himself. As Plotinus remarks during the latter part of *Enn.* v 3 [49] 10–17, self-intellection requires duality; a subjective, thinking element and an objective, thought element, which comprises the unity and simplicity of the Monad. This difficulty is illustrated by Nicomachus' highly-strained definition of the First Principle as νοῦς τε εἴη, εἶτα καὶ ἀρσενόθηλυς καὶ θεὸς καὶ ὕλη δέ πως, 'therefore a Mind and Androgyne and god and somehow matter'.[35] Numenius' First God is clearly an intellect, although one can see here the beginning of a move to regard intellection as the domain of the second principle; the Demiurge is specifically identified by Numenius as an intellect. The influence of this can be seen in Plotinus, as he claims that the One is superior to Intellect.

The nature of the 'inner life' of the First God is of vital importance for understanding demiurgic causality. Since he is the ultimate source of life, he cannot be regarded as inert (a problem faced also by Plotinus) and I think that Numenius is attempting to deal with this by postulating some kind of motion, (here intellectual motion). The exact nature of the First God also has important implications: if his nature transcends that of the Demiurge to such an extent, how exactly does the Second God interact with him?

In Fr. 15, the First God seems akin to the Demiurge of the *Timaeus* in permitting the Young Gods to exist forever; the stability of the Demiurge's production is guaranteed by the First God and not by the Demiurge himself. At this point, another passage of Plotinus might prove enlightening:

> The noetic object (contemplated by Mind) remains by itself and it is not deficient, just like what it sees and thinks – for I say that what thinks is deficient in comparison to the Intelligible – but it is not without sense; but everything belongs to it and is in it and with it. It is able to distinguish itself in every way (πάντη διακριτικὸν ἑαυτοῦ); there is life in it and everything is in it and its observation of itself occurs by means of a kind of conscious awareness (οἱονεὶ συναισθήσει) in an everlasting state of rest and according to a form of noetic activity which differs from the noetic activity of Mind. (*Enn.* v 4 [7] 2.13–19)

---

[34] Dillon: 1992b, 195   [35] ap. Phot., *Bibl.* 187 143 A. discussed by Rist: 1965, 337

Here the One seems like a sort of living 'table of contents' of world-generation, a self-conscious blueprint which the Demiurge can follow. Applying this to our original fragment, it seems that the Numenian First God comprises this all-encompassing element. He might not be involved in the practicalities of demiurgy, but he appears to regulate things in the same manner that the chairman of a board of directors might regulate a multinational. He has some limited role in world-production, since it is from him that σωτηρία spreads to all beings, but I am unclear as to what exactly Numenius means by this (although it is perhaps just a basic presentation in existence). It is difficult to see how exactly the First God can be responsible for universal salvation, even though he seems to generate the soul-principle, although perhaps this is merely an allusion to the fact that he prevents cosmic collapse. If this inherent stability is really an 'innate movement', perhaps it is even possible to postulate that the First God is involved in a sort of continual demiurgy: by constantly remaining stable, he prevents the destruction of the world.

At Fr. 16 (25L. = Eus., *Praep. Ev.* XI.22.3–5), there seems to be something of a demarcation dispute between Numenius' triad of principles:

εἰ δ᾽ ἔστι μὲν νοητὸν ἡ οὐσία καὶ ἡ ἰδέα, ταύτης δ᾽ ὡμολογήθη πρεσβύτερον καὶ αἴτιον εἶναι ὁ νοῦς, αὐτὸς οὗτος μόνος εὕρηται ὢν τὸ ἀγαθόν. Καὶ γὰρ εἰ ὁ μὲν δημιουργὸς θεός ἐστι γενέσεως, ἀρκεῖ τὸ ἀγαθὸν οὐσίας εἶναι ἀρχή. Ἀνάλογον δὲ τούτῳ μὲν ὁ δημιουργὸς θεός, ὢν αὐτοῦ μιμητής, τῇ δὲ οὐσίᾳ ἡ γένεσις, <ἣ> εἰκὼν αὐτῆς ἐστι καὶ μίμημα. Εἴπερ δὲ ὁ δημιουργὸς ὁ τῆς γενέσεώς ἐστιν ἀγαθός, ἦ που ἔσται καὶ ὁ τῆς οὐσίας δημιουργὸς αὐτοάγαθον, σύμφυτον τῇ οὐσίᾳ. Ὁ γὰρ δεύτερος διττὸς ὢν αὐτοποιεῖ τήν τε ἰδέαν ἑαυτοῦ καὶ τὸν κόσμον, δημιουργὸς ὤν, ἔπειτα θεωρητικὸς ὅλως. Συλλελογισμένων δ᾽ ἡμῶν ὀνόματα τεσσάρων πραγμάτων τέσσαρα ἔστω ταῦτα· ὁ μὲν πρῶτος θεὸς αὐτοάγαθον· ὁ δὲ τούτου μιμητὴς δημιουργὸς ἀγαθός· ἡ δ᾽ οὐσία μία μὲν ἡ τοῦ πρώτου, ἑτέρα δ᾽ ἡ τοῦ δευτέρου· ἧς μίμημα ὁ καλὸς κόσμος, κεκαλλωπισμένος μετουσίᾳ τοῦ καλοῦ.

And if essence and the Idea are on the level of the Intelligible and if Intellect has been recognised as prior and superior as their cause, it is only Intellect which is revealed as being the Good. In effect, if the Demiurge is the god of Becoming, it suffices for the Good to be the principle of Being. The demiurgic God bears the same relation to [the First Principle], being his imitator, just as Becoming is the image and imitation of Being. Well, if indeed the Demiurge of Becoming is good, without doubt also the Demiurge of Being will be the Good itself, as connatural to Being; because the Second, who is double, produces from himself his own idea and the universe, as a Demiurge, after which he devotes himself entirely to contemplation. In order to conclude our reasoning, let us posit four names corresponding

to four entities: (a) The First God, the Good itself, (b) his imitator, the
Demiurge, who is good, (c) the essence, one of the First, another of the
Second; (d) the copy of all this, the beautiful universe, embellished by its
participation in the Good.

These four entities are divided up amongst three gods: Good itself, the
Demiurge and the world or World-Soul. The double οὐσία shared by the
First and Second Gods does not seem to add a new reality to either.[36]
These four seem to be composed of two gods and two *ousiai*, but it is an
odd way of calculating. Krämer points out that since the Demiurge can
be confounded with the good World-Soul,[37] the Second and Third Gods
only count as one (Frs. 1, 4, 11), which leaves us with only two divinities:
an ultimate reality and a generative entity. However, I feel that all four
entities can best be understood in terms of demiurgic causality: there are
two causal principles, since, as has been stated before, the First God also
plays a limited role in world-production and the result is the Third God.

It is difficult to explain the third entity – the double οὐσία. I think
that Numenius wishes to point out that the Second God is in some way
consubstantial with the First, just as has previously been illustrated, the
Second and Third are substantially the same. This would be necessary
if the Demiurge also has to deal with the Intelligibles. The Demiurge is
referred to as the imitator of the First God; he imitates him, not only
in his contemplation of the Intelligibles but also in his need to generate.
Numenius tries to assign some kind of demiurgic role to the First God,
referring to him as 'the Demiurge of essence'. Numenius here regards
the Good, not as a Form which contains all the other Forms, but rather
playing a role similar to that played by the Second God in the realm of
Becoming. The First God is the Demiurge of the realm of Being, although
it is unclear here whether he is contemplating the Intelligibles or whether
the Intelligibles only exist because he contemplates them.

Des Places' position was that the First God is all contemplation; and
I think that this contemplation must be equivalent to the 'inner life' of
the First God.[38] Dodds suggests that it is only with the assistance of the
Second God that the first can contemplate (νοεῖν).[39] I also agree with his
contention that the Second only generates as a first step, after which he
returns to contemplation, in which he serves as a model for the philosopher
(*Rep.* vi.496d, 498b–c, 501a–c). Dodds' emendation ἐπεὶ ὁ ἄ (= πρῶτος)

---

[36] Des Places: 1973, 109   [37] Des Places: 1973, 109
[38] Des Places: 1973, 57   [39] Dodds: 1960, 14

θεωρητικὸς ὅλως ('since the [First God] is completely contemplative') needs to be seriously considered.[40] The text otherwise would make some sense, but not much, as there is no other indication of the Second God enjoying periods of total contemplation. ἔπειτα may not necessarily imply temporal succession; Des Places claims that the Demiurge engages in a first generative movement, by which he produces his own idea and the idea of the world, and then undergoes a conversion by which he turns away from matter towards the first νοῦς.[41] I fail to understand how the Demiurge produces his own idea when surely that is generated by the First God, unless this is related to the concept Plotinus picks up on, of the self-generation of lower hypostases through reversion on the higher. Secondly, I am unhappy with the phrasing. The idea that the Second God undergoes a conversion seems to imply that world-generation is the result of some kind of 'moral fall', and that the Numenian Demiurge is similar to his ignorant or fundamentally flawed Gnostic counterpart, which is clearly not the case here.

Numenius boldly attempts to use the *Timaeus* to justify the existence of an intellect superior to the Demiurge.[42] He claims that Plato drafted the *Timaeus* account in the way that he did, because he was aware that only the Demiurge was generally known, although he was aware of the existence of an older and more divine intellect (νοῦς πρεσβύτερος καὶ θειότερος). Numenius is alluding to *Tim.* 28c, which he interprets as referring to two distinct gods, the 'father' and the 'maker' being different. Plutarch draws a similar distinction at *Quaest. Plat.* 11 and it is seen subsequently in Neoplatonism. Plutarch distinguishes between the activity of a builder or weaver, whose product is separated from him and that of a parent, where a principle emanating from the parent inhabits the child (1001a), 'for, Chrysippus says, he who provided seed is not called father of the placenta, though it is a product of the seed' (*Quaest. Plat.* 1000f.). As God sows from himself into matter, he can be regarded as both 'father and maker'. Incidentally, this position is mentioned and rejected by Proclus at *In Tim.* 1 p. 319, 15–20 [Diehl]. Plutarch, however, justifies his position by pointing out that Plato regards the Demiurge as producer of both the body and soul of the universe. The former is composed from matter (1001b), while soul, as a partaker in intelligence, reason and concord, is both a work, but also a part of God, as it is produced not just by him, but from him.

---

[40] Dodds: 1960, 15–16   [41] Des Places: 1973, 109
[42] Fr. 17 (26L = Eus., *Praep. Ev.* XI.18.22–3)

The identification of the First God and Being comes from the Xenocratic tradition. Despite the slightly negative portrayal of the Demiurge here, there is no question that world-generation is evil in any way; it is just that the Demiurge is inferior to the First God. That said, it is possible to observe echoes of the Gnostic current in the reference to a superior god who remains unknown.

Fr.18 (27L. = Eus., *Praep. Ev.* XI.18, 24) provides an interesting description of the manner in which the Demiurge produces:

> κυβερνήτης μέν που ἐν μέσῳ πελάγει φορούμενος ὑπὲρ πηδαλίων ὑψίζυγος
> τοῖς οἴαξι διϊθύνει τὴν ναῦν ἐφεζόμενος, ὄμματα δ' αὐτοῦ καὶ νοῦς εὐθὺ τοῦ
> αἰθέρος συντέταται πρὸς τὰ μετάρσια καὶ ἡ ὁδὸς αὐτῷ ἄνω δι' οὐρανοῦ
> ἄπεισι, πλέοντι κάτω κατὰ τὴν θάλατταν· οὕτω καὶ ὁ δημιουργὸς τὴν ὕλην,
> τοῦ μήτε διακροῦσαι μήτε ἀποπλαγχθῆναι αὐτήν, ἁρμονίᾳ συνδησάμενος
> αὐτὸς μὲν ὑπὲρ ταύτης ἵδρυται, οἷον ὑπὲρ νεὼς ἐπὶ θαλάττης [τῆς ὕλης]·
> τὴν ἁρμονίαν δ' ἰθύνει, ταῖς ἰδέαις οἰακίζων, βλέπει τε ἀντὶ τοῦ οὐρανοῦ εἰς
> τὸν ἄνω θεὸν προσαγόμενον αὐτοῦ τὰ ὄμματα λαμβάνει τε τὸ μὲν κριτικὸν
> ἀπὸ τῆς θεωρίας, τὸ δ' ὁρμητικὸν ἀπὸ τῆς ἐφέσεως.

A helmsman, I suppose, who travels on the open sea, perched above the helm, directs the ship with the tiller, but his eyes, like his spirit, are directed up towards the aether, towards the celestial regions, and his route comes from above, across the sky, while he sails across the sea; in a similar manner, the Demiurge, who knits together links of harmony around matter, for fear lest it break its fastenings, and will be cast adrift, remains himself adjusting it, just as if in a ship upon the sea, he regulates harmony in it by governing it in accordance with the Forms, but looking at the God above in place of the heavens who attracts his gaze, and if he receives his judgement from this contemplation, he retains his impulse to act from desire.

Here the Demiurge generates by harmonising matter in accordance with the Forms, but it appears that he is only aware of what these Forms are as a result of his contemplation of the First God, who transmits this information to him. The First God's role in demiurgic causality seems to be that of generating or transmitting a coherent scheme for organising matter to the Demiurge, who then proceeds to carry out, if not his instructions, then at least his intentions. Clearly, the idea of a subsequent 'conversion' to philosophy on the part of the Demiurge propounded by certain commentators is out of place; he is 'philosophising' even at the moment of world-generation. Also, one cannot speak of a 'conversion' here; unlike the Gnostic Demiurge, the Numenian Second God is not only aware of the existence of a superior entity, but actually collaborates with it.

Numenius speculates on the relationship of the Demiurge to the Forms and positions his scheme within the structure of the *Timaeus*.[43] He reads Plato's qualification of the Demiurge as good in the *Timaeus* to indicate that he should be identified with the Form of the Good (ἀγαθοῦ ἰδέαν) of the *Republic*. Numenius deduces from this that if 'it is reasonable to suppose that if the Demiurge is good by participation in the First Good, then the First Intellect would be the Form of "the Good", being the Good itself'. Numenius introduces an important distinction between the Demiurge as ἀγαθός and the First God as αὐτοαγαθός.

Here the generative role of the Demiurge is once again placed in context. If he is 'good', it is only as a result of his interaction with the First God. Even though the Second God may be actually involved in generation, the productive role of the First God is stressed; the Demiurge is an instantiation of the Form of the First God. Numenius is clearly attempting to resolve the problem bequeathed by Plato of how the Demiurge actually relates to the Forms. His solution differs from the Middle Platonist refinement of representing the Forms as the thoughts of God. In Numenius' version, by representing the First God as the Form of the Second, he highlights the separation between both gods and he lowers the status of the Second God, though he seems to be following Plato's *Timaeus* more closely than the Middle Platonist development which makes the Demiurge the producer of the Forms.

At Fr. 21 (Test. 24 L. fr. 36 = Proclus, *In Timaeum* 1.303.27–304), Numenius is presented by Proclus as outlining the hierarchy of his three gods:

Νουμήνιος μὲν γὰρ τρεῖς ἀνυμνήσας θεοὺς πατέρα μὲν καλεῖ τὸν πρῶτον, ποιητὴν δὲ τὸν δεύτερον, ποίημα δὲ τὸν τρίτον· ὁ γὰρ κόσμος κατ' αὐτὸν ὁ τρίτος ἐστὶ θεός· ὥστε ὁ κατ' αὐτὸν δημιουργὸς διττός, ὅ τε πρῶτος θεὸς καὶ ὁ δεύτερος, τὸ δὲ δημιουργούμενον ὁ τρίτος. Ἄμεινον γὰρ οὕτω λέγειν ἢ ὡς ἐκεῖνος λέγει προστραγῳδῶν, πάππον, ἔγγονον, ἀπόγονον. Ὁ δὴ ταῦτα λέγων πρῶτον μὲν οὐκ ὀρθῶς τἀγαθὸν συναριθμεῖ τοῖσδε τοῖς αἰτίοις· οὐ γὰρ πέφυκεν ἐκεῖνο συζεύγνυσθαί τισιν οὐδὲ δευτέραν ἔχειν ἄλλου τάξιν.

Numenius proclaims that there are three gods and calls the first 'Father', the second 'maker' and the third 'product', because the cosmos for him is the Third God; while the Demiurge is double, the First God and the Second, and that which has been generated is the Third God. It is much

---

[43] Des Places, Fr. 20 (29L. = Eus., *Praep. Ev.* XI.22.9–10).

better, in effect, to express it in this way, rather than to speak like him in a melodramatic style of 'Grandfather', 'Father' and 'Grandson'. But he who says this first of all is not correct in numbering the Good with these causes: for it is not in its nature to be linked to anything nor to hold a rank second to anything else.

The hierarchy here is not that of Fragment 11 (20L), where the First God does not play a role in world-generation, while the Second and Third can be regarded as the same entity. Here the Demiurge is listed as comprising the First and Second Gods, while the Third plays no role in the regulation of matter. Des Places points out that the equivalence God-Father is admitted implicitly by Numenius, in contradiction to *Tim.* 28e3; where ποιητής precedes πατήρ,[44] while Numenius relegates the role of ποιητής to second place. However, this fragment is a paraphrase by Proclus whereas Fragment 11, as a verbatim citation (by Eusebius) has greater value. One must assume that Proclus has here deliberately distorted the *Dreigötterlehre* of Numenius or suffered a lapse of memory, but in a way the First God can be regarded as demiurgic, acting in collaboration with the Second God.

Matter

In considering Numenius' doctrine of demiurgy, it is necessary also to investigate his conception of matter. For Numenius, matter is not created by the divine triad and it is involved in some sort of opposition to it, although the nature of this opposition remains to be seen. Fortunately, in this regard, we possess some fragments quoted by Eusebius on the subject, but further information may also be obtained from Calcidius' *Commentary on the Timaeus*, which used Numenius as a source, although a difficulty here is that even though Calcidus refers to his predecessors, he does not tend to acknowledge his sources and we cannot always conclude definitive use of a specific text.[45]

Numenius characterises matter as in a state of flux and uses the recalcitrance traditionally associated with it, at least from a Platonic perspective, to deny a connection with Being. His argument is that if matter is infinite (ἄπειρος), it is indeterminate (ἀόριστος), therefore irrational (ἄλογος), and if irrational, unknowable (ἄγνωστος). If matter is unknowable, the reason why it is unknowable must be that it is without order (ἄτακτος). None of these attributes, according to Numenius, can be applied to Being. It requires an incorporeal power, which Numenius identifies with Zeus the

---

[44] Des Places: 1973, 113   [45] Van Winden: 1959, 13

Saviour, 'to separate corruption from these mixtures and to maintain them' (τὴν φθορὰν ἀμύνειν δύνηται καὶ κατέχῃ).[46]

Numenius attributes motion in matter to a recalcitrant principle, which renders bodies incapable of remaining in a fixed position. The Second God is clearly involved in continual temporal generation, rather than a once-off event, since deprived of the principle that he injects into matter, it will no longer retain its position. This raises the question: what is the nature of this principle? I think that it is quite possibly soul (which itself is a principle of number). Just like the Demiurge in numerous metaphysical systems, including Plato's own, the Second God orders, rather than creates, although the situation here is rather more complicated, since the Second God orders pre-existent matter using a principle which he himself has not created. While Plato's Demiurge may order according to the Forms, he is still an autonomous Demiurge, rather than simply an 'instrument' of a superior God, as is the case with Numenius' Second God.

Numenius explicitly states that soul is responsible for holding together matter and providing it with cohesion, although he indicates that there is a second principle, which maintains soul in its turn, but he is less clear about what that is.[47] It is probable that the principle supporting soul is the Second God, who implants it in the cosmos. Numenius regards soul as the basis of movement. This must mean that soul is only the cause of all orderly motion, since, as has previously been illustrated, matter is regarded as subject to an irrational motion which does not partake of Being.

Numenius has a problem here: how can he explain the action of an incorporeal (soul) upon a corporeal (matter). He is forced to concede that soul is three-dimensional, which allows it to permeate the 'host-body' of matter. On soul's tridimensionality, he claims 'it is not such by itself, but κατὰ συμβεβηκός', that is because of the body in which it is: . . . τῇ ψυχῇ καθ' ἑαυτὴν μὲν πρόσεστι τὸ ἀδιάστατον, κατὰ συμβεβηκὸς δὲ τῷ ἐν ᾧ ἐστι τριχῇ διαστατῷ ὄντι συνθεωρεῖται καὶ αὐτὴ τριχῇ διαστατή, 'and the soul by itself is without extension, but has it accidentally, since it resides in what has a threefold dimension, it appears to have a threefold dimension'.[48] Numenius is caught between the tendency to make matter corporeal and the opposing tendency to make soul corporeal.[49] This same problem is evident in Calcidius, who uses Numenius as his main source

---

[46] Fr. 4a (13L. = Eus., *Praep. Ev.* xv.17.3–8)

[47] Fr. 4b (Test. 29L. = Nemesius, Περὶ φύσεως ἀνθρώπου, 2, 8–14). Despite coming from Nemesius, this passage can be regarded as reliable, since it is supported from Fr. 4a, a citation by Eusebius.

[48] Fr. 4b (Test. 29L. = Nemesius, Περὶ φύσεως ἀνθρώπου 2.18).

[49] Van Winden: 1959, 160

here. Calcidius, in a similar position, believes that matter is *inpetibilis*, but believes that one may state 'silva patibilis est'.[50] Plotinus radically breaks with this in his statement ὕλη ἀπαθής ἐστι, 'matter is impassible'. It is clear that Calcidius is inspired by Numenius here. For Chrysippus matter was indifferent due to its lack of quality: οὐ γὰρ ἥ γ' ὕλη τὸ κακὸν ἐξ ἑαυτῆς παρέσχηκεν· ἄποιος γάρ ἐστι καὶ πάσας ὅσας δέχεται διαφορὰς ὑπὸ τοῦ κινοῦντος αὐτὴν καὶ σχηματίζοντος ἔσχε, 'for matter has not out of itself brought evil forth. For it is devoid of quality and all the variations which it receives it has got from that which moves and moulds it'.[51] Van Winden raises the possibility that Numenius reacts against these words.[52]

This hypothesis is rendered more credible by the distinction between essence and matter present in Numenius, which must come from Stoic sources. Essence for the Stoics was *fundamentum operis*, 'that out of which something is made' while matter was 'the means by which the Maker operates'.[53] I think that we can see the influence of this distinction upon Numenius in his attempts to posit a second principle supporting soul which also works upon matter. In this context, it is worth citing Calcidius *In Timaeum* 293:

> Therefore, according to the Stoics, the body of the world is limited and one and the whole and a substance: it is a whole, since no single part is missing; one, because its parts are inseparable and cohere together, an essence because it is the first matter of all bodies, through which – they say – stabilising and universal reason passes, just like seed passes through the genitals. Therefore they suppose that this reason is a craftsman, and a coherent and qualityless body, completely passive and changeable, is matter or substance.

This passage is interesting for the light that it sheds upon Stoic demiurgic causality, but it can help us to better understand the fragments of Numenius. Clearly, he is opposed to the notion of passive matter.[54] Matter cannot be without quality in his dualistic system. However, the Stoic speculation

---

[50] *Cf. Ad. Par.* 309, 148   [51] Plut., *De Comm. Notit.* 10765 c–d

[52] Van Winden: 1959, 100 following a suggestion originally made by Leemans. Leemans adds: 'Materiam fontem esse malorum iam veteres Pythagorei adserunt (*Dox.* Gr. 302), quibus consentiunt omnes Platonici et Pythagorici recentiores', 'The ancient Pythagoreans claim now that the origin of evil is matter; all the more recent Platonists and Pythagoreans agree with this position.')

[53] Van Winden: 1959, 97

[54] Calcidius goes on to say (*in Tim.* 295) 'Numenius ex Pythagorae magisterio Stoicorum hoc de initiis dogma refellens Pythagorae dogmate' ('Numenius, who placed himself amongst the Pythagoreans, refutes this Stoic theory of principles with the help of a doctrine of Pythagoras'; as Van Winden successfully demonstrates (p.103–4), Calcidius is dependent upon Numenius for these sections on Aristotle and the Stoics, a dependence betrayed by Calcidius' statement 'ut in Timaeo loquitur Plato' (327, 3), which stands out in a commentary on the *Timaeus*, and indicates that Calcidius is here either following closely or merely translating Numenius.

on essence has left its mark, even on the limited fragments that we possess. The penetration of the Demiurge into matter uses a sexual metaphor and this also cannot be Numenius' view (although it can be seen as part of the Stoic's preference for the biological, rather than technological, image of the *Timaeus*).[55] For Numenius, matter is not generated; he distinguishes between two states: one ordered and the other unarranged, and states that this unarranged state is *aequaeva deo*. This unarranged matter (chaos) of the *Timaeus* is actually something concrete.

In Timaeum 296 contradicts somewhat this image we have constructed of Numenian matter:

> Numenius says that Pythagoras also thinks that matter is fluid and without qualities. However, he did not suppose, unlike the Stoics, an intermediate nature, between good and evil, which they classify as 'indifferent', but which, on the contray, is completely malevolent. However, for Pythagoras – and for Plato as well – God is the principle and cause of the good but that which proceeds out of form and matter is indifferent. As a consequence, it is not matter, but the world which as a mix of Form's goodness and the evilness of matter, is indifferent. Finally, the world has been generated out of Providence and Necessity, according to the doctrine of the old theologians.

Numenius' view that Pythagoras would regard matter as without qualities appears problematic in light of his view that it is also evil; this reminds one of Plotinus' attempts to reconcile both aspects of matter. Numenius breaks away from the Platonic supposition that the world is good, regarding it as merely indifferent. The Demiurge in the process of world-generation orders by allowing form to become enmattered, but he cannot neutralise completely its inherent evil. Matter is improved as a result of this mixture, though the evilness inherent in its nature could not be removed throughout. Calcidius refers to the Stoic view that evil is caused by the malign influence of the stars. Since Numenius too regarded stars as consisting of matter, he was not particularly open to this attempt to blame evil on malevolent astral influence. Sidereal motion, after all, is caused by the instability of matter, so even this explanation of evil regards matter as its cause.[56] The Demiurge produces order out of disorder, but there must exist a second principle which is the cause of disorderly motion. As Calcidius remarks *anima silvae neque sine ulla substantia est*, 'the soul of matter is not without

---

[55] Numenius uses the image of seed in an agricultural and not a sexual sense; *cf.* Fr. 13.
[56] Van Winden: 1959, 115

any substance.'[57] This *malitia* for Numenius is more than mere disorder; rather it is due to a 'volition' existing in the soul of matter.[58]

> And so God adorned matter with his miraculous power and he corrected its faults in every way, without destroying them completely, so that material nature might not be completely destroyed, but not allowing them to extend and to spread out everywhere, but maintaining its nature, able to change its condition from a troublesome into a desirable state, he transformed it completely, adorning and decorating it by joining together order with disorder, measure with lack of measure and beauty with ugliness. Finally, Numenius says – and with good reason – that what comes into being free from defects can not be found anywhere, not in the crafts of man or in nature, not in the bodies of animals, nor in trees, plants or fruits, not in the thread of air, nor in the current of water, nor in heaven itself, for everywhere a lower order of nature mixes with Providence as a kind of contamination. And when, then, he wishes to show, and as it were bring to light a bare image of matter, he says that all bodies which in the bosom (of matter), change and cause change, should be removed one by one and we should consider in our mind that which has been emptied by this removal; this he calls 'matter' and 'necessity'. The work which is the world is from this matter and from God; God uses persuasion and Necessity obeys. This is Pythagoras' assertion about the origin of things. (Calcidius, *In Timaeum* 299)

Here the God attempts to improve matter during the process of world-generation in order to make it as good as possible, but defects remain, through no fault of the Demiurge, but rather in spite of his best efforts. The image of demiurgic causality ascribed to Numenius here is similar to that of the *Timaeus*: Reason moulding Necessity as far as is possible through the use of persuasion. However, while Plato posits recalcitrant, pre-existent matter, to my knowledge, he never equates it explicitly with Necessity. Numenius posits animated matter, which is more than an Aristotelian δύναμις.[59] To apprehend matter it is necessary to 'think away all bodies'. Numenius clearly envisages the essence of matter as non-corporeal. In reference to pre-cosmic chaos, he states that the bodies of matter are continually changing from [one form] to another in the womb of the *silva*. This would mean that matter is now being identified with the Receptacle; a modification observable also in Plutarch, but there the situation is somewhat different, as he regards Receptacle-matter as either passive or inclining towards the good. Numenius has blurred the distinctions between the space *in which*

---

[57] *In Tim.* 298
[58] Van Winden: 1959, 117, uses the term 'will', although I am rather uncomfortable with using this word, since it denotes a concept that did not really exist in Greek philosophy.
[59] Van Winden: 1959, 117

generation occurs and the substance *out of which* it occurs. Why? Perhaps it is under the influence of the Stoic distinction between matter and essence, although here again Plato's use of 'spatial' terms (such as ἐκμαγεῖον) to refer to material concepts makes such an interpretation justifiable.

Clearly for Numenius, the principle opposed to the Demiurge in the sensible world is more than just matter. There is an echo of the maleficient soul in precosmic matter posited by Plutarch. The Demiurge appears to produce, not by adding anything to matter, but by removing its recalcitrance. Even if Calcidius is not a completely reliable source for Numenius, we can follow his statement here since it agrees with fragments we possess from Eusebius, such as Fr. 4b and Fr. 49. In any case, Calcidius at this point does not try to mask the fact that Numenius stresses recalcitrance, while he, due to his attempt to free matter from evil, focuses more on its pliability.[60]

Matter is also linked to Numenius' daemonology, as illustrated by Fr. 37 (Test. 59L. = Proclus, *In Timaeum*, 1.76.30–77.23 Diehl):

Οἱ δ' εἰς δαιμόνων τινῶν ἐναντίωσιν, ὡς τῶν μὲν ἀμεινόνων, τῶν δὲ χειρόνων, καὶ τῶν μὲν πλήθει, τῶν δὲ δυνάμει κρειττόνων, καὶ τῶν μὲν κρατούντων, τῶν δὲ κρατουμένων, ὥσπερ Ὠριγένης ὑπέλαβεν. Οἱ δ' εἰς ψυχῶν διάστασιν καλλιόνων καὶ τῆς Ἀθηνᾶς τροφίμων καὶ γενεσιουργῶν ἄλλων, αἳ καὶ τῷ τῆς γενέσεως ἐφόρῳ θεῷ προσήκουσι. Καὶ ἔστι τῆς ἐξηγήσεως ταύτης προστάτης Νουμήνιος. Οἱ δὲ καὶ μίξαντες τὴν Ὠριγένους, ὥσπερ οἴονται, καὶ Νουμηνίου δόξαν ψυχῶν πρὸς δαίμονας ναντίωσιν εἶπον, τῶν μὲν δαιμόνων καταγωγῶν ὄντων, τῶν δὲ ψυχῶν ἀναγομένων... καὶ ἅπερ οἱ παλαιοί, φασι, θεολόγοι εἰς Ὄσιριν καὶ Τυφῶνα ἀνήγαγον ἢ εἰς Διόνυσον καὶ Τιτᾶνας, ταῦτα ὁ Πλάτων εἰς Ἀθηναίους καὶ Ἀτλαντίνους ἀναπέμπει δι' εὐσέβειαν· πρὶν δ' εἰς τὰ στερεὰ σώματα κατελθεῖν, <ἐναντίωσιν> παραδίδωσι τῶν ψυχῶν πρὸς τοὺς ὑλικοὺς δαίμονας, οὓς τῇ δύσει παρῳκείωσεν... ἐπὶ δὲ ταύτης ἐστὶ τῆς οἰήσεως ὁ φιλόσοφος Πορφύριος, ὃν καὶ θαυμάσειεν ἄν τις εἰ ἕτερα λέγοι τῆς Νουμηνίου παραδόσεως.

Some explain [the fable of Atlantis] as representing the opposition between the two parties of *daimones*, a better and a worse, one superior in numbers, the other in power, one victorious, the other defeated: this was Origen's theory. Others speak of an opposition of souls, the fairer ones who are nurslings of Athena against others who are attached to generation, and who belong to the god who oversees generation. The champion of this doctrine is Numenius. Others combine the opinions of Origen and Numenius to produce a conflict between the souls and the *daimones*, the *daimones* causing a downward motion, while the souls are led aloft ... According to these men, where the theologians (θεολόγοι) spoke of Osiris and Typhon or

---

[60] *In Tim.* 301

Dionysus and the Titans, Plato referred through reverence to the Athenians and the inhabitants of Atlantis. And [the proponent of this theory] says that before they enter solid bodies the souls are engaged in a war with material *daimones*, whom he locates in the west . . . This opinion is held by the philosopher Porphyry, whom one would not expect to contradict the tradition received from Numenius.

This fragment illustrates the manner in which the Osiris/Isis allegory of Plutarch and the lost work of Numenius, which acted as the prototype for Porphyry's *Cave of the Nymphs*, both expound the same philosophical element: world-generation results from a conflict between the forces of order and disorder. The nursling of Athena is Odysseus, who is protected by her against Poseidon, the god of generation. Poseidon is not actually mentioned here, but clearly the plot of the *Odyssey* is the basis for this allegory. The sea is frequently used as an image of the generated universe in Numenius (e.g. Frs. 2 and 18), and Plato refers to Poseidon as the patron god of Atlantis (*Critias* 113c).[61]

If Poseidon is meant to be the god of generation here, it is difficult to see how he could represent the same entity as the Demiurge, in spite of his title. Athena is evidently intellect, and as such must be identifiable with the First God. In this case, Poseidon cannot be the Second God, since he works in collaboration with the First, not in opposition to him. I do not see how he can even be identified with the Third God; he must rather represent an irrational World-Soul like Seth-Typhon; the counter-motion ascribed by Numenius to matter. Numenius probably borrowed this image from Pherecydes of Samos, who represented the conflict between the gods and the giants as an allegory for the tension between the Demiurge and the Errant Cause.[62] This acts as further evidence strengthening the interpretation of Fr. 37 as an excursus on demiurgic causality in terms of the ordering of disorder. The pagan Celsus even saw the presentation of the peplos to Athena at the Panathenaic procession as a representation of demiurgic triumph over disorder: 'For he says that this depicts the rule of the motherless and immaculate *daimon* over the arrogance of the giants.'[63]

Celsus attributes this allegory to Pherecydes:

---

[61] Edwards: 1990, 258

[62] 'And [Celsus] says that Pherecydes composed a myth of two armies engaged in battle, Cronus led one and the other was led by Ophioneus . . . and they agreed that whichever of them should sink into the Ocean (*Ogēnos*) would be defeated, and the one which had driven them out and defeated them would possess heaven. [Celsus] says that these mysteries concerning the war waged by the Titans and giants against the gods and the Egyptian stories concerning Typhon, Horus and Osiris signify the same thing.' (*CCels.* vi.42 = Vol. ii. P.iii.13 Koetschau = Pherecydes Fr. B4 DK)

[63] *CCels.* vi.42 = p. 112.30 Koetschau = Pherecydes Fr. B5 DK

And [Celsus] interprets Homer's words as follows: the words of Zeus to Hera [*Iliad* 1.590–1 and 15.18–24] are those of god to matter, and they mean that God took it at the beginning, when it was disharmonious and bound it with mathematical proportions and ordered it, and he cast forth the *daimones* who were insolent on the path to this place. And he says that Pherecydes interpreted Homer in this way when he said 'the region of Tartarus is below the region . . . where Zeus casts down any of the gods who are insolent'.[64]

Here we are dealing with a model of demiurgic causality to which Numenius owes a certain debt, since he borrowed material for his image of the Cave of the Nymphs.[65] The Cave itself represents matter or the generated world, which is seen as home to evil forces, while the road to it is the descent of the soul to the sensible world. This reveals a negative view of the generated world also observable in Numenius.[66] Porphyry's interpretation of the Cave of the Nymphs can probably be regarded as the same as that of Numenius, since Celsus is never mentioned by Platonists as an original philosopher and since Porphyry admits that some of his knowledge of Pherecydes comes from Numenius. It is probable that Numenius is responsible for the interpretation of this allegory as a metaphor for the descent of the soul and the generation of the sensible world.[67]

Numenius attempts to explain the nature of soul.[68] For Numenius, soul was a mathematical entity, serving as an intermediary between physical and suprasensible realities which partakes of the Monad in so far as it is indivisible and of the Indefinite Dyad, in so far as it is divisible. Des Places notes that the indivisible Monad is God, the Indefinite Dyad is matter.[69] There is nothing particularly unusual about regarding soul as a number principle. Numenius, according to the testimony of Proclus at any rate, views it also as a principle intermediate between the suprasensible and sublunar worlds. Again the stress here is on the geometric nature of soul. Just as Plutarch stresses the fact that the Demiurge continually engages in geometry, Numenius seems to regard ordering matter as some form of mathematical activity. However, it would appear that Proclus has distorted somewhat Numenius' actual theory. He cannot have regarded soul or even the soul-principle as a mixture between matter and the Monad, since soul is explicitly said to come from the First God. I think that Proclus, for whatever reason, glosses over the fact that Numenius posited a lower, irrational soul,

---

[64] *CCels.* vi.42 = p.112.20ff. Koetschau = Pherecydes Fr. B5 DK
[65] 'Pherecydes of Syros talks about recesses, and trenches and caves and grotto entrances and through these alludes to the generation and return of souls' (p.77.18 Nauck = Pherecydes Fr.B6 DK.). This fragment appears in Porphyry's *Cave of the Nymphs* 31.
[66] E.g. Fr. 35.10 Des Places   [67] Edwards: 1990, 262
[68] Fr. 39 (= Proclus, *In Tim.*, ii.153.17–25)   [69] Des Places: 1973, 121

which can be said to come from matter (this is the principle which imparts a motion to matter), but clearly even if the Numenian higher soul can be said to act as an intermediary between the two realms (which is probably true since it emanates from the First God and is implanted in matter by the Demiurge), it is wrong to regard it as merely a mixture of matter and of the First Principle.

Some further details concerning the nature of this incorporeal essence may be gleaned from Fr. 41 (Test. 33L. = Iamblichus, Περὶ Ψυχῆς, ap. Stob., *Anthol.* 1.49.32). Numenius is supposed to have held the view that the incorporeal essence (ἀσώματον οὐσίαν) was homogenous (ὁμοιομερής) and that the totality could be found in the parts (ὡς καὶ ἐν ὁτῳοῦν αὐτῆς μέρει εἶναι τὰ ὅλα). Numenius, according to this fragment, located the sensible world, gods, *daimones*, the Good and the superior species (πάντα τὰ πρεσβύτερα) in the soul, following the line of reasoning according to which the soul does not differ from any of these in its essence. Each of these is instantiated in the world differently, based on the role which it is to fulfil (οἰκείως μέντοι κατὰ τὴν αὐτῶν οὐσίαν ἐν ἑκάστοις).

The fragment comes from Iamblichus' Περὶ Ψυχῆς, and appears to contradict the fragment taken from Proclus quoted above, which alleges that Numenius regarded soul as a mixture between Monad and Dyad. According to Fr. 41, soul is equivalent to Intellect, which in Numenian terms would make it identical to the First God. However, it is stressed several times in the fragment that what we are discussing is not necessarily soul, but rather its essence. While Fragments 39 and 41 may not illuminate the issue of demiurgy considerably, taken together they can be useful for cautioning one not to place excessive credence on fragments which do not come from Eusebius, since they (may) have been distorted.

Proclus offers another interesting comment on the mixture of divinity with matter. After mentioning the Stoic claim that sublunar gods do not have their essence mixed with matter, Proclus mentions Numenius' formulation that it is the powers and activities (τὰς δὲ δυνάμεις καὶ τὰς ἐνεργείας) of the sublunar gods which are mixed with matter.[70] This fragment indicates that Numenius did not view either the Demiurge or the Third God as being enmattered, although their activities are mixed with it; a clear indication that Numenius did not envisage the need for additional hypostases or an equivalent of Philo's *Logos*-Cutter in order to insulate the deities that were engaged in sublunar activity from matter; probably because his First Principle is already separated from matter by the two lower gods.

---

[70] Fr. 50 (Test. 26 L.) Des Places = Proclus, *In Tim.* III.196.12–19, Diehl

The only other fragment of interest concerning matter is Fr. 51 (Test. 28L.): 'Numenius thought that all the elements are mixed and that not one of them is in a pure state.'[71] Clearly, the Demiurge must then generate (or order) the world by mixing the various elements in due proportion. In any case, in the Platonic system, the world is constructed from a mixture of elements, since unlike its Aristotelian counterpart, there is no room for the primacy of any one element.

Conclusion

Numenius, a Neopythagoreanising Platonist, attempted to combine elements from the great world religions with which he was familiar. In doing so, as far as can be observed from the surviving fragments, he produces an original account of demiurgic causality, while still claiming a Platonic provenance. He cites the Second Platonic Letter (312e) as evidence that the concept of three gods was actually the doctrine of Socrates and that Plato was the only one of his pupils astute enough to follow it. Valentinus and Justin Martyr both used this Epistle to advocate a similar view, but it is unclear who first devised this manoeuvre.[72]

Evil enters Numenius' system not through any fault of the Demiurge, but due to an opposed evil principle. However, it does seem that Numenius believed in the existence of superlunary evil. Just as the Hermetists argue that the rational soul acquires accretions during its passage through the planetary sphere (e.g. *CH* 1.25*f.*), Numenius argues that evil enters the soul as ἀπὸ τῶν ἔξωθεν προσφυομένων ('beings attached from outside'). Calcidius states that Numenius located evil in the heavens, which Proclus regarded as an absurd opinion. It is unhellenic to believe in superlunary evil, and it has been suggested that this may stem from Iranian influence, where the sun and moon are the only beneficent planets.[73] However, such a problem can be resolved by considering Numenius' view of demiurgy. The superlunary evil he posits arises not due to the intention of the Demiurge as in the Gnostic systems, but rather as a result of matter, which he viewed as composing the stars.

In any case, such astral speculations lower Numenius' standing in Dodds' eyes.[74] Yet leading Neoplatonic philosophers are not in the habit of plagiarising from charlatans. Numenius propounded two postulates which became fundamental to Neoplatonism, both of which are linked to his

[71] Νουμήνιος μὲν οὖν πάντα μεμῖχθαι οἰόμενος οὐδὲν οἴεται εἶναι ἁπλοῦν.
[72] Frede, M.: 1987, 1056   [73] Dodds: 1960, 54   [74] Dodds: 1960, 11 (quoted above, pp. 139–40)

view of demiurgy. Firstly, the notion that by participation in the intelligible world each thing possesses all things, though modified by its special characteristics, as expressed by Proclus' *Elements of Theology*, prop. 103 or Plotinus' ἐξέχει δ' ἐν ἑκάστῳ ἄλλο, ἐμφαίνει δὲ καὶ πάντα, 'in each of them a being of a different kind stands out, but in each one all are manifest' (v 8 [31] 4.10). This argument was used by later Platonists to bridge gaps in their system.

The second postulate was that of 'undiminished giving', whereby the transmission of divine goods does not impoverish the giver, just as fire transmits light without being diminished. Plotinus uses the example of communicated knowledge (IV 9 [8] 5.4–9). It is this Numenian postulate which prevents Neoplatonism becoming pantheism and ensures that Numenius' status as a philosopher is much greater than that with which Dodds credits him.

Numenius represents a major development in terms of the doctrine of the Demiurge. While Philo's *Logos* and Plutarch's Osiris both have demiurgic functions, neither is a fully-fledged secondary demiurgic deity comparable with the Second God. Philo's *Logos* is certainly a mediator, but Numenius' demiurgic entity is more than a tool in the hands of God. Numenius emphasises the separation between the Demiurge and the First Principle, portrays world-generation in negative terms (as the result of an act of lust) and sees the Demiurge as negatively affected by matter in the process of cosmic structuring (if we interpret the division between the Second and Third Gods as some fragmentation of the godhead). These are all of importance in the Gnostic and Hermetic systems.

CHAPTER 7

On the fringes of philosophy
Speculations in Hermetism

Introduction

The revelations of Hermes Trismegistus to his son Tat form part of the same intellectual current from which Gnosticism emanates. The fourteen treatises of the *Corpus Hermeticum* were attributed by the Greeks to the god Hermes. They were rediscovered in Western Europe when the manuscript containing them was brought to Florence in 1460 by Leonardo of Pistoia. Cosimo de' Medici ordered Marsilio Ficino to suspend his project on the dialogues of Plato to translate them and it was via this translation that these texts became the basis of the speculations in astrology and alchemy that were at the core of Renaissance Hermeticism, a fact which reduced scholarly interest in Hermetism until recently by stripping it of intellectual respectability.

The influence of Hermetism was weakened in 1614 by the discovery of the Genevan Calvinist, Casaubon, that the *Corpus Hermeticum* should be dated to after the beginning of the Christian era, thus denuding it of the lustre of its perceived antiquity. However, certain Hermetic doctrines could be significantly older than the corpus in which they are contained. For example, the view that the world emanates as an overflow from God could be an ancient Egyptian one.[1] The 'Throne Mysticism' of esoteric Judaism is another case in point; the seven initiated palaces of Heaven behold the 'Kabod' (the glory of God in the guise of Man).[2] In addition, Jewish mysticism contains numerous speculations about Adam Qadmon (archetypal Man). In this light, Casaubon's views become less cogent.

The most striking appropriation of Hermetism from the Platonic tradition is the equation of *Nous* with the demiurgic entity. As with Gnosticism, it is an interesting tradition to study, due to its reliance upon an alternative 'creation myth', which at points takes on a character of its own. While the

---

[1] Salaman *et al.*: 1999, 12   [2] Copenhaver: 1992

main Hermetic texts do not appropriate specific passages or episodes of the *Timaeus*, as is the case with, for example, Philo or Plutarch, they do borrow the synthesised mass of Platonising interpretations of the dialogue. For example, the *Nous* (Mind) of the *Poimandres* which produces a second demiurgic *Nous*, is reminiscent of Numenius' theory. This secondary *Nous* generates the world on behalf of the First *Nous*. The Governors can be associated with the planetary gods of the *Timaeus*. Like Gnosticism, Hermetism has a heritage which lies outside the realm of Greek philosophy, and this explains why the correspondences between this tradition and the Platonist one are not as strong as in other branches which drew inspiration from the *Timaeus*. However, in the rest of the *Poimandres* myth, the Demiurge appears largely redundant. Though he does produce the world, the focus is on the descent of Man, in order to explain the high point of world-generation (the birth of mankind or more specifically the entrapment of that part of the godhead which goes on to become the human soul).

Of particular interest in Hermetism is the manner in which various features of the demiurgic myth could be incorporated. There is a considerable difference in perspective between the Hermetic myths and philosophical interpretations. Firstly, Hermetism is devoid of the notion of a Demiurge who is continually active in the sense of continually ordering matter to prevent some kind of cosmic collapse. World-generation occurs as the result of an error leading to division within the godhead, resulting in a less desirable state within the *supralunar* realm, and Hermetism envisages, indeed aspires to, a return to this state. Unlike the philosophical traditions, the interaction of immaterial entities upon material ones does not require explanation, and, in fact, the position they occupy within the myth can provide an impetus for altering their metaphysical function. Examples include the redundant Demiurge or the position of *Logos* between the lighter and heavier elements in the *Poimandres* (although this could also be interpreted in terms of a mediating entity). Again, the *Logos* is redundant due to the existence of the Second *Nous*.

Hermetism welcomes Platonic elements into a structure developed out of the Egyptian religious tradition. Rather than developing the metaphysical aspect of the demiurgic concept, this tradition marshals the entities of philosophical discussions on the topic and uses them to people its myths. Hermetism welcomes such familiar features, as the concept that the cosmos is the Son of God (*CH* iv.8), who aids God in world-generation (*CH* x.1.9), the role of Necessity in the *Asclepius*, or envisages demiurgy as the differentiation of unordered nature. What makes it particularly noteworthy is that it is the only tradition here analysed that posits a Demiurge, who is largely irrelevant to its structure (the Gnostic Demiurge at least occupies a central position in the myth of Sophia), and testifies to how pervasive the concept was at this period with regard to speculations on the origin of the cosmos.

Hermetism differs from Gnosticism in the use to which salvational knowledge can be put. It is possible for God to be revealed to the Hermetist through contemplation during life, rather than for this 'knowledge' to be only of real benefit after death, as is the case with Gnosticism. Rather than stressing that the nature of man is alien to the world, the Hermetist expresses his oneness with God, which tends to lead to a less severe anti-cosmic stance than is found in Gnosticism. Finally, Hermetism is not an elaborate metaphysical system, but a mechanism for achieving spiritual progress, which is rather sparse on technical metaphysical elements. Gnosticism, or at least certain systems thereof, had certain quasi-philosophical pretensions and this explains the greater emphasis on theoretical speculations.

The *Hermetica* have traditionally been divided into two classes: the philosophical *Hermetica* and the 'popular', or perhaps more correctly, the technical *Hermetica*. Although I am not in principle in favour of drawing such a sharp distinction between the two, as has been done by earlier scholars working in this area, such as Festugière, nevertheless only the philosophical texts need concern us here. As Fowden has shown, since the Hermetic texts cater for initiates at different levels of spiritual growth, attempts to categorise various sections of the corpus are doomed to fail.[3] Yet for the purposes of analysing demiurgic causality in the Hermetic tradition, it is, I feel, justifiable to focus on the more technical treatises.

The *Poimandres*

Of particular interest for understanding the issue of demiurgic causality is the *Poimandres*; actually only the first tract of the *Corpus Hermeticum*, although when the *Corpus* was rediscovered in Western Europe, Marsilio Ficino was mistakenly led to believe that the title referred to the entire corpus. This is perfectly understandable. *Poimandres* not only plays a pivotal role in the first Hermetic treatise, but is referred to implicitly in the eleventh and is mentioned twice (by name) in *CH.* XIII. As Kingsley notes, it appears that the figure of *Poimandres* was much better known in antiquity than emerges from the surviving remnants of Hermetic literature.[4] It is important to bear in mind that Hermetism is not 'serious philosophy',

---

[3] Fowden: 1986, especially 97–104   [4] Kingsley: 1993, 1

but a spiritual conviction, which contains philosophical elements. In the *Poimandres*, then, we have an example of revelation literature, in which Poimandres, the world-generator, reveals the truth concerning the structure of the universe to Hermes; rather than a heavyweight metaphysical analysis.

The role of the figure of Poimandres is key, not merely to understanding the tractate, but also other elements of the Hermetic corpus, is evinced by the concentrated efforts, not only during antiquity, but also in more recent scholarship, to discover the etymology of the name. In the thirteenth treatise, *Nous* is portrayed in the role of a shepherd (*poimainein*), while Zosimus provides an etymology, revealing Poimandres to be the ποιμήν (shepherd) of men (ἄνδρες).[5] However, an accusative *Poimenandra* would imply a nominative *Poimenâner* and following the normal evolution of Greek etymology, we need *Poimandros*, *Poimānor* or *Poimenanōr*. It is clear, then, that the Greek etymologies of the name are folk, or secondary, etymologies, and to understand the name, Poimandres, we need to look for an Egyptian origin.[6]

'P' is the masculine singular definite article, which has been constructed using the name of a divinity. Res is probably a Greek transcription of Re.[7] It is proposed that Poimandres is actually a corruption of *P-eime n-rē* – 'The intelligence of Re'. Parallels for a shift in Coptic 'ei' to Greek 'oi' (which were both pronounced 'ī' by this time) exist and the genitive -*nterē* could easily have been altered to -*ndres* in Greek. This would make Poimandres a philosophical abstraction. When he identifies himself: 'I am Poimandres, the intelligence of the supreme authority', his name and title are equivalent. In this sense, he parallels *Pi-nous nte-piot*, 'the intelligence of the father', found in the *Gospel of Truth*, or *T-Pronoia n-t-authenteia*, 'the foreknowledge of the Supreme', found in the *Apocryphon of John*.[8] It is usually considered a Greek trait to personify abstract philosophical ideas, but there are also Egyptian parallels, such as *Sia* 'Intelligence' and *Hu* 'Word'. These two figures can, in a sense, be viewed as responsible for demiurgic causality in the *Poimandres*, where *Nous* and *Logos* are responsible for world-generation. During the Graeco-Roman period, Sia was often equated with Thoth, who is usually identified with Hermes Trismegistus, or else viewed as the initial revealer of Hermetism, while Hermes was its translator into Greek. One of Thoth's titles was 'ib nRa, 'the heart of Ra', which made him the First Principle's generative Intelligence. Poimandres must be another

---

[5] Berthelot and Ruelle, 1887–88, ii. P.245, 6–7 = Tonelli: 1988, pp. 120.28 – 122.2
[6] Kingsley: 1993, 3   [7] Kingsley: 1993, 4   [8] Kingsley: 1993, 5

title of Sia or Thoth cast in the same role as a generative Intelligence. The etymology of the name is important in terms of understanding who exactly Poimandres is, helping to clarify certain strange elements which make no sense in terms of the Greek philosophical tradition.

Initially, one is struck by the differences between the *Poimandres* and other Gnostic/Hermetic texts. The Demiurge may be separate from the supreme principle, but there is no indication that he is in any way opposed to it. Indeed, the division of the godhead, which can be seen as a fall, since it makes the godhead less perfect, can be blamed on the supreme principle itself, since it seems to be partially responsible for it. It is also difficult to be sure how radically dualist one should consider the treatise. It is not entirely clear whether matter is the product of the First Principle, which of necessity would be less radically dualist than treatises which posit pre-existent matter. However, in the *Poimandres* matter is actually real, as opposed to the *Gospel of Truth* where it is only real as long as one deems it real; a more dualistic stance. In the *Poimandres*, the material world is only inferior to the immaterial one; it is not actually described as evil. It could be argued that world-generation in the *Poimandres* actually fulfils a positive role, allowing the improvement of the godhead, as each of the parts of divinity trapped in the material world finally return to compose a more united godhead. However, it could equally be argued that with the restoration of the godhead, we return to the stage before world-generation; and therefore the production of the world, in fact, accomplishes nothing.

The *Poimandres* is rich in material which helps to elucidate the nature of demiurgic causality, especially the cosmological section of the treatise (4–11). Poimandres first of all identifies himself as light, Mind, the shining reason-principle (emanated) from Intellect and the son of God. This primordial light gives way to darkness, and has often been interpreted in dualist terms as can be observed by the subsequent comment at §4: εἶτα βοὴ ἐξ αὐτῆς ἀσυνάρθρως ἐξεπέμπετο, ὡς εἰκάσαι φωνῇ πυρός ('Then he uttered a cry of appeal, without articulation, such as I would compare to a voice of fire'). Festugière regards this as the mark of opposition between a brutal elemental character, as evinced by the cry, and the sanctity of *Logos*, which he regards as speech denoting Reason. This plaintive cry, rather than denoting opposition, may be a sign of some sort of prior attachment between Light and Darkness; existing in the dramatic time before the opening of the treatise, as this generation myth commences *in medias res*. Darkness must therefore have existed prior to its appearance and the agitation it experiences seems to be a kind of primordial chaos. This attachment could explain why the Light becomes involved in the material realm; perhaps producing the world by ordering matter as some kind of compassionate response.[9]

The Light is the First Principle which then gives way to Darkness, the irrational, disorderly element, matter. Matter is not created by the Light, since it arises separately and there is no indication that it actually arises out of the Light. A dualism is set up through the opposing states of Light and Darkness, or the Nature it becomes. Light is serene (εὔδιος) and happy (ἱλαρός), while Darkness is indescribably agitated (ἀφάτως τεταραγμένον) and fearful and gloomy (φοβερόν τε καὶ στυγνόν). Light produces the hypostasis, *Logos*, by means of which it orders matter to produce the elements. It appears to be a compassionate response on the part of the Light to the agitation experienced by Darkness. *Logos* enables Nature to release fire and air, while earth and water remain behind intermingled, though it is unclear whether *Logos* acts as a mate or a midwife. In any case, their birth is equivalent to their differentiation from unordered Nature and so *Logos* is the mechanism of God's world-generation. In this sense, it is equivalent to Philo's *Logos*-Cutter. However, the author of the *Poimandres* did not need to postulate such an entity in order to insulate God from matter, since he later postulates the existence of a separate Demiurge. It seems that he adopts the terminology and personified abstractions of Greek philosophy, in order to adapt them to his mythological framework, but without actually understanding the reason for their introduction in the first place. These passages make very little sense in terms of Greek philosophy, and should, I feel, be read in terms of the Egyptian religious tradition. There is no strife between light and darkness; in fact the light turns into darkness and the fire (again a form of light) arises out of the darkness. This can be explained in terms of the Egyptian notion of cosmology paralleling the daily appearance of the sun, where darkness is not just the opposite of light, but also its primeval form. Since God is equated with the light and light is everything, God and the world are one: God is not actually a transcendent deity.[10]

Fire and air, the lighter elements, attempt to reach the Light, and even though they fail in their attempt, they ascend above the *Logos*. This appears like a precursor to the entrapment of Man. The *Logos* is produced out of the Light and by the Light alone, while fire and air are produced out of Nature and so the *Logos* should occupy a position closer to God than they do. The *Logos* can be viewed as mating with Nature, just as subsequently Man does.

---

[9] Plotinus also uses light imagery (in relation to the Soul's descent to Matter e.g. *Enn.* 11 [53] 12.24–30).
[10] R. A. Segal: 1986, 24

The *Logos* is, in a sense, entrapped in matter, since even though fire and air form the supralunar realm, this is still a material realm. Earth and water, as the heavier elements, sink to form the sublunar realm.[11] This leaves *Logos* as a separative element between the supra- and sublunar worlds.

Earth and water, for the moment, however, remain undifferentiated, their intermingling is only ended later (§11). In terms of Stoic cosmology, which shares numerous parallels with the generative account of the *Poimandres*, this is incomprehensible, but the same situation occurs in *Gen.* 1. Indeed, the *Poimandres* account reflects in many ways the structure of the *Genesis* account (and it must be the case that the *Poimandres* is influenced by *Genesis*, rather then the case that similarities are simply due to both narratives outlining world-generation; elements from other comogonical myths, such as a primeval monster or a cosmic egg, are here absent.)[12] The order of generative events in both accounts is similar: in *Poimandres*, the world is generated in five stages: (1) the separation of light and darkness, (2) the separation of upper elements from lower, (3) the production of heavenly bodies, (4) production of birds and fish and (5) land animals. This differs only slighty from the arrangement of the six days in *Genesis*: (1) separation of light and darkness, (2) the separation of the waters above from those below, (3) generation of land, water and plants, (4) heavenly bodies, (5) birds and fish, (6) land animals. It will be noticed that the main difference is that the *Poimandres* simply assumes the production of land and water, but does not describe it. Dodds has also analysed the latter part of the *Poimandres* tractate, which does not deal with the generation of the world, but rather consists of a sort of 'Gospel of Poimandres'. He demonstrates that the ethical vocabulary overlaps to a considerable extent

---

[11] A similar creation myth is mentioned by Copenhaver: 1992, 97–8 which he finds in the first part of *Papyri Graecae Magicae* XIII ('Eighth Book of Moses'): 'When the god laughed, seven gods were born (who encompass the cosmos . . .). When he laughed first, Phōs-Augē [Light-Radiance] appeared and irradiated everything and became god over the cosmos and fire . . . Then he laughed a second time. All was water. Earth, hearing the sound, cried out and heaved, and the water came to be divided into three parts. A god appeared; he was given charge of the abyss [of primal waters], for without him moisture neither increases nor diminishes. And his name is Eschakleo . . . When he wanted to laugh a third time, Nous or Phrenes [Mind or Wits] appeared holding a heart, because of the sharpness of the god. He was called Hermes; he was called Semesilam. The god laughed the fourth time, and Genna [Generative Power] appeared, controlling Spora [Procreation] . . . He laughed the fifth time and was gloomy as he laughed and Moira [Fate] appeared . . . But Hermes contested with her . . . And she was the first to receive the sceptre of the world . . . He laughed the sixth time and was much gladdened, and Kairos [Time] appeared holding a sceptre, indicating kingship, and he gave over the sceptre to the first-produced god, [Phōs] . . . When the god laughed a seventh time, Psyche [Soul] came into being, and he wept while laughing. On seeing Psyche, he hissed, and the earth heaved and gave birth to the Pythian serpent who foreknew all things . . . ' Lines 161–205 (trans. Betz: 176–8).

[12] Dodd: 1935, 100

with that of the Septuagint, but concludes that since much of this terminology is simply characteristic of the Hellenistic period, it is not possible
to draw further conclusions.[13] The fall of Man is cleary inspired by the
story of Adam and Eve; the apple has been regarded as an allegory for a
sexual transgression and has simply been discarded. The *Poimandres* is also
similar to Jewish apocalyptic literature, especially 2 *Enoch*, as outlined by
Pearson.[14] In the *Poimandres*, Hermes is almost asleep when he receives
a vision, he is called by name by a large being and God then reveals a
cosmology to him. In 2 *Enoch*, Enoch is at first asleep and then awakes
to receive a vision; he is called by name by two very large men and God
then reveals a cosmology to him. In both, the making of man is sevenfold
(*Poimandres* §§12–19; 2 *Enoch* 30:8–9).

The separation of Word from God by fire and air, which rise up to
occupy the position between God and his *Logos*, is strange in the context
of §6: 'This is what you must know: that in you which sees and hears is the
Word of the Lord, but your mind is God the Father; *they are not divided
from one another, for their union is life.*' Here Word and Mind are portrayed
as united, but perhaps this refers to the union within the individual. Yet,
since man is the microcosm of the universe, if Word and Mind are united
within him, they should also be united in the overall metaphysical scheme,
which is clearly not the case.

CH 1.7 presents the role of fire during world-generation: 'But when he
raised his head, I saw in my mind the light of powers beyond number and
a boundless cosmos that had come to be. The fire, encompassed by great
power and subdued, kept its place fixed.' The countless powers in the light
must be the Forms. The relationship between the Forms and the Fire is
unclear. It is also unclear what exactly the great power which subdues the
fire is. The Demiurge is subsequently presented as lord over the fire and
so he is one candidate. Unfortunately, he does not exist at this stage. As
elsewhere in the *Poimandres*, the interaction of an immaterial entity upon
a material one is not properly explained.

Poimandres responds to the issue of *creatio ex nihilo* claiming that the
elements of nature have arisen 'from the will of God, which having taken
the *Logos* and having seen the beautiful cosmos, copied it, having been
made into a cosmos by means of its own elements and its production of
souls'.[15] It is implied that the Demiurge does not produce the archetype of
the sensible world, but it does seem that he actually makes the elements

---

[13] Dodd: 1935, 173–5   [14] Pearson: 1990, 138–9
[15] *CH* 1.8. This raises the question of where the Word came from.

(though he may accomplish this merely by ordering pre-existent matter, like the Demiurge of the *Timaeus*), since it is claimed that they arise from the desire of God. The question here is whether βουλή can be regarded as a hypostasis of God. It may actually have the force of 'Will'. In any case, it is clearly a female generative principle, perhaps part of the Sophia figure in Philonic terms. It may be another term for Nature, which is also female.[16] Like Nature, Will receives the Word of God. However, it is not clear that Nature actually arose out of God, while the Will must have. The Will and the Word cannot be identical; aside from the fact that Word is masculine and Will is feminine, they are described as mating with each other. Will must be an entity that already exists, rather than an unmentioned entity which arises along with Word, and so this leaves Nature as the only suitable candidate. The highest principle then proceeds to produce a second demiurgic *Nous* (ἕτερον Νοῦν δημιουργόν), rather like the system found in Numenius. The androgynous Mind, identified with life and light, produces this Demiurge by speaking. The second Nous produces the planetary entities, referred to here as Governors (διοικητάς).

The Governors' rule of the world constitutes Fate. The term ἡ διοίκησις τοῦ κόσμου is a standard Stoic expression for the 'government' of the world'. It is the Demiurge who produces the planets ('governors/heavenly gods'), although it is not explicitly stated who generates the sensible world. I think that we must assume that it is the Demiurge, since the Governors only seem to encircle or take control of what was already there. In any case, the situation is clarified further on in the text:

ἐπήδησεν εὐθὺς ἐκ τῶν κατωφερῶν στοιχείων [τοῦ θεοῦ] ὁ τοῦ θεοῦ Λόγος εἰς τὸ καθαρὸν τῆς φύσεως δημιούργημα, καὶ ἡνώθη τῷ δημιουργῷ Νῷ (ὁμοούσιος γὰρ ἦν), καὶ κατελείφθη [τὰ] ἄλογα τὰ κατωφερῆ τῆς φύσεως στοιχεῖα, ὡς εἶναι ὕλην μόνην. ὁ δὲ δημιουργὸς Νοῦς σὺν τῷ Λόγῳ, ὁ περιίσχων τοὺς κύκλους καὶ δινῶν ῥοίζῳ, ἔστρεψε τὰ ἑαυτοῦ δημιουργήματα καὶ εἴασε στρέφεσθαι ἀπ' ἀρχῆς ἀορίστου εἰς ἀπέραντον τέλος· ἄρχεται γάρ, οὗ λήγει· ἡ δὲ τούτων περιφορά, καθὼς ἠθέλησεν ὁ Νοῦς, ἐκ τῶν κατωφερῶν στοιχείων ζῷα ἤνεγκεν ἄλογα (οὐ γὰρ ἐπεῖχε τὸν Λόγον), ἀὴρ δὲ πετεινὰ ἤνεγκε, καὶ τὸ ὕδωρ νηκτά· διακεχώρισται δὲ ἀπ' ἀλλήλων ἥ τε γῆ καὶ τὸ ὕδωρ, καθὼς ἠθέλησεν ὁ Νοῦς, καὶ <ἡ γῆ> ἐξήνεγκεν ἀπ' αὐτῆς ἃ εἶχε ζῷα τετράποδα <καὶ> ἑρπετά, θηρία ἄγρια καὶ ἥμερα.

From the downward-tending elements, the Word of God immediately leapt up to the pure demiurgy of Nature and united with the demiurgic Mind (for it was of the same substance) and the downward-tending elements of Nature

---

[16] Segal: 1986, 30

were left behind so that they were only matter. But the demiurgic Mind, together with the Word, encompassing the circles and rotating them in a rushing motion, turned around his own demiurgy and permitted them to turn from a beginning without an end to an end without limit. For it begins where it terminates. And revolving exactly as Mind wished, they brought forth from the downward-tending elements living things devoid of reason, (for they did not retain the Word/Reason), and the air produced winged creatures and the water swimming ones. And earth and water were separated from each other, exactly as Mind desired, and 'earth' brought forth from itself the four-footed and crawling creatures, wild and tame animals, which she held within herself, (*CH* 1.10–11)

According to this, the First *Nous* remains the sovereign cause of world-generation, even though he acts via his son, the *Nous* Demiurge.[17] This is seen in the constant emphasis on everything occurring according to the desire of Mind. The Word seems to be another hypostasis of the First Mind, which is closely associated with the Demiurge. The collaboration between Word and the Demiurge in world-generation is perhaps to be explained as a remnant of the role played in creation by Sia (Intelligence of the First Principle) and Hu (Word of the First Principle), rather than in Greek metaphysical terms. It seems that the author may have perhaps had enough knowledge of Greek philosophy to posit a divine *Logos* to separate his First Principle from matter, but then goes on to posit a second demiurgic *Nous* which renders this principle redundant.

The *Poimandres* is attempting to integrate two rival cosmological traditions and that is the reason for two separate demiurgic figures. Since the Demiurge is described as ἕτερος νοῦς, he functions as the mind of the material world, much as God acts as the mind of the immaterial one. The Demiurge is more of an independent entity than the Word, which is really just a tool of God. Unlike Word, although the Demiurge descends, he does not sink below the realm of fire. The manner in which Word leaps out of earth to unite with him echoes the manner in which fire and air escaped from Nature.

It also implies that Word was trapped in matter and needed to be rescued. Such a reading would at least have the benefit of providing a good reason for the generation of the Demiurge; though it is still unclear how an instrument of God could become entrapped. Yet it seems that the Demiurge arises to generate the material world out of the elements released

---

[17] Nock and Festugière: 1946, 21 n. 33. *cf.* §12: παρέδωκε τὰ ἑαυτοῦ πάντα δημιουργήματα, 'and he entrusted him with all his demiurgic productions'.

by Word, and Word utilises this opportunity to escape, rather than that the Demiurge was generated in order to release the Word.

The Demiurge also appears morally better than Man since he never sinks into the material world. The evilness of his production cannot be reconciled with his presentation here. He never appears as evil or even ignorant in the *Poimandres*. If he is merely following God's orders, then the evilness of the material world has to be blamed on God, rather than on him. By setting the planets in rotation, the Demiurge impels Earth and Water to separate and bring forth living beings. This mode of production is only indirect.

ὁ δὲ πάντων πατὴρ ὁ Νοῦς, ὢν ζωὴ καὶ φῶς, ἀπεκύησεν Ἄνθρωπον αὐτῷ ἴσον, οὗ ἠράσθη ὡς ἰδίου τόκου· περικαλλὴς γάρ, τὴν τοῦ πατρὸς εἰκόνα ἔχων· ὄντως γὰρ καὶ ὁ θεὸς ἠράσθη τῆς ἰδίας μορφῆς, παρέδωκε τὰ ἑαυ-τοῦ πάντα δημιουργήματα, καὶ κατανοήσας δὲ τὴν τοῦ Δημιουργοῦ κτίσιν ἐν τῷ πυρί, ἠβουλήθη καὶ αὐτὸς δημιουργεῖν, καὶ συνεχωρήθη ἀπὸ τοῦ πατρός· γενόμενος ἐν τῇ δημιουργικῇ σφαίρᾳ, ἕξων τὴν πᾶσαν ἐξουσίαν, κατενόησε τοῦ ἀδελφοῦ τὰ δημιουργήματα, οἱ δὲ ἠράσθησαν αὐτοῦ, ἕκασ-τος δὲ μετεδίδου τῆς ἰδίας τάξεως· καὶ καταμαθὼν τὴν τούτων οὐσίαν καὶ μεταλαβὼν τῆς αὐτῶν φύσεως ἠβουλήθη ἀναρρῆξαι τὴν περιφέρειαν τῶν κύκλων, καὶ τὸ κράτος τοῦ ἐπικειμένου ἐπὶ τοῦ πυρὸς κατανοῆσαι.

Mind, the Father of everything, light and life, produced Man; similar to himself, whom he loved as his own child. For he was most beautiful, and had the appearance of his father. For God was really in love with his own image, and he entrusted him with his demiurgic productions. And Man, having observed the productions of the Demiurge in the fire, himself wished to engage in demiurgy, and this was agreed to by the father and entering into the demiurgic sphere, having been awarded complete authority, he observed the demiurgic productions of his brother, and the Governors loved him and each gave him something of his own order and learning completely their essence and partaking of their nature, the man wished to burst through the circumference of the circles and to inspect the power of the one placed over the fire. (*CH* I.12–13)

Perhaps surprisingly, the highest principle is here identified as *Nous* (in Gnosticism, *Nous* is normally only the highest aeon). Outside the *Poiman-dres* the only other parallel, to my knowledge, is the Naassene νόμος ἦν γενικὸς τοῦ παντὸς ὁ πρωτότοκος νοῦς.[18] However, there are stronger connections within Greek philosophy. Anaxagoras posited *Nous* as the highest God: καὶ ὅσα γε ψυχὴν ἔχει καὶ τὰ μείζω καὶ τὰ ἐλάσσω, πάντων νοῦς κρατεῖ, 'and Mind has power over all things, both greater and lesser, which

---

[18] 'The generative principle of everything was the First-born Mind', Ps.-Hipp. *Ref.* v.10; 102, 23 W.

have soul'.[19] Plato expresses the same idea at *Phileb*. 28c6: πάντες γὰρ συμφωνοῦσιν οἱ σοφοί, ἑαυτοὺς ὄντως σεμνύνοντες, ὡς νοῦς ἐστι βασιλεὺς ἡμῖν οὐρανοῦ τε καὶ γῆς, 'for all the wise men are in agreement – feeling awe in this – that Mind is king of heaven and of earth'. The identification is also found in Middle Platonism (*cf.* Alcinous 10.2 and Numenius Fr. 17 Des Places). The tendency is also observable in the Church Fathers, Clement of Alexandria at *Strom.* 4.25 (317.11 Stählin) states: Πλάτων τὸν τῶν ἰδεῶν θεωρητικὸν θεὸν ἐν ἀνθρώποις ζήσεσθαί φησι· νοῦς δὲ χώρα ἰδεῶν, νοῦς δὲ ὁ θεός, 'Plato says that the God able to perceive the Forms lives in man, and Mind is the place of the Forms and Mind is God.'

This passage is problematic, since unlike in other systems which posit a fall which occurs within the godhead itself, such as Valentinianism, where a lower entity is responsible, here the First *Nous* is responsible for the fall as the result of an act of narcissism. God falls in love with Man, because he sees in Man the reflection of his own beauty. God has to make Man, since if he was produced by the Demiurge, he could only be his equal, not better than him. Word and the Demiurge are both subordinate to God. The Demiurge is another Mind. However, Man is God's equal (ἴσος §12). Even though God brings forth (ἀποκυέω) both the Demiurge and Man, it is only Man who bears the image of his father and whom God loves as his son. Since God is perfect, it is acceptable for him to love Man, although the sense here is sexual (ἐράω §12). What is wrong is that in his love of Man, God forgets that Man is only a part of God, not a separate entity, and it is this that allows God to grant Man permission to separate from the godhead, which necessarily results in a less perfect order than that which existed before.

Man here is clearly the ancestor of archetypal man. If the Demiurge has already generated the material world, it is unclear what remains for Man to produce. Furthermore, there seems to be an element of rivalry in Man's desire to engage in demiurgy in order to emulate the Demiurge. It seems rather as if he is to oversee his brother, since he was to have all authority in the craftsman's sphere. It is not apparent why God should hand over the generated world to Man and dispossess the Demiurge from a philosophical perspective; this can only be explained, I think, as a result of God's love for Man.

Another problem concerns the gifts of the Governors. Normally, in the Gnostic tradition this is negative; the mechanism by which the Governors trap Man. But that is quite clearly not the case here. The Governors act

---

[19] Anaxagoras, Fr. 12

out of love and since they are the productions of the Demiurge, I think that they must do this with his consent. This problem is linked to why God lets Man engage in demiurgy in the first place. If Man is ensnared by the machinations of the Governors, then the First Principle cannot be held completely responsible for the fall of Man. From §13, it seems that the error may not have been Man's initial descent, but his second descent into the realm of fire, which I interpret to mean the sublunar realm, since he does not do this with the permission of the First Principle, and it seems to be motivated by nothing other than idle curiosity. In trying to trace the point at which the error that involved world-generation, or the generation of Man at any rate, occurred, it is useful to turn to the eschatological section of the *Poimandres*:

> καὶ οὕτως ὁρμᾷ λοιπὸν ἄνω διὰ τῆς ἁρμονίας, καὶ τῇ πρώτῃ ζώνῃ δίδωσι τὴν αὐξητικὴν ἐνέργειαν καὶ τὴν μειωτικήν, καὶ τῇ δευτέρᾳ τὴν μηχανὴν τῶν κακῶν, δόλον ἀνενέργητον, καὶ τῇ τρίτῃ τὴν ἐπιθυμητικὴν ἀπάτην ἀνενέργητον, καὶ τῇ τετάρτῃ τὴν ἀρχοντικὴν προφανίαν ἀπλεονέκτητον, καὶ τῇ πέμπτῃ τὸ θράσος τὸ ἀνόσιον καὶ τῆς τόλμης τὴν προπέτειαν, καὶ τῇ ἕκτῃ τὰς ἀφορμὰς τὰς κακὰς τοῦ πλούτου ἀνενεργήτους, καὶ τῇ ἑβδόμῃ ζώνῃ τὸ ἐνεδρεῦον ψεῦδος.

> And then the human rushes up through the framework (of the universe) and he surrenders the activity of increase and decrease at the first zone and at the second the contrivance of evils, now a device no longer actualised and at the third the now inactive deceit of longing and at the fourth the eminence of the Archon, now devoid of excess and at the fifth impious courage and the headlong rush of daring and at the sixth the now inactive wicked impulses of wealth and at the seventh zone ensnaring falsehood. (*CH* 1.25)

The shedding of the 'gifts' of the Governors as the soul ascends towards salvation, as well as the description of what the 'gifts' actually are indicates that they are evil. The gifts comprise 'the energy of increase and decrease', 'machination', 'arrogance', 'unholy presumption', 'daring recklessness', 'the evil impulses that come from wealth' and 'deceit'. These impulses become inactive as the soul ascends. This contrasts with §13 describing the bestowal of the gifts. If Man's fall began with his descent into the sublunar realm, then to be saved he only needs to return to the supralunar realm; he does not need to shed the gifts of the Governors. The fact that he does indicates that these played a role in his fall. In order to enter the (region of) the Ogdoad, the human soul has to be stripped of the effects of the cosmic framework. They are then transformed into 'powers' before they can enter into the godhead.

The First Principle is transcendent, since he is described as located beyond the ogdoadic region. The return of the human soul to the godhead is the restoration of Man to his rightful place in the cosmic scheme. Certain scholars, such as Segal, have been tempted to see in this a denial of the validity of world-generation, since it marks a return to the position before it occured. But surely, the material world would continue to exist; it is just that humanity would no longer possess a material form. All that would be undone would be the fall of Man, which was not foreseen or intended by the First Principle. This indicates that the descent of Man in order to engage in demiurgy was a mistake, and along with the fact that he casts off the gifts of the Governors in order to return to God, reveals that his fall occurred with his desire to participate in world-generation, not with his entry into the sublunar region.

This is in keeping with the treatise's denunciation of the material world, since it means that Man's desire to engage in demiurgic activity (not just the jealousy that motivates this desire) is evil. Segal goes a step further, claiming that Man's fall may, in fact, begin with his separation from God,[20] that is to say with his birth, in which case the First Principle is actually culpable on two accounts: for the generation of Man, which seems to be utterly pointless in terms of demiurgic causality and motivated by nothing other than narcissism, and secondly, for consenting to Man's desire to create. Perhaps this scheme was meant to be along the lines of the Numenian one, with the First Principle handing over all of creation to Man, in order to retire and contemplate the Intelligibles. However, there is no evidence for this in the text, and there is no reason why God should hand over the material world to Man, rather than to the Demiurge. It seems, then, that no justification can be found for the generation of Man.

καὶ ὁ τοῦ τῶν θνητῶν κόσμου καὶ τῶν ἀλόγων ζῴων ἔχων πᾶσαν ἐξουσίαν διὰ τῆς ἁρμονίας παρέκυψεν, ἀναρρήξας τὸ κύτος, καὶ ἔδειξε τῇ κατωφερεῖ φύσει τὴν καλὴν τοῦ θεοῦ μορφήν, ὃν ἰδοῦσα ἀκόρεστον κάλλος <καὶ> πᾶσαν ἐνέργειαν ἐν ἑαυτῷ ἔχοντα τῶν διοικητόρων τήν τε μορφὴν τοῦ θεοῦ ἐμειδίασεν ἔρωτι, ὡς ἅτε τῆς καλλίστης μορφῆς τοῦ Ἀνθρώπου τὸ εἶδος ἐν τῷ ὕδατι ἰδοῦσα καὶ τὸ σκίασμα ἐπὶ τῆς γῆς. ὁ δὲ ἰδὼν τὴν ὁμοίαν αὐτῷ μορφὴν ἐν αὐτῇ οὖσαν ἐν τῷ ὕδατι, ἐφίλησε καὶ ἠβουλήθη αὐτοῦ οἰκεῖν· ἅμα δὲ τῇ βουλῇ ἐγένετο ἐνέργεια, καὶ ᾤκησε τὴν ἄλογον μορφήν· ἡ δὲ φύσις λαβοῦσα τὸν ἐρώμενον περιεπλάκη ὅλη καὶ ἐμίγησαν· ἐρώμενοι γὰρ ἦσαν.

And Man, having complete authority over the cosmos of mortals and over irrational animals, when he had burst out of the vault, he peered out of

---

[20] Segal: 1986, 37

the framework (of the cosmos) and he exhibited to the downward-tending nature the beautiful form of God, and Nature, seeing the one whose beauty is insatiate and who contains within himself all the activity of the governors and the form of God, she smiled with love, since she saw the appearance of the most beautiful form of Man upon the water and his shadow upon the earth. And Man, seeing a shape similar to himself upon the water, as it was in Nature itself, he fell in love and he wished to inhabit it. And the desire and the activity occurred simultaneously and he dwelt in the irrational form. And Nature, seizing her beloved, embraced him completely and mingled with him. For they were lovers. (*CH* 1.14)

Nature's love is understandable – she is drawn to a superior entity, as Man is the final emanation of the supreme principle, who resembles it in form. It seems that what we have here is some attempt by the inferior world to order itself in response to what is above. This union between Man and Nature symbolises the descent of the most perfect creature of the First God into matter.

However, Man's love is less noble than that of φύσις. He initially falls in love not with Nature, but with his own reflection. In this sense, he parallels the Father of All, *Nous*, who falls in love with Man, as the reflection of his own image. In the *Poimandres*, this marriage of Man with matter can be viewed in cosmological terms; explaining the manner in which the human form became enmattered; although here it is through no fault of the Demiurge's. In later accounts of the myth, the focus tends to be more on anthropological aspects; the *Poimandres* is viewed as an explanation of the dual nature of humanity (immortal and mortal elements). This was possibly borrowed from Persian speculation.

Bousset[21] records a treatise of the Emperor Julian, *The Hymn to the Mother of the Gods*, which deals with the Attis myth.[22] Here a similar situation is observable. Attis lusts after the Nymph and sinks into matter as a

---

[21] Bousset: 1907, 184–5

[22] Sallustius, *De deis et mundo* 4.8–9 draws heavily upon the treatise of his friend, the Emperor Julian
Εἰς τὴν Μητέρα τῶν θεῶν· Ἡ μὲν οὖν Μήτηρ τῶν Θεῶν ζωογόνος ἐστὶ Θεά, καὶ διὰ τοῦτο Μήτηρ καλεῖται·ὁ δὲ Ἄττις τῶν γινομένων καὶ φθειρομένων δημιουργός, καὶ διὰ τοῦτο παρὰ τῷ Γάλλῳ λέγεται εὑρεθῆναι ποταμῷ· ὁ γὰρ Γάλλος τὸν γαλαξίαν αἰνίττεται κύκλον . . . Ἐρᾷ δὲ ὁ Ἄττις τῆς Νύμφης· αἱ δὲ Νύμφαι γενέσεως ἔφοροι . . . ἐπεὶ δὲ ἔδει στῆναι τὴν γένεσιν καὶ μὴ τῶν ἐσχάτων γενέσθαι τι χεῖρον, ὁ ταῦτα ποιῶν δημιουργὸς δυνάμεις γονίμους ἀφεὶς εἰς τὴν γένεσιν πάλιν συνάπτεται τοῖς Θεοῖς.

'For the Mother of the gods is the life-producing divinity and for this reason she is called "Mother"; and Attis is the Demiurge of what is generated and of what decays and on account of this he is said to be found beside the river Gallus; for Gallus represents the galaxy (Milky Way) . . . Attis loves a nymph and the nymphs are the overseers of generation . . . but since it is necessary that generation be stopped at some point and that it does not generate something lower than what is worst, the Demiurge, having made these things, casts off his generative powers into generation and is joined to the gods once again.'

result of this love. This sets into motion the generation of the world. The divine Mother is angry at this and Attis has to abandon the Nymph and return to her. This parallels the *Poimandres* in its postulation of a return of the divine part of Man to the godhead, and can be interpreted as the desire of Primeval Man to escape from Matter. Again, this postulates an anthropological interpretation, even though the myth also has a cosmological role, explaining as it does the events that set world-gemeration in motion.[23]

The actual mating of Man with Nature is problematic. Nature is attracted to Man, not just because of his beauty, but also because of his power (ἐνέργεια §14). Segal claims that Man sees Nature himself, not his projection of himself onto her. Upon the sight, he then spontaneously projects this image onto her, which then becomes enmattered in Nature. Segal regards this as the moment of Man's entrapment.[24] However, I think that Man sees a projection of himself (his reflection in the water) and falls in love with it. Once he formulates this desire, he becomes spontaneously embedded in Nature, since his wish and action are simultaneous.

This descent into Nature is motivated by Man's sexuality. However, Man's initial descent is motivated by his desire for power; to either emulate or replace his brother, the Demiurge. Man is the 'Son of God' and Nature is female. Since the result of this union is archetypal Man, who is androgynous, Man must surely be an androgyne. This means that he should not really experience sexual desire (in the sense of the 'desire for the missing half' illustrated by Aristophanes' speech in the *Symposium*). In any case, as an immaterial entity, he should be asexual (unless sexual desire is interpreted as some sort of spiritual lust; Sophia's desire to know the Father in the Valentinian myth has strong sexual overtones). Furthermore, it is not clear how he could appease the sexual desire of a material entity or actually mate with her.

The gifts of the 'Governors' (subordinate Archons headed by the Demiurge, each of whom resides within a planetary sphere) cannot, I think, be

---

[23] Julian himself explains the situation as follows at *Hymn to the Mother of the Gods* 8 : Οὐκ ἄτοπον οὖν [εἰ] καὶ τὸν Ἄττιν τοῦτον ἡμίθεόν τινα εἶναι, βούλεται γὰρ δὴ καὶ ὁ μῦθος τοῦτο, μᾶλλον δὲ θεὸν μὲν τῷ παντί· πρόεισί τε γὰρ ἐκ τοῦ τρίτου δημιουργοῦ (as Bousset notes at this point 'das klingt bereits ganz gnostisch') καὶ ἐπισυνάγεται πάλιν ἐπὶ τὴν Μητέρα τῶν θεῶν μετὰ τὴν ἐκτομήν· ἐπεὶ δὲ ὅλως ῥέπειν καὶ νεύειν εἰς τὴν ὕλην δοκεῖ, θεῶν μὲν ἔσχατον, ἔξαρχον δὲ τῶν θείων γενῶν ἁπάντων οὐκ ἂν ἁμάρτοι τις αὐτὸν ὑπολαβών.

'It is not surprising that Attis is a certain demigod, for this is what the myth means, or rather he is in fact a god, because he proceeds from the third demiurge and he is called back to the mother of the gods after his castration. When he seems to wholly incline and to tend towards matter, someone who supposes him to be the last of the gods, but the first of all divine genera would not be wrong.'

[24] Segal: 1986, 38

responsible here. There is no indication that they implant sexual desire in Man, and, in fact, he falls in love with the image of his material self. Nature is not responsible for what seems to be a pre-existent sexual desire in Man, though there is no indication how it came to be there. In any case, if Nature is guilty of having tempted Man, it is equally clear that Man is only too happy to be tempted (ἐρώμενοι γὰρ ἦσαν). I think that Nature is the means by which Man brings to fulfilment his own narcissistic desires, a repetition in some sense of the role that Man plays for the First Principle. The mating of Man with Nature creates more philosophical difficulties than it solves. Ironically, it means that the highest point of world-generation, humanity, was not actually envisaged either by the Demiurge or by the First Principle. I think that the whole episode can best be explained in terms of the mythic framework of the *Poimandres*, where Man has a complete persona and is more than just an abstract philosophical entity.

The mechanics of demiurgy

At *CH* 1.17, we are provided with a description of the manner in which the elements interact during the generation of the world. Earth is the female element, water does the fertilising (and is therefore the male component), Fire allows what has been generated to mature, while Nature works as an efficient cause, taking spirit from aether and producing bodies in the form of Man. Nature confusingly takes spirit from the aether, when she already has an immaterial element in the form of enmattered Man. In most Gnostic texts, the body of Man is the product either of the Demiurge or the Archons/Governors (identified with the planetary gods), but here the human body is the product of Nature. Nature's borrowing of spirit from the aether reminds one of the relationship which Aristotle envisages between *pneuma* and aether. Pneuma appears similar to Aristotle's fifth element, although its activity focuses more in the sublunar domain.[25] The Demiurge of the *Poimandres* plays a relatively unimportant role in the cosmogonical myth. Once he has produced the Governors, he retires into a passive obscurity.

CH 1.18 outlines the mechanism of world-generation by division adopted by the supreme god:

τῆς περιόδου πεπληρωμένης ἐλύθη ὁ πάντων σύνδεσμος ἐκ βουλῆς θεοῦ· πάντα γὰρ ζῷα ἀρρενοθήλεα ὄντα διελύετο ἅμα τῷ ἀνθρώπῳ καὶ ἐγένετο

---

[25] For more on this, see Edel: 1982, 53–4 and 412 n. 22; Aristotle, *GA* and *MA*; Solmsen: 1957; Solmsen: 1961, especially 169–78.

τὰ μὲν ἀρρενικὰ ἐν μέρει, τὰ δὲ θηλυκὰ ὁμοίως. ὁ δὲ θεὸς εὐθὺς εἶπεν
ἁγίῳ λόγῳ, Αὐξάνεσθε ἐν αὐξήσει καὶ πληθύνεσθε ἐν πλήθει πάντα τὰ
κτίσματα καὶ δημιουργήματα, καὶ ἀναγνωρισάτω <ὁ> ἔννους ἑαυτὸν
ὄντα ἀθάνατον, καὶ τὸν αἴτιον τοῦ θανάτου ἔρωτα, καὶ πάντα τὰ ὄντα.

Upon the completion of the cycle, the bond of all things was dissolved by the
counsel of God. For all living creatures, being androgenous, were divided,
including humans, and part became male and in a similar manner, part
became female. But God immediately delivered a holy oration: 'increase in
increments and become numerous in numbers, all you generated things and
demiurgic productions and let the one who is thoughtful recognise that he
is immortal and that love is the cause of death and let him recognise all that
is in being'.

There is no reason why the First Principle should suddenly introduce the
division of the sexes at this point. Humans are already in existence as a result
of the fall of Man, and there seems to be no reason why the First Principle
should split them. All living beings, according to this, were originally
androgynous. In the case of Man, this is easily explained as the result of the
fall of his archetypal ancestor, but why should this be the case with other
living beings? If it was the case, as the result of the design of the Demiurge,
there seems to be no point in changing it at this stage. In the Gnostic and
Hermetic traditions, reproduction is often presented as a source of evil
and it is unclear why the First Principle should be the one to divide the
androgynes, and advocate sexual reproduction. Equally strange is the fact
that just after doing this, he then delivers a tirade against it. I think that
it is likely that it is only sexual intercourse among humans that is actually
condemned. In any case, the idea of a primordial androgynous ancestor is
not uncommon. It occurs in the Gnostic creation myth mentioned in the
Refutation of Pseudo-Hippolytus during his discussion of the Naassenes:
'For man is androgyne, they say . . . Attis was castrated . . . and has passed
over to the eternal substance above, where there is neither male nor female
but a new creation, a new man, who is androgyne' (5.7.14–15). The same
notion can also be found in biblical texts.[26] Under the influence of *Gen.*
1:27, Philo thought that humans were created in a divine image that was
either bisexual or sexually undetermined.

The mechanism of reproduction by sexual intercourse is then established
by Providence, through the instrument of Fate and 'through the cosmic
framework' (ἁρμονία).[27] As in the *Asclepius*, it is apparent that Providence
and Fate are only instruments of the supreme god, not independent entities

---

[26] Cf. *Gal.* 3.28, 6.15; *Eph.* 2:15, 4:24   [27] *CH* I.19

existing outside his control. Providence only acts after God has spoken. The allusion to Fate and the cosmic framework echoes again the *Asclepius*: the Demiurge or higher powers influence the world through the revolution of the stars.

It is difficult to understand the explanation of demiurgy presented in the *Poimandres* in terms of Greek philosophy. God appears to be both omnipotent and omniscient. He wilfully produces a world, which he then decides to oppose. The *Poimandres* never explains or resolves this paradox. To a certain extent, world-generation is presented as a *fait accompli*. However, as Segal points out, once the *Poimandres* is read in terms of myth, it becomes possible to find a solution. The god of the *Poimandres* may be omnipotent and omniscient, but he is still capable of acting contrary to his knowledge, as in myth even the chief god may act under the influence of emotion. The *Poimandres* does not attempt to conceal this paradox, but neither does the author seem to perceive the need to resolve it. As Jonas notes: 'The Plotinian descensus of Being, in some respects an analogy to the Gnostic one, proceeds through the autonomous movement of impersonal concept by an internal necessity that is its own justification. The Gnostic descensus cannot do without the contingency of subjective affect and will.'[28] In the *Poimandres*, we have a perfect example of the flaws which Plotinus perceived in Gnosticism, not merely their radical dualism, but also the emphasis on revelatory assertion, rather than rational argumentation.

The myth of the *Poimandres* is so problematic in philosophical terms as an explanation of demiurgy that there are those who prefer to read it in psychological terms. Jung regarded Gnosticism as the predecessor of alchemy. Just as alchemy sought to turn a base metal into gold, Gnosticism sought to liberate the soul from the baseness of matter. He mistakenly equated the Demiurge with Anthropos.[29] For Jung, the *Poimandres* explains not world-generation, but the development of man's psyche. The interrelation of the immaterial godhead and unordered matter represents the emergence of the ego out of the consciousness. As he comments: 'Gnosticism long ago projected this state of affairs into the heavens in the form of a metaphysical drama: ego-consciousness appearing as the vain Demiurge, who fancies himself the sole creator of the world and the self as the highest

---

[28] Jonas: 1967, 193

[29] 'The primordial figure of the quaternity coalesces for the Gnostics with the figure of the Demiurge or Anthropos. He is, as it were, the victim of his own creative act, for, when he descended into Physis, he was caught in her embrace. The image of the *anima mundi* or Original Man latent in the dark of matter expresses the presence of a transconscious centre, which because of its quaternary character and its roundness, must be regarded as a symbol of wholeness.' (Jung: 1969, 197–8.9)

unknowable God, whose emanation the Demiurge is.' Jung radically alters
the meaning of the *Poimandres* because he reads it in psychological, rather
than metaphysical terms. Whatever the merits of Jung's theory, it does
show that the *Poimandres* lends itself more easily to being read in terms
other than metaphysical and should be treated more as a myth than as
'serious' philosophy.

Other texts

CH ii attempts to discover whether God is an essence or not. At *CH* ii.6,
the author denies that God exists as a spatial area (τόπος), but rather as a
form of energy (ἐνέργεια), which is responsible for motion in the cosmos,
although he himself remains motionless. At §12, this point is reiterated,
but it appears that the Receptacle of the *Timaeus* has somehow become
equated with Aristotle's Unmoved Mover:

> τὸν οὖν τόπον τὸν ἐν ᾧ κινεῖται τὸ πᾶν, τί εἴπομεν;...Νοῦς ὅλος ἐξ
> ὅλου ἑαυτὸν ἐμπεριέχων, ἐλεύθερος σώματος παντός, ἀπλανής, ἀπαθής,
> ἀναφής, αὐτὸς ἐν ἑαυτῷ ἐστώς, χωρητικὸς τῶν πάντων καὶ σωτήριος
> τῶν ὄντων, οὗ ὥσπερ ἀκτῖνές εἰσι τὸ ἀγαθόν, ἡ ἀλήθεια, τὸ ἀρχέτυπον
> πνεύματος, τὸ ἀρχέτυπον ψυχῆς.

> What have we said concerning that place in which the universe is
> moved?... For the entire Mind encloses itself entirely, free from all body,
> unwandering, free from affectation, untouched, being at rest in itself, able
> to contain all things and preserving everything in being, so that the good,
> the truth and the archetype of spirit, as well as the archetype of soul are its
> rays.

In the Hermetic texts, τόπος has three separate functions. It is (1) the space
occupied by a body, (2) the divine *Logos* with which God fills the universe
with incorporeal powers and (3) God, as that which contains all things and
which is his own place (αὐτός ἐστι χώρα ἑαυτοῦ, κεχωρηκὼς ἑαυτόν).[30]
This Intellect, τόπος, is a god, but he is not the First God. This shift from
passive Receptacle to an independent divine entity is as interesting as it is
unnecessary. It does, however, help to explain the interaction between the
supreme transcendent God, and the cosmos. It is evident that the First God
does not occupy a place in this world, and that He is above all Intellect, as
well as all essence (§5).

The same idea can be found at *CH* v.10 where there is no space around
God because He embraces everything: οὐ τόπος ἐστὶ περὶ σέ, 'there is no

[30] Nock and Festugière: 1946, 39 n.14

space around you'.[31] At XI.18, there is the comment that if all things are contained in God, they are not contained in the same manner as in a spatial area. Finally, as Festugière points out, in the *Excerpta ex Theodoto* 34, 37, 38 ss, τόπος is used as a name for God.

At *CH* III we have an account of world-generation which parallels that of the *Poimandres*; the light elements separate themselves from the others by rising, and the heavy ones sink down, and all this division is accomplished by fire. However, here world-generation is performed by a number of subordinate Demiurges:

> ἀνῆκε δὲ ἕκαστος θεὸς διὰ τῆς ἰδίας δυνάμεως τὸ προσταχθὲν αὐτῷ, καὶ ἐγένετο θηρία τετράποδα καὶ ἑρπετὰ καὶ ἔνυδρα καὶ πτηνὰ καὶ πᾶσα σπορὰ ἔνσπορος καὶ χόρτος καὶ ἄνθους παντὸς χλόη· τὸ σπέρμα τῆς παλιγγενεσίας ἐν † ἑαυτοῖς ἐσπερμολόγουν †

> Each god sent forth by his own power that which had been assigned to him, and the four-footed and crawling beasts were generated and the aquatic and the winged and every productive seed and grass and all flowering plants. They all acquired in themselves the seeds of rebirth. (§3)

The Demiurge makes the cosmos not by hand, but by speech and through his will.[32] It is clear that this passage is modelled after *Genesis* 1.

At *CH* IV.1, we have a further discussion of the manner of world-generation:

> ἐπειδὴ τὸν πάντα κόσμον ἐποίησεν ὁ δημιουργός, οὐ χερσὶν ἀλλὰ λόγῳ, ὥστε οὕτως ὑπολάμβανε ὡς τοῦ παρόντος καὶ ἀεὶ ὄντος καὶ πάντα ποιήσαντος καὶ ἑνὸς μόνου, τῇ δὲ αὐτοῦ θελήσει δημιουργήσαντος τὰ ὄντα· τοῦτο γάρ ἐστι τὸ σῶμα ἐκείνου, οὐχ ἁπτόν, οὐδὲ ὁρατόν, οὐδὲ μετρητόν, οὐδὲ διαστατόν, οὐδὲ ἄλλῳ τινὶ σώματι ὅμοιον· οὔτε γὰρ πῦρ ἐστιν οὔτε ὕδωρ οὔτε ἀὴρ οὔτε πνεῦμα, ἀλλὰ πάντα ἀπ' αὐτοῦ. ἀγαθὸς γὰρ ὤν, <οὐ> μόνῳ ἑαυτῷ τοῦτο ἀναθεῖναι ἠθέλησε καὶ τὴν γῆν κοσμῆσαι . . .

> Since the Demiurge made the entire cosmos not by hand, but by reason/speech, so that at present you might understand him as always existing and as having made everything and as one alone, and as having crafted that which is by means of his will. For this is his body, intangible, invisible, immeasurable, unextended, dissimilar to any other body. For it is neither fire nor water nor air nor spirit, but everything comes from it. For being good, he did not wish to set this up as a votive gift for himself alone and to order the earth . . .

---

[31] Parallels to this can be found in Philo *Leg. All.* 1.44, Arnobius of Sicca, *Adversus Nationes* 1.3: 'prima enim tu causa es, locus rerum ac spatium', 'for you are the first cause, the place and space of things'. Nock and Festugière: 1946, 39 n.14

[32] 'οὐ χερσὶν ἀλλὰ λόγῳ', *CH* IV.1

Here cosmos and Demiurge are closely identified. The Demiurge's body is not the visible cosmos (as it is not sense-perceptible), but it is the source of the physical world. The cosmos can be said to be the body of the Demiurge, in so far as he is the Reason pervading the universe. As the Demiurge's body is immaterial (illustrated by the comment that it is not one of the elements) all things only come from his body in so far as he transmits the powers of the suprasensible world to the sublunar realm and orders matter. The stress on the fact that God does not create like a craftsman is noteworthy, since it echoes the comments of Plutarch that the Demiurge does not produce like a man, but through the use of mathematical principles. It seems here that the Demiurge merely has to command and matter obeys him. This is stated again at *CH* v.4, where Hermes acknowledges that matter is deficient but nevertheless it obeys the Maker.

Imperfection in the world occurs when bodies are no longer able to contain the Monad (*CH* iv.11). This same idea occurs throughout the corpus. At *CH* vi.2, there is no place in that which has come to be for the Good. The world is not good since it is in motion, but it is not bad since it is immortal. At *CH* vi.3, the world is only good in relative terms; absolute goodness in the material realm is impossible. This same idea is also expressed at *CH* x.10: even if the world is beautiful, it is not good since it is constructed from matter. CH xi.3 is more optimistic – the cosmos is ordered by Eternity, which is a constitutent of God's wisdom, by introducing immortality and permanence into matter.

CH viii *and* ix

CH viii presents the Stoic idea that there is no such thing as absolute death, merely the dissolution of elements. God generated the world because He wanted to adorn the beings lower down on the ontological scale with every quality (§3). He made the world in the form of a sphere which is immortal. The only point worthy of note is the manner in which God constructs the world modelled on the intelligible archetypes implanting 'in the sphere the qualities of forms, shutting them up as in a cave'.[33] This comment is made against the background of the usual platitudes concerning the disorder of matter and its retention of this quality even after it has been ordered. The reference appears to indicate that the images of the Forms become enmattered against their will, but this line is probably a sophisticated literary allusion. It recalls not only Plato's myth of the *Republic* (514–17),

---

[33] *CH* viii.3

but also looks forward to Porphyry's exegesis of *Odyssey* 13.102–12, *On the Cave of the Nymphs*, where the darkness of the cave represents the unstable state of matter.[34] In Mithraism, the cave also represented the world.[35]

CH IX shares numerous parallels with *CH* VIII. It relates the three terms: Man (§1–2), World (§6–8) and God (§9) in the same manner. God is the father of the world, just as the world is the father (surely mother would be more appropriate) of the beings which it contains.[36] The treatise also refutes the notion that God is unthinking and without thought (§3–6) since being all things and in all things, He is necessarily intellective. §3 outlines the influence of God on individuals:

> ὁ γὰρ νοῦς κύει πάντα τὰ νοήματα, ἀγαθὰ μέν, ὅταν ὑπὸ τοῦ θεοῦ τὰ σπέρματα λάβῃ, ἐναντία δέ, ὅταν ὑπό τινος τῶν δαιμονίων, μηδενὸς μέρους τοῦ κόσμου κενοῦ ὄντος δαίμονος † τῷ ὑπὸ τοῦ θεοῦ πεφωτισμένῳ δαίμονι † ὅστις ὑπεισελθὼν ἔσπειρε τῆς ἰδίας ἐνεργείας τὸ σπέρμα, καὶ ἐκύησεν ὁ νοῦς τὸ σπαρέν, μοιχείας, φόνους, πατροτυπίας, ἱεροσυλίας, ἀσεβείας, ἀγχόνας, κατὰ κρημνῶν καταφοράς, καὶ ἄλλα πάντα ὅσα δαιμόνων ἔργα.

> For Mind conceives every thought: the good, when Mind receives seeds from God and the opposite, when they are received from some *daimon* and there is no part of the cosmos which is without a *daimon*, which entering imperceptibly sows the seed of its own activity and Mind conceives what has been sown, adulteries, murders, beating one's own father, temple-robberies, ungodliness, suicide by hanging or jumping off a cliff and other works of *daimones* similar in kind.

Here Mind is clearly not the First Principle, as in the *Poimandres*. The positing of evil *daimones* helps to protect God from responsibility for the existence of evil. The author then adopts the Socratic stance that God is the cause only of a few things, i.e. of the Good: 'Few seeds come from God, but they are potent and beautiful and good.'

The author of *CH* IX believes firmly in the goodness of the cosmos, and therefore in the goodness of the Demiurge.[37] It is only the sublunar region which is evil. The products of the Demiurge are originally good, but the motion of the cosmos soils some with vice (ῥυπαίνουσα τῇ κακίᾳ, *CH* IX.5). This account echoes that of the *Timaeus*, God, being good, fashions everything for the best, but it is Necessity which is responsible for evil. This cosmic motion is rather vague and could indicate either recalcitrant matter or malign astral influence.

---

[34] Porphyry is only building on previous exegeses, such as that of Cronius.
[35] Copenhaver: 1992, 149
[36] Nock and Festugière: 1946, 92   [37] *CH* IX.4

All matter is used in world-generation. The cosmos is a closed system in which the matter that it contains is continually reused, as cosmic motion renews and dissolves everything. God uses the cosmos as an instrument (ὄργανον),[38] which makes everything itself (ἵνα πάντα παρ᾽ ἑαυτῷ) through preserving (φυλάττων) the seeds which it has received from God. After God has set everything in order, the cosmos is capable of functioning on its own to maintain the life contained within it as a sort of second Demiurge; it is explicitly referred to as a craftsman of life (δημιουργὸς ζωῆς). Just as in the *Poimandres*, cosmic motion was the means by which the Demiurge produces, so here too it is the mechanism by which the cosmos ensures the preservation of life; engaging in a sort of continual temporal world-generation, as it were, through its motion.[39]

The motion of the cosmos produces various kinds of bodies from different combinations of the elements; heavier bodies are more composite and lighter bodies are simpler.[40] God transmits the Forms to the cosmos, which is only responsible for producing the individual instantiations. The cosmos does not produce the type, but by its revolutions it modifies each type to produce new individuals, and by this process ensures that each kind is preserved, since it is continually replenished. This partnership between God and the cosmos is stressed in the presentation of a father–son relationship between the two; the cosmos' role as a secondary Demiurge is represented by the claim that the cosmos is the father of the things within it.[41]

This text seems to do no more than reproduce Platonic platitudes, but it is precisely this fact which renders it noteworthy. Unlike most Gnostic or Hermetic texts, there is no separation here between the First Principle and the Demiurge. Were it not for the fact that this text was attributed to Hermes Trismegistus, one would have difficulty claiming that it belongs to the same tradition as the *Poimandres*. Even *CH* VIII, with which *CH* IX shares so many correspondences, draws a distinction between a First and Second God. Though the Second God is clearly the cosmos, it is stressed that man's relationship with the First God is of a far superior order.

CH x

CH x.3 returns to the more familiar Hermetic concept, distinguishing between the Demiurge and the Good:

---

[38] *CH* IX.6
[39] One is reminded of the Aristotelian notion of a motor that is engaged in continuous noetic activity in order to ensure continuous, eternal motion in the world (*Met.* L.6).
[40] *CH* IX.7   [41] *CH* IX.8

αἴτιος δὲ ὁ πατὴρ τῶν τέκνων καὶ τῆς σπορᾶς καὶ τῆς τροφῆς, τὴν ὄρεξιν
λαβὼν τοῦ ἀγαθοῦ διὰ τοῦ ἡλίου· τὸ γὰρ ἀγαθόν ἐστι τὸ ποιητικόν·
τοῦτο δὲ οὐ δυνατὸν ἐγγενέσθαι ἄλλῳ τινὶ ἢ μόνῳ ἐκείνῳ, τῷ μηδὲν μὲν
λαμβάνοντι, πάντα δὲ θέλοντι εἶναι·

The Father is the cause of the insemination and the raising of his children,
having received the desire for the Good from the sun. For the Good is the
principle of generation. And it is not possible for the Good to come to be in
anything other that the one who alone receiving nothing, desires all things
to be.[42]

This is the doctrine found at *CH* I.11; the First *Nous* remains the supreme
cause of world-generation, even if he produces through his son, the *Nous*
Demiurge. In this context, I prefer Festugière's translation of ἀγαθόν ἐστι
τὸ ποιητικόν '*le Bien . . . le principle efficient*', which stresses the demiurgic
role of the First Principle. The boundary between God the Father and the
Good is blurred: 'and God the Father is the Good in that he "wills" all
things to be'.[43] The First Principle is even described as the one managing
the universe like a statesman and through the use of Intellect: 'And this is
the regulation of the universe, dependent upon the nature of the one and
extending through the one mind.'[44]

At *CH* XI.2, God generates the world with the assistance of another agent:
'God makes Eternity, and Eternity makes the cosmos; the cosmos makes
Time and Time makes generation.'[45] Eternity is described as a power of god
(δύναμις δὲ τοῦ θεοῦ (§3)) and Eternity is not only its creator, but also the
guarantor of survival, because Eternity is imperishable. Eternity here retains
the same signification as philosophical Eternity, as the immaterial model
from which cosmic time was formed. However, it has been transformed
into a hypostasis of God, and functions as a co-Demiurge. It is a kind
of Hermetic hybrid between divine wisdom and the World-Soul, since it
is Eternity which sets the world in order by introducing immortality and
duration (τὴν ἀθανασίαν καὶ διαμονὴν (§3)) to matter. Eternity, however,
is not an independent agent, but is completely dependent upon God (§4).
Using Providence, Necessity, and Nature, Eternity is able to preserve the
world. God and his energy (ἡ δὲ ἐνέργεια θεοῦ (§5)) are responsible for
the actions of eternity, and so there is no question, as in the *Timaeus* or

[42] This image resurfaces at *CH* XVI.18, where God is described as the father of all, and the sun is
identified as the Demiurge. God there provides the Sun with his craftsmanship by providing him
with the Good (§17).
[43] ὁ δὲ θεὸς καὶ πατὴρ καὶ τὸ ἀγαθὸν τῷ εἶναι τὰ πάντα.
[44] *CH* X.23 καὶ αὕτη ἡ τοῦ παντὸς διοίκησις, ἠρτημένη ἐκ τῆς τοῦ ἑνὸς φύσεως καὶ διήκουσα δι' ἑνὸς
τοῦ νοῦ·
[45] ὁ θεὸς αἰῶνα ποιεῖ, ὁ αἰὼν δὲ τὸν κόσμον, ὁ κόσμος δὲ χρόνον, ὁ χρόνος δὲ γένεσιν.

the *Poimandres*, of Necessity or of Nature acting as independent entities which thwart God's plan. The moon also seems to function as an agent in the ordering of matter: (σελήνην δὲ ἐκείνων πρόδρομον πάντων, ὄργανον τῆς φύσεως, τὴν κάτω ὕλην μεταβάλλουσαν, 'The moon races ahead of them all, the instrument of nature, transforming the matter below' (§7)). The moon must just act in the same way as the cosmic spheres elsewhere in the *Corpus Hermeticum*, as the mechanism by which the higher powers are able to regulate lower beings.

CH xi.9 continues the line of argumentation that these entities are responsible to God, by arguing against the dualism of various Gnostic sects:

> ἐνδιαφόρων γὰρ καὶ πολλῶν οὐσῶν τῶν κινήσεων καὶ τῶν σωμάτων οὐχ ὁμοίων, μιᾶς δὲ κατὰ πάντων ταχύτητος τεταγμένης, ἀδύνατον δύο ἢ πλείους ποιητὰς εἶναι· μία γὰρ ἐπὶ πολλῶν οὐ τηρεῖται τάξις· ζῆλος δὲ τοῖς πολλοῖς παρέπεται τοῦ κρείττονος.

> For motions are varying and numerous and bodies are not similar, and a single speed has been regulated for each of them, for it is impossible for there to be two or more makers. For it is not possible to maintain a single order amongst many. For envy of the better is the consequence of multiplicity.

The text adopts a classic Aristotelian formulation against the existence of multiple Demiurges; if there is one order, there can only be one Maker, established at Arist. *Metaphysics* l.10,[46] (though naturally this applies to coordinate, rather than subordinate demiurges). The text argues against the possibility of a Demiurge of immortal entities and a Demiurge of mortal ones; a position which in fact runs counter to that adopted by the *Timaeus*. Since matter is one and soul is one, the treatise cannot envisage the possibility of two Demiurges. The One God is the sole producer of soul and all living beings provided with it (*CH* xi.11). In fact, giving life to all living things and providing them with movement takes the place of motion and life for God (§17).

CH xii.14 adopts the same position. The entire succession of entities sometimes seen as exercising an influence on causality independent of the Demiurge are placed firmly under his control. Necessity, Providence and Nature are the instruments of the organisation of matter. God energises matter by permeating it (§22–3). This viewpoint may actually be a positive reading of the *Poimandres* myth, where Man is, after all, a part of the godhead. The same notion can be found at *CH* xiv.6, where the entity

---

[46] *Cf.* also Cic., *ND* ii.43–4; ii.90.

who generates and the one which is generated are described as one in their unification (ἕν ἐστι τῇ ἐνώσει).

CH xiv.7 accepts cosmic evil as a necessary fact of generation:

> . . . αὐτῷ δὲ τῷ ποιοῦντι οὐδὲν κακὸν οὐδ᾽ αἰσχρὸν νομιζόμενον. ταῦτα γάρ ἐστι τὰ πάθη τὰ τῇ γενέσει παρεπόμενα, ὥσπερ ὁ ἰὸς τῷ χαλκῷ καὶ ὁ ῥύπος τῷ σώματι. ἀλλ᾽ οὔτε ἰὸν ὁ χαλκουργὸς ἐποίησεν, οὔτε τὸν ῥύπον οἱ γεννήσαντες, οὔτε τὴν κακίαν ὁ θεός. ἡ δὲ τῆς γενέσεως ἐπιδιαμονὴ καθάπερ ἐξανθεῖν ποιεῖ καὶ διὰ τοῦτο ἐποίησε τὴν μεταβολὴν ὁ θεός, ὥσπερ ἀνακάθαρσιν τῆς γενέσεως.

> . . . but do not believe that there is something evil or shameful about the maker himself. For such things are byproducts of generation, just like rust on bronze or filth on the body, but the bronzesmith did not make the rust, nor did the parents make the dirt, nor did God make evil. However, the continued existence of generation makes it degenerate, on account of which God made change for the repurification of generation.

The Demiurge combats evil by eternal temporal generation in order to maintain the *status quo*. It is as if matter is continually attempting to break its bonds and the Demiurge has to continually order it. This passage also counters the belief of some Gnostics that extending divine unity into creative diversity would taint the supreme god, leading to the standard Gnostic postulation of the Demiurge.

Asclepius

The *Asclepius* is the Latin translation of the Greek treatise *Logos teleios* (Perfect Discourse). Lydus and Lactantius both reproduce passages from it in Greek.[47] The *terminus ante quem* for the Greek text, then, is the early fourth century, but a Latin version of the *sermo perfectus* corresponding to our version of *Asclepius* can first be found in Augustine's *City of God* (413–26). Due to the number of early references to this text which come from North African Christians, the Latin version may have been produced there. In any case, the treatise covers a great many topics, leading some scholars to suggest that the *Asclepius* is a synthesis of other works.

At §2–3 the text outlines the composition of the world from the four elements.

As elsewhere in the Hermetic corpus, it is fire that is represented as the life-giving element. Most interesting of all is the reference to 'one matter,

---

[47] Copenhaver: 1992, 214 – *Divine Institutes* 2.14.6; 4.6.4; 7.18.4 (*cf. Asclep.* 28,8,26); *De mens.* 4.7.149 (*cf. Asclep.* 19, 39, 28).

one soul and one god'; the *Asclepius* exhibits monotheistic tendencies; even though it does refer to numerous gods; as elsewhere in the Hermetic corpus, these seem to be understood as merely instantiations of the supreme God.

At *Asclepius* §8, the author outlines the manner of world-generation:

> When the master and framer of everything, whom we rightly call God, made a second after himself, who is able to be seen and perceived . . . this second after himself seemed beautiful to him, since it was most full of the goodness of all things and he loved it as the offspring of his divinity. Therefore, he was so great and good, that he wished that there might be another who might be able to gaze upon him, whom he had made from himself and immediately he made Man, the imitator of his reason and diligence.

This passage outlines a different method of generation from that contained in the *Poimandres*. The First God is evidently the Demiurge, since he is the shaper of all things and the text goes on to state that God's goodness is the reason for his production. The Second God seems to adopt somewhat the role of Man in the *Poimandres*; God falls in love with him as a reflection of his own beauty. In any case, this passage was misread by Christian interpreters such as Lactantius, who cites it as evidence that Hermes Trismegistus was aware that the supreme God had a son.[48] The Second God here is obviously the cosmos, as is explicitly stated at §10. Scott viewed this passage as modelled on *Tim.* 29e–31b, 37c, 92c and it is easy to observe numerous correspondences between both texts, particularly the emphasis given to the concept of Plenitude.

The passage then goes on to outline the manner in which God made man:

> And so when he 'had made' man *ousīodes* and observed that he was not able to take care for all things, unless he covered him with an earthly shelter, he covered him with a bodily home and he directed that humans be of such a kind, combining and mixing both natures in one to the extent that was appropriate. And so he formed man from the nature of soul and body, that is from the eternal and mortal, in order that the animal so formed might prove satisfactory to both his origins and might admire and adore the celestial things and might care for and govern earthly things.

Again here, it is the First Principle who functions as the Demiurge. The description of the mingling of two substances of a separate order recalls Plato's account of the blending of soul substance out of Sameness and Difference in the *Timaeus*. The *Asclepius* seems to take a more positive

---

[48] Lactantius cites from *Logos teleios – Divine Institutes* 4.6.4 – Copenhaver: 1992, 222

stance regarding the cosmos than is usual in Hermetism. Here mankind's physical incarnation is not the result of some kind of fall (as it is in the *Poimandres*), but rather part of the rational design of a demiurgic First Principle. The material wrapping (*mundano integimento*) is not regarded as a prison, but rather as a mechanism allowing Man to fulfil his designated role in the ontological scheme.

The conflict between Reason and Necessity found in Plato's *Timaeus*, which left its mark on many other Platonic metaphysical schemes with more pronounced dualistic tendencies, is opposed by the author of the *Asclepius* (§8): 'Necessity follows God's pleasure; result attends upon his will. That anything agreed by God should become disagreeable to him is incredible since he would have known long before that he would agree and that it was to be'. Here there is no question of any entity being capable of opposing the supreme God. The passage, unfortunately, does not really explain the mechanism of demiurgic causality: the will of God is itself sufficient to produce the end result. God generates Man as a 'well-ordered world'.[49] This is clearly modelled on Plato's description of man as a microcosm of the well-ordered world in the *Timaeus*.

A more detailed description of demiurgy is provided at §14. The two standard Platonic principles are posited: God and a pre-existent matter, which contains some kind of motion of its own. (The text refers to a spirit existing within it.) The account is garbled at this point: 'spirit was in matter, but it was not in matter, as it was in God'.[50] It is difficult to find a philosophical explanation for this and perhaps the best solution is to regard this as an attempt to create the illusion of a religious mystery, especially since the text goes on to make further statements in a similar vein: 'But *hylē* (or the nature of matter) and spirit, though from the beginning they seem not to have come to be, nonetheless possess in themselves the power and nature of their coming to be and procreating. For the beginning of fertility is in the quality of nature, which possesses in itself the power and the material for conceiving and giving birth.' This statement is problematic. It not only makes matter a co-Demiurge with God, but it states that nature is capable of production itself. In the *Poimandres*, Nature is incapable of world-generation herself, but requires Man. The Demiurge must not be the producer of soul, if that is what the author means by spirit here. Since matter possesses spirit, there may be some kind of idea of matter attempting to order itself by responding to the upper world and attempting to imitate it.

[49] *Asclepius* 10   [50] trans. Copenhaver

The lesser gods also seem to play a limited role in demiurgic causality:

> There are gods who are leaders of all classes, after these follow gods, whose
> *ousia* is a leader; these are sensible gods and they are similar to their double
> origin and they produce all things throughout sensible nature, one through
> the medium of another and each one of them illuminates his own work.
> The *ousiarch* [First Principle of the Essence] of heaven is Jupiter, for through
> heaven Jupiter supplies life to all things. The *ousiarch* of the sun is light, for
> the bounty of light pours down upon us through the sphere of the sun. The
> Thirty-Six, which are called horoscopes, that is the stars which are always
> fixed in the same place, have as their *ousiarch* or leader Pantomorphos or
> Omniform, who makes diverse forms in the different classes. What are called
> the seven spheres have as their *ousiarchs* or leaders what they call Fortune
> and *Heimarmenē*, by which all things change according to the law of nature
> and the surest stability, disturbed by everlasting variation. Air is the true
> instrument or mechanism of all, by means of which all things are made; its
> *ousiarch* is the second ... (§19)

Here we have a distinction between hypercosmic intelligible gods and cosmic sensible gods, introduced in the passage preceding the one cited.[51]
The term *ousiarchēs* may be a translation of an Egyptian term. In the
manuscripts five *ousiarcha*i are mentioned: Jupiter, Light, *Pantomorphos,
Heimarmenē* and a Second (?). A second Zeus, perhaps, would fill the
lacuna here. The five sensible gods are: Heaven, Sun, and the thirty-six
(the Decans), seven planetary spheres and Air.[52] Each sensible god is paired
with a corresponding intelligible god, but unfortunately a lacuna in the
manuscripts prevents us from being certain whether there were further
pairings of sensible and intelligible gods. Scott modified the schema to
produce the following pairings of intelligible and sensible gods: (Pantomorphos, Decans), (*Heimarmenē*, Spheres), (Zeus *Neato*s (probably Hades
ruling the air), sublunar atmosphere), (Zeus Chthonios, Earth and Water).
Scott compared this to similar structures in the Stoic Posidonius and the
Platonist Xenocrates, although Festugière did not accept either Scott's
position that *ousia* was Stoic corporeal substance or Murray's that it was
Platonic intelligible essence.[53] Festugière compared *ousia* here to its usage in
Iamblichus, designating secondary deities, and I think that this is probably
the case. I am less clear concerning the manner in which air can be used
as the mechanism of all the gods, unless as the lowest-ranking sensible god

---

[51] 'There are many kinds of gods, of whom one part is intelligible and the other sensible. Gods are
not said to be intelligible because they are considered beyond the reach of our faculties; in fact, we
are more conscious of these intelligible gods than of those we call visible, as you will be able to see
from our discussion if you pay attention.'
[52] Copenhaver: 1992, 231–2   [53] Copenhaver: 1992, 232

all connections between all other entities in the ontological system and the higher-ranking gods have to take place through it. For example, the light produced by the planets is radiated into the air, and transmitted by the air to the earth.

The *ousiarchai* or 'Departmental Rulers' have specifically delineated functions. The uppermost *ousiarch* transmits the generic forms of the ideal world to the *ousiarch* below him, to be modified by individual differences before being implanted in matter to form individual bodies. The passage can equally be read in terms of Stoic doctrine: that the outermost *ousiarch* emits fire, which passes through the chain of lower-ranking *ousiarchai*, before combining with air to form πνεῦμα. The *Asclepius* attempts to combine elements from different philosophical schools, but they are not always completely harmonised and the details do not seem to have been fully worked out, as is the case here.[54]

The individual forms are bestowed by the *ousiarch* of the fixed stars. He does this through the revolution of his sphere which modifies the form-type, since each individual is born under a different aspect of the Decans. *Heimarmenē*, the *ousiarch* of the planets, governs the alterations that the form will undergo during its existence. Air receives all these influences and then redistributes them. The *ousiarch* of earth and sea supplies nutriment to the material bodies.

The reason Scott attributed this scheme to a Stoic source was that the nearest analogies can be found in Stoic systems.[55] Zeus is named here as the god who governs the cosmos, which is more characteristic of Stoicism[56] than Hermetism, where Zeus normally only occurs as the name of the planet Jupiter.[57] The scheme is vaguely reminiscent of the myth of the *Phaedrus*, and Scott suggests that Xenocrates (c. 330 BC) may have been inspired to produce his version under the influence of Orphic theology.[58] (Xenocrates' system in which the World-Soul receives the Forms and

---

[54] Scott: 1968, 109   [55] Scott: 1968, 110

[56] For example DL. 7.88: ὁ νόμος ὁ κοινός, ὅσπερ ἐστὶν ὁ ὀρθὸς λόγος, διὰ πάντων ἐρχόμενος, ὁ αὐτὸς ὢν τῷ Διί, 'the common law which is correct reason, pervading everything, is identical with this Zeus.'

[57] *Kore Kosmou* 28

[58] Xenocrates, *Testimonia, doctrina et fragmenta* 216: ἦ καὶ Ξενοκράτης Δία τὸν ἐν μὲν τοῖς κατὰ ταὐτὰ καὶ ὡσαύτως ἔχουσιν ὕπατον καλεῖ νέατον δὲ τὸν ὑπὸ σελήνην, 'and Xenocrates calls the uppermost Zeus . . . and the lowest that below the moon'. See also Clement of Alexandria, *Strom.* 5.14.116: Ξενοκράτης δὲ . . . τὸν μὲν ὕπατον Δία, τὸν δὲ νέατον καλῶν, ἔμφασιν πατρὸς ἀπολείπει καὶ υἱοῦ, 'and Xenocrates . . . in referring to the supreme and inferior Zeus, leaves behind an indication of the Father and Son.' A different scheme is attributed to Xenocrates by Aetius (second-century BC doxographer), Diels *Doxogr. Gr.* 304: ἀρέσκει δὲ καὶ αὐτῷ <θείας εἶναι δυνάμεις Zeller> καὶ ἐνδιήκειν τοῖς ὑλικοῖς στοιχείοις. τούτων δὲ τὴν μὲν <δι' ἀέρος ἐνεργοῦσαν δύναμιν "Ηραν Meineke> ἀειδῆ ('Ἅιδην Diels) προσαγορεύει, τὴν δὲ διὰ τοῦ ὑγροῦ Ποσειδῶνα, τὴν δὲ διὰ τῆς

projects them upon matter is also derivable from a non-literal reading of the *Timaeus*).[59]

The scheme presented here exhibits some differences with the type of metaphysical speculation found in Stoicism. Firstly, the Stoics did not posit the existence of incorporeal beings, while the author of our treatise postulates two classes of gods, with the *ousiarchs* as νοητοὶ θεοί. The Hermetic scheme also postulates a supracosmic god in addition to the cosmic god found in Stoicism.

The *De Mysteriis 8.2* contains a summary of a theological system which has pretensions to be from Egyptian sacred writings, but which is more likely from a more recent Neoplatonist interpretation of the 'Books of Thoth'.[60] The author calls the First God of the system (the ἕν of Plotinus) νοητάρχης, as the ἀρχή of τὰ νοητά and the Second God (Plotinian νοῦς), αὐτάρχης as the cause of himself, as well as οὐσιοπάτωρ in his role as ἀρχὴ τῆς οὐσίας, the Demiurge of the sensible world. The system of the *De Mysteriis* contains sufficient significant differences from that of the *Asclepius* for it to be unlikely that either system was derived from the other. However, the similarity of terminology leads one to believe that they were modelled on an earlier system using the term *ousiarch*.[61]

Scott's hypothesis concerning the origin of this system is that Posidonius' list of departmental gods (first century BC) was reproduced, with modifications, by the Egyptian Stoic Chaeremon (c. 50 AD), who may have introduced the Decani and the term οὐσιάρχης. In Stoic terminology, and that of Posidonius, οὐσία is synonymous with ὕλη. It seems, therefore, that the *ousiarchs* of the *Asclepius* are the overseers of material substance: fire, air, earth and water.

All the various entities in the ontological system are interconnected into a harmonious whole: 'mortals are attached to immortals and sensibles to sensibles'.[62] The contradiction between the monotheistic stance adopted at the commencement of the treatise and the postulated existence of many gods is reconciled: 'the whole of it complies with the supreme governor, the

---

γῆς φυτοσπόρον Δήμητρα. ταῦτα δὲ χορηγήσας τοῖς Στωικοῖς κ.τ.λ., 'and he expresses the opinion that there are divine powers and that they are pervaded by material elements. And of these he calls the formless power active in the air Hera, and that active in moisture Poseidon and that active in the plant-bearing earth Demeter; and, in this, he followed the lead of the Stoics.' The Orphic verses that may have influenced Xenocrates can be found in Stob. 1.I. 23, vol. I, p. 29 W.: Ζεὺς πρῶτος γένετο, Ζεὺς ὕστατος ἀργικέραυνος, Ζεὺς κεφαλή, Ζεὺς μέσσα, Διὸς δ' ἐκ πάντα τέτυκται·,'Zeus was born first, Zeus the last with vivid lightning, Zeus the head, Zeus the middle, and from Zeus all things are born.' Dillon suggests that Aetius was attempting 'to make sense of an already garbled text'. Dillon: 2003a, 103
[59] Dillon: 2003, 105   [60] Scott: 1968, 113   [61] Scott: 1968, 114   [62] *Asclepius* 19

master, so that really there are not many but rather one'.[63] The *Asclepius* is not so much monotheistic as syncretistic. All the lesser deities are really just the result of the volition of the supreme god.

Having examined the hierarchy of deities, it now remains to consider spirit, as the mechanism by which these deities act upon matter (§16–17):

> Spirit supplies and animates everything in the world, just like an instrument or mechanism, it is subjected to the will of the highest god. This is a sufficient level of understanding for us for the present. Understood by mind alone, the god who is called the highest is the ruler and governor of that sensible god, who embraces within himself all place, all substance of things and the whole matter of things that generates and creates and every sort of quality and quantity. Indeed Spirit rouses and governs all kinds in the world, and each in accordance with the nature which has been allotted to it by God. Hylē or matter is the Receptacle of all things and agitates and concetrates them and God is their governor. And he apportions to all things in the world as much as is necessary for each one of them. He fills everything with his spirit, breathing into each one in accordance with its natural quality.

Spirit is the mechanism by which the First Principle acts on matter. §17 reiterates Plato's standpoint in the *Timaeus* that the sensible cosmos occupies the Receptacle and uses up all available matter. *Agitatio atque frequentatio*, 'agitation and concentration' denotes a much more active agent than matter which passively, as a *receptaculum*, 'receives' the Forms. Spirit plays some role in the nourishment of soul – perhaps by allowing it to communicate with entities higher up on the ontological scale, since it is the instrument of the supreme God.[64]

After making the gods, God uses a mixture of 'the more corrupt part of matter' and of the divine to make man. The account of the generation of Man parallels the *Poimandres*, where even though Man is produced after the heavenly gods, he is the one whom God loves most. Just as there he is better than the Governors, the same situation is observable here: 'for among all living things God recognized mankind by the unique reason and learning through which humans could banish and spurn the vices of bodies and he made them reach for immortality as the hope and intention'.[65]

However, what is most interesting here is the description of Necessity as the generation of the First Principle in order to control the lesser deities. It is described as an order framed in law to prevent the gods from becoming detached from learning and understanding and plays no role in limiting the scope of the Demiurge's production. However, it seems that in the

---

[63] *Asclepius* 19   [64] *Asclepius* 18   [65] *Asclepius* 19

Asclepius, the role played by Necessity in the *Timaeus* is taken over by *Heimarmenē*.[66] This is defined as 'the necessity in all events' and it collaborates with Necessity. *Heimarmenē* begins everything and Necessity forces these productions into activity, thereby producing order.[67] Interestingly, *Heimarmenē* is a creation of the Demiurge, not an opposed evil or recalcitrant principle. *Heimarmenē* must be equivalent to the Fate regarded as originating from the circles of the Governors elsewhere in the Hermetic corpus, though the author of the *Asclepius* is not so specific. It seems somewhat akin to a separate entity which assists the Demiurge in world-generation, using order and necessity. These three principles *Heimarmenē*, Necessity and Order, resemble Xenocrates' triad of Fates.[68] *Heimarmenē* and Necessity are agents of the Demiurge who assist him in the generation of the cosmos and are completely under his control. *Heimarmenē* seems to be the entity that acts on matter, sowing the seed of generation (perhaps even soul) into it. Necessity is the divine plan which seems to compel matter into subjection. This vitiates the image hinted at early on, where matter seemed to respond itself to the generative impulse. Their activity is circular, so that it is impossible to observe the beginning of their activity, which hints at continual temporal generation – just as in the *Statesman* myth disorder creeps into the world at regular intervals and God has to intervene.

In fact, §26 outlines this possibility, during the old age of the world, when '*the god whose power is primary and governor of the First God*' will restore the world to its original state, destroying vice by flood, fire or disease. The italicised quote is problematic. The Latin reads *deus primipotens et unius gubernator dei*. *Gubernator* is the Latin translation of the Greek δημιουργός. The problem is that the text does not explain what the Demiurge is first in relation to. Lactantius' Greek reads ὁ κύριος καὶ πατήρ καὶ θεός καὶ τοῦ πρώτου καὶ ἕνος θεοῦ δημιουργός: 'The lord and father and god and Demiurge of the first and one god'. Amongst the numerous attempts to solve this passage, we can note that of Scott, substituting τοῦ κόσμου for the underlined portion of the Greek. Gersh saw in τοῦ πρώτου the positing of a consubstantial relationship between the first and second principles, but that in the wider context the Second God is the cosmos and is only first

---

[66] The notion of ἀνάγκη occurs elsewhere in Plato, not just in the *Timaeus*, often in connection with Fate. *Cf. Rep.* 566a, (the necessary transformation of a protector into a tyrant, through the allegory of the transformation of a cannibal into a wolf), or *Laws* 904c, where the context is the necessary change of those things that share in soul. The notion is also to be found at *Stat.* 272e (the turning backwards of the earth by fate (εἱμαρμένη) and innate desire, after the helmsman of the universe (τοῦ παντός ὁ κυβερνήτης) 'drops the tiller'.

[67] *Asclepius* 39   [68] *Asclepius* 40

in the sense of being the first product of the Demiurge.[69] I am grateful for Dillon's suggestion to take *demiourgos* with the genitive phrase which precedes it as 'Craftsman *in the sense of* or *as the representative of* the first and one god'. Otherwise, the text must be corrupt.

The general sense of this passage at first reading appears to be one of continual temporal generation. The Demiurge has to re-order the world as disorder starts to creep in over the course of time. However, I think that this is one occasion when the text has to be read both with an eye to the Hermetic tradition and to that of Greek philosophy. In the Hermetic corpus there are frequent references to the coming neglect of the ancient Egyptian religion and the subsequent desertion of Egypt by the traditional gods. This was interpreted by Christian readers as a pagan prediction of the future fall of their religion, but is probably due to tension felt by Egyptians of the period when confronted with Hellenic culture, which was increasingly becoming dominant in the region. A hint that this is what the author had in mind can be found in the reference to irreverence and disregard of the good which will soon take over the world.

Placing *Heimarmenē* and Necessity under the authority of the supreme God leaves the author of the *Asclepius* with a problem: how to account for evil in the world. At §40, he notes that accident and chance are mixed in with everything material. However, the *Asclepius* adopts the response of a manual for spiritual progress and not that of a metaphysical treatise. The author makes little effort to explain the origin of evil, instead stressing the fact that the Demiurge did what he could to protect humanity against evil by endowing it with enough intelligence to avoid its effects.[70]

Clearly, it is problematic to state that nothing in the world can come into being that is not pleasing to God and then subsequently to state that evil is an inherent part of the world, but God cannot really be held responsible for its existence. Evil must originate from somewhere and quite clearly at this point it is useful to place the blame on the philosopher's favourite scapegoat, matter: 'Just as there is a fertile quality in the nature of matter, so also is the same matter equally fertile in malice' (§15). Here the standard anti-materialistic stance of Hermetic literature creeps in. Since matter is not the production of the Demiurge, as is explicitly stated in §15 and elsewhere in the *Asclepius*, this absolves him neatly from responsibility for the existence of evil. In spite of the anti-material strain observable here, the author's attitude remains somewhat ambivalent: matter is still fertile and productive.

---

[69] Copenhaver: 1992, 243–4   [70] *Asclepius* 16

Conclusion

Apart from the *Poimandres* and the *Asclepius*, the *Corpus Hermeticum* can, in general, be viewed as a sort of 'school-level' philosophy. It does not provide a particularly sophisticated account of demiurgy. However, it does offer interesting insights into the perceptions of the Platonically-influenced underworld. The texts are often contradictory, since they cater to initiates at different stages of their spiritual progress. One can distinguish two separate trends, although I am reluctant to divide the texts into separate categories. Firstly, there are texts such as the *Poimandres* and the *Asclepius* with a much more sophisticated version of demiurgic causality, which see the need for a generative entity distinct from, even if dependent upon, the supreme principle. The other texts tend to stress the unity of world-generation and regard all the other generative entities merely as agents, or better yet, as tools of the supreme God.

The more pro-cosmic treatises can probably be regarded as intended for earlier on in the initiate's career. The basic version that emerges from their more sophisticated counterparts is of a First Principle, which must be regarded as the efficient cause of world-generation. He does not always employ a Demiurge (his son) to generate on his behalf, and in such cases he relies on a team of secondary, generative entities formed from all the usual suspects: Providence, Necessity, Fate and Eternity. There is no notion that these act independently of his volition and so they must accomplish their tasks with his approbation.

Indeed, world-generation itself is not really a mistake; the problem is that Man became enmattered, and texts such as the *Poimandres* do not fully explain why the omniscient and omnipotent First Principle should allow the fall of a hypostasis. By submitting Necessity and the Demiurge to the control of the First Principle, one is left only with the recalcitrance of matter as an explanation for the existence of evil in the material world. This is not utilised very much by the Hermetic authors, and in the *Poimandres* it is clear that the dissolution of the godhead begins with the emanation of Man, for which God would have to bear full responsibility. In the Hermetic corpus, we are no longer dealing with the abstract entities of Greek philosophy, but with emotional characters in the drama of world-generation; a transformation which affects even the supreme god. This has to be the favoured explanation for elucidating demiurgic causality in the Hermetic tradition, rather than a philosophical one.

CHAPTER 8

The ignorant Demiurge
Valentinus and the Gnostics

Introduction

I am aware of the current trend, particularly in North American scholarship, to question the utility of a term such as Gnosticism. Gnosticism,
after all, consisted of numerous divergent sects, which could also claim
to belong to the Christian church. Such sects should therefore not be
regarded as heretical, but rather heterodox. In any case, heterodox belief
was widespread and also tolerated in early Christianity. Indeed, it was quite
normal for divergent beliefs to exist amongst early Christian groups and
only became problematic with the attempt to develop an 'orthodox' fate.[1]
These are all valid points, but an analysis of this phenomenon in terms
of religious history falls outside the scope of my study. 'Gnosticism' is
still a convenient 'label' to represent an anti-cosmic tradition in which the
Platonic Demiurge undergoes a radical transformation and in which the
separation between the First Principle and the demiurgic one appears to
reach its most extreme. Admittedly, it is difficult to see anything in the
Timaeus text which could have led to the ignorant Gnostic Demiurge.
Since the Timaean Demiurge cannot overcome Necessity completely, in
order to produce a more rationally ordered cosmos, this may have led to a
less positive appraisal of his role. The Gnostic Demiurge, though, probably owes more to the prevailing intellectual-religious trend among certain
groups receiving the text than it does to anything indicated in the dialogue
itself.

One might argue that the term 'Demiurge' has been applied to a different sort of entity from the generative one of the *Timaeus* and its only
Platonic legacy is that of titular appropriation. Against this, one can set
the following considerations: (1) The recalcitrance of matter, as mentioned
in the *Timaeus*, has developed into a claim that the entire material world

---

[1] For discussions of how Gnosticism should be categorised, see Turner: 1992, or Brakke: 2010, esp.
4–5. Smith: 1980 and King: 2005 resist the use of Gnosticism as a category.

is fundamentally evil. (2) The Demiurge, in some versions of the Gnostic myth, actually does produce a world in imitation of the higher realities of which he is ignorant (due to the intervention of Sophia). I would contend that this has originated to some extent from the notion of the Demiurge modelling the world upon the Forms. (3) The Young Gods of the *Timaeus* are paralleled in the host of entities (such as Archons) which assist the Demiurge during the act of world-generation (although the original justification, that they produce the mortal element in humanity, finds no place in this myth, where the Demiurge himself is responsible for what is blameworthy in the material realm). (4) The descending ontological rank of the demiurgic principle can be observed even in monotheistic thinkers, such as Philo and Origen. The low-ranking Gnostic Demiurge is part of this tradition.

Gnosticism can be seen as an extreme evolution of the concept of the Demiurge. The attempt to insulate him from the contamination of matter and responsibility for the production of evil leads, via the distinction between two complementary powers championed by Numenius, to the view that these two entities are antagonistic, in order to account for the inherent imperfection of the world. This may be observed in the parallel development in mainstream philosophy, whereby terms such as 'begotten of himself' were applied increasingly by pagan philosophers to a divine mediator, rather than the supreme principle.[2] Porphyry refers to *Nous*, the Neoplatonic second principle as *autogennêtos* and *autopatôr*.[3] In these thinkers, we have the notion that it is somehow beneath the dignity of the First Principle to move or beget (perhaps related to Epicurean criticism of Plato, *cf.* Cicero, *ND* I). Pétrement observes this idea in Numenius, although Logan claims that this cannot be proved to have existed in philosophy prior to its adoption by the Barbelognostics. Even in Philo, we encounter the position that the universe is inherently evil; for example at *Somn.* II.253, although he generally advances the view that the world, as the creation of a beneficent and omnipotent God, is good.

Many elements of Gnosticism are explained by Christian hostility to Judaism, and hence this distinction between the true God (the Father of Christ) and the Demiurge (Yahweh), influenced by philosophical speculation emphasising the separation between the First Principle and a secondary

---

[2] Logan: 1996, 80

[3] Porphyry, *Historia Philosophiae* Frag. 223 Smith: προῆλθε δὲ προαιώνιος ἀπ' αἰτίου τοῦ θεοῦ ὡρμημένος. αὐτογέννητος ὢν καὶ αὐτοπάτωρ, 'it proceeds before time, rushing forth from God, its cause, since it is self-generated and self-engendered'.

demiurgic figure. However, it is possible to trace its origins as a development of dissident Judaism. *The Tripartite Treatise* (112, 33–113, 1) claims that God did not create alone, but with the assistance or through the agency of angels. This is not heretical and is found in Rabbinical doctrine. The view found justification in the Septuagint's statement ποιήσωμεν ἄνθρωπον: 'Let us make Man.' Philo maintained this position, although he may have been regarded as heterodox (Christians preserved his works). Philo regarded this as referring to the planetary gods (pure souls/angels). The doctrine is related to an attitude that denigrated the value of the human body. According to Justin, heretical Jews claimed that the human body was created by angels (*Dialogue* 62).[4] This view, as well as the attendant belief that the human body was unworthy of creation by God, can be traced back to Plato's position on the demiurgic role of the Young Gods at *Tim.* 41.

A major problem in studying Gnosticism is the biased nature of the sources. When Irenaeus refers to their 'wisdom', he adds 'falsely so-called'. He attacks their unity: their opinions are inconsistent (*Adv. Haer.* 1.11), they dispute amongst themselves (*Adv. Haer.* 1.12), they are inspired by evil spirits (*Adv. Haer.* 1.9.5) and their Biblical exegesis is described as akin to breaking up a mosaic of a king to construct one of a fox or dog (*Adv. Haer.* 1.8.1).[5] Nor does Irenaeus stop there; he attacks the morality of the Gnostics: they not only associate with idolators and attend gladiatorial shows, but are even sexually promiscuous (*Adv. Haer.* 1.6.3f.).[6] Irenaeus parodies the tendency of Gnosticism to multiply the chain of Being through the postulation of entities, Aeons, syzygies and angels with names such as 'Abyss', 'Silence' and 'Limit'. At *Adv. Haer* 1.11.14, in a satire of the Gnostic creation myth, he describes the emanation of Valentinian melons from the primeval beings, Gourd and Utter-Emptiness.

Hostility to the Gnostics was not limited to the Church Fathers and heresiologists. Plotinus comments on acquaintances who 'chanced to come upon this way of thinking before becoming our friends and I do not know how they manage to continue upon it'.[7] Plotinus composed a treatise *Against the Gnostics* (*Enn.* ii 9 [33]) and frequently criticised Gnostic viewpoints.[8] Plotinus' main objection seems to be the number of levels of Being in the Gnostic systems, as well as their world-negating stance.[9] He himself posited only three levels of Being: the One, Nous and Soul. Such

---

[4] Petrément: 1991, 41   [5] Perkins: 1976, 196   [6] Perkins: 1976, 195
[7] *Enn.* ii 9 [33] 10   [8] According to Porphyry, *Vita Plotini* 16.
[9] 'And through naming a multitude of intelligibles, they suppose that they have found the very truth, but by means of this multiplicity, they turn intelligible nature into the likeness of the sensible and inferior world.' (Plotinus, *Enn.* ii 9 [33] 6.29–31).

philosophical opposition to Gnosticism is illustrated by Van den Broek's comment that 'Gnosticism is not even a depraved form of philosophy. It is something quite different, though the Gnostic writers often make use of philosophical ideas.'[10]

As Filoramo comments, the Gnostic Demiurge is always problematic and never a venerable figure.[11] This difficulty can mask some of the obvious differences in his role in various sects. He is central to Valentinian and Sethian systems, but possibly absent in the systems of Menander and Saturninus. He lacks a primary role in the triadic systems, of which our evidence derives from Pseudo-Hippolytus.[12] For Ptolemy, the Demiurge was merely the ignorant creator of the seven heavens:

> They say that the Demiurge thought that he had constructed all of this himself, but he had made it as a result of Achamōth directing his course. For he made heaven without knowing Heaven and he moulded man although ignorant of Man and without knowing the Earth, he brought it to light. And they say that in each case he did not know the Forms (of the things) which he made, or even his own mother, and he thought that he alone was everything. (*Adv. Haer.* 1.5.3)

However, this neutral position becomes more ambivalent and even overtly hostile in other sects.

The origins of Valentinian Gnosticism

Gnostic motifs can be traced in mainstream philosophy, particularly in the language and imagery of Stoicism. For example, Zeno claims:

> God and Mind and Destiny and Zeus are one and he was also called by many other names. Therefore, in the beginning, being by himself, he transformed all substance through air into water, and just as sperm is contained in the engendering fluid, so too was the *spermatikos logos* of the cosmos and this remains behind in the moisture and makes matter serviceable to himself, for the generation of the remaining things. And first he generated the four elements. (*SVF* 1.102f = DL VII.135)

We also have a further metaphor from the Stoics, portraying world-generation in sexual terms:

> Zeus, remembering Aphrodite and genesis, softened himself and having quenched much of his light, transformed (it) into fiery air of less intensive fire. Then, having had intercourse with Hera he ejected the entire seminal

---

[10] Van den Broek: 1998a, 4   [11] Filoramo: 1990, 218 n. 20   [12] Filoramo: 1990, 77

fluid of the All. Thus he made the whole substance wet, one seed of the All; he himself running through it, just like the forming and fashioning spirit in seminal fluid. (*SVF* 2.622)

Imagery exploited by the Gnostics is clearly exhibited by this passage – not just the sexual imagery but also the role played by moisture in creation. Here, Hera does not actually provide anything towards the creation; she merely causes the fluid to be released.

The Stoic doctrine of natural place with the various elements separating of their own accord also echoes the transgression of Sophia:

> They fled and turned away from each other and they endured unusual and stubborn impulses since they were in a state in which, according to Plato (*Tim.* 53b), all things which do not have God are, just like bodies that do not have mind and soul, until what was longed for came to nature out of Providence, when affection and Aphrodite and Eros were generated, as Empedocles and Parmenides and Hesiod say. (Plut., *De facie in orbe lunae* 926f–927a)

This is similar to the imagery of the Sophia myth, and in a way it is Sophia's inability or rather unwillingness to accept her natural place that is the cause of all the trouble. It should be noted that any similarity between Stoicism and Gnosticism is unlikely to be the result of any direct connection between the two, since apart from Basilides, Gnostic thinkers' contact with Greek philosophy was limited to either Pythagoreanism or Platonism.

The Stoics' viewpoint is shared to a certain degree by Philo, another important figure in tracing the development of Valentinian gnosis. Even though Plato had envisaged God as dealing with the world through intermediaries, illustrated by the Demiurge's relationship to the created realm through the Young Gods of the *Timaeus*, it was Philo who managed to harmonise such a conception with a staunch monotheistic viewpoint. For Philo such intermediaries could be equated with the angels. However, God could also deal with the world through a predominant hypostasis, such as the *Logos*, who could also be personified as a Servant of God (or the Son, as exemplified in the Christian tradition by Origen).

Another hypostasis, Ruach Jahweh, is not easily translated from Hebrew into Greek by πνεῦμα. Since *Logos* and Sophia do not share the same gender in Greek, it is difficult for Philo to present them as synonymous. Philo's *Logos* is to some extent the ancestor of Valentinus' Horos. At *Abr.* 143, it is not God but his subordinates who punish Sodom, and create human free will;[13] just as it is the *Logos*-Cutter which handles matter (*Spec.* 1.329). Evil

---

[13] Stead: 1969, 97

cannot originate with God, but Philo is prepared to entertain the notion that his subordinates may be responsible for it (*Opif.* 75, *Conf.* 179, *Fuga* 68*ff.*, *QE* 1.23). Similarly, Horos maintains discipline within the Pleroma and separates the primary Dyad from the lesser Aeons, which it would be beneath the dignity of the First Principle to do. The name Horos is a suitable one, since it also refers to the boundary separating the Pleroma from Sophia and the generated world.

As Stead points out, various traces of Philo's conceptions of Sophia could have given rise to Gnostic themes, particularly the notion of Sophia as the mother of all, as well as the idea of a fallen Sophia.[14] The interesting question to pose is why these two elements should have entered the Valentinian tradition, rather than others. Sophia is generally thought to be the original representation of God's primary agency, with the *Logos* being posited subsequently. This is because of the obvious advantage that if Sophia is posited as God's consort, it explains where the *Logos* came from, if it is claimed as the son of these two, whereas if the *Logos* emerges first, as a masculine entity, it cannot be claimed to be the consort of the Father, and the relationship between the three entities cannot be explained in human terms. Even Philo refers to Sophia as God's consort.[15] It is this sort of concept that Irenaeus attacks at 1.30.2*ff*, when he comments on the notion that the Father is the First Man, the Son the Second Man, and the Holy Spirit the First Woman with whom both have intercourse to generate the created universe. Such a consideration explains the pivotal role Sophia plays in the creation myth of Valentinianism, despite her significant ontological demotion.

The notion of an Oriental mother-goddess, such as Isis, has been grafted onto Sophia, as have Pythagorean speculations concerning the Dyad as the first 'feminine' number and therefore as the mother of plurality. Xenocrates describes this concept at Heinze Fr. 15, describing the Dyad as the mother of the gods and the soul of the universe. Armstrong proposes that the origins of Gnosticism may be found amongst those forcibly Judaised by John Hyrcanus and Aristobulus during the second century BC, such as the Idumaeans, Ituraeans or Peraeans, although he notes that this is merely speculation.[16] There is no need to go to such exotic lengths to find the origins of an anti-Judaic Gnosticism, since it could have originated within

---

[14] Stead: 1969, 97

[15] ἦν γὰρ ἀναγκαῖον τῆς μητρὸς καὶ τιθήνης τῶν ὅλων πάνθ᾽ ὅσα εἰς γένεσιν ἦλθεν εἶναι νεώτερα. 'For it was necessary that all the things which pertain to generation are younger than the mother and nurse of the whole', *Ebr.* 31.

[16] Armstrong: 1978, 92 n. 7

Christianity and Pythagorean or Platonic accounts of demiurgy conveniently provided the framework for the Gnostic myth.

The life and works of Valentinus

Valentinus (AD c. 100–175) was born at Phrebonis in the Egyptian Delta. He received a Greek education at Alexandria, where he may have met his contemporary, Basilides. This helps to explain the curious amalgam of Platonic philosophy and Gnostic mythology that he exhibits in his writings. He later taught at Rome, but is said to have left the city after Anicetus (154–165) was elected bishop instead of him. This reveals the extent to which he could have claimed to be part of the mother church. One theological work *On the Three Natures* has been attributed to him, which deals with the three hypostases and persons (Father, Son and Holy Spirit) of the Trinity. The *Tripartite Tractate* (*NHC* 15) is unrelated, although it probably has a Valentinian (c.150–180) provenance. Additionally, the *Gospel of Truth* (*NHC* 13) has been attributed to Valentinus, though without adequate justification. In spite of the name, this 'gospel' is really a homily. Other attributed texts include the *Gospel of Philip* and the *Letter to Rheginos* (*NHC* 113, 1, 4, xi, 2).

It is difficult to distinguish an 'original' Valentinian doctrine. In any case, much useful work in this area has been accomplished by Stead and Quispel.[17] Each disciple seems to have made his own alterations; an acceptable procedure within the liberal environment of Valentinianism. A great preoccupation of research in this area has been a comparative study of the various Valentinian 'schools', with the admittedly logical view that the lowest common denominator must be Valentinus' original teaching. For the purposes of my examination, I shall treat Valentinianism as a single unit, incorporating all the various strands, as well as whatever may have originally been the position of Valentinus himself, but concentrating more on the system in its entirety, than on the contributions of any single individual.

Valentinus' followers claimed that he had an apostolic accreditation for teaching, since it was asserted that he had been instructed by Theudas, a disciple of St Paul.[18] Layton v Fr. A[19] = Völker Frag. 7 reveals a similar claim, despite its author's hostile stance: 'For Valentinus says that he saw a newborn babe and questioned it to find out who it was. And the babe answered him saying that it was the Word. Thereupon, he adds to this a certain pompous tale, intended to derive from this his attempt at a "sect".'

---

[17] Quispel: 1951 [18] Layton: 1987, 217 [19] v Fr. A = (Layton) Valentinus Fragment A

This fragment was preserved in a quotation by Pseudo-Hippolytus *Ref.*
VI.42.2. Whatever the reality of the situation, it does stress that the Valentinians did not see themselves as a schismatic group, however they may have
been viewed by others, and expressly attempted to legitimise themselves in
terms of the mother church.

What Pétrement refers to as the Valentinian turning-point,[20] the attempt
by Valentinians to reduce the distance between Christianity and Gnosticism, is also an attempt by some Christians to raise their own theology to
the same academic level as that of pagan philosophical systems with which
they were familiar. The Valentinians originally seem to have been a sect
within the church, rather than a separate group (heterodox rather than
heretic), although in 692 AD, we learn from Canon 95 passed at the Trul-
lan Synod which dealt with the treatment repentant Valentinians should
receive from the Catholic Church, that the sect still persisted.

The Valentinians consciously attempted to link themselves with the
'mother church', as well as mainstream Greek philosophy, as can be seen
from this fragment, fortuitously preserved by Clement of Alexandria, *Mis-
cellanies (Stromateis)* 6.52–3 (vol. 2, 458, 11–16 Stählin):

> Much of what has been written in the books available to the public is
> found in the writings in the Church of God. For this common matter is
> the statements from the heart, the law written in the heart. This is the host
> of the beloved, which is beloved and loving him. (Layton v Fr. G = On
> Friends – Völker Frag 6)

The publicly available books are the non-Christian works of Greek philosophers. Like Philo and others before them, the Valentinians sought to reconcile the truth they perceived in mainstream philosophy with their own
religious beliefs by claiming that earlier intellectuals whose beliefs agreed
in whole or in part with their own were inspired by God.

Given the fragmentary remains of writings that may be attributable to
Valentinus, it can be easy to underestimate the extent of their influence on
the Christian intellectual tradition, a fact attested by the hostility which
they managed to evoke in the Church Fathers. In 229, for example, Origen
travelled to Athens to debate with Candidus, an influential Valentinian.[21]
There is evidence of their survival into the fourth century, as we hear of
feuds between the Arians and Valentinians of Syrian Edessa during the
reign of the Emperor Julian (361–363), while during that of Theodosius I
(379–395), a Valentinian Church was destroyed by monks at Callinicum

---

[20] Pétrement: 1991, 370–8   [21] Rudolph: 1983, 325

on the upper Euphrates.[22] Interestingly, this is one of the few references we have for specifically Valentinian worship and indicates their relationship to the 'mother church' of the period. Unfortunately, no archaeological site has been definitively identified as a Valentinian building. Layton raises the possibility that the sect survived into the fifth century, with its members in hiding; although Valentinus' disciples come towards the end of the innovative period of western Gnosticism. They may have seen themselves not as a religion in competition with Christianity, but rather a sect offering a particular interpretation of its teaching.[23]

The Valentinians' most distinctive doctrine was their myth of Sophia. Their teachings can be grouped into two branches: Italic and Oriental, both of which varied the myth. The main source is Irenaeus *Adv. Haer.* 1.11.1, although Irenaeus is not concerned with producing a comprehensive account, but with merely highlighting some differences between the position of Valentinus and that of the main body of the Gnostics. Layton breaks the entire saga down into four 'acts', which are the sections relating to the Demiurge proper: the generation of the spiritual and material realms, the production of humans, which Irenaeus does not include in his account, and the Christian-soteriological section outlining the role of the Holy Spirit and Jesus.

Despite the lack of acceptance by many scholars of Pétrement's Valentinian 'turning-point', it does point to the problems surrounding Valentinus' position within Gnosticism. Irenaeus is deliberately confusing in his application of the term 'Gnostic' and the Western Church Fathers tended to follow him in his inexactitude. Secondly, in the Eastern Church, the term had more favourable connotations than in its Western counterpart. The Valentinians, however, are the first sect to be mentioned by Irenaeus in connection with the term 'Gnostic'.[24] That the term 'Gnostic' was conventionally used is indicated by Irenaeus' use of λεγομένης, although he provides no evidence for when or by whom this name was first utilised.

Irenaeus associates Valentinus with the Gnostics here for his own particular reasons. He accuses the Valentinians of plagiarism with the line λεγομένης γνωστικῆς αἱρέσεως, but at the same time claims that they have been excessively original: ἴδιος χαρακτήρ. The Gnostics lack originality;

---

[22] Rudolph: 1983, 325
[23] This is in spite of the fact that according to the *Gospel of Philip*, they celebrated additional sacraments.
[24] ὁ μὲν γὰρ πρῶτος, ἀπὸ τῆς λεγομένης Γνωστικῆς αἱρέσεως τὰς ἀρχὰς εἰς ἴδιον χαρακτῆρα διδασκαλείου μεθαρμόσας Οὐαλεντῖνος . . . 'For Valentinus was first of the so-called Gnostic sect to correct the principles of his own school' *(Adv. Haer.* 1.11.1).

but the Valentinians seem to be regarded by Irenaeus as a separate sect.[25] He states that they were similar to the Gnostics, which suggests that he did not regard both groups as identical. Irenaeus was aware that Valentinus could differ from mainstream Gnostic thought on important matters. For example:

> De ea autem quae est ex his, secunda emissione Hominis et Eccle-siae, ipsi patres eorum, falso cognominati Gnostici, pugnant adversus invicem . . . aptabile esse magis emissioni dicentes, uti verisimile, ex Homine Verbum, sed non ex Verbo Hominem emissum . . .

> Once again, concerning the second (generation) which is emitted from these [Aeons], that of Man and Church, their fathers themselves, falsely called the Gnostics (i.e. the knowing ones), fight amongst themselves . . . , saying that it is more suitable to the theory of emission, as being similar to the truth, that the Word was emitted out of Man, and not Man out of the Word. (*Adv. Haer.* II.13.10)

'Gnostic' for Irenaeus denotes a group of diverse heterodox beliefs, con-nected by their claim of a false *gnōsis*.[26] Valentinus himself seems to have avoided use of the term 'Gnostic'. The epithets they applied to themselves were traditionally used by members of the early Church; for example 'peo-ple endowed with spirit', 'spirituals' (= πνευματικοί, 1 *Co* 2:15) and 'the perfect' (= τέλειοι).[27] The term 'Valentinians' emerges c. 160 AD, coined by opponents in critical pamphlets, in order to imply that this group were followers of Valentinus, rather than of Christ. According to Epiphanius, the Valentinians referred to themselves as 'Gnostics'.[28] However, Epipha-nius cannot be viewed as a reliable authority in this case, given his need to maintain eighty sectarian titles in order to allude to the eighty concubines in the *Song of Songs*.

Although Gnosticism seems to be generally presented in classical scholar-ship, or for that matter in philosophy and theology, as a 'fringe movement', Valentinianism was too important to ignore for figures such as Clement of Alexandria or Origen. In this we are fortunate, since it provides us with a source of information; as opposed to the situation regarding Gnosticism within Judaism. The rabbis had a much more effective way of dealing with heretics; by simply ignoring them, the details of the heresy would not spread — quite correctly, as it turns out.

---

[25] . . . ἀριστερὸν Ἄρχοντα ἐδογμάτισεν ὁμοίως τοῖς ῥηθησομένοις ὑφ' ἡμῶν ψευδωνύμοις Γνωστικοῖς, 'And he [i.e. Valentinus] had a doctrine of a left-sided Archon; in this he agreed with the falsely-called Gnostics about whom we have been speaking.' (*Adv. Haer.* I.11.1)
[26] Brakke: 2010, 4   [27] Layton : 1987, 270
[28] Epiph. *Pan.* 31.1.1, 31.7.8, 31.36.4, 33.1.1, 31.5.5

Sources

The myth of Sophia, in addition to being distinctly Valentinian, also demonstrates the development of Valentinian thought in the various 'schools'. The main source is the work of Irenaeus, Bishop of Lyons, *Exposure and Refutation of the falsely so-called Gnostics (Adversus Haereses)* in five books. The original Greek version for the first part of Book I was preserved by Epiphanius' *Haer.* 31, although the complete Latin version survives. The work also survives in Armenian and Syriac. It is generally thought to expound the doctrines of the founder of the Italian branch, Ptolemaeus. It was composed over a lengthy period; Rudolph suggests during the reign of the Emperor Commodus (180–192).[29]

It seems to have been written to combat the Gnostic heresy, which from the second half of the second century, during the reign of Marcus Aurelius, having originated in Asia Minor, began to spread towards Lyons, where Irenaeus was consecrated bishop in 177–178. It was also reported that he died during a persecution c. 200. The ostensible motive for composing the work was to satisfy a friend's request for information concerning Valentinian doctrine. Irenaeus deals with a variety of sects that fall under the term Gnostic. He claims to have relied on the written and oral accounts of the Valentinians, which independent research has confirmed.

Second in order of importance is the *Refutation of all Heresies* (incorrectly) attributed to Hippolytus, Book VI, 29–36. There are also a set of extracts from Clement of Alexandria's *Excerpta ex Theodoto*. The problem with these is that they are completely out of context and they are interspersed in a confusing manner with Clement's views, although they have the great advantage of providing information on Theodotus' oriental branch, while Irenaeus and Pseudo-Hippolytus have an Italian bias.

In addition to the above-mentioned sources there are some others, of which unfortunately not enough survives to draw firm conclusions from. These include the fragments of Heracleon, taken from a *Commentary on John*, and the fragments of Valentinus. Irenaeus *Adv. Haer.* 1.11.1 contains some details concerning Valentinus, and he also mentions some other systems derived from Valentinianism. There is also a Valentinian letter at Epiphanius, *Haer.* 31.5–6 and an *Adversus Valentinianos* by Tertullian, which is based on Irenaeus' version. W. Völker's traditional numerical order of the Valentinian fragments is not followed by Layton, who prefers to arrange the fragments based on the order of the Gnostic myth, while

---

[29] Rudolph: 1983, 11

Völker Fr. 8 is listed as a separate section, VHr by Layton, as he regards it as a complete work, rather than a fragment.[30] In the interests of clarity, my practice here will be to provide both numerations.

Valentinian myth of Sophia

There are two variations of the Valentinian myth, deriving from the two main branches. Irenaeus is the main source for A, while Pseudo-Hippolytus is the main source for B. However, it should be noted that elements of version B can be identified in Irenaeus – in II.3 and II.4.[31] The Valentinian system posits a plethora of entities between the First Principle and the Demiurge (see Fig. 8.1), although in comparison with the Basilidean system, where the material realm is fabricated by the three hundred and sixty-fifth generation of angels, it could be viewed as rather restrained. These hypostases, which represent modes of God, are paired into syzygies and then grouped together into larger formations, which could be viewed as families. First comes the Primal Ogdoad[32] (Abyss = Silence/Thought, Intellect = Truth, the Word = Life, Human Being = Church).[33] Word and Life then emanate a second group of ten Aeons (the Deep-Sunken = Intercourse, the Unaging = Union, the Self-Produced = Pleasure, the Motionless = Mixture, the only-Begotten = Blessed). The Twelve Aeons are emanated from Human Being and the Church (the Intercessor = Faith, the Fatherly = Hope, the Motherly = Love, the Ever-Flowing = Intelligence, the Ecclesiastical = Blessedness, Theletos (the Desired) = Sophia).

Such a system can be seen as an attempt to convey the various conceptions of God without compromising the simplicity of the First Principle. However, unlike Origen who locates them all within his Christ-*Logos* and thereby dispenses with the need for numerous hypostases, the Valentinians are able to adopt this approach since a fragmented godhead is one of the cornerstones of their theology. Even though they posit such an elaborate system, it fails to work even within the terms which the Valentinians set themselves, or perhaps it would be fairer to say that while it is possible that such a system might function within a mythic framework, when tested with the touchstone of metaphysics, it feels as though the entire structure begins to break down.

[30] The so-called *Summer Harvest*.
[31] Stead: 1969, 78 outlines the extent of the influence of version B on Irenaeus' account.
[32] I use the equals sign to indicate the consort of the male hypostasis which appears on the left.
[33] This is only in version A (Irenaeus); in version B (Pseudo-Hippolytus), there is no primal octet.

The Abyss = Silence/Thought

↓

Intellect = Truth

Primal Tetraktys

The Word = Life

Human Being = Church

Primal Ogdoad

Group of ten Aeons (emitted by Word and Life)

The Deep-Sunken = Intercourse

The Unaging = Union

The Self-Produced = Pleasure

The Motionless = Mixture

Christ and Holy Spirit ←   The Only-Begotten = Blessed

(Emitted by Only-Begotten through the Abyss's foresight)

INNER BOUNDARY

(Emitted in image of parent through agency of Only-Begotten, Iren., *Adv. Haer.*1.2.4)

_____

Group of twelve Aeons (emitted by Human Being and Church)

The Intercessor = Faith

Fig. 8.1 The Valentinian myth of Sophia

	The Fatherly = Hope
Fullness of Aeons contribute	The Motherly = Love
'most beautiful and splendid	The Ever-Flowing = Intelligence
that it had within itself' to	The Ecclesiastical = Blessedness
emanate the 'perfect fruit,	The Desired (Theletos) = Wisdom (Sophia)
Jesus'	↓
(and angels as his bodyguards)	

PLEROMA

_____

Achamōth

SUBLUNAR REALM

↓

Matter, Demiurge

Six other Archons

World Ruler (Devil) and Demons

Material and Inanimate Adam (all products of the Demiurge)

Fig. 8.1 (*cont.*)

Leaving aside the question of whether the First Principle should be above the law of the syzygy, there is the question of how these various groups relate to one another. Where do Human Being and Church emerge from to emanate the group of twelve Aeons? Christ plays a role later on in the Sophia myth, but at least he is described as emerging from Intellect. This makes Intellect the Father, which might be acceptable in this scheme where he is described as the parent and the source of the entirety. However, he can only be the third-highest ranking aeon, since Silence and Abyss come first. Indeed Abyss is referred to as prior source.

This is perhaps a throwback to the persistent attempts within philosophy to outdo Plato by going back further than him in attempting to uncover the origin of the universe, and describing the First Principle as Forefather or Pre-First Principle. Abyss is described as prior source. It is problematic in a 'Christian' document for Christ to not be emanated directly from the First Principle. It is also unclear how the Holy Spirit is generated, though it seems to be floating around in the Pleroma, and given Origen's system, it does not seem to have been unusual to have assigned it no metaphysical role at all. It is also unclear how, when or by whom Horos is produced, although since he separates the primary Dyad from Intellect, there are good grounds for assuming that it is emanated fairly early on. In analysing this system, the hypostases which are actually of importance are the First Principle and Sophia.

The Valentinian First Principle is described in negative terms – it is located 'within indivisible and unnameable heights, where there was – they say – a pre-existent, perfect eternity; this they call also prior source, ancestor and Abyss. And it existed uncontained, invisible, everlasting and unengendered. Within infinite eternal realms, it was in great still-ness and rest: And with it coexisted thought, which they also call loveliness and silence.'(1.1.1)

This thought is the consort of the First Principle; together they emanate the next principle:

> And at some point the Abyss thought to emit from himself the Beginning of everything, and he placed this emanation, which he had decided to issue forth, just like sperm, in the womb of Silence, which existed together with him. And she received the sperm and conceived and brought forth Mind, which was of a similar nature and equal to the one who had emitted it and which alone understood the magnitude of his father. And they call this Mind the only-begotten and Father and principle of everything. (Iren., *Adv. Haer.* 1.1.1)

This primary divine couple is an allegory for a Dyad as the First Principle, rather than a single First Principle or two antagonistic principles. This is indicated by the statement: 'For sometimes they claim that the father is with a consort, Silence, and at other times that it is beyond male and female' (Iren., *Adv Haer.* 1.2.4). I think the Valentinian group which suggested this formulation were attempting to adopt a more monistic stance. The version described by Pseudo-Hippolytus also envisages the cosmos as originating

from a single male principle and therefore allocates no female consort
to Abyss: ἄθηλυν καὶ ἄζυγον καὶ μόνον τὸν Πατέρα, 'a non-female and
unjoined and only father' (Ps.-Hipp. *Ref.* VI.29.3.4). For Irenaeus, however,
the First Principle is ὑπέραρρεν καὶ ὑπέρθηλυ, 'beyond male and female',
(Iren., *Adv. Haer.* I.I.3.17). In the version where the parent has no female
counterpart, he emits a boundary which purifies Sophia and reunites her
with Theletos, but expels her unlawful passion.

> They say that the forefather was only known by the only-begotten, which
> was generated from him, that is by Mind and to the others he remains
> invisible and unreachable. According to them, Mind alone delighted in
> contemplating the father and glorified in comprehending its immeasurable
> magnitude, And he decided to communicate to the other Aeons the magni-
> tude of the father and how great he was and that he was without a beginning
> and uncontained and impossible to see. But by the will of the father, Silence
> restrained him on account of the father's wish to lead them up to thought
> and to the desire to seek the aforementioned forefather. (Iren., *Adv. Haer.*
> I.2.I)

This is similar to Origen's view that only the Son knows the Father.[34] The
Gospel of Truth explains how the First Principle actually emanates these
entities:

> All the ways are his emanations. They know that they have emanated from
> him like children who were within a mature man, but knew that they had
> not yet received form nor had been given name. It is when they receive the
> impulse towards acquaintance with the Father that he gives birth to each.
> Otherwise, although they are within him, they do not recognise him. The
> Father himself is perfect and acquainted with every way that is in him. If
> he wills, what he wills appears, as he gives it form and name. And he gives
> it name and causes it to make them come into existence. (GT 27; trans.
> Layton)

There is some difference in terminology between the *Gospel of Truth* and
the version of Irenaeus, with the Aeons being referred to as ways. Both
versions also differ in the details that lead to the fall of Sophia:

> But Wisdom (Sophia) – the last and youngest Aeon of the twelve which
> had been emitted by the Human Being and the Church – surged forward
> and underwent a passion without the union of her consort, the Desired
> (Theletos). The passion began in the region of Mind and Truth, but it

---

[34] This parallel is brought out more forcefully at the *Gospel of Truth* 16 'that they might learn to know
him through the power of the Word that emanated from the fullness that is in the Father's thought
and intellect – the Word who is spoken of as "saviour".' (trans. Layton)

plunged into this (Aeon), which had been deflected, ostensibly on account of love, but in reality on account of recklessness, because she did not have the same communion with the perfect father as Mind had. The passion was the quest for the father. For, they say that she desired to comprehend his magnitude. Then, since she was not able, since she had thrown herself into an impossible matter, she became embroiled in great distress on account of the magnitude of the Deep, and the inscrutability of the father and her love for him. (Iren., *Adv. Haer.* 1.2.2)[35]

Here it is as a result of her unacceptable desire to know the First Principle that she transgresses (the Limit) and falls. In Pseudo-Hippolytus' version, she attempts to imitate the Creator by producing an offspring without her consort. Sophia is less culpable in version A, where even if she acts out of ignorance, she also acts out of love. Version B reveals her as hubristic; assuming that she is capable of emulating the creative power of the Father, and in acting above the law of the syzygy (she produces without her consort). There is no element of jealousy in Sophia's attempt to emulate the Creator; similar divine beneficence can be observed in Plato's *Tim.* 28e–29a (although there evidently in a less antagonistic or culpable context) and reminds one of the descent of Man in the *Poimandres* to emulate the activity of his brother, the Demiurge.

Sophia is then kept out of the ineffable magnitude and turns back to herself. In version A only the guilty intention of Sophia is expelled, not Sophia herself. This lower entity is forced outside the outer boundary of the Pleroma. (In a sense, this is the first time that the outer boundary of the Pleroma acquires any importance, since it is the first moment in the cosmology that an entity exists outside the fullness of the Pleroma). This lower Sophia is also known as Achamōth (a garbled form of the Hebrew *Hokhma*, meaning wisdom or Sophia); a spiritual essence since it results from the natural impulse of an aeon, but on account of her lack of comprehension, she is without form and imageless and is described as a weak and female fruit.[36] It is expelled from the Pleroma, like an aborted foetus.

---

[35] In *The Gospel of Truth* 17, the error is that of the whole Pleroma: 'Inasmuch as the entirety had searched for the one from whom they had emanated, and the entirety was inside of him – the inconceivable uncontained, who is superior to all thought – ignorance of the Father caused agitation and fear. And the agitation grew dense like fog, so that no one could see. Thus error found strength and laboured at her matter in emptiness. Without having learned to know the truth, she took up residence in a modelled form, preparing by means of the power, in beauty, a substitute for truth.' (trans. Layton)

[36] *Adv. Haer.* 1.2.4

This parallels the description of the Demiurge as an ἔκτρωμα or abortion – whatever offspring Sophia gives birth to is of necessity defective, since it is conceived without the participation of her consort or the will of the supreme principle.[37] The myth now requires the emanation of two further Aeons to rectify the situation: Christ and the Holy Spirit or Pneuma. The Holy Spirit and Christ set the Pleroma in order by equalising the Aeons (1.2.5–6). As a result of this equalisation all of the Aeons become intellects, Words, human beings and Christs; in other words they become 'equal in form and intention' (1.2.6), which indicates some sort of unification of the godhead. It is interesting to find a demiurgical role attributed to the Holy Spirit in the Christian tradition or rather quasi-Christian tradition, since in Origenian thought it has no such function and is not even a metaphysical principle. However, for Origen, it does have a soteriological role, and if one was to be exact that is just what it is engaged upon here.

The Aeon Christ descends out of the Pleroma in order to stabilise Sophia. There should really be no need for this action, as it seems to be merely a duplication of the activity of the Holy Spirit. It seems to be part of the development of the elaborate Gnostic systems, which appear to contain redundant entities (perhaps as the result of the combination of Christian and philosophical entities):

> Then the (higher) Christ pitied her and extended himself through the cross and by means of his own power he shaped it into a form, only according to essence, but not according to knowledge (*gnosis*). And having accomplished this, he ran back up, and withdrew his power and he abandoned 'her' so that she might perceive the passions around her, in which she was struggling, on account of her separation from the Pleroma and desire something different, for she possessed a certain perfume of immortality, which had been left behind for her by Christ and the Holy Spirit. (Iren., *Adv. Haer.* 1.4.1)

The emergence of these Aeons is significant in numerous ways. Firstly, Christ and the Holy Spirit need to be written into the Gnostic myth, so to speak, in order to explain the emergence of the Christian Trinity. It would seem, then, that in spite of their age, they must be promoted to a senior rank in the Pleroma, just below the Father (who himself, as we have already seen, may be only the second-ranking principle). If this event

---

[37] *Hypostasis of the Archons* (*NHC* II.4, 94 (142), 5–13: 'Sophia (Wisdom) which is called "Pistis" wished to create a work alone without a consort. And her work became an image of heaven, (so that) a curtain exists between the heavenly and lower regions (Aeons). And a shadow came into being beneath the curtain, and that shadow became matter.' (trans. Rudolph)

takes place in version A, it means that the number of Aeons totals thirty-two. If one includes Jesus, that provides thirty-three Aeons; significantly the age at which the Saviour died.[38] The Valentinians are displaying the same evidence of rationality in their account of creation as Plato does in the *Timaeus*. However, here we are discussing the godhead, which should display rationality; whereas the entire act of creation within Valentinianism is irrational. The role played by Christ was a Valentinian development and was seen as a prefiguration of the soteriological role which he plays later on when dealing with humanity.

The Pleroma's structure also displays Pythagorean influence in both versions. The primary Ogdoad can either be divided into two tetrads or four pairs, both of which reveal the significance of the numbers two and four, although all numbers up to ten in Pythagorean numerology have some significance. The pairing of male and female through the entire structure of the Pleroma, including the First Principle, reflects the importance of συζυγία (sexual union) within the Valentinian system, illustrated by the letter of Epiphanius.[39] Version B traces Being to a Monad which produces a Dyad. Even though this Dyad (*Nous* and *Aletheia*) is composed of male and female, it is collectively female.[40] Version A, as Stead notes, is less acceptable to the Jewish or Christian reader, who would raise no objections to claiming an ultimate Monad, but could not really agree with the claim of an ultimate Dyad.[41]

Sophia is conscious of the wrong that she has committed and attempts to turn around. In Pseudo-Hippolytus' version, all of the Aeons are thrown into confusion by the transgression of Sophia. Achamōth undergoes manifold passions because she is cut off from the Pleroma. It is these emotions that become matter.[42] This is important, since it indicates that the material realm is created not merely as the result of a split within the godhead, rather than due to the divine plan, but also as the result of a mistake perpetrated by this fragmented section of the godhead.

> They say that this is how the composition and essence of the matter came about, from which the world was assembled. For from this reversion, the whole World-Soul and the Demiurge arose, and other things had their origin from her fear and from her grief. For all moist essences were generated from her tears, and bright ones from her laughter, and from her grief and shock

---

[38] This total, however, disagrees with the account at I.3. or III.I, although this may come from version B.

[39] Pythagoreanism also contained a series of pairs of syzygies.

[40] κυρία καὶ ἀρχὴ καὶ μήτηρ, 'power and principle and mother' (Ps.-Hipp. 29.6).

[41] Stead: 1969, 80   [42] *Adv. Haer.* I.5.4

the bodily elements of the cosmos. For they say that sometimes she cried and mourned that she had been left behind alone in the darkness and emptiness and sometimes when she thought about the light which had left her, she was put in a good humour and she laughed and once again at other times, she was afraid and on still other occasions, she was perplexed and driven out of her senses. (Iren., *Adv. Haer.* 1.4.2)[43]

However, every thought in the divine world, even a guilty one or one not authorised by the supreme principle, becomes a hypostasis. As a result, expelling the thought is only the second-best option, because even the Aeon Christ is unable to remove it completely:

> He separated (the passions) from her, but did not ignore them, for it was impossible to obliterate them like those of the first (Sophia), since they were already consitituted and powerful, but instead he separated them and mixed them and stabilised them and from incorporeal passions, he changed them into incorporeal matter. Then he supplied them with appropriate characteristics and with a nature, so that they might enter into compounds and bodies, from which two essences came about, an evil one from the passions and a passionate one from the reversion. It is on account of this that they say that the saviour acted with the power of a demiurge. (Iren., *Adv. Haer.* 1.4.5)

Here Christ can be regarded as a sort of Demiurge within the divine world, given his attempt to stabilise it and impose order upon disorder; the reference to compounds and essences reminds one of the *Timaeus*. Yet, strictly speaking, there should be no need for this type of ordering activity not just within the divine world, but within the very godhead. It is an example of the extent to which a rather commonplace philosophical motif has been seized upon by the Gnostics and used in an unsuitable context, which quite frankly produces bizarre consequences.

Jesus is the joint emanation of the entire Pleroma, their 'common fruit', produced from the fullness of the Aeons, each contributing the best that it has within itself and simultaneously producing the angels as His bodyguard.[44] It seems that he supersedes Christ and Word, since he assumes these titles, despite the pre-existence of these entities. This agrees

---

[43] *Cf. Gospel of Truth* 26: 'All the ways moved and were disturbed, for they had neither basis nor stability and Error became excited, not knowing what to do [she] was troubled, mourned and cried out that she understood nothing inasmuch as acquaintance which meant the destruction of her and all the emanations had drawn near to her' (trans. Layton). Interestingly, the author does not refer to the fallen Aeon by the contradictory name of Sophia –Wisdom, but rather Error, which more accurately reflects her situation.

[44] Iren., *Adv. Haer.* 1.2.6

with the view that, as divine messenger, he is endowed with the power of all the Aeons, as well as the Father.[45] At Pseudo-Hippolytus, *Ref.* VI.32.1–2, it seems that the power described is Carpos, which is also Jesus, since he is the καρπός (fruit) of the Pleroma, as is pointed out at Pseudo-Hippolytus, *Ref.* VI.32.2.4. Jesus is seen by Sophia (σύν ὅλῃ τῇ καρποφορίᾳ αὐτου, 'with the whole of his fruit-bearing nature') and marries her.[46] It is difficult to understand why such a marriage is necessary, unless to ensure that she has a consort and to parallel the restoration of the first Sophia to Theletos. In this context of duplication, Jesus may not be intended to supersede Christ, but to act as a second Christ, replicating the saving work of the first Christ in the physical realm.

Sophia then initiates world-creation:

> Of these three (essences) which, according to them, existed at this point, one derived from her passions, which was matter, another from her reversion, which was the psychic and that which she had borne, which was the pneumatic and she turned to the shaping of these essences. But she was not able to shape the pneumatic, since it was of the same sort of essence as she was. (Iren., *Adv. Haer.* 1.5.1)

This is important for Gnostic eschatology, since it explains the three classes of soul. Evidently, this differs greatly from Origen, who regards souls as the same in their essence. For the Gnostics, then, individual salvation seems predetermined, having been fixed at the moment of creation. Sophia produes a god who is both a Demiurge and parent; drawing on the Timaean distinction between 'maker and father'. He is the 'mother-father' of the 'animates' (i.e. Gnostics) referred to as 'those on the right' and craftsman of the 'materials' (i.e. non-Gnostics).[47]

This reference to the right and left seems to be an attempt to incorporate the notion of the Cosmocrator or the left-sided ruler. In this version, there is no real need for him, since the Demiurge is the creator of the material realm. The Cosmocrator is depicted as the brother of the Demiurge;[48] he is more evil with a 'spiritalis malitia', but he is also superior since he knows more concerning the higher powers than the Demiurge. In systems which acknowledge the Cosmocrator, the Demiurge is usually envisaged as ruling on the right-hand side; though here he appears to have jurisdiction on both sides: he is described as king of all (i.e. both 'animates' and 'materials'). The Cosmocrator seems to be a later addition to the system, only included when Valentinianism began to propound the doctrine that

---

[45] Iren., *Adv. Haer.* 1.2.6   [46] Iren., *Adv. Haer.* 1.1.8; Ps.-Hipp. 34.4
[47] Iren., *Adv. Haer.* 1.5.1   [48] Iren., *Adv. Haer.* 1.5.4

the Demiurge was not evil; not good, but just. This left a vacancy, which was supplied by an entity found in the writings of St Paul. While St Paul clearly never regards the world as the product of any entity other than the God of the Christians,[49] he does frequently regard the (Judaic) law as the product of the angels (though this does not imply that it was designed without the consent of God). This subjected Man to the rule of the angels,[50] and may lie in the background of the emergence of a figure (Demiurge or Cosmocrator) ruling the world in opposition to the supreme God.[51]

Strangely, the Saviour acts through Achamōth to make images in honour of the Aeons. She keeps the image of the invisible parent with which the Demiurge is not acquainted, while he keeps an image of the only-begotten child and the archangels and angels retain images of other Aeons.[52] There seems to be an element of parallelism common in Gnostic myths in this passage. The Saviour acts through Achamōth, just as she acts through the Demiurge to mitigate the effects of creation. One must ask what are the images of the Aeons that she is creating here. It would appear to be a second Pleroma (but inferior because it is merely an image of the first). The images must be an equivalent to the Platonic Forms, so it would seem that she is transmitting the Forms to the Demiurge to ensure that some of the goodness of the Pleroma is replicated in created reality.

This is not unusual in Gnostic myth; what is not so commonplace is a description of how she transmitted those images, such as we have here. It is not the case that Achamōth communicates these forms to the Demiurge in an attempt to repent of what she has done (nothing, in fact, since the fault is that of the older Sophia). Rather she performs this activity under the orders, as it were, of the Saviour. Each entity's retention of an image seems related to its ontological rank. The Demiurge's retention of an image of the only-begotten child (i.e. intellect) echoes his original characterisation as an intellective entity (even if in the Gnostic myths this is not so immediately apparent). A variant of the myth suggests that Achamōth has intercourse with the angels: 'But Achamōth (i.e. the lower Sophia), having been freed from her passions, took pleasure in the sight of the lights, that is the angels who were with him (the Sotēr), was impregnated by them and bore fruit after their image.'[53] As Achamōth has been freed from passions, perhaps no sexual fault is implied here.

---

[49] *Romans* 1:20
[50] *Gal.* 4:3: 'So with us, when we were children, we were slaves to the elemental spirits of the universe.' Cf. *Gal.* 4:9 –11
[51] Pétrement: 1991, 62–3.   [52] Iren., *Adv. Haer.* 1.5.1   [53] Iren., *Adv. Haer.* 1.4.5

The Demiurge

This brings us to the Demiurge, who is essentially a creator-angel. He tends to be identified with titles given to God in the Old Testament, most frequently Ialdabaoth (probably from a Semitic root *ialad* 'child' and *baoth* 'chaos', hence 'child of chaos').[54] He is also referred to as Esaldaios (= El Shaddai), Elohim, Iao, Sabaoth. As Ialdabaoth (an Ophite/Sethian appellation), he is frequently identified with Saturn and depicted as a lion. Since Yahweh's day, the Sabbath, is celebrated on Saturn's day, Saturday, this helps to explain how the identification took place.

Ialdabaoth is the 'father of the powers'. In some sects, he fathers seven sons, the Archons, the eldest of whom, Sabaoth, the 'god of the powers' is actually the Demiurge. It makes little sense, however, to have a Demiurge whose sole metaphysical purpose is to emanate another Demiurge. In some versions Pistis Sophia and her daughter Zoe intervene to allow Sabaoth to take his father's place. This is because he does penance when he realises his father's delusion; he becomes a Christian in advance of Christianity. This division may stem from the Gnostic perception that Yahweh, God of the Law, was the least acceptable aspect of the Old Testament God, while the God of the prophets after Moses or the Creator (the Demiurge proper) was more satisfactory. The Demiurge generates the physical universe as follows:

> So they say he became a father and god of things outside the Pleroma, being the maker of all psychic and material things. For he separated the two compounded essences and he made bodies out of the incorporeal and he wrought as a craftsman the heavenly and earthly and caused the material and the psychic to come into being, Demiurge of the right and left, of the light and the heavy, of the upward- and downward-tending. For he fabricated seven heavens, above which is – they say – the Demiurge. On account of this they call him the Hebdomad (the seventh) and they call Achamōth the mother the Ogdoad (the eight) and she preserves the number of the primal and the first Ogdoad of the Pleroma. (Iren., *Adv. Haer.* 1.5.2)

The reference to the seven heavens was by now standard. Each contained its own ruling Archon (an adaptation of the Jewish archangels). However, the importance of Sophia in terms of creation is such that in certain accounts it is she who is envisaged as physically moulding matter.[55] These seven heavens are described as intellectual and as angels, while the Demiurge is an angel resembling God. Paradise is located above the third heaven and Adam is described as having 'got something from it when he passed time within it'.[56]

---

[54] Pétrement: 1991, 43   [55] Cf. *Gospel of Truth* 17 quoted above (note 35).
[56] Iren., *Adv Haer.* 1.5.2. Cf. 1.71.

What could Adam have gotten from the fourth heaven if not some kind of gift, similar to that bestowed upon Man in the *Poimandres*? Clearly this motif has remained on in the Valentinian myth, but not much is said concerning it because it has become redundant, since Sophia is now the entity whose fall is responsible for creation, and not Man. The Demiurge constructs the physical world 'through Achamōth's act of emission', though he believes that he is generating of his own accord and he remains ignorant of his mother's existence.[57] This ignorance is characteristic of the Gnostic Demiurge: 'For he made heaven without knowing Heaven and he moulded man although ignorant of Man and without knowing the Earth, he brought it to light.'[58] It is because the Demiurge is not acquainted with the 'ideal Forms' that the physical world is deficient. However, in this version the Demiurge is not to blame for his ignorance, but rather Achamōth, since she conspires to keep him in this state. This contrasts with the usual view that Sophia conspires when the Demiurge is creating Man to place a spark of spirit in him so that Adam becomes superior to creation and a son of the true God. This text has been influenced by an alternative strand of the tradition, in which the spark implanted in mankind is something negative (a spark of the female sex), and so Achamōth can be viewed as an almost malevolent entity.

The Valentinian Demiurge is the unconscious instrument of divine will. He is directed in the act of creation by the *Logos* of God. In systems influenced by Valentinianism, he is ignorant, rather than evil. Yet in the *Apocryphon of John*, Ialdabaoth's position is motivated by jealousy of the higher God. He safeguards his status by cheating the other Archons in what he apportions:

> He apportioned to them some of his fire, which is his own attribute and of his power, but of the pure Light of the power which he had inherited from his Mother, he gave them none. For this reason he held sway over them, because of the glory that was in him from the power of the Light of the Mother. Therefore he let himself be called 'the God' renouncing the substance from which he had issued. And he contemplated the creation beneath him and the angels under him, which had sprung from him, and he said to them 'I am a jealous god, besides me there is none' – thereby already indicating to the angels beneath him, that there is another God: for if there were none, of whom should he be jealous? (41:13*ff.*; 44:9*ff.* Till)

This is a Gnostic motif with Christian imagery. Ialdabaoth's claim to be the sole God is met with a retort from on high or from the soul of the Gnostic returning to its origin, which invokes its knowledge of Sophia and

---

[57] Iren., *Adv. Haer.* 1.5.3   [58] Iren., *Adv. Haer.* 1.5.3

of the unknown God.[59] Sometimes his mother, Sophia responds: 'Do not lie, Ialdabaoth: above you is the father of all, the First Man and Man, the son of Man.'[60] The mention of Man invokes the primordial Man of the *Poimandres*. The term arises from the view that since God created Man in his own image, then God can be referred to as Man. Reading *Genesis* from a Gnostic viewpoint, however, suggests that Man is the Demiurge. Saturnilus changed the Biblical text so that the Archons say 'Let us make man in the image and likeness' rather than 'in our image and likeness'. Man is created in the image of God (*Gen.* 1:26–7), rather than of his creator, the Gnostic Demiurge. This is because Sophia or the true God tricks the Demiurge into creating a being greater than himself by supplying the pneumatic element. It is this that is 'alien' to the world. Man's superiority to the Archons who made him is stressed also at Layton v Fr. C = Völker Frag 1 = Clem., *Strom.* 2.36.2–4 (133.6–16 Stählin):

> And just as panic overcame the angels on account of the moulded form, since it uttered what was greater than its moulding on account of the one, who unseen, deposited in it a seed of the essence from above and who spoke openly, in this way too in the races of earthly men the works of men become objects of terror to the ones who made them, such as statues and images and everything which hands make as a pretence of God. For Adam, having been moulded as a pretence of Man, rendered them fearful of the pre-existent Man, since this stood in him and being terrified, they quickly spoilt the work.

Despite this superiority, Man is still inferior to the 'pre-existent human being' envisaged by God and the actual production, a theme one can also observe in Philo. However, in this case the Archons can be blamed for the inferiority of Man, just as in the *Timaeus* the work of the Young Gods was responsible for Man's mortality. Man is still formed according to the divine image and the God rectifies his inadequacy, since he improves upon what has been modelled (Layton v Fr. D = Völker Frag 5 = Clem., *Strom.* 4.89.6–4.90.1 (vol. 2.287.21–7 Stählin)):

> Just as much as an image is inferior to the living face, to this extent too is the comos inferior to living eternity. What, then, is the cause of the portrait? It is the greatness of the face that has provided the impression to the painter, so that it might be honoured under his name. For the shape is not authoritatively secured, but the name completes the deficiency in the representation. And the unseen (activity?) of God works together with what has been moulded to make it credible.

---

[59] Iren., *Adv. Haer.* 1.21.5   [60] Iren., *Adv. Haer.* 1.30.6

Man's members (i.e. the Church) remain in the world as prisoners, but can escape through *gnosis*. The story of Man is a prefigurement of the fate of Christ and the myth is probably inspired by it.

The end of creation

The Valentinian concept of creation also envisages what will occur at the end of the world, when the Demiurge and the souls of the just will move to the midpoint, occupied by Sophia, but will remain outside the fullness.[61] Philosophically, this is particularly interesting. Many metaphysical systems have a cyclical concept; for example, Stoic *ekpyrosis* or Platonic metempsychosis. Here the goal of Valentinianism is the negation of creation. Unlike Origen, a second fall is not envisaged or at least never made explicit. Creation is totally pointless, although at least Valentinus envisages some hope of salvation for the creator. Unlike other Gnostic sects, he also recognises the possibility of some (albeit limited) salvation for the just (non-Gnostics). Still, unlike in Plato's system, they never get a second chance. Once all human souls have escaped, the material fabric of created reality will be destroyed by fire and matter will enter into 'definitive non-existence'.[62] It is an indictment of creation when the entire goal of the Valentinian system is to seek to undo it. In the Valentinian system, no doubt as part of its *rapprochement* with the Jewish tradition, the Demiurge is allowed to repent at the arrival of the Saviour and be rewarded by a place at the midpoint.[63]

   The Demiurge is not an antagonistic power, but it seems that a particular divine role has been allotted to him; he is something like the caretaker of the *Cratylus*. While this may not prove Pétrement's 'Valentinian turning-point', the notion of the Jewish Yahweh acting as a protector for the Christian Church certainly indicates a change in outlook that has taken place since the emergence of Christian Gnosticism. The spirits of the Gnostics become detached from their souls and enter the Pleroma with Achamōth; and are bestowed as brides on the angels around the saviour. According to the *Gospel of Truth*, the material world will be dissolved, rather like the system in Origen.[64]

---

[61] Iren., *Adv Haer.* 1.7.1   [62] Iren., *Adv. Haer.* 1.7.1

[63] Iren., *Adv. Haer.* 1.7.4. This is similar to the mother's readmission into the Pleroma when she is viewed as having become completely rehabilitated in the Barbelognostic system. *Cf.* Iren., *Adv. Haer.* 1.29.4.

[64] GTr 25: 'But when unity makes the ways complete it is in unity that all will gather themselves, and it is by acquaintance that all will purify themselves out of multiplicity into unity, consuming matter within themselves as fire, and darkness by light, and death by life.' (trans. Layton)

The significance of the Sophia myth

Intense debate has been sparked off by both variants of the Sophia myth as to which is the original Valentinian version. As Stead has illustrated, it is likely that it is neither, but that both are sophisticated versions of a much simpler original doctrine held by Valentinus himself.[65] Stead advances several cogent arguments in favour of such a view. Firstly, both versions are organised in two phases (events within the Pleroma and activity subsequent to the fall). Secondly, the myth employs formal parallelism at several points. The First Sophia and the other Aeons do not know their origin, which is known by Monogenes (*Adv. Haer.* 1.3.13), in order that they may long to see the Father. Likewise, the younger Sophia is not informed about her origin by Christ so that she may long for better things (*Adv. Haer.* iv.1.33–4).

The First Sophia acts without her consort (*Adv. Haer.* 1.2.2), while the younger Sophia is without a consort (*Adv. Haer.* 1.4.1). Indeed, it might be said that she is below the law of the syzygy. Thirdly, there is the parallelism between Sophia's attempt to know the Father, which is stopped by Horos, and Achamōth's attempt to re-enter the Pleroma to find the Aeon who has left her, until she is stopped by outer Horos (who must clearly be a duplication). Fourthly, there is the parallelism between the expulsion of Sophia's guilty thought from the Pleroma, which creates younger Sophia or Achamōth and the expulsion of Achamōth's passions which then go towards the creation of the material realm. Finally, when younger Sophia is expelled she appeals to Christ to expel her passions and he sends the Paraclete or Soter. This indicates that the versions which we have are a development of a much simpler original involving only one Sophia, one Horos and a single expulsion of passions.

Sagnard propounded a theory of '*les lois de la gnose*'.[66] This is the notion that in the Gnostic myths there is a tendency to draw a correspondence between both the upper and lower worlds. However, in this myth, there is only duplication in the events relating to Sophia. There is no equivalent to the Pleroma functioning at a lower level, and the Demiurge has no counterpart within the Pleroma. This leaves one to draw the conclusion that the myth of Sophia is a deliberate reconstruction. This may have been to cater for inconsistencies between the various traditions. It is possible, for example, that some versions regard the guilty intention of the first Sophia as expelled from the Pleroma, while others may have regarded her passions as being expelled. One tradition claims that Sophia had four passions;

[65] Stead: 1969, 81   [66] Sagnard: 1947, 255–65

another that she had three (and repentance). This all seems to indicate that
the passions were those of the First Sophia, but have been assigned to the
younger Sophia in the versions which we have.

According to Irenaeus, Valentinus believed in an ultimate Dyad and
thirty Aeons, which is closer to the system subsequently advocated by
Ptolemaeus. Valentinus does posit two Horoi, one between the other Aeons
and Bythos and another between the Mother and the Pleroma.

> ... καὶ τὸν Χριστὸν δὲ οὐκ ἀπὸ τῶν ἐν τῷ Πληρώματι Αἰώνων προβεβλῆσ-
> θαι, ἀλλὰ ὑπὸ τῆς μητρός, ἔξω [suppl. δὲ] γενομένης, κατὰ τὴν γνώμην
> τῶν κρειττόνων ἀποκεκυῆσθαι μετὰ σκιᾶς τινος.

> ... and Christ was sent forth not in the Pleroma of the Aeons, but by the
> mother outside, and due to the judgement of the powers, she was put away
> with a certain shadow. (Iren., *Adv. Haer.* 1.5.1.19–22)

In this version, Christ is the son of Sophia (and therefore the younger
brother of the Demiurge), and is not the product of the Pleroma. Sophia
has been expelled from the Pleroma, indicating that in this version, we are
only dealing with a single Sophia. If one turns to the *Excerpta* of Clement,
the situation becomes more complex. In one passage, Christ is emanated
from the Ennoia (Thought) of Sophia.[67] Stead suggests that this might
indicate that the Ennoia is to be distinguished as a separate entity from
Sophia and that the resemblance between the two passages suggests that
the Mother and Sophia can be equated.[68] If this is the case, then perhaps
in the Ennoia we have the origin of the younger Sophia. At *Excerpta* 39,
the Mother produces Christ.[69] Christ ascends to become the adopted son
of the Pleroma. This version is problematic, since Christ's origin would be
inferior to that of the other Aeons, and would seem to make him incapable
of fulfilling the role which he has to play.

All of this reveals that a creative approach towards Gnostic mythology
was adopted by Valentinus and his successors, rather like the approach
towards Plato's dialogues that was adopted by Platonists. In the myth of
Sophia, we have the ultimate indictment that the world is bad from its
beginning. It results, not as part of the divine plan, but as the product
of fragmentation within the godhead, which ultimately leaves part of the
godhead trapped, as in Hermetism. Similarly, Gnosticism's whole goal is a
return to the situation before creation occurred. (In Valentinianism, this is

---

[67] ... τὸν Χριστὸν ἐξ ἐννοίας προελθόντα τῆς Σοφίας..., 'Christ comes forth from the thought
of Sophia' and ... ἐκ τῆς μητρῴας γενόμενον ἐννοίας..., 'being generated out of the maternal
thought' (*Excerpta* 2.32.2.1)
[68] Stead: 1969, 85   [69] ἡ Μήτηρ, προβαλοῦσα τὸν Χριστόν...

not strictly speaking true, since the Demiurge will receive a promotion of sorts.)

This world does not result from God's perfect wisdom, but from another Sophia, who must be an inferior sort of wisdom, since not only is she the last and youngest of the Aeons, but we are explicitly told that she suffers from ignorance.[70] This ignorance results from impudence, and the materials of the physical world are derived from the negative emotions of the even lower form of wisdom which is expelled. On top of this, the world is created by the Demiurge, who lacks the better aspects of Achamōth, so that what we are left with in the created world is a cosmos that reveals some aspects of a divine, ordering power (such as the images of the Forms), but which was unperceived by the entity who actually moulded the world.

Sophia can be interpreted not just as a failed emanation which has to be expelled from the godhead, but also as a divine mediator. The lower Sophia/Achamōth (that is the substance which is emanated from the higher Sophia is described as a 'heavenly Jerusalem', and 'the good land flowing with milk and honey'.[71] Indeed, as a divine mediator and creative agent, she eclipses the Demiurge in the Valentinian creation myth. Sophia contains numerous concepts. The term Mother is often allocated to her and it seems that she may have been conflated with the consort of the Father. She also is a failed female entity. As the *Gospel of Philip* 60:10–14 states: 'Echamoth is one thing and ech-moth another. Echamoth is simply Sophia, but Echmoth is the Sophia of Death – that is the Sophia who is acquainted with Death, and who is called the little Sophia' (trans. after Layton, slightly modified).[72] The perfect consort may have been altered into this Sophia of Death based on the view that, since the most powerful principle after Good is Evil, it must originate from the second most powerful cosmic power.[73] It would have been quite natural to make this second power female, since the second principle was traditionally regarded as a Dyad (which is female).

Since Sophia connects the world of matter and the Gnostic equivalent of the world of the Forms, she can be regarded as the last of the Aeons. In attempting to interpret this myth, Platonists assigned various roles to Sophia. She can be viewed as the Receptacle of the *Timaeus*, hence the use of the term 'mother' to refer to her. Because of her fall, she can be regarded

---

[70] ἄγνοια, Iren., *Adv. Haer.* 1.2.3, 1.4.1, 1.5.4, Ps.-Hipp., *Ref.* VI.31.1–2, ἀπορία, Iren., *Adv. Haer.* 1.4.1, 1.5.4, Ps.-Hipp., *Ref.* VI.32.5, 32.6.

[71] Ps.-Hipp., *Ref.*, VI.25. *Cf. Exodus* 33:3.

[72] Only the Coptic translation (MS *NHC* II (pp. 51–86) survives, not the original Greek. The *Gospel of Philip* is a Valentinian anthology; Layton has suggested that its contents may possibly be drawn from different branches of Valentinianism. *Cf.* Layton: 1987, 325.

[73] Stead: 1969, 99 cites the Naassene psalm at Ps.-Hipp., *Ref.* V.10.2 in this context.

as recalcitrant matter. Pseudo-Hippolytus at *Ref.* vi.30.9 refers to her as μήτηρ καὶ τιθήνη, which evokes the 'formless matter' of *Tim.* 51a. Stead also adds that she can be identified with the World-Soul; just like the human soul she falls due to her attachment to matter.[74] Plutarch, too, regards the Receptacle as a disorderly soul.

It is tempting to discern Philonic influence on the Valentinian myth. Philo uses 'God's shadow' to denote either the *Logos* or the world *vis-à-vis* the *Logos* (*Leg. All.* iii.96, 100). In Philo, the world is God's younger son, while the eldest is *Logos* (*Deus* 31), God's four offspring being *Logos*, Shadow, Demiurge and Prince. The Valentinian myth is composed within the context of an interest in the origin of evil and within the framework of the temptation of Eve. For example, Eve's celestial counterpart is Zoe, who is connected with Sophia in Gnostic texts. In the *Hypostasis of the Archons* and *On the Origin of the World*, she is generally represented as the daughter of Sophia, though on occasion in *On the Origin of the World*, Sophia is called Sophia Zoe. Another indication of the similarity is that in both cases a female figure initiates the sin, and the guilt is transmitted to a husband/consort. Ultimately, both myths try to explain the emergence of disorder. For the Gnostics the fall of Man becomes simply a copy of the fall which occurred within the Pleroma, and both myths connect the Pleroma and the material world.[75]

Sophia also owes something to the Holy Spirit, which Simon and Menander both regarded as the Mother of all beings.[76] Christ in *The Gospel of the Hebrews* refers to 'my mother the Holy Spirit'. Aphraates, a fourth century writer, claims that God is man's father, but the Holy Spirit is his mother.[77] The conception of the Holy Spirit as the Mother is a natural one, since *rûah* (spirit) is feminine in Hebrew. Since *pneuma* in Greek is neuter, *rûah* can be rendered in Greek by Ennoia or Sophia, which helps to preserve the female aspect. Theophilus of Antioch and Irenaeus' *Apostolic Demonstration* list Wisdom as the third person of the Trinity.[78] The Holy Spirit is equivalent to creative Wisdom. Once the act of creation was devalued, a distinction was drawn between the supreme Mother as first emanation and a second divine Mother inferior to the first.[79] It is only once *pneuma* is translated by the masculine Latin *spiritus* that the concept of the Spirit as a female divine principle disappears.

---

[74] Stead: 1969, 100   [75] Macrae: 1970, 99

[76] Pétrement: 1991, 75 gives references: *Apocryphon of John* (BG p. 117 and parallels); *Gospel of Philip* 107.18–27; 118.24–5; 119.16–28; *Apocryphal Epistle of James* 6.20–1.

[77] Aphrahat, *Homilien*, übers. V. G. Bert, TU 3, 3–4 (Leipzig, 1888), 297

[78] Theoph., *Ad. Autol.* 1, 7, 11, 15 and 18 Irenaeus, *Demonstr. apos.* 5 and 10

[79] Pétrement: 1991, 77

This is replaced to some extent in later Christian thought by the Virgin Mary by certain heretics who worshipped her as a goddess and regarded her as the incarnation of a cosmic power, Michael. The Father, Christ and Mary were regarded as the Trinity by groups mentioned by Epiphanius of Salamis in the mid-fourth century. The Christian concept of Mary contains elements of the Mediterranean mother-goddess.

An element of this occurs in the Barbelo, the second entity in the onto-logical scheme of the Barbelo-Gnostics. Although sometimes described as a male virgin, it is essentially a female generative principle. The *Apocr. Joh.* 5.56 describes it as 'mother–father', 'a womb for the Pleroma' and the 'thrice-androgynous name' which indicates a dyadic nature.[80] From v Fr. B Layton (= Frag 9 Völker = Marcellus of Ancyra, *On the Holy Church*, 9), it would seem that Valentinus was quite close to the Barbelognostics' three-fold division. In *On the Three Natures*, Valentinus is supposed to have pro-pounded a belief in three subsistent entities (hypostases) and three persons. This might even be a version of the triad: Being, Life, Intellect. The source for the text is Marcellus of Ancyra, a fourth-century theologian. The title is all that survives of *On the Three Natures*. While it is possible that this work refers to the Trinity, it may also have dealt with the earlier tripartite division of this Barbelo Aeon, which does not correspond to either the persons of the Trinity or to the Platonic triad.[81] Sophia is also an indefinite female dyad and this is how she comes to represent a cause of instability, thereby suggesting the myth of her fall.

Letter to Flora

Another major witness to the Platonising element within Gnosticism was Ptolemy (*floruit* c. 136–180 AD). Previously regarded as one of Valentinus' most important disciples and as the founder of its Italic version, his precise relationship to Valentinus has been cast into doubt by the recent research of Christoph Markschies.[82] Markschies suggests that when Irenaeus refers to 'the people around Ptolemy' (οἱ περὶ Πτολεμαῖν) he is differentiateng them from the Valentian school (ἡ τοῦ Οὐαλεντίνου σχολή) at *Adv. Haer.* I *praef.* 2, not suggesting that Ptolemey was the founder of a branch of Valentinianism. Despite this, Markschies is willing to accept a close connection between Valentinus and Ptolemy.

An important source for Ptolemy's ideas is his *Letter To Flora*. Despite its name, it reads more like a treatise. The text was preserved in a quotation

---

[80] Dillon: 1999, 70 n. 2 [81] *Cf.* e.g. *Gr. Seth* 50:23–4. [82] Markschies: 2000. esp. 251–2

by Epiphanius of Salamis (*Against Heresies* 33.3.1–33.7.10).[83] Although it
does not deal solely or even primarily with the Demiurge, it is valuable
for our purposes, since it concentrates on one of the burning issues of
the Christianity of its day: the importance of the Jewish Torah and its
relationship to the Christian Bible. The addressee of the letter appears to
be a mainstream Christian, to whom Ptolemy is expounding the details
of Valentinianism. The language is non-technical and rather frustratingly
alludes to a sequel, which will concentrate more heavily on metaphysics,
but which does not seem to have survived (if it was composed at all).

Ptolemy raises the question of whether the law and the world are the
creation of God or if the devil is 'the father and maker of the universe', a
clear allusion to Plato's terminology at *Tim.* 28e.[84] Ptolemy alludes to the
belief advocated by certain Gnostic sects, most notably the Cathars and
Bogomils, that the world is so imperfect that it must have been created by
the devil, usually in this context known as the Cosmocrator. The majority
of Gnostic sects, including the Valentinians, would reject this claim, seeing
the Demiurge as a separate entity. Ptolemy defends the Demiurge, whom he
equates with Yahweh. The law is regarded as the product of the Demiurge
or Old Testament God.[85] The true Demiurge, however, is the father of
Christ, who allows Yahweh to create the world:

> And the apostle says that his is the demiurgy of the cosmos and that 'all
> things were generated by him and nothing was generated apart from him',
> and in this way undermined in advance the wisdom of these liars which
> is without sure foundation and the demiurgy is not of a god who causes
> destruction, but of one who is just and who hates wickedness. But these
> unthinking people do not take account of the forethought of the Demiurge
> and so they are incapacitated, not only in the eyes of the soul, but also those
> of the body. (33.3.6)

It is of particular interest that the father of Christ can be regarded as
the true Demiurge. In the more fundamentalist Gnostic tradition, the
Demiurge's malevolence (or sometimes ignorance) is responsible for the
inherent imperfection of the universe. The Valentinians, as part of their
attempt to bridge the gap between the Christian heritage of Judaism,
Gnosticism and Greek philosophy, sought to reconcile the concept of
an imperfect world formed by an ignorant Demiurge and the Platonic
notion that the design of the world revealed the existence of the rational
intelligence which had created it. The myth of Sophia allows him to regard

---

[83] Since the text is a word for word quotation, it is, in fact, reliable.
[84] Ptolemy, *Letter to Flora* 33.3.2   [85] Ptolemy, *Letter to Flora* 33.3.4

the First Principle as ultimately the Creator, since the Demiurge creates after being inspired by the supreme God, although he is unaware of this.

Ptolemy does not regard the Demiurge as the devil; they are both distinct entities. Ptolemy is also more favourable to Yahweh than is typical for the Gnostics, not referring to him as ignorant, but as just (although not good). While an element of ignorance is conveyed in Ptolemy's description of the Demiurge as administering the cosmos according to the sort of 'justice that is his',[86] he does display the *rapprochement* towards Judaism that led Pétrement to refer to this as the Valentinian turning-point.

Although positioning the Demiurge between the devil and the true God is to be found in Gnostic systems that do not posit a Cosmocrator, Ptolemy is heavily influenced by the Platonic myth of world-generation in this description of three essences:

> For the essence of the opponent is destruction and darkness (for he is material and split into many parts) and the essence of the ungenerated father of the all is both incorruptible and self-existent light and the essence of this produced a triple power, and he is an image of the better god. (37.7.7)

It seems that Ptolemy has been influenced here by the three elements of Sameness and Difference, and the mixture intermediate between the two at *Timaeus* 35aff. in his explanation for the variance between these entities here. Ptolemy then tantalisingly alludes to an esoteric Valentinian metaphysics concerning which he will inform Flora in the next instalment. He is on the verge of explaining the origin of evil and how corruptible and intermediate essences can come to be from a First Principle which is 'ungenerated and indestructible and good'.[87]

The main value of the *Letter to Flora* is the information it provides on the relationship between the Demiurge and the First Principle. It is of particular interest since it is a document created by the Gnostics themselves, rather than information relayed via the hostility of the Church Fathers. In it, Ptolemy adopts a stance which differs from the dualistic type of approach that one might expect from a Gnostic, identifying three separate entities: God, Devil and Demiurge, rather than the more usual two of God and Demiurge. It is never quite clear how there is space in the Gnostic scheme for both Devil and Demiurge, but it is a product of Ptolemy's attempt to rectify the harsh dichotomy between Yahweh and the highest principle more usually found in Gnosticism.

---

[86] Ptolemy, *Letter to Flora* 33.3.5   [87] 33.7.8

Summer Harvest

<αἰ>θέρος πάντα κρεμάμενα {πνεύματι} βλέπω,
πάντα δ᾽ ὀχούμενα πνεύματι νοῶ·
σάρκα μὲν ἐκ ψυχῆς κρεμαμένην,
ψυχὴν δὲ ἀέρος ἐξεχομένην,
ἀέρα δὲ ἐξ αἴθρης κρεμάμενον,
ἐκ δὲ βυθοῦ καρποὺς φερομένους,
ἐκ μήτρας δὲ βρέφος φερόμενον.

By means of my spirit I see all that are hanging,
By means of my spirit I know all that are being carried,
For flesh hangs from soul,
And then soul clings to air,
And air hangs from aether,
And fruits rush forth from the deep,
And a foetus rushes forth from its mother.

This text (Layton v Hr[88] = Völker Frag 8) is a cosmological poem in which the writer, whom it has been suggested is Valentinus himself, describes the generation of the universe.[89] It actually has nothing to do with a summer harvest and Layton plausibly suggests that it may have been a tune to which this poem was intended to be sung, although noting that this school frequently makes use of agricultural metaphors when considering emanations.[90] The text itself has been preserved by Pseudo-Hippolytus, who quotes it *Refutation of all* in *Heresies* VI.37.7, and it forms a useful comparison to the theme of the Demiurge presented in the myth of Sophia. The text differs from traditional Gnostic material, being written in regular verse, and the speaker claims a personal authority for his knowledge ('I see in spirit'), rather than resorting to pseudepigraphy, which would be more common among the Gnostic sects. The author (I hesitate to write Valentinus) describes the ontological structure of the universe from below 'flesh-soul-air-upper atmosphere') while the 'crops' are the elements emanated from the godhead into the realm of phenomena. The 'Deep' is the Valentinian First Principle. Aether represents the Pleroma in its entirety, including Sophia.

According to Pseudo-Hippolytus' interpretation, flesh refers to matter which hangs from the soul of the craftsman (Demiurge) – by this he means that the craftsman clings to the spirit of the outer fullness. The infant child may be a reference to Valentinus' vision from which he is said to have derived his authority, although it is far more likely to represent the *Logos*

---

[88] V Hr = Valentinus, *Summer Harvest*, not a fragment, but a complete work.
[89] The Greek text can be also found at Heitsch: 1963, 155.
[90] Layton: 1987, 346

(as it does in his supposed vision), and to indicate that he placed it next to the Father, but above the other Aeons. According to Pseudo-Hippolytus, Valentinus distinguished three levels of reality, but these are not the triad of spirit, soul and matter. Stead suggests that the emendation Σιγήν for the MS πᾶσι γῆν is wrong, although this leaves the genitive which follows unexplained.[91] He inclines towards Hilgenfeld's view that the emendation may be πηγήν, which would imply a triad of the Father, the Aeons and the cosmos, which could be seen as equivalent to the Middle Platonist triad of God, the Forms and matter. This would suit what we know of the Valentinian sect, which is more heavily Platonised than other Gnostic groups. The soul in such a case, though, may not necessarily refer to the Demiurge, but rather to the Platonic World-Soul, which would equate to what is otherwise introduced as a 'power' in Gnostic myth or 'verbal substance' in Fr. v.

The Sethians

Prior to concluding, it will be beneficial to examine briefly Sethian Gnosis, a much more dualistic system with markedly less Platonic features than its Valentinian counterpart. However, it is an alternative example of Christian Gnosis, although it does not seem to have attracted the same hostility as Valentinianism from the 'mother church', probably because it was not as influential, exemplified by the limited records or references to it in the ancient sources, in comparison to the Valentinians.

In the *Paraphrase of Shem* (*NHC* VII.1) Derdekeas, the son of the highest entity (Pleromatic Light) is allowed by his father to grant a revelation to Shem. In this system there are three principles: Light and Darkness with intermediate Spirit. Darkness wants to retain the *Nous* revealed to Shem, while Light attempts to recapture it. This produces the conflict which leads to creation. After the first clash, sky and earth are created and subsequent clashes produce living beings. This is reminiscent of Mandean dualism. Perates (the Self-Generated), intermediate between Supreme Good and Matter, descends to impress his father's seals upon matter,[92] echoing Man's descent in order to create in the *Poimandres*. Perates recovers the formal principles and returns. Here creation is allegorised as a circular self-generating process.

Basilides adopts elements of this, expressed in a less dualistic form. He depicts the non-existent God creating the world by hurling his seed into the immaterial substratum. The First Sonship, *Nous*, returns to him

---

[91] Stead: 1969, 81   [92] Filoramo: 1990, 84

immediately. The Second, Anima Mundi, is unable to follow, but ascends to a place near God. The Second Sonship is the Holy Spirit, but for Basilides, it is not consubstantial with the Father.[93] It is more akin to the veil of the Sethian system or the Horos of the Valentinians than Sophia.

The Third Sonship requires purification because 'that has remained in the huge mass of seeds to make and receive benefits'. This Third Sonship allows creation to take place and it is also the one which becomes incarnate in Jesus: in the Sethian system, man is created by the demon-angels, who divide up the task amongst themselves. *NHC* ii.1.15. 29–17.6 provides the details: 'The first one began to create the head: Eteraphaope Abron created his head; Meniggestroeth created the brain; Asterechme the right eye; Thaspamocha the left eye; Yerormos the right ear; Bissoum the left ear; Akioreim the nose . . . ' The text goes on to outline the creation of each segment of the human body by a demon in a similar manner right down to the toe-nails. It contains a detailed section on the creation of the genitals. Each demon controls that part which it created. Their mother, Onortocrasi, is pure matter, while the four chief demons are Efememphi (Pleasure), Iocho (Greed), Nenentophni (Pain), and Blaomen (Fear).[94]

According to the *Apocryphon of John*, the Mother tricks the Demiurge by informing him through the five luminaries that to give Adam life, he should breathe his spirit into Adam's face.[95] The Mother's power leaves Ialdabaoth and passes to Adam. Realising their mistake the Archons imprison Adam in the material world. The Demiurge or Ialdabaoth or the chief Archon – the terminology refers to the same entity – extracts Adam's rib in his attempt to seize the Epinoia of Light, which flees. As a compromise the Demiurge makes a copy of the Epinoia: terrestrial Eve.

Ialdabaoth and Eve mate and produce Elohim (Cain, the bear-faced just god) and Jahweh (Abel, the cat-faced unjust god). Elohim and Jahweh are two Old Testament names for God. It is understandable that as God of the Law Jahweh should represent the unjust god, since that was the aspect of the Jewish God most objectionable to the Gnostics. But why is Abel unjust, when the Biblical Cain is the unjust brother? Perhaps this is a deliberate inversion. Cain presides over the higher elements (fire and wind), Abel over the lower ones (earth and water). It is difficult to see, though, how Cain can be just when he unites with Abel to deceive humanity.

Epinoia-Zoe returns to Eve, who produces a child, Seth, with Adam. In other similar variants, carnal Eve produces Cain and Abel and spiritual

---

[93] Filoramo: 1990, 85   [94] Filoramo: 1990, 92   [95] *BG* 51.1*ff.*

Eve bears Seth. The Demiurge or Protarchon consults with the seven planetary Archons and produces Necessity (*heimarmenē*), which seems to be a version of Plato's *Anankē*. It cannot eradicate the people of *gnosis*, so the Archons ravish the daughters of men, which produces sickness and death[96] (*NHC* 11.1.30.4–7). Eve is somehow possessed of *gnosis*, which she communicates to Adam. The Demiurge retaliates by splitting the androgynous Aeon. This has the effect of making Adam and Eve oblivious of *gnosis*.[97]

Three angels (these appear to be different to the Archons or demon-angels) announce *gnosis* to Adam and the future destiny of Seth's descendants. This is clearly a duplication as exhibited so frequently in Gnosticism; in the original version, Adam must have learnt *gnosis* from Eve and then revealed it to Seth. Where does Eve derive *gnosis* from? The androgynous Aeon must be Man, though it is unclear what ontological system would allow the Demiurge power to divide an Aeon.

Noah's generation ridicule the power of the Demiurge, and he decides to eradicate them. Noah is either warned of the flood by Light or else reassures the Demiurge and is allowed to survive. Noah's sons serve the Demiurge, but four thousand of the descendants of Shem and Japhet join with the people of *gnosis*. The Demiurge once again attempts to eradicate them, but they are saved from fire, sulphur and asphalt by Abrasax, Sablo and Gamaliel, who descend on clouds and convey them to the higher Aeons where 'they will be like those angels, for they are not strangers to them, but they work in the imperishable seed' (*NHC* v.5.76 3ff.).[98] The Third Intervention occurs when the 'Illuminator of Knowledge' defeats the Demiurge by performing miracles. The Illuminator appears to be the Saviour, who is an incarnation of Seth. However, the end will occur only during the time of the fourteenth kingdom when sinners will repent and be judged by the honest angels.

The Sethian system is less interesting for our purposes than that of Valentinus. Of note here is the extreme hostility to the Demiurge, who resembles an evil principle, like the devil-cosmocrator of the Cathars and Bogomils. Here Eve is an illuminating principle, with no element of a fall expressed even in her mating with Ialdabaoth. Sethianism owes more to Iranian dualism than to Platonism. It is the Platonism of Valentinus which leads him away from the hardline dualism of this system.

[96] *NHC* 11.1.30.4–7
[97] 'We became darkened in our hearts. Now I slept in the thought of my heart.' (*NHC* v.5.65.21ff.)
[98] Filoramo: 1990, 97

Conclusion

Gnosticism, especially its Valentinian variant or development, is particularly interesting in tracing the development of the Demiurge. Firstly, the Valentinian system itself was relatively liberal, allowing scope for subsequent thinkers to develop or reinterpret the teachings of the master. Irenaeus complains that 'every day one of them [the Valentinians] invents something new and none of them is considered perfect unless he is productive in this way' (1.18.15). Here we have evidence of the similar type of phenomenon that was occurring in contemporary Platonism and which helps to account for the divergent traditions. In spite of the state of the evidence and the evident hostility of Irenaeus, through whom much of our information is conveyed, it is still possible to draw a number of firm conclusions concerning the Valentinian view.

Firstly, while we may be dealing with a heterodox sect, what we are discussing here is creation in the Judaeo-Christian sense and not mere demiurgy. The Valentinians were after all 'wolves in sheep's clothing', very much a part of the mother-church in their original incarnation. This, I would suggest, is one of the reasons why the Demiurge is a less important agent in the generation of the world than Sophia or Achamōth. It is Sophia who initiates the sequence of events that leads to creation; one cannot really expect the Demiurge to accomplish more than he does. Since he was conceived by Sophia without the will of her consort or the consent of the supreme principle, he is destined to be defective. He is forced to construct the world without any knowledge of the Forms since he was either expelled from the Pleroma at birth or was born outside it. The material from which he constructs the world is drawn from the negative emotions of Achamōth. It is not the case that the Demiurge is malevolent; rather he is an entity with limited resources.

The Demiurge's role is undermined by his relationship to other figures. In variants which posit the Cosmocrator, both entities appear to be on a level of equality, although the Cosmocrator has the advantage of greater knowledge. This would seem to leave him incapable of combating evil within the material realm, which since he is described as good, one would presume that he would wish to do. He is also not the sole creator of the material realm, since Sophia is responsible for instilling spirit in man, which is the only positive aspect of creation. Christ is the true Demiurge in the suprasensible realm, since in his stabilisation of the Pleroma he performs the standard demiurgic action of imposing order upon disorder. The Gnostic

Sophia is probably derived from an interpretation of the Pythagorean–Platonist Indefinite Dyad, as well as the Wisdom of intertestamental Jewish Wisdom literature (upon which Philo draws).

Valentinianism is an extreme development of the concept of the Demiurge as an insulator of the supreme God from the inherent evil of his creation. Still, in fulfilling that role, he is unsatisfactory as a divine mediator; a role which is fulfilled jointly by Christ in the soteriological sense, and by Sophia metaphysically. This helps to account for his role in the Valentinian creation myth, where he is certainly not a central character, and where he emerges on the scene in what can only be described as an epilogue, after the main events within the Pleroma have already taken place. Perhaps one should expect nothing less from a system which undermines the very value of the creative act. The sole result of creation during *Endzeit* will be a more united Godhead, since presumably Sophia will have repented adequately for her transgression. In Gnosticism, there is no notion of world-cycles, so that this entire universe can be viewed as nothing other than a divine aberration.

CHAPTER 9

Origen, the Demiurge and Christian theology

Introduction

The work of Philo provided a foundation for his fellow-Alexandrians' attempts to reconcile the divine revelation offered to the Judaeo–Christian tradition with the insights of Greek philosophy. Origen's predecessor Clement had, it is true, drawn heavily upon Greek philosophical motifs, but was unwilling to engage in a systematic exposition of Christian theology, due to the dangers of allowing the general public access to an account of divine mysteries.[1] Origen was not so inhibited, though his Christian Platonism made his works 'suspect' to some. The perceived heresy of Origen's works accounts for the loss of large sections, and these heretical elements themselves owe a great deal to his attempts to unite Platonic philosophy and Christianity, or to put it another way, to give Christianity a philosophical pedigree, which culminated most famously in his portrayal of Christ as the 'creature' of the Father. Whatever doubts one might have about his orthodoxy, one cannot question Origen's intellectual ability; unlike with Plutarch, or Maximus, here we have a 'serious' philosopher, prepared to resolve the most perplexing questions relating to demiurgy in a unique and original way.

This Christian interpretation of the Bible in philosophical terms was part of a struggle for credibility and legitimacy. The Bible was a major advantage in the drive to convert: as Origen comments, the Church's principal mechanism for conversion was reading the Bible and explaining these readings.[2] The contradictions between the Bible and Greek philosophy could also at times be something of an Achilles heel, exposing the Christians to ridicule or hostility, when trying to win converts from the

---

[1] The earliest Christian thinker whom we know to have enjoyed a philosophical education in the Greek tradition, Justin Martyr, was influenced by the Timaean scheme of world-generation, though unlike his successor, Tatian, he does not seem to have recognised the problems it posed for a Christian, in terms of its positing of co-existent matter.

[2] *CCels.* 3.50

upper-classes. The Christians were also involved in scriptural debates with the Jews. Christians like Origen were trying to win over pagan converts through unlocking the universal philosophy contained in the Bible, while claiming to be worthier heirs of Judaic wisdom than the Jews themselves. Origen himself famously compiled the *Hexapla*, containing multiple versions of the Bible, to ensure the accuracy of his scriptural references. One thinks of Yohanan ben Zakkai's comment that 'a heathen who studies the Torah deserves death' (*Sanhedrin* 59a), since his actions are comparable to one who violates a bethrothed maiden.[3] Despite Origen's heavy dependence on the *oeuvre* of the hellenised Philo, and naturally on the Old Testament itself, he refers to Jewish teaching itself as μύθοι καὶ λῆροι, 'myths and rubbish'.[4] His main exposition of the Judaeo–Christian creation account is outlined in *Peri Archôn*, although he discusses related issues in other works, most notably in the *Commentary on John* and *Contra Celsum*.

It seems to me that Origen's interpretation of Scripture can best be understood against a Platonist background, although this is not universally agreed. Edwards and Tzamalikos, in particular, downplay the Platonic influence upon Origen, although they do not deny the significant role played by philosophy (or indeed Platonic language) in his thought. Tzamalikos also questions the extent to which Philo's *Logos* served as a direct influence on Origen, rather than the *Gospel According to John*. The main contribution of the position adopted by Edwards and Tzamalikos has been to stress the extent to which Origen's views have been misrepresented by his opponents,[5] as well as to highlight passages where Origen does not adhere to a Platonist view; however it is clear that Origen as a Christian must necessarily disagree with Platonist views which contradict the Bible. Origen used Platonist language and concepts to expound Scripture in much the same way that a modern Jesuit (one thinks of Teilhard de Chardin here) might explain the Bible in a manner which takes account of scientific theories, in order to attract educated followers. Edwards and Tzamalikos do, however, concede that Origen's thought has been radically influenced by Platonism.

One of the major arguments which Tzamalikos relies upon to support his position that Origen is an anti-Platonist is the claim that for Origen creation comes about from non-Being:

---

[3] Rabbi Yohanan clearly did not mean this literally; rather he seems to have been concerned that Gentiles could use Jewish law against the Jews.
[4] *CCels* 2.5
[5] For example, Methodius of Olympus' claim that Origen espoused the doctrine of transmigration. *Cf.* Edwards: 2002, 2.

This is one more point on which Origen dissents from the Platonic mode of thought. To Plato it was an axiom that 'everything that has a beginning has also an end'. Against the background of that proposition, Origen affirms creation out of non-being (an unPlatonic concept) and explicates that, although this creation had a beginning, it will have no end. The notions of 'beginning' and 'end' related to creation are expanded in a context dissimilar to the Platonic mindset.[6]

Tzamalikos relies on Origen's statement *selPs* 138; PG 12:1661 to support this position: 'He is Creator because He brought creatures into being out of non-being'. Since the Greek reads καὶ δημιουργός μὲν διὰ τὰ γεγονότα ἀπό τοῦ μὴ ὄντος εἰς τὸ εἶναι, it would sound far more Platonic if simply translated 'He is the Demiurge, since he has brought generated things to be out of non-Being'. In any case, to call Origen an anti-Platonist on this basis does not seem to my mind to accurately reflect the Platonic tradition. In the *Timaeus* (on a literal reading) the world comes into being from non-being (i.e from pre-cosmic chaos). Even if the majority of Platonists rejected this reading, Plutarch and Atticus did not. Thus Tzamalikos' point actually demonstrates that Origen adhered to a view that was held by a minority of Platonists, but which could be justified based on a literal reading of a particularly influential dialogue of Plato's. This method of proceeding also highlights the difficulty in evaluating Origen's cosmology: Origen can refer to the world being generated out of non-being in the generally-understood sense of the term (i.e. nothing, so *creatio ex nihilo*) or in the Platonic sense (i.e. non-being in the sense of lacking a definite structure).

Similarly, Edwards notes that 'it is dangerous to count Plato as a monotheist or a theist of any kind, when he did not, in any sense that the Bible knows, believe in God'.[7] However, it is clear that Plato exhibits strong monotheistic tendencies (he reinterprets the traditional gods of Greek religion as manifestations of a supreme rational principle) and it is certainly possible to be a theist without believing in an anthropomorphic deity.

Peri Archôn

Origen's main discussion of creation is found in *Peri Archôn*; of his *Homilies on Genesis*, only *Homily* 1 is really concerned with creation (and it does not address philosophical concerns, but rather expounds *Genesis* as an aid to morality, as St Basil would later do in the *Hexaemeron*). For example, the

---

[6] Tzamalikos: 2007, 331   [7] Edwards: 2002, 48

'great whales' of *Genesis* 1:21 are interpreted as thoughts which are against God. Some comments in *Homily* 3 are relevant, such as the declaration that God is incorporeal and omnipotent and 'that he cares about mortal affairs and that nothing happens in heaven or earth apart from his providence',[8] but the homily deals with the circumcision of Abraham). The title of *Peri Archôn* is itself a reference to matters of philosophical debate. Rufinus translated it as *vel de Principiis vel de Principatibus*. Here we have an allusion to the two possible interpretations of the title: the principles of the Christian faith, or the metaphysical principles necessary for existence and knowledge. The Platonists recognised three ungenerated principles: God, Matter and the Forms. However, as Eusebius comments, Origen has retained the plural, even though he only recognises one principle necessary for existence: God, since he regards matter and the intelligible world as the creation of the Father.

That the principles of Christianity are really intended is suggested by the contents of the work. The preface of the treatise deals with matters of faith which are studied in the second part. The treatise itself also deals with matters essential to the Christian faith, such as the Church, and the redemption mentioned by Christ.[9] Despite the plural, there is never any doubt that we are dealing with the *arche* of the cosmos: God. In fact, the *arche* here is not to be confused with the Trinity, since for Origen it is only the Father and the Son, which he identifies with the *Logos*, which play a metaphysical role. The Holy Spirit is an entity which explains the workings of divine soteriology in the world through the influence of the Saints, but Origen does not attempt to assign it a metaphysical function.

Origen reveals his awareness of the multiple senses of the term *arche* at *Comm. Jn.* 1.(x) v 90, where he points out that it is not only among the Greeks that it has multiple significations. *Peri Archôn* aims at creating a system which can explain God's working in the world, in terms of Greek philosophy, while at the same time remaining loyal to Christian thinking. For Marcellus of Ancyra, the *archai* were evidently the Platonist ones: God, Matter and the Forms.[10] The Aristotelians and the Stoics also had their *archai*. Although Origen only recognised God as a principle, he is aware of the numerous interpretations of *arche*, as emerges from his discussion at *Comm. Jn.* 1.90–105. It is clear, then, that the title is deliberately ambiguous, evoking both metaphysics and Christianity. Additionally, Origen is playing

---

[8] *Homily* 3.2   [9] Crouzel and Simonetti: 1978, 14   [10] Crouzel and Simonetti: 1978, 13

on a third sense of the term, although in this case it has to be taken in the singular: the beginning of creation.[11]

The use of the term 'principle' is a technique on Origen's part to locate his work within a specific tradition. The fragments of a Περὶ ἀρχᾶν, composed in Doric Greek and falsely attributed to Archytas, is preserved in Stobaeus. Porphyry's *Life of Plotinus* also attributes a *Peri Archôn* to the Neoplatonist Longinus. Since Origen regards matter as uncreated and the intelligible world as created atemporally by the Son-*Logos*, contained in the Father who generated him, it would seem strange that Origen speaks of several principles when he clearly only posits one. However, he does use the term 'principle' to refer to matter and the Forms on the grounds that they are considered principles by others.

The work appears to be written without a plan. However, once the confusion of the book divisions is removed, the actual structure emerges. In any case, the book divisions are subsequent, probably from the fourth century, if the reception of the *Peri Archôn* followed the pattern of other works of Origen, such as the *Apology*. The *Peri Archôn* does have an overarching editorial structure, however, with two main sections – a general exposition, followed by a focus on particular questions, in this case echoing Pseudo-Aristotle's *De Mundo*, or more closely paralleling Salustios' *Concerning the Gods and the World*. Given this context, the *Peri Archôn* is particularly suitable for a study of demiurgic causality, as after having outlined the main concepts of his system, Origen then proceeds to resolve specific objections. The *Peri Archôn* consists of a number of relatively autonomous tracts which are arranged in the inverse order of the subject-matter of the six books of Plotinus' *Enneads*. (Plotinus' treatment consists of (1) Ethics, (2)–(3) the World, (4) Soul, (5) Intelligence and the Forms which it contains, (6) Being, One or Good.)

The reliability of Rufinus' translation

The next question which needs to be addressed before turning to the *Peri Archôn* is the reliability of Rufinus' Latin translation, the only complete (but not necessarily completely unabridged) version of the treatise that we have. Rufinus began a translation of the *Apology* at the end of 397 and then started on the *Peri Archôn* in 398. This detail is important, since Rufinus inserted into the *Peri Archôn* certain passages taken from his translation of the *Apology*.[12] Rufinus himself claims greater accuracy than Jerome, whom

---

[11] *Comm. Jn.* 1.95   [12] Crouzel and Simonetti: 1978, 23

he asserts in his version aspires to be more 'the father of the discourse than its translator'.[13]

Fortunately, it is possible to assess Rufinus' reliability independently. The discussion of free will at *Princ.* III is also found at *Philocalia* XXI. A comparison with Rufinus' version reveals the suppression of passages that would have been imprudent to reproduce doctrinally. He also ignores passages which contradict more orthodox selections of Origen concerning the Trinity; these passages, however, are probably heretical interpolations in any case and so need not concern us. At points where Origen is obscure, Rufinus adds explanations, although this is unproblematic, since he tends to glean them from Origen's corpus itself. He acknowledges this technique in the *Praefatio*.[14] The main problem with Rufinus from our perspective is his treatment of Greek philosophical terms, which lose their precision when translated. Although he sometimes retains the Greek or latinises it, he often translates it with a Latin paraphrase. This leads to a lack of consistency, since the same term is not always translated in the same manner.

More generally, however, Rufinus' version is reliable as an overall account which paraphrases Origen's work, rather than a faithful translation. In any case, it is generally more reliable than Jerome's version. Jerome claims to have produced a literal version of the *Peri Archôn*, but a comparison between the *Philocalia* passage and his and Rufinus' version would not be in support of this viewpoint. Rufinus is substantially faithful to his Greek original at III.1.22, while Jerome makes an explicit allusion to the pre-existence of souls only hinted at in the Greek. Jerome seems to alter the treatise in order to make it sound more strongly heretical. At IV.3.10 Rufinus is again more faithful than Jerome, although Jerome contains some items omitted by Rufinus.[15] For all its shortcomings, then, Rufinus' version is still the most important and useful version that we possess. Attempts have been made to produce a more reliable version. Examples include Merlin (1512), Erasmus (1515), C. Delarue (1733) reprinted by *Patrologia Graeca, Volume XI* (1857), and E. Redepenning (1836).[16] The most thoroughgoing attempt to provide a reliable text was that of Paul Koetschau (Berlin 1913), which attempted a reconstitution of the original text, weaving in all sorts of citations to fill in the lacunae left by Rufinus. Although all modern editions owe something to Koetschau, his radical method has been somewhat discredited. The best modern editions are those of Görgemanns and Karpp (1976) and of Crouzel and Simonetti (1978), the edition which I have principally relied upon.

---

[13] I *Praef.* 1.16–18   [14] *Princ.* 1.59–64
[15] Crouzel and Simonetti: 1978, 28–34   [16] Harl *et al.*: 1976, 15

Creation in *De Principiis*

origen opens with a programmatic statement, positioning himself within the metaphysical debate on the Demiurge.[17] He refers to God as 'the God of all the Just: Adam, Abel, Seth, Enos, Enoch, Noah, Shem, Abraham, Isaac, Jacob, of the twelve patriarchs, of Moses, and of the prophets'. These Judaic references hint at the technique Origen utilises. He relies on Biblical revelation to provide himself with the authority he needs, but in fact his toolkit is inherited from philosophy, using reason and logic to expand this revelation in metaphysical terms and to go further than other Christian thinkers, although in practice Origen tends to point out that philosophy alone can only bring one so far. For example at *Homilies on Genesis* VI:1–2, Origen interprets the Biblical account (*Genesis* 20) of Abraham, Sara and Abimelech allegorically. It will be remembered that Abimelech, king of the Philistines, takes Sara as his wife, since Abraham had claimed that she was his sister, but God 'would not let him touch her'. Sara represents virtue and Abraham did not wish her to be called his wife, since otherwise she could not be shared. Abimelech represents philosophers who 'do not reach the complete and perfect rule of piety' but 'nevertheless perceive that God is the father and king of all things'.[18] God has compassion for Abimelech – he does after all cure his handmaidens after making them barren, but he still does not let the king of the Philistines attain virtue. Origen's own work is 'a philosophy towards Christianity' (φιλοσοφία πρὸς Χριστιανισμόν).[19] Creation is difficult to understand 'even by those who are trained in philosophy, unless by means of divine inspiration'[20] because it is hidden in scripture.[21] Origen, indeed, is concerned about discussing it openly since it is similar to giving holy things to dogs or casting pearls before swine.[22] He was clearly concerned about his views being misrepresented, as, in fact, occurred.

Origen chiefly employs two techniques in his use of philosophy (principally Platonism) to better understand the Trinity and Christian creation. By avoiding the identification of the Christian and Platonic divine triads, he is able to accommodate Platonic principles within a Christian theological system and by drawing on Philo's concept of the instrumentality of the *Logos*, he is able to explain *Genesis* with the aid of philosophy.

Origen also moves against Gnosticism by stressing the goodness of the Creator and outlining that he is also the Father of Jesus as well as the

---

[17] *Princ.* I, *Praef.* 4   [18] *Homilies on Genesis* VI.2, trans. Heine
[19] *Epistula ad Gregorium Thaumaturgum*, section 1 (*Philocalia* 3.1)
[20] *CCels.* IV.65; trans. Tzamalikos   [21] *Comm. Gen.* 3   [22] *CCels.* V.29, quoting *Matt.* 7.6

God of both Testaments. Origen portrays the Father as the creator of the world, even though he goes on to state that everything else, including the Holy Spirit, is created by the Son. Since the Father is the principle of the Son, the Father can be viewed as both creator by extension, as well as the highest transcendent principle. The Son adopts the role of a metaphysical mediator and is a co-creator with the Father: 'He helped the Father in the creation of all things, because everything was created by Him.'[23] In any case, the Father creating all things by means of his Word is found in the New Testament (*Cf. John* 1:304; *Hebrews* 1:2).

Here the First Principle creates a second, demiurgic god in a pattern familiar from the *Dreigötterlehrer* of Numenius.[24] The Son aids the Father during the act of creation: a common contention in pre-Nicene writers, which one finds even during the Arian crisis. What is particularly interesting here is the question of the manner in which the Son is created. In pagan metaphysics, subordinating the Demiurge to the First Principle is a standard approach. However, for a Christian, such a stance has significant doctrinal implications. As Jerome comments 'and at once in the first book Christ, the Son of God, is not born but made'.[25]

What is the manner of this creation? It seems that Origen might be addressing two themes – that of corporeal generation (Valentinus) or that of the creation of the Son *ex nihilo* (the Arian theory). Origen posits an incorporeal, transcendent God, but at the same time, he needs to protect His unity. The Son is for Origen, in a sense, similar to divine sons in Plutarch, not produced by sexual relations or by a normal emanation – as if the οὐσία of the Father is simply divided.[26] He is born by[27] or from[28] the will of the Father or else is this will itself.[29]

The Son is produced by the Father without causing any change in His nature or weakening Him.[30] Although both the Son and the Numenian Second God are created atemporally, this creation has to be different, as the Son is not the result of a split in the godhead, as is the case in the Numenian and Gnostic systems. God's nature is immutable and so it would not undergo the sort of change undergone to produce the Son-*Logos*. Since it is part of God's nature to be a father (this, I think, needs no

---

[23] *Princ.* 1.4.72–7
[24] Origen comments on this also at *CCels.* II.9, V.12, VI.60, *Comm. Jn.* I.19 (22), 110 –11; II.3, 19; II.10 (6), 77; II.30 (24), 183.
[25] Jerome, *Letter* 124: this is not an accurate reflection of Origen; Jerome here has his own axe to grind.
[26] Justin, *Diad.* 128, 4   [27] Justin, *Diad.* 400, 4, 127, 4   [28] Clement, *Protr.* X, 110, 3
[29] Hippolytus, *Contra Noetum* 13, PG 10, 280C, Clement, *Ped.* 14, 12, 98, 1, *Protr.* XII, 120, 4
[30] Pamphilus, *Apologia pro Origene* 5 (IV.92 Delarue)

justification from a Christian perspective, nor does Origen give it any), he must have always been the Father of a Son. This Son is equated with the Word; the influence of Philo's *Logos* theology is evident here. While the status of this Son-*Logos* as an independent entity is not denied, he remains within the Father. He is actually contained within Him, in his breast (τὸν κόλπον, *Comm. Jn.* vi.14.17–18). It is because the Son has this special relationship with the Father as First-born (but not as actually created) that only the Son can know the Father, since they have both existed since the beginning.[31] He is to be regarded as the Wisdom of the Father. In this way, Origen avoids positing two separate gods, which would be closer to Gnosticism, since it would be another formulation of the two-powers-in-heaven theory, and according to Rabbinic documents this notion of two complementary powers is actually older than that of two antagonistic ones.[32]

After this preliminary section, the first treatise, *De Deo*, investigates the nature of the Trinity. Initially, it points out that God is incorporeal:

> ... uti ne maius aliquid et inferius in se habere credatur, sed ut sit ex omni parte μονάς, et ut ita dicam ἑνάς et mens ac fons, ex quo initium totius intellectualis naturae vel mentis est. Mens vero ut moveatur vel operetur, non indiget loco corporeo neque sensibili magnitudine vel corporali habitu aut colore, neque alio ulla prorsus indiget horum, quae corporis vel materiae propria sunt.

> ... not believing that there is more or less in Him, since He is entirely a Monad and to speak in this way a henad, an intelligence, which is the source from which all intellectual nature or all intelligence proceeds. In order to move and in order to act, intelligence has no need of corporeal space, nor of perceptible grandeur nor of colour nor of sensible magnitude, nor of a corporeal container, nor of anything which is appropriate to matter. (1.1.6.151–8)

God here is νοῦς (like the Numenian First God), although this itself is problematic, since at *CCels.* vii.38, Origen states that he is above both νοῦς and οὐσία. This was an issue on which speculation amongst both the Middle Platonist and early Christian writers was unresolved and goes back to Plato's comments at *Rep.* 509b 6*ff.*[33] At *Exh. Mart.* 47, he is above both the νοητά and the intelligibles and at *Comm. Jn.* xix 6, iii, 37, He is again stated to be above οὐσία.[34]

---

[31] Origen discusses this at *Princ.* 1.1.8.280–92.   [32] Segal: 1977, 2

[33] For a detailed discussion of this issue, see Whittaker: 1969: Ἐπεκείνα νοῦ καὶ οὐσίας, *VChr.* 23, 91–104.

[34] Crouzel and Simonetti: 1978, 30

It is unfortunate that Origen displays a lack of precision in his terminology here, and I do not think that we can blame Rufinus, since Philo
and Clement both exhibit the same terminological inexactitude in this case
and it occurs elsewhere in Platonism and Gnosticism. The point Origen
wishes to make is not whether God can be identified with Mind or should
rank above it, but rather that God as the First Principle must be incorporeal, since if He was composed of elements, the elements from which
he was composed would be anterior to Him (1.1.6.190–3). In any case,
Origen envisages God as light,[35] and seems to play upon the contemporary
Platonist doctrine that it was incorporeal.[36]

Origen compares God's working on the world to vision: 'But Mind does
not require physical magnitude in order to achieve something or to be
more itself just as is the case with the eye which dilates in order to observe
large bodies, but to observe smaller ones contracts and closes itself. In the
same way, the mind requires intelligible magnitude, so that it grows not
corporally, but intelligibly' (1.1.6.194–9). The Origenian Demiurge acts
on matter by expanding and contracting to set events in motion by its
oscillation. The description implies that the Demiurge must encompass
that which it wishes to act on intelligibly, whatever Origen might mean
by that, but it is clear that the Will of God alone is powerful enough to
stimulate creation. This is, after all, how He gives birth to the Son.

Once the Son is regarded as a secondary divine mediator, the unusual
nature of Origen's metaphysical system becomes clear. This divine mediator
has no beginning, not just temporally, but even conceptually:

> In hac ipsa ergo sapientiae subsistentia quia omnis virtus ac deformatio futu-
> rae inerat creaturae, vel eorum quae principaliter exsistunt vel eorum quae
> accidunt consequenter, virtute praescientiae praeformata atque disposita:
> pro his ipsis, quae in ipsa sapientia velut descriptae ac praefiguratae fuer-
> ant, creaturis se ipsam per Salomonem dicit creatam esse sapientia initium
> viarum dei, continens scilicet in semet ipsa universae creaturae vel initia vel
> rationes vel species.

> It is necessary to believe that Wisdom was engendered without any beginning
> which one can affirm or conceive. In this subsistent being of Wisdom, all
> of future creation was virtually present and formed both the beings which
> existed in the first place, as well as the accidental and accessory realities. As a
> result of these creatures, which were in it like descriptions and prefigurations,

---

[35] 'God is light as John says in his Gospel (1 *John* 1:5), and in Him is no darkness.' See Dillon: 1988a,
218*ff*.
[36] Not a notion derived from the presentation of light in either the *Timaeus* or the *Republic*. For a full
treatment of this topic, see Dillon: 1988a.

> Wisdom says through the mouth of Solomon that it was created as the principle of the paths of God, since it contains in itself *the principles, the reasons and the species of all creation.* (1.2.2.50–8)

The Father is above the Intelligibles, since the intelligible world of the (Platonic) Forms are contained in the Son. Origen modifies the traditional Platonist view that the Forms are the thoughts of God, since he locates it in His Wisdom, which he identifies with the Son, rather like the position in Philo. Origen is attempting to harmonise several strands of Greek philosophy with Christian thinking. The *rationes* that Origen locates in the Son are a Stoic borrowing corresponding to the seeds of the beings who will emerge at the creation of the world.[37] There is no contradiction between the identification of the Son with *Logos* and then subsequently with Wisdom. Origen collects the different names given to the Son in Scripture and uses them as the basis for his Christology; applying the different names to different ἐπίνοιαι, each of which denotes a particular activity of Christ, usually either demiurgic or soteriological.

Origen mentions God's Wisdom here, partly because it is what he perceives to be the central *epinoia* to which the others are subordinate, but also because it relates so strongly to the creation of the demiurgic Son. Since there could never have been a time when God existed without His Wisdom, the Son must always have existed. Origen is perhaps also attempting to score a hit here against the Valentinian Gnostics, who posit Sophia (Wisdom) as the last of the Aeons, while he places it first (although the notion is also Philonic). The notion of a pre-temporal noetic image of creation contained in the Son also allows Origen to avoid the illogicality of positing a sudden divine temporal creation (and here we really are discussing creation in a Judaeo–Christian sense, rather than simply Platonic demiurgy), while at the same time permitting him to remain loyal to the account of *Genesis*.

Origen regards the *Logos* as subordinate to Wisdom, since at *Prov.* 8.22, Wisdom is said to be the main ἀρχή of God's Will and *Jn.* 1.1 reads 'in the Wisdom (the Principle) was the Word' (discussed by Origen at *Comm. Jn.* 1.90–4).[38] Origen explains that the *Logos* refers to its function as interpreter of the secrets of Wisdom.[39] While God the Father parallels the absolute simplicity of the Platonic Monad or the Plotinian One, the Son contains the binary nature of the Dyad; a single hypostasis with multiple aspects: Wisdom, Truth, *Logos* and Resurrection. This multiplicity of nature would seem to make him inferior in many respects to the Father, although his

---

[37] Crouzel and Simonetti: 1978, 31   [38] Crouzel and Simonetti: 1978, 30–1
[39] *Princ.* 1.2.3.59–67

unity is not compromised by these multiple aspects (*Comm. Jn.* 1.28 (30), 196–7),[40] something that emerges elsewhere in Origenian thought. This inferiority appears to be supported by the New Testament.

The role of Wisdom in creation is outlined at 1.2.3.59–67:

> Quali autem modo intelleximus sapientiam initium viarum dei esse, et quo-
> modo creata esse dicitur, species scilicet in se et rationes totius praeformans
> et continens creaturae: hoc modo etiam verbum dei eam esse intellegendum
> est per hoc, quod ipsa ceteris omnibus, id est universae creaturae, mysterio-
> rum et arcanorum rationem, quae utique intra dei sapientiam continentur,
> aperiat; et per hoc verbum dicitur, quia sit tamquam arcanorum mentis
> interpres.

> We have therefore understood how Wisdom is the principle of the paths of
> God and how it is said to be created; in so far as it performs and contains
> in it the species and the reasons of all creation. It is necessary to understand
> that it is also the Word of God by the fact that it opens to all other beings,
> that is to say all creation, the reason of the mysteries and of all the secrets, all
> contained without exception in the Wisdom of God, and by that it is called
> *Logos* (Word), since it is like the interpreter of the secrets of intelligence.

The Forms do not exist in an autonomous manner; they are contained within the oldest ἐπίνοια (II.118). There is a distinction between *initia* and *rationes*, a contrast between the Platonic Forms and the Stoic germs of being. The *rationes* contained in Wisdom are a pattern of creation more detailed than that of the Forms; they are the λόγοι σπερματικοί of the individual beings which will be created.[41] At *Prov.* 8. 22, Wisdom is said to be produced (κτίζειν). Origen reserves ποιεῖν to denote creation, but in spite of this, Arius seized upon this passage to prove that Christ is a creature of the Father. What interests me here are not the intricacies of Christian theology, but precisely what form of creation is intended. Rufinus translated *creata esse dicitur*, a doctrinally safe option. In this context the Son is created, but only in the sense that He is a prefiguration of the created world to come, not in any other way, since He has always existed in the bosom of the Father (1.2.3.72–7). For the Father to exist without the Son would be to deny Him absolute perfection. This differs from the viewpoint of apologists, such as Athenagoras (*Legatio* 10), Tatian (*Oratio* 5) and Theophilus (*Autol.* II. 50), who all draw a distinction between the

---

[40] Crouzel and Simonetti: 1978, 33

[41] For further examples, see *Princ.* 1.4.5 (Rufinus and Justinian); II.3.6; *Comm. Jn.* I 19 (22), 113–15; 34 (39), 24, 4; 38 (42), 283, II 18 (12), 126; V, 5; XIX, 22 (5); 146–50; *CCels.* V, 22; V, 3, 9; VI, 64; *Fragm. Ephes.* VI (JTS III, 341).

moment when the *Logos* was immanent in the Father and when it was engendered as a separate being.[42]

At 1.2.4.109–24, Origen states that the Son is not generated by God by sexual means. The Son is Son, not as the result of adoption by the Holy Spirit, but by nature, since He is generated eternally and perpetually (aeterna ac sempiterna generatio), just as a ray is generated by a source of light. At *Comm. Jn.* 11.2–18, this continual generation of the Son by the Father is compared to His unceasing contemplation of the Father; the Son has moved to occupy a role similar to that of the Numenian Second God. In this case, the Son must be ordering Himself in response to the Father and it explains how the Father can still be regarded as the Demiurge since He is involved in the continual creation of the world of the Forms contained in the Son. Origen has demoted the Forms, which in the Numenian system were located above his Second God,[43] but by doing this, he has given the Father a much more active role in generation than that of having merely produced a Demiurge, although the leitmotif of generation in contemplation can be found elsewhere: in Plato (*Phaedrus* 249c), Alcinous (*Didasc.* 14.1) and Plotinus.

At 1.2.6.161–8, Origen outlines the manner in which the Father and the Son collaborate during creation:

> Si enim omnia quae facit pater, haec et filius, facit similiter in eo quod omnia ita facit filius sicut pater, imago patris deformatur in filio, qui utique natus ex eo est velut quaedam voluntas eius ex mente procedens. Et ideo ego arbitror quod sufficere debeat voluntas patris *ad subsistendum hoc, quod vult pater*. Volens enim non alia via utitur, nisi quae consilio voluntas profertur. Ita ergo et filii ab eo subsistentia generatur.

> In fact, if everything which the Father does, the Son does in the same manner, then the Son does everything like the Father, the image of the Father is distorted in the Son, who surely is born like a will of the Father, proceeding from intelligence. It is why, I think, *that the will of the Father must suffice in order to create what the Father wants*. In His desire, He does not use a means other than the Will which He brings forth in His counsel. It is in this way that the subsistent being of the Son is engendered by Him. (my italics)

The Father can create merely by wishing it. The Son accomplishes the same actions as He does. The italicised expression is used in Greek to refer to the creation of matter.[44] The Son is dependent for His existence upon

---

[42] Crouzel and Simonetti: 1978, 37, n. 16   [43] Numenius Fr. 18 Des Places

[44] Crouzel and Simonetti: 1978, 41 n. 37

the Father, rather like the Young Gods of the *Timaeus*. At 1.2.6.178–84,
Origen states that the Father produced the Son by the Will resulting from
intelligence, not cutting or isolating a part. Origen explains that the Father
is like an immense statue, which because of His dimensions cannot be seen
by anyone, so he creates a similar statue which resembles Him perfectly
[1.2.8]. In this way, the noetic realm must be in some manner present in God
the Father, although Origen never tells us that. Origen cleverly combines
Greek philosophy and Christian thought by linking the demiurgic role
with God's fatherhood. Origen also moves against the Gnostic notion that
the production of the phenomenal realm was the result of an attempt by
the Demiurge to imitate the production of the suprasensible world by the
Father [1.2.12.432–8]:

> Ea sane quae secundum similitudinem vel imitationem discipuli ad mag-
> istrum a quibusdam dicta sunt, vel quod in materia corporali ea a filio
> fiant, quae a patre in substantiis spiritalibus prius fuerint deformata con-
> venire quomodo possunt, *cum in evangelio filius dicatur non similia facere,*
> *sed eadem similiter facere?*

> Some speak of the similarity in the imitation of the master by the disciple
> or say that the Son accomplished in corporeal matter what the Father had
> already shaped in spiritual substances. How could this be imagined *since the*
> *Scripture does not say that the Son makes similar works, but that He similarly*
> *makes the same works?* (my italics)

The Son is not a Demiurge in imitation of the Father, nor even involved
in carrying out the instructions of the Father, as the italicised lines reveal.
He is the instrument through which the Father creates (as is found in
the New Testament). In a sense, the Son, as *Logos*, has adopted the role of
Philo's *Logos*-Cutter. Creation is produced through the collaboration of the
Father and the Son, perhaps akin to Numenius' principle of πρόσχρησις.
This is an anti-Gnostic move, since the Gnostics envisaged demiurgy as
the application to the psychic realm of the principles which created the
hylic one.[45] This blurs to some extent the traditional Platonist distinction
between the noetic realm and the sensible one, since here the sublunar
world is produced as a continuation of its suprasensible counterpart, not
in opposition to it.

Origen revisits this notion of the demiurgic instrumentality of the Son
in *Commentary on John.*[46] Christ as Wisdom is generated by the Father

---

[45] Iren., *Adv. Haer.* 1.5.5
[46] πλὴν δυνατὸν ὡς τὸ 'ὑφ' οὗ', ὅπερ ἐστὶ ποιοῦν, εἴγε 'ἐνετείλατο ὁ θεὸς καὶ ἐκτίσθησαν'.
Δημιουργὸς γάρ πως ὁ Χριστός ἐστιν, ᾧ λέγει ὁ πατήρ· 'Γενηθήτω φῶς' καὶ 'Γενηθήτω

before time. Ἀρχή is both a principle and the beginning, and this further explains Christ's role, as that which was generated first and atemporally (11.36). The Father creates *ex ipso*, as the First Cause, while the Son creates *per ipsum* as the means through which everything else is created, *per* reflects the Greek pronoun *dia*, taken from *John* 1:3.[47] Christ can even be called the προσεχῶς δημιουργός 'immediate craftsman', as He is at *CCels.* VI, 60. As Blanc points out, one can even refer to him as an executor (fragment III), as διά indicates not a service (διακονία) but rather collaboration (συνεργία).[48]

This raises the whole question of participation. The *Logos* is not just the ontological link between the Father and the rest of creation, but additionally a spiritual one. Even though everything might receive God's spirit (*Princ.* 1.3.68), this does not suggest any sort of material pantheism.[49] As Lyman points out, Origen stresses participation, not to claim that the cosmos is consubstantial with God, but to prove that all creation intentionally results from God the Father and sustains its existence from Him in a dynamic relationship.[50]

Origen identifies the Son with the Numenian Second God; this is implied at 1.3.1–4 where he mentions that other philosophers have regarded creation as the work of God's *Logos*, and at *HomGen* XIV.3, though it is obvious that he has this in mind, since he would have encountered it via the *Platonic Letter* II.312e– 313a, which is quoted by Celsus and to which point Origen responds at *CCels.* VI.8. Some of the difficulty in understanding Origen's hypostatic triad comes from the merging of two 'Ones', which owes something to the first two hypostases of the *Parmenides*. The entire moment of creation can be viewed in terms of a tried and tested Platonic formula, with a merging of a Mind that thinks the world and a Mind which is the Demiurge who actually created it.

The Holy Spirit

Many Platonists, including Numenius, interpreted the three kings of the pseudo-platonic *Epistula* II.312e as referring to a divine triad: 'All things

---

στερέωμα'. Δημιουργὸς δὲ ὁ Χριστὸς ὡς ἀρχή, καθ' ὃ σοφία ἐστί, τῷ σοφία εἶναι καλούμενος ἀρχή.

'However, it is possible that he is "He by whom", that is to say He who creates, because "God commanded and it was created". Christ is, in a certain sense, a Demiurge, since the Father said to Him "Let there be light", "Let there be a heaven". It is as a principle that Christ is the Demiurge, in so far as he is Wisdom, because it is because He is Wisdom that he is called a principle.' *Comm. Jn.* 1.110–11.

[47] Blanc: 1966, 252–3   [48] Blanc: 1966, 252–3
[49] Denied at *CCels.* 6.71 (SC 147. 356–60).   [50] Lyman: 1993, 48

are related to the King of all things and the all are on account of him and he is responsible for all good things. And the second things are related to the Second and the third things to the Third.'[51] In Christian literature prior to Origen, we can find evidence of similar speculations. For example, Justin Martyr claims that Plato obtained the idea of the Trinity from Moses, suggesting an equation between Platonist and Christian triads of hypostases. After quoting *Epistula* II, Clement goes on to comment 'I at least do not understand it any other way than that the Trinity is disclosed; for the Holy Spirit is third and the Son is second, through whom 'everything was made' [*John* 1:3] in accordance with the will of the Father' (*Stromateis* V.102.3–103.1).

Origen's response differs from his Christian predecessors in his opposition to a simple identification of both triads.[52] Despite repeatedly admitting Plato's stylistic superiority over scripture,[53] he is able to regard Christian doctrine as superior, since it alone has knowledge of the Holy Spirit.[54] Pagan philosophers were unaware of its existence because it has no demiurgic function; its activity is soteriological and confined to the saints.[55] Origen's influence on the Christian tradition ensured that, due to the differing Third Hypostasis, the Platonic and Christian triads are not equated. By not identifying the Third King with the Holy Spirit, Origen can retain a version of the Platonic principles which does not conflict with Christian theology and claim superiority for Christianity in that it alone knew of the existence of the Holy Spirit. Origen is clearly drawing on the triadic thinking of Numenius of Apamea, whose theology speculates on these three kings. While Origen rarely mentions his sources in his extant works, we do know that he consulted Numenius as he is mentioned second to only Plato in the *Contra Celsum*.

Numenius' combination of an intellect at rest, which can be regarded as possessing a demiurgic function insofar as it generates the Demiurge, influenced Origen in positing a Father who is a creator insofar as he uses

---

[51] Kritikos: 2007: περὶ τὸν πάντων βασιλέα πάντ' ἐστὶ καὶ ἐκείνου ἕνεκα πάντα, καὶ ἐκεῖνο αἴτιονἁπάντων τῶν καλῶν· δεύτερον δὲ πέρι τὰ δεύτερα, καὶ τρίτονπέρι τὰ τρίτα.

[52] Tzamalikos: 2007, 17, bases some of his opposition to the claim that Origen exhibits strong Platonic tendencies by pointing out the 'hackneyed assertion that his Trinity was a Plotinian triad' which is often made. He has a point here, in that Origen does not attempt to incorporate the Holy Spirit into a metaphysical system.

[53] *CCels.* VI.1 *ff.* [54] *Princ.* 1.3.1

[55] The subordinate nature of the Holy Spirit comes across at *Comm. Jn* II.10.76: 'And perhaps this is the reason why he himself does not bear the name Son of God, for only the only-begotten is Son by nature from the beginning, and it seems that the Holy Spirit has need of him to minister to him his substance.' (trans. Widdicombe: 1994, 97)

the Son as an instrument. Origen links the unity of the Father with the multiplicity of Creation through the *epinoiai* which he posits in Christ. These *epinoiai* (Greek = thoughts, purposes) are denominations of Christ which correspond to an aspect of his activity. The first two of these, Wisdom and Word, betray the influence of Numenius' Second and Third God in that Wisdom is the Son's creative potential, whereas the Word is actually involved in the act of creation. Word is then the lower aspect of Wisdom, just as the Third God is the lower aspect of the second. In positing the Word or *Logos* as the instrument through which a transcendent God creates, Origen additionally reveals the debt which he owes to Philo.[56]

There is another reason why Origen may have wished to avoid associating the Holy Spirit with the third hypostasis of the Platonist triad (the World-Soul) and why he may have viewed a simple equation between the Trinity and the Platonist triads as inadequate for his metaphysics. The only possible parallel to the World-Soul in Origen is the human soul of Christ. I think that since the Platonist World-Soul contains individual human souls (Plato, *Tim.* 34b; picked up later by Plotinus at *Enn.* IV 9 [8]), Origen would not relish the prospect of making the Holy Spirit substantially the same as individual human souls, whereas for the human soul of Christ, this presents no problem. The Holy Spirit does represent, however, the beginning of creation, since it is the first entity co-produced by the Father and Son. Origen makes it quite clear that the Holy Spirit only owes its existence to the continual mediation of the Son.

The Son participates in the divinity of the Father and is not merely one of the created, though the Holy Spirit appears to be one. The Father and Son share a substratum (or lack of a material substrate), denoted by the terms ὑποκείμενον, ὑπόστασις and οὐσία, although it is unclear whether the Son is actually generated from the οὐσία of the Father.[57] In fact, Origen did not believe that the Son could be created *ex nihilo*: 'we do not therefore say, as the heretics think, that a part of the substance of God changes itself into a Son, or that the Son was created by the Father from nothing' (*Princ.* IV.4.1.(28).3–19). Even though it is clear that the Father does not produce the Son from outside His substance, Origen does not actually say that He was produced from the substance of the Father. This idea of the generation of the *Logos* from nothing was an Arian notion, frequently linked with the non-eternity of the Son.

---

[56] Clearly the *Logos* is to be found in the Fourth Gospel also, but Philo, I think, can rightly be viewed as the innovator of a theory of the *Logos* within a Biblical context.

[57] Lyman: 1993, 69

Origen rules out the idea of pre-existent matter at 1.3.2.56–62, relying on reference to Scripture to refute belief in a matter which is co-eternal with God. Origen moves against the traditional Platonist perception of demiurgy (ordering something pre-existent) in preference to his belief in *creatio ex nihilo*, a prudent move for a monistic system. This is stressed by Origen, who does not wish for fragmentation to creep into the godhead, stressing the unity of purpose shared by the Trinity. However, despite this radical shift, Origen's system is influenced by the concept of demiurgy, rather than an entirely independent creational model: he refers to the Trinity at 1.4.3.46–50 as εὐεργετικὴ δύναμις et δημιουργική, 'a beneficial and demiurgic power'. Rufinus uses the Greek terms in his Latin text, indicating that they originate with Origen himself. It is of note that Origen applies the term to the whole Trinity, as well as to the Father. Even though the Father and Son are co-Demiurges, Origen can apply the term to the Trinity as a whole, since they are one.

God's activity prior to creation

Origen then deals with one of the vital issues facing all those who posit creation at a given point in time: what was God doing beforehand. For Origen, it is impious to think that God was actually idle.[58] Origen has to view the Demiurge as active for all eternity since, as he points out further on in the same passage, to say otherwise would lead one to suppose that he had been prevented from creating by external powers, which would go against belief in His omnipotence. The other alternative, that God had simply not wished to create until a given moment in time, would go against His immutability. To claim that God is active for all eternity, as Origen does here (an excellent philosophical choice), would be to claim that creation is co-eternal with God; a claim contrary to the Christian faith.

Origen manages to evade this problem by means of a solution already hinted at in section 1.2.10. Creation is co-eternal with God, but only insofar as this refers to the intelligible world, containing the blueprint of creation, which itself is contained within the Son, who is produced by continual generation. Origen also points out that temporal vocabulary cannot be applied to the Trinity.[59] We are fortunate that Rufinus leaves several of the terms of this section in the original Greek, which reveals the numerous influences which lie behind the composition of this section – that of Philo (in the reference to God as a ποιητική and βασιλική power),

---

[58] *Princ.* 1.4.3   [59] *Princ.* IV.4.1

and of the Platonic tradition (*Tim.* 29), in the description of the world as an emanation from divine goodness. This solution is given explicitly at 1.4.4.80–5. If creation was always present in God's Wisdom, then there never was a time when creation did not exist (even if this only refers to the noetic realm). The conclusion to this argument advanced with some caution at 1.4.5.100–5 is that if the noetic realm always existed, then the 'genera' and 'species' must also have done so. This raises the question of whether individualities (*singula*) could possibly have always existed. Origen only mentions the issue, but does not attempt to provide a solution; he is here in an area where the Church of his day had not yet produced a dogmatic response. Tzamalikos does not regard the question of what God was doing before creation as one which Origen takes seriously, referring to it as a 'pseudo-question'[60] and a 'fake question'.[61] This seems to me to be unduly dismissive – the claim that the world had been created at a point in time was a difficult one to defend within the Greek philosophical tradition (probably a reason why the literal reading of the *Timaeus* had been abandoned by the Old Academy). It is true that Origen is not unduly worried about having to interpret the creation accounts of *Genesis* as literally referring to a temporal creation: 'Scripture does not speak here of a beginning in time, but states that the heaven and earth and everything which was made, was made, "in the beginning", that is in the Saviour' (*Homilies on Genesis* 1.1).[62] Tzamalikos is, however, right to point out that Origen separates the conception of God from his will to create; in other words God does not need to create to be God.[63] By contrast, it is hardly possible for the Demiurge not to generate the world and still be the Demiurge.

However, perhaps the Origenian system itself provides the answer. For Origen, the world is created through the free choice of individual souls who fall; some to become angels or stars and others still further to become men or demons.[64] Therefore it is possible that all individuals existed before the creation of this world, since the end of the cosmos will represent a return to the state of the beginning, as individual souls chose the path of righteousness, although as free will shall remain, the *possibility* of a future fall and further worlds is preserved, though the *probability* of this occurring is disputed (see my discussion below). This fall is contested by Edwards and

---

[60] Tzamalikos: 2006, 147   [61] Tzamalikos: 2006, 153
[62] non ego hic temporale aliquid principium dicit, sed 'in principio', id est in Salvatore, factum esse dicit caelum et terram et omnia quae facta sunt.
[63] Tzamalikos: 2006, 153
[64] It is uncertain whether Origen envisages the souls of all angels as remaining in the initial state of blessedness or whether this applies only to their higher orders.

Tzamalikos on the grounds that the texts supporting a fall have largely been drawn from opponents of Origen and that this belief in a fall was largely sustained by the anathemas which were decreed by the second Council of Constantinople.[65] An example of this is the second anathema against Origen, which appears in Koetschau's edition as Fragment 23a.[66]

> The production of all rational creatures consisted of incorporeal and imma-
> terial minds without any number or name, so that they all formed a unity on
> account of the identity of their essence and power and activity and by their
> union with and knowledge of God the Word; . . . they took bodies, either
> consisting of finer or grosser particles, and become possessed of a name,
> which accounts for the differences of names, as well as of bodies among the
> higher powers; and thus the cherubim, with the reigns and authorities, the
> lordships, thrones and angels and all the other heavenly orders came into
> being and received their names.[67]

Even if we must bear in mind that this passage is not a literal citation, it must reflect Origen's views (otherwise there would not have been much point in decreeing these anathemas against him).[68] According to Tzama-likos, the souls are originally 'in God'; the soul of Christ comes out, since it is sent from the Father 'but other souls came out of God in a dissimilar manner, neither being sent or escorted by the divine will'.[69] For Tzamalikos argues that any reference to the fall of souls really refers to the emergence of souls out of God and is not a fall, but rather an expression of divine economy, since 'before' the fall or 'after' the end of this aeon, there is only a divine reality.[70] This is clear also from Origen's argument: 'Therefore in this Wisdom, which was always with the Father, creation was always present in outline and form and there was never a moment when the prefiguration of those things which were to come to be was not in Wisdom.'[71] Creation is continuous, since it reflects the eternal Wisdom of God, where the *Logos* always is.[72] 'The God who made the universe did not require time in order to make such a great heaven and earth . . . for even if it might seem that these things were made in six days, there is need of intellect to understand in what way "in six days" is meant.'[73]

A related topic has been the cause for one of the major disputes in recent Origen scholarship. Edwards and Tzamalikos reject the notion that

---

[65] Tzamalikos: 2007, 340
[66] *Cf.* the anathemas which appear at the end of Justinian *Ep. ad Mennam* (Mansi IX.533).
[67] Trans. after Butterworth: 1966, 125   [68] *Cf.* Butterworth: 1966., 125, n. 7.
[69] *Comm. John 20,* xix, trans. Tzamalikos. *Cf.* Tzamalikos: 2007, 334ff.
[70] Tzamalikos: 2007, 340   [71] *Princ.* 1.4.4
[72] Bostock: 2007, 223   [73] Origen, *CMt* 14,9: trans. Bostock

Origen believed in the incorporeal Platonic world of the Forms, citing the following passage in support:

> Designat sane et alium quendam mundum praeter hunc visibilem etiam dominus et salvator noster, quem re vera describere ac designare difficile est; ait namque: Ego non sum ex hoc mundo. Tamquam enim qui ex alio quodam esset mundo, ita dixit quia non sum ex hoc mundo. Cuius mundi difficilem nobis esse expositionem idcirco praediximus, ne forte aliquibus praebeatur occasio illius intellegentiae, qua putent nos imagines quasdam, quas Graeci ἰδέας nominant, adfirmare: quod utique a nostris rationibus alienum est, mundum incorporeum dicere, in sola mentis fantasia vel cogitationum lubrico consistentem; et quomodo vel salvatorem inde esse vel sanctos quosque illuc ituros poterunt adfirmare, non video.

> Our Lord and Saviour indicates another world, apart from this visible one, which is truly difficult to describe and define. For he says 'I am not of this world' and in so far as he said 'I am not of this world', he is from another world. I said before that it is difficult for us to explain this world here, lest perhaps it might supply to some people the occasion to suppose that we are asserting the existence of certain images which the Greeks call 'ideas'. For it is completely foreign to our mode of reasoning to speak of an incorporeal world, which exists solely in the fantasy of the mind and in the fluidity of thought, and I do not see how they could assert that the Saviour came from there or that the saints will go there. (*Princ.* II.3.6.236–48)

However, this corresponds with Origen's unitary view of a single world: at *Princ.* II.4.3 everything in heaven and earth constitutes the world and at *Princ.* II.3.6 both celestial and supercelestial, along with the earthly and infernal can be generally referred to as a single world, though Origen concedes that the other worlds that are in it are contained within this single perfect world. This problematic passage at *Princ.* II.3.6 can be reconciled with the noetic world posited at *Princ.* I then, since Origen elsewhere frequently refers to the world as consisting of spaces on different levels – celestial and supercelestial ones at *Princ.* II.3.6, or placed above the aether at *CCels.* III.4.2; V.4.

Another passage which Tzamalikos uses to support an anti-Platonic reading is *CCels.* V.21 'Furthermore the followers of Pythagoras and or Plato assert that the cosmos is indestructible, but they trip up in a similar manner.'[74] This passage refers to the succession of identical worlds in which the same events are fated to occur: Socrates will once again be accused by Anytus and Meletus, and will once again be condemned. Clearly, Origen could not accept such a deterministic account, given his views on free

---

[74] Tzamalikos: 2006, 280

will – but this should not lead to him being considered an 'anti-Platonist' as such. It is also that case that Origen continually represents Christian wisdom as being superior to, or as surpassing Greek thought, while at the same time being profoundly influenced by Greek philosophy.

The question of evil

At *Princ.* 1.5.374–88, Origen asks whether God designates some of his creatures as virtuous and others malicious. Clearly, he replies, it cannot be the case that some souls were evil from the very moment of their creation, since this would make God ultimately responsible for evil. There is no necessity for them to be evil; rather they fall as a result of making the wrong choices; the Creator is not responsible for this; He has merely given them free will.[75] At 1.5.3.129–37, Origen points out that there is nothing in the nature of the Trinity which would lead them to produce beings which are evil by nature. Saints were not saints since the beginning, rather they were souls which fell further than the angels, but not so far as the rest of mankind.

This idea is clearly inspired by Plato's *Phaedrus* 246b–d and an echo of the same thought is expressed at *CCels.* iv.40. This fall is what motivates God to produce the material world, thus vitiating the claim that it would be illogical for Him to arbitrarily create it at a given point in time (though Origen could have simply used Plato's point that it was produced along with Time, not in Time). He could similarly have availed himself of Philo's response that the events of *Genesis* are depicted in a hierarchical, rather than a temporal order. Metaphysically, Origen is still faced with the problem of having his First Principle intervene directly in the material world. Of course, God intervening directly in the sublunar realm is precisely what occurs during the Incarnation, but this would not deter Origen from attempting to harmonise Christianity and a philosophical view of creation. This intervention is not problematic for Origen. The creative intervention does not posit a change in God's nature and is not the result of God changing His mind. After all, God's decision to create is as as the result of His mercy, which is part of His nature. Nor should Origen's view be seen

---

[75] At *CCels.* iii.69.1–11, blame is placed squarely on Man, when Origen asserts that no soul was created evil, but they became so as a result of habituation or perversion, and even for such individuals, the divine *Logos* has a purificatory function, actually nourishing the human soul (*CCels.* iv.18.12–26). In this passage, Origen plays upon the nurse imagery of the Receptacle, although it is the *Logos* who is the nurse of creation, nourishing individual human souls, just as a nurse provides milk to an infant.

as particularly unusual; the same idea occurs for example in tenth-century Arabic philosophy. The Incarnation is not an aberration, but rather it is part of God's divine plan, intended all along to take place when the time was right. (In this way, it is similar to Teilhard de Chardin's 'Omega Point' as the goal of history.) Christ is furthermore never in time, but stretched out alongside (συμπαρεκτεινόμενος) time.[76]

As a result of their fall, the pre-existing intelligences are placed in bodies: the angels have the lightest, followed by men and demons. It would seem that the weight of the material body should be linked to the distance of the fall from God in the first book of *Peri Archôn*.[77] However, elsewhere Origen refers to demons as having a lighter body than ours.

In this sense, Origen does not differ from the Gnostics in regarding the material world as essentially evil, since it is under the power of the devil.[78] The devil is evil through his own free choice. As Origen later affirms, the devil can be regarded as the creature of God, as a being, but not in his role as the devil.[79] He owes his existence to God, but not his choice, and so God is not responsible for the existence of evil in the sublunar realm.[80] Origen makes this point more forcefully at *Princ.* I. 5.5.283–6: 'it is only the Father, the Son and Holy Spirit who are pure in a substantial manner, but the holiness *of every creature* is an accidental reality and that which is accidental can fall.' The italicised phrase has often been overlooked, when Origen has been attacked for claiming that the Son is a creature of the Father. Clearly from this section everything other than the Father, Son and Holy Spirit are created. They are the only entities capable of possessing goodness substantially, because goodness depends on the correct exercise of free will and only the Trinity is capable of always making the correct

---

[76] *John* 1.26, *Comm. Jn.* VI.30

[77] Koetschau Fr. 15, which he inserted at *Princ.* I.8.1, although not paralleled in Rufinus' Latin. *Cf.* discussion at Edwards: 2002, 91.

[78] *Princ.* 1.5.5.273–81

[79] *Comm. Jn.* II.97: καὶ τάχα τοῦτο ἔσηνε τοὺς εἰπόντας τὸν διάβολον μὴ εἶναι θεοῦ δημιούργημα· καθ᾽ ὃ γὰρ διάβολός ἐστιν οὐκ ἔστι θεοῦ δημιούργημα· ᾧ δὲ συμβέβηκε διαβόλῳ εἶναι, γενητὸς ὤν, οὐδενὸς κτιστοῦ ὄντος παρὲξ τοῦ θεοῦ ἡμῶν, θεοῦ ἐστι κτίσμα· ὡς εἰ ἐφάσκομεν καὶ τὸν φονέα μὴ εἶναι θεοῦ δημιούργημα, οὐκ ἀναιροῦντες τὸ ᾗ ἄνθρωπός ἐστι πεποιῆσθαι αὐτὸν ὑπὸ θεοῦ.

'This is perhaps the motive which persuaded those who affirm that the devil is not the work of God; in effect, as the devil, he is not the work of God; but the one who became the devil, since he has an origin, and there is no creator other than our God, is a creature of God; just as if we say that a murderer is not the work of God, we do not deny that, in so far as he is a man, he was created by God.'

[80] God's Providence, in fact, defends the world against the spread of evil at *CCels.* IV.6.4.18–23, although at IV.70.11–14 God is said to use the malice of evil individuals to preserve cosmic order. In this sense, even though God is not responsible for the existence of evil, it plays a role in the divine scheme. God is no more responsible for the existence of evil than a carpenter is responsible for the existence of sawdust which results from his woodworking (*CCels.* VI.55.17–24).

choices. In this way, Origen does away with the Necessity which dogs the Platonic Demiurge's attempts at creation.

Origen's other argument to protect God from responsibility for the existence of evil is simply to argue that it does not exist, on the grounds that 'whatever has not received its constitution from God or from His *Logos* is nothing'.[81] Plotinus was strenuously opposed to this non-existence of evil, since, as he argued, if evil did not truly exist, then neither did good, although Aristotle did not posit evil as one of his principles. Origen may have adopted this formulation, which essentially regards evil as an errant cause, as a response to Gnostic dualism.

Creation, *apokatastasis* and the material realm

Origen has his own version of Stoic *ekpyrosis*, with the possibility of an infinite number of worlds being created and destroyed, although they do not exist simultaneously. (Origen vacillates between this view and the position that there is only a single fall and a single creation).

> Finis ergo mundi et consummatio dabitur, cum unusquisque pro merito peccatorum etiam poenis subicietur; quod tempus deus solus agnoscit, quando unusquisque quod meretur expendet. In unum sane finem putamus quod bonitas dei per Christum suum universam revocet creaturam, subactis ac subditis etiam inimicis.

> There will be an end and a consummation of the world, at a time which God alone knows, during which each shall be submitted to the punishments merited by his sins. We think that the bounty of God will assemble by His Christ all creation in a single end, after having reduced and subjected even His enemies. (1.6.1.20–5)

I think that here we have a democratic version of Gnosticism. In Origen, just as in Valentinus, the soul does not belong in the material realm, but has entered it as the result of a fall. Just as in Gnosticism, creation is in a sense pointless, since the aim is to undo it, and for the soul to escape back to the noetic realm from which it came. However, there are important differences. Creation in Origen is not created by a split within the godhead itself and the need for the godhead to reunite does not motivate Christian soteriology. Creation is worthwhile; if at the end, intelligible creatures, including presumably demons based on the passage quoted above, learn to make the morally correct choices.

---

[81] *Comm. Jn.* 11.93

Just because *Endzeit* is similar to the beginning in Origen does not mean that creation is not worthwhile. God's salvation here is open to all, not just a select elite, as is the case in Gnosticism. It is justified because at the end of this current world, the intelligences choose to return to God of their own free will, opening themselves to His mercy and leaving behind the material world, although the continued existence of free will leaves open the possibility of a further fall, and thus the positing of multiple worlds, although of course there is no reason why an identical succession of events should take place in each new world (as Origen is quick to point out).

> Semper enim similis est finis initiis; et ideo sicut unus omnium finis, ita unum omnium intellegi debet initium; et sicut multorum unus finis, ita ab uno initio multae differentiae ac varietates, quae rursum per bonitatem dei, per subiectionem Christi atque unitatem spiritus sancti in unum finem, qui sit initio similis revocantur. . . .

> The end is in fact always the same as the beginning: and it is why, in the same manner that the end of all things is one and the same, in the same way it is necessary to understand that the beginning of everything is one and the same. As this single end is that of numerous beings, in this way starting from a unique beginning, there are many differences and varieties, which again, by the bounty of God, the submission of Christ and the unity of the Holy Spirit, are called back to a single end similar to the beginning. . . . (1. 6.2.46–52)

At the end of creation, all intelligences are united. What does Origen mean by this? If the end is similar to the beginning, this would indicate that the souls exist in the noetic realm within the Son-*Logos*. It would indicate, just as in Gnosticism, that they would be absorbed back into the godhead, However, this cannot be the case, since the souls were not produced by the splitting of the godhead and are its creatures, and secondly, if they existed in the Son-*Logos*, they would be ontologically superior to the Holy Spirit. At 1.6.4.164–7, Origen states that this is not his view: 'if the exterior form of the world passes away, it will not be a complete destruction, nor a loss of material substance, but a certain change of quality and a transformation of the outward appearance.'[82] Clearly if some aspect of the material world is to be retained at the end, this cannot be reintegrated in the Son-*Logos*. The Origenian creation cycle can be viewed as the distribution of pre-existent intelligences into corporeal bodies, which culminates in their reintegration into the supralunar realm. But if Origen is not concerned with the absorption of individual souls into the godhead (and I think that

---

[82] . . . si habitus huius mundi transit, non omnimodis exterminatio vel perditio substantiae materialis ostenditur, sed inmutatio quaedam fit qualitatis atque habitus transformatio.

he is not), then does he regard the individual entities as merged at the end? Under such a reading, at the commencement, individual souls would not be distinguished, and we have already seen that they are, even in the noetic realm of the Son-*Logos*.

A related point is the consideration of what happens to the material realm after the end. In Gnosticism it seems to keep ticking away under the Demiurge, since it exists in opposition to God the Father and not because of Him. The passage quoted above is clearly inspired by St Paul's comment that the external form of the world will pass away and God will be all in all.[83] Yet, material substance will continue to exist, in the sense that corporeal bodies will become more refined, like the bodies of angels. It is not the case, as in Gnosticism, that the material world shall continue to exist in conflict with the noetic one, even when the pneumatics are saved, but that the entire material world shall be reintegrated, not into the noetic realm contained in the Son-*Logos*, but into the supralunar realm.

Origen is quite clear on the necessity of the continued existence of material nature, even at the end of the world. That only the Trinity could be incorporeal is a commonplace concept in Origen and he does not see how it is possible for a great number of substantial beings to survive without body.[84] He suggests that the 'corporeal substance will be so pure and purified that it can be envisaged in the manner of aether', but notes that 'only God knows with certainty what will occur'.[85] It has been the opinion of numerous scholars that Origen regarded the end of the world as the final incorporeality of rational creatures.[86] This has the merit of making the end of the world the same as before the initial creation. Yet it is disproved by Origen's speculations regarding aethereal corporality. Ultimately the question of corporality is left somewhat open. The end cannot be the same as the beginning, since the intelligences do not exist at the beginning (except perhaps in the noetic realm of the Son-*Logos*); they are created by God the Father through the medium of the Christ.

Secondly, these aethereal bodies must have been created at some point, but this raises the question of whether souls can ever have existed without some element of corporality. Based on Origen's view that only the Trinity can exist without corporeality, it would seem that this could never be the case. The end, on this reading then, is only like the beginning of that specific world, but not like the initial commencement of cosmic creation. Matter becomes refined to the point of becoming aether. However, I do

---

[83] 1 *Corinthians* 7:31; 1 *Corinthians* 15:28   [84] *Cf. Princ.* I.6.4.163–7; II.2.27; IV.3.15.
[85] *Princ.* I.6.4.163–7   [86] Crouzel and Simonetti: 1978, 102

not think that it is the case that God creates matter from pre-existent aether, although He may create aether Himself as an initial stage. Matter cannot be ungenerated, since it would be coeval with God and outside His control. In any case, everything has been created by God (1.7.2.41–6 *et passim*), including soul.[87]

What Origen seems to have in mind, on a literal reading, is that God creates matter initially, but at the end of each successive world, it becomes aether, only to become matter again during a subsequent fall. In such a case, we cannot strictly speak of a soul becoming enmattered, rather the soul is already in an aethereal body, which then transforms into matter. If we envisage, as Origen sometimes does, only a single creation followed by a single *apokatastasis* (abolition of evil after the judgement and purification of souls), there would be no question of God continuously converting matter to aether and vice-versa.

Book II of the *Peri Archôn* is also useful for the question of demiurgy, since it is concerned with the world and matter:

> Quamvis ergo in diversis sit officiis ordinatus, non tamen dissonans atque a se discrepans mundi totius intellegendus est status; sed sicut corpus nostrum unum ex multis membris aptatum est et ab una continetur ita et universum mundum velut animal quoddam inmensum atque inmane opinandum puto, quod quasi ab una anima virtute dei ac ratione teneatur.

> Even though the state of the universe is composed of diverse functions, it is however not necessary to believe that it would be in disaccord and in disharmony with itself, but as our body formed from numerous limbs is one and maintained by a single soul, in the same way, it is necessary to regard the universe as an immense and enormous animal governed by the power and reason of God as by a single soul. (II.1.3.58–64)

This idea of a harmonious cosmos owes much to Stoic thought, although evidently the concepts of a World-Soul and the cosmos as a Living Animal are drawn from *Tim.* 30b. Origen also treats the World-Soul here as something allegorical, cleverly drawing on Platonic imagery and not contradicting it, even though evidently he did not believe in a World-Soul. Crouzel and Simonetti argue that the Son as the Power and Reason of God constitutes the Origenian World-Soul, since this is the mechanism through which God governs the world.[88] This may well be true as regards function, but as regards an exact parallel, it is the human soul of Christ

---

[87] *Princ.* 1.7.1.10–11. Omnes animae atque omnes rationabiles naturae factae sunt vel creatae, sive sanctae sint, sive nequam., 'All souls and all rational creatures, were made or created, whether they are good or bad.'

[88] Crouzel and Simonetti: 1978, 133, n.15

which can best be viewed as a World-Soul. For Origen, the Son is really a transcendent, personalised *Logos*.[89]

Origen, rather conveniently for our purposes, then supplies us with a definition of matter: a substrate of the body, i.e. that which exists with the insertion of qualities. Origen mentions four qualities: heat, cold, dry and wet, and notes that although matter itself is without qualities, it never exists without them.[90] In reality, it has to always be informed by qualities; the intellect can only grasp this *simulata quodammodo cogitatione.*

This view of matter is in line with standard Middle Platonist teaching. Matter is an amorphous substrate which has to be informed by a specific quality: it can be arranged as an instantiation of any particular Form, without being engendered by it.[91] Since matter has been created by God, it cannot be responsible for evil. Origen criticises the standard Platonic notion of an uncreated matter as well as the view that it is unregulated: 'I do not know how so many great men thought that it was uncreated, that is to say, that it was not made by God, Creator of the universe, and how they thought that its nature and its activity were the products of chance.'[92]

Origen drew on the Stoic view of matter as uncreated but amorphous, while its qualities are created by God. This allows him to defend Christianity in terms which are also acceptable to those trained in Greek philosophy, which regards matter as uncreated. He argues that once his opponents are forced to concede that matter is nothing other than an assemblage of qualities, one dispenses with the substrate; if matter only consists of qualities, then these qualities are created by God. Therefore, matter is created by God.[93] However, Origen's claim that one can dispense with the substrate differs from his usual view of matter and is clearly adopted here for the purposes of polemic.[94]

Origen has to tackle also the notion of an idle Demiurge, a problem known more famously from the *Ad Theopompum* in which his student, Gregory the Thaumaturge, attacks a figure called Isocrates, who is accused of holding this position.[95] The argument, refuted at *Princ.* II.1.4.125–56, is that God is incapable of *creatio ex nihilo* and so if He had not been

---

[89] *Princ.* II.II.6, *Comm. Jn* VI.30(TS), 154; VI.38 (22), 188–9, *HOM PS*, 36, II, *Ser Matth*, 36

[90] *Princ.* II.1.4

[91] *Cf. CCels.* III.41 ; IV.47, *Comm. Jn.* XIII.21, 27; XIII.61 (59), 429, *Frag. Gen.*, PG 12, 485, P. Arch. IV.4, 5–8, III, 6, 4

[92] *Princ.* II.1.4. *Cf.* Origen's discussion of God's creation of matter at *Princ.* II.4.3.

[93] *Princ.* IV.4.7, (34), 252–8

[94] Further arguments on this subject can be found at Plutarch, *De Communibus Notitiis* 50, Diogenes Laertius, *Vitae* (Zeno), VII, 137, Marius Victorinus, *Ad Candidum* 10 (SC 68).

[95] It is not clear who this Isocrates was, but he seems to have impressed the addressee of the letter to Theopompus.

conveniently presented with matter, He would have remained idle, unable
to create. Origen responds by suggesting that matter would not be suitable
to be ordered by God's Wisdom, if it had not been created by divine Providence. He sides with the Platonists and the Stoics against the Epicureans
and their denial of a divine Providence which regulates the world. However,
he is also undermining the Platonic/Stoic position, since it is contradictory
to posit both Providence and an uncreated matter which limits its actions.
For Origen, matter has to have a divine origin, since it is all used up in
creation, as no other worlds exist [1.3.1]; therefore its quantity has been
precisely calculated.

It could be argued that the Demiurge merely uses up all matter in
creation, but the quantity of matter used to make each body is directly
linked to the depth of the fall of the soul, therefore only God would be
capable of calculating the precise quantity of matter necessary for creation.
II.3.3.130–42 elaborates:

> Sed videamus quid eis occurrat, qui haec ita asserunt. Videbitur enim
> esse necessarium ut, si exterminata fuerit natura corporea, secundo iterum
> reparanda sit et creanda; possibile enim videtur ut rationabiles naturae, a
> quibus numquam auferetur liberi facultas arbitrii, possint iterum aliquibus
> motibus subiacere, indulgente hoc ipsum deo, ne forte, si inmobilem sem-
> per teneant statum, ignorent se dei gratia et non sua virtute in illo fine
> beatitudinis constituisse; quos motus sine dubio rursum varietas corporum
> et diversitas prosequetur, ex qua mundus semper adornatur, nec umquam
> poterit mundus nisi ex varietate ac diversitate constare; quod effici nullo
> genere potest extra materiam corporalem.

> But we see the difficulties which are presented to the one who reasons in
> this manner. If corporeal nature is completely destroyed, it would seem
> necessary to restore it and to create it a second time, for it seems possible
> that rational natures, which are never denied the faculty of free will, could
> again be submitted to certain movements and God would allow this, lest, if
> they would remain always in a state of immobility, they would lose sight of
> the fact that their continuation in this final state of bliss depends on God
> and not on their own proper virtue: these movements will involve once
> again without any doubt the variety and diversity of bodies, which always
> decorate this world, because a world can never consist of anything other
> than variety and diversity, and that cannot be generated out of anything
> other than corporeal matter.

Here the importance of matter in the creation of the sensible world is
stressed, but it is only an element in the divine plan, not an independently-
existing entity. Origen successfully adapts the Stoic notion of a succession
of worlds to a Christian and Platonist context. In place of the strict Stoic

determinism, Origen has greater spiritual dynamism. All that has been determined is the precise number of rational creatures created by God at the beginning. Each successive world cannot be the same given the existence of free will. At *Princ.* II.3.4, Origen compares this to throwing wheat and expecting the grains at each successive throw to form exactly the same pattern. The final state will be an assimilation to the state of the Trinity, with the important caveat that for creatures this state is not one of nature, but of character. Just as Origen modifies the Stoic notion of successive worlds for his own purpose, so he combats the trend of increasing the separation between the sensible and suprasensible worlds, which found its fullest expression in the Pleroma and Kenoma of the Gnostics.

Origen seems to have these Gnostic realms in mind when he points out that such an incorporeal world is 'strange to our manner of speaking' and he opposes the view that the Saviour comes from it or that the Saints return to it.[96] This, at first sight, appears to break with the Platonic distinction between two realms, but discussions of such realms can be traced back to misunderstanding Greek statements concerning the Forms. However, it is clear from the Origenian conception of the noetic cosmos that it would be untenable for the Saints to return to the realm of the Forms, when this is contained within the Son-*Logos*, which in turn is contained in the Father. For Origen, the world of which the Saviour speaks is the suprasensible one and is evidently different from its material counterpart, but this does not preclude a clearly-defined relationship between the two, 'suggesting to us that the whole universe of that which is and exists, of celestial and supracelestial, terrestrial and infernal, forms in a general sense a single perfect world, in which and by which the others, if these exist, are contained'.[97]

Here Origen again raises the possibility of other worlds, this time existing simultaneously. I do not think that he is seriously prepared to countenance this view, although it is possible that there are other worlds into which man cannot cross ([II.3.6] where he cites Clement as his authority), but these cannot properly be regarded as independent *cosmoi*. It is essential for Origen's conception of the Demiurge that the entire cosmos can be viewed as a logical system.

This raises the question of the longevity of the world:

> Sane hoc quod dicunt quidam de hoc mundo, quoniam corruptibilis quidem est ex eo quod factus est, nec tamen corrumpitur, quia corruptione fortior

---

[96] *Princ.* II.3.6   [97] *Princ.* II.3.6.262–7

ac validior est voluntas dei, qui fecit eum et continet illum, ne ei corruptio dominetur, rectius ista sentire possunt de eo mundo, quam ἀπλανῆ spheram supra diximus, quia ex voluntate dei nequaquam corruptioni subiaceat, pro eo quod nec causas corruptionis accepit. Sanctorum quippe est et ad liquidum purificatorum mundus ille, non etiam impiorum, sicut iste noster.

Certainly some say concerning the world that it is corruptible, because it was made, but that it does not decay, because the Will of God which made it is stronger and more powerful than corruption and maintains it so that it is not dominated by corruption: but it would be more correct to think this concerning the world which we mentioned above, the sphere of the fixed stars, because by the will of God, it is not subject to decay. In effect, this world belongs to the saints, to those who have been completely purified and not to the impious, like our world. (II.3.6.295–304)

Origen borrows the distinction of the *Timaeus* between what is immortal and what is merely everlasting at the pleasure of the Demiurge. Here, of course, the world cannot be, strictly speaking, everlasting, since it will ultimately give way to a superior sort of world, but it is capable of falling into disorder, although it is unclear how exactly it is maintained by the Will of God. There is no hint that God's Will has to engage in geometry or in continual temporal creation, intervening in favour of order, as is the case with the Plutarchean Demiurge, rather, it seems that the Will of God simply forbids decay to set in and protects the world by His continual care.

At III.5.3.59–66, Origen raises the question of what God was doing before the creation of the world.[98] Although Origen suggests that He is involved in the construction of successive worlds, he does not consistently maintain this view.[99] Origen follows in the Platonist tradition (and himself set the agenda

[98] Sed solent nobis obicere dicentes: Si coepit mundus ex tempore, quid ante faciebat deus quam mundus inciperet? Otiosam etiam et immobilem dicere naturam dei impium est simul et absurdum, vel putare quod bonitas aliquando bene non fecerit et omnipotentia aliquando non egerit potentatum. Haec nobis obicere solent dicentibus mundum hunc ex certo tempore coepisse et secundum scripturae fidem annos quoque aetatis ipsius numerantibus.

But they tend to say to us by way of objection: If the world began in time, what did God do before the world began? To say that the nature of God is idle and immobile is both impious and absurd, just like saying that there never was a time when Goodness did not do good or when the All–powerful did not exercise His power. One constantly makes this objection to us when we say that the world began at a certain time and when we consider the years and the duration according to the accounts of Scripture. (*cf. Princ.* 1.4.5)

[99] Cum visibilem istum mundum fecit deus, coepit operari, sed sicut post corruptionem huius erit alius mundus, ita et antequam hic esset, fuisse alios credimus.

'It is not when God created this visible world that He began to work, but just as after the destruction of this world there will be another, even so before this world existed, there were, we believe, others.' (III.5.3.70–3).

for the Cappadocian Fathers) as regards his distinction between Time and Eternity. The Trinity is eternal, so Origen points out that his claim that 'there never was a time when the Son never existed must be understood with indulgence' ('*cum venia*'). Like Plato, he laments the difficulty of describing the divine with inadequate language; here temporal vocabulary '*temporalis vocabuli*'.[100] God, like Plato's Demiurge, exists outside time and language can only refer to him in a tenseless kind of way, which in itself is impossible for language. Before Aquinas, Origen expresses the same notion with reference to the God of the Christians; it is not appropriate to say that He is everlasting, rather He exists outside time. Time itself only came into being with the creation of the cosmos.

Scholars are divided on the issue of whether Origen really envisages the possibility of successive worlds as the result of further falls.[101] His own works are contradictory and he even adopts opposed positions within the same work.[102] Stefan Svendsen has extensively analysed the reasons which contribute to Origen's vacillation.[103] If free will continues after the *apokatastasis* (which Origen has to believe in order to avoid strict determinism), then there could always be the possibility of a future fall.[104] However, Svendsen observes, if future falls take place, God would be guilty of unnecessary suffering in allowing humans to lead 'painful lives' in the material realm, which could only be justified on the grounds that they would be purified from sin, while all along He would have known that this response on His part would not prevent this.[105] If there are repeated falls, it seems to me that it would make creation pointless, rather like the situation in Gnosticism, since the whole point of creation becomes the attempt to undo it.

In order to avoid the determinism that the alternative theory would necessitate, Svendsen suggests that Jesus' 'perfection of love', which prevented Him from falling, will characterise the other souls after *apokatastasis*.[106] This would ensure that free will remains, but ensures that

---

[100] *Princ.* IV.4.1.34–43
[101] For example Bigg, Daniélou and Crouzel are opposed to successive falls, but their view is by no means unanimous.
[102] Svendsen points to *Princ.* II.66 and III.66 as well as CCels. VI.20 with IV.69.
[103] I am grateful to Dr Stefan Svendsen for raising this issue with me during the course of a seminar at the University of Copenhagen, which has led me to reconsider views on this issue expressed elsewhere (O'Brien: 2007a, 174), as well as for providing me with a copy of his research data 'Origen and the Possibility of Future Falls'.
[104] Svendsen's argument places Origen's views within the context of ancient speculations concerning fate and human autonomy.
[105] Svendsen, S. N. (unpublished data), 16
[106] Svendsen bases his argument on *Commentary on Romans* 5.10.15 and *De Principiis* II.6.4–5. Svendsen, S. N. (unpublished data), 18

because of the excellence that their natures have now attained, the souls no longer direct it towards evil purposes, because 'love never fails'.[107] Each soul becomes a 'pillar in the temple of God which will not go out'.[108] This also provides a teleology to creation: by providing a purificatory lesson to rational intelligences, it is part of the divine plan and results from God's compassion, thereby explaining temporal creation without positing a change in God's nature. Origen is not actually the inventor of the Christianised version of *apokatastasis*: it is found in Clement and the Greek-Ethiopic *Apocalypse of Peter*, although Origen developed the concept.[109] Since Origen posits a temporal beginning to the cosmos, he also accounts for the end; unlike Plato he does not envisage an everlasting cosmos. Origen's vacillation on the issue, though, indicates discontentment with the solution which he had proposed.

Origen uses the term καταβολή to refer to creation, which he etymologises as a 'throwing down towards the lower regions'. This passage, though evidently referring to the fall of souls, makes God a much more active agent than the idea of a fall would normally suggest. It seems less that the souls fell, than that they were cast out, but this might also refer to the manner in which the Son-*Logos* informs the substrate with Forms from the noetic realm by a sort of 'throwing down'. This 'throwing down' produces two natures (III.6.6.222–36), the invisible, that of rational creatures, and the corporeal, that of animals.

Origen regards the stars (amongst which he includes the planets) as rational living beings, since they are capable of receiving the commandments of God, which Origen bases on the Biblical phrase 'I ordered all the stars'.[110] For Origen, the stars have to be rational, since they exhibit order in their movements. He regards them as animate because the notion that soul is the source of all motion had by this stage become commonplace. What is interesting is Origen's focus on the rational design behind the rotation of the stars and planets. He breaks with Plato's idea that the stars are the habitations of human souls, while the planets are the heavenly gods, for obvious reasons. However, he still needs them to be ensouled, if he still wishes to believe that they are alive, in order for the mechanics of the situation to work. This leads him to argue that stars are a separate order of living being, which accept some sort of material body in order to be of service to men. For Origen, the stars are intermediate beings between angels and men.

---

[107] I *Cor.* 13:8   [108] *Comm. Jn.* x.42; trans. Tzamalikos.
[109] *Cf.* Ramelli and Konstan: 2007, 119   [110] *Princ.* I.7.3

Origen gives a detailed account of their creation at 1.7.4.107–12:

> ... fecit deus duo luminaria magna, luminare maius in principatum diei et luminare minus in principatum noctis, et stellas, an non cum ipsis corporibus, sed extrinsecus factis iam corporibus inseruerit spiritum, pervidendum est. Ego quidem suspicor extrinsecus insertum esse spiritum, sed operae pretium videbitur de scripturis hoc ostendere.

> ... God made two great lights, a larger one to govern the day and a smaller one to govern the night, as well as the stars. So then God did not create the soul together with the bodies, nor did he insert it from the outside, once the body was created. I myself suspect that the soul is inserted from the outside, but it seems a worthy task to demonstrate this from Scripture.

I find this account fascinating, but the whole notion proved to be problematic for Origen, since the Church condemned the notion that the stars were alive. The above passage points out that the soul is older than the body as in the *Timaeus*, and both are constructed separately. The idea of the insertion from outside is particularly interesting, since the stars seem to exist at some point without corporeality. However, it is necessary to be cautious, since Rufinus may use *spiritus* here to translate νοῦς rather than πνεῦμα (although he usually translates νοῦς by *mens* or *animus*), so this cannot be taken as a conclusive affirmation of the pre-existence of souls. The stars are material, although their bodies are composed of aether.[111] Whereas in conventional Platonic thought the variety of rational beings comes about through the instantiation of all possibilities (irrespective of whether or not these possibilities are also produced by the Demiurge), for Origen the devil, demons, man, the saints, the stars and the angels all have the same divine origin; it is only as a result of the choices that they make that they become enmattered in a specific way.

Animals, however, are the result of a secondary creation; they are distinguished from the reasonable natures which possess free will and soul.[112] They merely possess visible nature, and no invisible element; being nothing more than a modification of matter, not the insertion of a soul into a material form. Origen was opposed to the Platonic notion of metempsychosis. No matter how far a soul falls, it will still be implanted into a rational animal (although this includes demons), but it will not be implanted into animals for the sake of punishment. According to *selPs.* I (PG 12, 1081 or *Philoc.* 11.51), it is not possible to understand why there are so many ferocious animals. This is a valid point; since animals have no free will, there is

---

[111] *Princ.* 1.7.5.156–7: licet aetherium sit corpus astrorum, tamen materiale est.
[112] *Princ.* III.6.7

no reason why God should have created them. Since this part of creation is completely under his control, it would seem that it should be perfect. Though other thinkers such as Justinian see in them a positive value, since they inculcate virtues such as courage, Origen does not trouble himself with the question.

It seems that matter is capable of preventing union in the godhead, since God is incorporeal, but Christ takes a material form, and it seems that the godhead must remain in what is to some extent a state of disunity, until the suppression of Christ's human body. However, just like Plato and unlike the Gnostics, who also see in matter a threat to the unity of the godhead, Origen is positive concerning the human body.

Even though the material world is not ideal, Origen still admires the physical instantiation of Man since it is capable of becoming something much greater: 'a very subtle, very pure and very resplendent body' (qualitatem sublatissimi et purissimi ac splendidissimi corporis).[113] Indeed, Origen stresses that the substrate is capable of being informed by God with all possibilities from the noetic realm and seems almost to regret the loss in diversity that the dissolution of the world will entail.[114] The reference to matter 'delivering itself' to the Father 'in complete readiness to the different aspects and kinds of things which He accomplished on it, since He is its lord and creator, in order that He could draw from it the diverse forms of celestial and terrestrial beings' echoes a Middle Platonist notion observable in Plutarch (and picked up by the Neoplatonists also); that of world-generation from below, since matter wants to be ordered and may even play a role in demiurgy by ordering itself in response to the inherent order of the One.[115]

The soul of Christ

At *Princ.* ii.6.3.106–14, Origen expresses the relationship between both realms in terms which suggest the influence of Plato's *Tim.* 35a:

> Hac ergo substantia animae inter deum carnemque mediante (non enim possibile erat dei naturam corpori sine mediatore misceri) nascitur, ut diximus, deus-homo, illa substantia media existente, cui utique contra naturam non erat corpus assumere. Sed neque rursum anima illa, utpote substantia rationabilis, contra naturam habuit capere deum, in quem, ut superius diximus, velut verbum et sapientiam et veritatem tota iam cesserat.

[113] *Princ.* iii.6.4   [114] *Princ.* iii.6.4.133
[115] *Princ.* iii.6.4. Cf. Isis' desire to be ordered at Plutarch *De Iside* 374cff.

Concerning this substrate of the soul, serving as an intermediary between God and flesh, because it was not possible that the nature of a God mixes itself with flesh without a mediator, so the God-man was born, as we have said, and in so doing this substance was the intermediary, because it was not against nature that this soul, a reasonable substance, would be able to contain God, since as we have said above, it was already completely changed itself, as in the Word, the Wisdom and Truth.

This passage proved to be problematic for Origen. If the final absorption of the human nature into the divine one in which God is all in all could be accused of monophysitism, then this section could be accused of Nestorianism, (which propounded the view that Christ had two separate natures, one human and the other divine). Origen commences a discussion on the soul, but goes on to discuss the nature of Christ. Origen seems to stray away from divine mediation and on to considering how the soul of Christ could reconcile both human and divine elements. The problem is that he actually could be construed as positing two Christs.[116]

It seems that the substance of the soul is in some way akin to God, since it was capable of containing God. There is a parallel between the interrelation of Christ and His human soul in Origen and the assumption of the psychic Christ by the Valentinians. However, while psychic Christ is abandoned by the Saviour prior to his death (*Excerpta ex. Theodoto* 615), Christ's human soul for Origen remains connected to the *Logos*. This is interesting metaphysically, since the human soul of Christ, which is to a certain extent the Origenian World-Soul, is actually an integral part of God's Word. Unfortunately, it does not shed any further light on how the human soul first came to be. However, the question of God's soul is not so simple and needs to be interpreted allegorically. Just as His arms, legs and eyes actually are allegorical references [II.8.5.204*ff.*], so too is His soul: 'just as the soul inserted in all of the body makes everything move and works and accomplishes all things, even so the only Son of God, His Word and His Wisdom, reaches and brings to all the power of God, because He is inserted.'[117]

For Origen, then, God is not soul. He does not even have one (or to be more precise, the Father does not have one, although the *Logos* does). By placing the Son in the same relation to the Father as soul to Man, Origen provides a hint of his conception of how the Father–Son relationship works on a demiurgic level. Just as the soul mediates between the mind and the

---

[116] A charge from which he was defended by Pamphilus *cf. Apol.* VI. 5, *TPG* 1.7.586, *Exc.ex Theod.* 58, Iren., *Adv Haer.* 1.6.1.

[117] *Princ.* II.8.5

body (being inferior to Mind), the Son mediates between God and the world (but is beneath the Father). The parallel works outside the realm of Origen's metaphysics, applying also to his soteriology; the descent of the Son to earth parallels to some extent the fall of the soul.

The limits of demiurgic knowledge

At *Princ.* II.9.1, it seems that Origen recommences a rambling view of creation, summarising points that he has already raised, although he is now concerned with the extent of demiurgic wisdom. Since for Origen, that which is infinite is by nature unknowable and since God in order to create everything must know it, then, from the beginning, there must only be a finite number of creatures, all of which owe their existence to God. This argument seems perfectly reasonable, with its focus not only on demiurgic limitations, but equally on the manner in which, for creation to be understood, even by God, it must be embraced within these limits. The notion was attacked in Justinian's *Letter to Menas*:[118] 'And he (Origen) adds to his blasphemies that which follows in the first volume on the following principles.' What is this first book of which Justinian speaks? We are already in the second book, but Justinian must have made an error, since he goes on to say: 'The power of God the Father is limited according to the second volume of the same book.' Justinian then provides a quotation of the text in Greek, which, for the sake of comparison, I include in the footnotes alongside Rufinus' translation.[119]

---

[118] Mansi: 1758–98, 489–525
[119] Justinian's quotation: *Just. Ep. ad Mennam* (p. 190, 7–14 Schw. [= I] und p. 209, 1–6

Schw. [= II] = Koetschau Fr. 24): Ἐν τῇ ἐπινοουμένῃ ἀρχῇ τοσοῦτον ἀριθμὸν τῷ βουλήματι αὐτοῦ ὑποστῆσαι τὸν θεὸν νοερῶν οὐσιῶν, ὅσον ἠδύνατο διαρκέσαι· πεπερασμένην γὰρ εἶναι καὶ τὴν τοῦ θεοῦ δύναμιν λεκτέον καὶ μὴ προφάσει εὐφημίας τὴν περιγραφὴν αὐτῆς περιαιρετέον. Ἐὰν γὰρ ᾖ ἄπειρος ἡ θεία δύναμις, ἀνάγκη αὐτὴν μηδὲ ἑαυτὴν νοεῖν· τῇ γὰρ φύσει τὸ ἄπειρον ἀπερίληπτον. Πεποίηκε τοίνυν τοσαῦτα, ὅσων ἠδύνατο περιδράξασθαι καὶ ἔχειν ὑπὸ χεῖρα καὶ συγκρατεῖν ὑπὸ τὴν ἑαυτοῦ πρόνοιαν· ὥσπερ καὶ τοσαύτην ὕλην κατεσκεύασεν, ὅσην ἠδύνατο διακοσμῆσαι.

'(Saying this) that in the beginning, as it is envisaged, God, by means of His Will, gave existence to the number of intelligible essences which he consider sufficient. For one must state that the power of God is limited and one must not strip away its limitiations from the motive of avoiding impious language. For if the power of God were unlimited, it would necessarily be unable to intelligise itself. For the unlimited is by nature uncircumscribed. Therefore he created as many as He could grasp and hold in His hand and weld together under His Providence and He furnished just as much matter as he was able to order.'

Rufinus' translation: Sed nunc ad propositae disputationis ordinem redeamus, et intueamur initium creaturae, quodcumque illud initium creantis dei mens potuerit intueri. In illo ergo initio putandum est tantum numerum rationabilium creaturarum vel intellectualium, vel quoquomodo

It is not my purpose here to enter into a debate upon textual matters. However, it is evident that although Rufinus does go on to mention that God created a number of beings suitable to being governed, ruled and surrounded by His Providence, this Greek text does contain material that Rufinus does not, and considering what is at stake here, it is necessary to investigate it further. In the first instance, the Greek citation may not be completely trustworthy. The phrase ἐὰν γὰρ . . . ἑαυτὴν νοεῖν is not contained in the fragment of the *florilegia*, although its omission is perhaps indicated by the phrase καὶ μετ' ὀλίγα.[120] According to Koetschau, the Rufinian text runs as far as *incompraehensibile erit*.

In any case, the evidence of both passages reveals that creation is not infinite: Origen is frequently accused of asserting that the infinite is unknowable, even by God, and that his power is finite, since otherwise he cannot understand it.[121] God cannot control an infinite number of beings.[122] Under such a system, the quantity of matter would in a sense be pre-determined, since God can only control a certain defined quantity and there is in any case need only for a sufficient amount to enmatter all the souls which will be created. This would make God the Father akin to James Clerk-Maxwell's calculating demon – read in this light, he would be a mathematician, rather than a divinity. If matter is created by God, there seems to be no reason why He cannot control it, no matter how great the quantity. Secondly, the fact that God cannot control an infinite quantity of matter ultimately

appellandae sunt quas mentes superius diximus, fecisse deum, quantum sufficere posse prospexit. Certum est enim quod praedefinito aliquo apud se numero eas fecit: non enim, ut quidam volunt, finem putandum est non habere creaturas, quia ibi finis non esti, nec conpraehensio ulla vel circumscriptio esse potest. Quodsi fuerit, utique nec contineri vel dispensari a deo quae facta sunt poterunt. Naturaliter nempe quidquid infinitum fuerit, et inconpraehensibile erit. Porro autem sicut et scriptura dicit, numero et mensura universa condidit deus, et idcirco numerus quidem recte aptabitur rationabilibus creaturis vel mentibus, ut tantae sint, quantae a providentia dei et dispensari et regi et contineri possint.

'But now let us turn again to the order of the proposed discussion and let us look closely at the beginning of creation, to the extent to which the mind can gaze closely at this beginning of God's creation. In this beginning, must one suppose that there was such a number of rational or intellectual creatures or whatever they are to be called, which we called minds above, created by God as He saw to be sufficient. It is certain that they were made in accordance with a fixed number, which he himself prescribed. For one must not suppose, as some have, that there was an unlimited number of creatures, since this could be neither understood nor delineated. For if it was (infinite), what has been made could be neither encompassed nor regulated by God. For whatever is infinite by nature is incomprehensible. Furthermore, Scripture also says that God has organised the universe in accordance with number and measure and for this reason; Number will be applied appropriately to both rational creatures or minds, in order that they might be so many, that they might be arranged and ruled and contained by the providence of God.'

[120] Crouzel and Simonetti: 1978, 211   [121] III.5.2.48–58   [122] *Princ.* II.9.1

makes it the source of evil, even though it is envisaged as unintelligible and disorderly, and places blame for its creation upon God.

The claim that Origen believed that divine knowledge was finite is partly based upon the Justinian passage quoted above which Koetschau inserted at *Princ.* II.9.1 (= Koetschau Fr. 24), a reason advanced by Koetschau for dismissing it. However, at the very point where this fragment was inserted by Koetschau, Origen comments that what is infinite is beyond comprehension. Rufinus' translation (quoted in note 119, along with the passage from Justinian) downplays the blasphemous overtones of the Greek version. The issue of God not comprehending what is infinite does not appear so problematic, as Rufinus' translation goes on to state: 'it is necessary to believe that everything was created by God in such a quantity that He knew would be sufficient for ordering the world. Therefore it is necessary to imagine that all of this was created by God at the beginning, that is to say before everything.'[123] Origen argues that this is hinted at in the Biblical reference to the creation of heaven and sky. Fortunately, the Rufinian text manages to allay some of the worries that one might have after reading Justinian's version, and this might reflect a deliberate alteration. Justinian's account runs contrary to Origen's statement at *CCels.* III.77 that God is 'infinite'. The world is finite since it was generated and it is directed towards an end, therefore divine knowledge is of what is finite, since only the Trinity is infinite and its knowledge is without limit.[124]

I agree also that the quantity of matter must be finite, but only because a finite quantity is needed, since it will all be used up in demiurgy, with nothing to spare. The argument that Origen posits in the Greek version seems to be one of the weakest which he could have fielded to make this particular point. It seems that Origen, in light of views expressed elsewhere, had been unduly influenced by the negative view of matter expressed within the Platonic tradition.[125]

Not only are rational creatures created by God, but they also have a beginning [II.9.2.31–6]. Again this differs from conventional wisdom concerning the Demiurge, since having a temporal beginning rules out the possibility of continued temporal creation, although of course this could still be the case in the noetic realm. Origen adopts a much more Platonist

---

[123] *Princ.* II.9.1.21–5: . . . quam utique tantam a deo creatam esse credendum est, quantam sibi sciret ad ornatum mundi posse sufficere. Haec ergo sunt, quae in initio, id est ante omnia, a deo creata esse aestimandum est.

[124] *selPs*, 144, PG 12.673

[125] Plato, *Tim.* 49; Aristotle, *Physics* III.6.206b.25*ff.*, Plutarch (regarding exhaustion of material resources) *QC* 718a, Numenius as quoted by Eusebius *Praep. Ev.* XV.17.

formulation in relation to God's motivation for creating the world; his goodness.[126] All reasonable natures (*rationabiles naturae*) were made equal and the same, since he did not have in himself variety or diversity. The cause of the diversity amongst reasonable natures results from their own choice, which drags them down as a result of their own negligence.

Aside from Origen's typical stress on the damning effects of free will, which in his philosophy takes the place of the recalcitrance of matter as the root of all evil, of note here is the stress on God's goodness as the reason for the creation of the world, just as is the case at *Tim.* 29e. Origen does not have the Platonic insistence on God's desire to enact His goodness in material creation. Rather, the material realm is a second-best option, after created souls exercising their free will reject the superior kind of existence which He has provided. God then creates the world as a result of compassion due to the fall of the soul, rather like the case in the creation-account of the tenth-century Islamic philosopher, Muhammad ibn Zakariyā al-Rāzī. (Al-Rāzī propounds the belief that the soul became so enamoured with matter, it sought unity with it in order to indulge in bodily pleasures. God then is compelled to come to the aid of the soul by creating the material world.)[127] However, God's creation is not limited in any way, by matter or by any other factor; it is exactly as he envisages through his divine foreknowledge.

Here God creates everything in His likeness, which is why all entities are equal at the outset. Yet if some creatures fall further than others due to the choices made according to their character, then surely God could be held responsible for giving some a nature more susceptible to corruption than others. However, at II.9.6.198–212, Origen attempts to rebut a possible charge of divine favouritism by adopting the Stoic view of the cosmos as a house for human and divine inhabitants, which not only contains gold and silver vases, but also those of wood or earth. God governs all of these creatures according to their merits. Therefore God cannot be blamed for any injustice in the lot that falls to individuals, while at the same time, the treatise constitutes an anti-Gnostic attack by showing how, in spite of a combination of positive and negative elements, God has still created a harmonious world. As Origen points out at III.1.21.699–706, a vase of a humbler material can ultimately turn into one of gold; it is not created in this way by God, but merely becomes so as the result of its own choices.

---

[126] *Princ.* II.9.6.183–98
[127] Fakhry: 1968, 18. *Cf.* Black: 2005, 323, n.5. Unfortunately, the myth is only known from the accounts of his opponents.

Contra Celsum

Some further details on demiurgy can be gleaned from *Contra Celsum*, the latest work of Origen's that we possess, which can be dated to c. 248 and which has been preserved in its entirety and in its original language. The treatise was composed, as it seems, at the request of Ambrosius, in response to Celsus' *True Logos*, an attack on Christianity. It seems strange that Origen should have composed such a defence: Celsus was dead by this stage, as *True Logos* had been composed seventy to eighty years previously, but the fact that it was still in circulation may have worried Christians like Ambrosius. Origen uses the opportunity not only to defend Christianity from Celsus' portrayal of it as a threat to Graeco-Roman values (including the belief that religion should be open to rational examination), but also to criticise the opinions of other (less sophisticated) Christians.

Perhaps one of the most striking comments of *Contra Celsum* is the reference at 1.19.1–9 to the fact that the world is less than ten thousand years old, according to the account of Moses, which leaves one wondering how Origen was capable of such great precision in determining the date of creation.[128] At 1.23.16–24, Origen affirms the unity of the creator, on the grounds that the world enjoys good order (κατὰ τὴν εὐταξίαν τοῦ κόσμου) and harmony, and this could not be the work of multiple Demiurges.[129] This helps to stress the unity of purpose of the persons in the Trinity. At 1.23.24–30, Origen further stresses the unity of God, this time drawing upon a Stoic argument; the totality of God is not reducible to the sum of his parts,[130] while His existence is proved by the existence of order in the created world.

The *Contra Celsum* continues the *De Principiis*' portrayal of Christ as effectively a second God, and the unnamed assistant of God in the creation of man, described at *Genesis*:

ἐγκαλοῦμεν οὖν Ἰουδαίοις τοῦτον μὴ νομίσασι θεόν, ὑπὸ τῶν προφητῶν πολλαχοῦ μεμαρτυρημένον ὡς μεγάλην ὄντα δύναμιν καὶ θεὸν κατὰ τὸν τῶν ὅλων θεὸν καὶ πατέρα. Τούτῳ γάρ φαμεν ἐν τῇ κατὰ Μωϋσέα κοσμοποιΐᾳ προστάττοντα τὸν πατέρα εἰρηκέναι τό· 'Γενηθήτω φῶς' καὶ 'Γενηθήτω στερέωμα' καὶ τὰ λοιπά, ὅσα προσέταξεν ὁ θεὸς γενέσθαι, καὶ τούτῳ εἰρηκέναι τό·'Ποιήσωμεν ἄνθρωπον κατ' εἰκόνα καὶ ὁμοίωσιν ἡμετέραν'.

---

[128] One is reminded of Archbishop James Ussher's attempt in *Annales veteris testamenti a prima mundi origine deducti* ('Annals of the Old Testament, deduced from the first origins of the world', 1650), to calculate the date of creation, which he fixed at the night before Sunday 23 October 4004 BC.
[129] *CCels.* 1.23.16–24   [130] Cf. Sext. Emp., *Adv. Math*, IX.4 (338–49).

We reproach therefore the Jews for not having regarded him as God, while the prophets stated that He was a great power and a god beneath God and Father of the universe. To Him, we say, in the account of creation told by Moses, the Father ordered, 'let there be light', 'let there be a heaven' and all the rest which God ordered at the creation. To Him, He said 'Let us make Man in our image and likeness'. (II.9.29–36)

The translation 'a god beneath God' is problematic, and is not accepted by all scholars as it creates a problem of subordination. Other possible interpretations are 'gemäss' [Koetschau], 'like' [Chadwick], 'par l'order de' [Bouhéreau] and 'secundo loco post' [Thuillier]. I am grateful for Dillon's suggestion of 'in the train of' or 'coordinated with', since the Son is God's unnamed assistant during creation: 'To him, He said "let us make Man in our image and likeness".' In any case, it is clear that Origen views Christ, as a production of the Father, as in some way beneath Him, and no particular interpretation of this passage can avoid addressing that fact, just as in the *De Principiis*, Christ, as the *Logos*, is God's instrument during creation.[131] Origen explicitly affirms the superiority of the Father: 'the Son is not more powerful than the Father, but He is inferior to Him' (τὸν υἱὸν οὐκ ἰσχυρότερον τοῦ πατρὸς ἀλλ᾽ ὑποδεέστερον). This is based on the statement that 'the Father who sent me is greater than I'.[132]

In general terms, there is little point in discussing at length all passages relating to demiurgy in *Contra Celsum*. To a great extent, they merely echo sentiments expressed much more fully in the *Peri Archôn*. However, there are some exceptions. At *CCels.* II.9.62–73, for example, Origen considers the question of the relation between the *Logos* and the incarnation of Jesus, pointing out that they form a single, united spirit; it is not the case that a part of the *Logos* is divided in order to become enmattered. Under no circumstances can the Son-*Logos* be ever conceived of as divided.

[131] II.9.36–46: . . . προσταχθέντα δὲ τὸν λόγον πεποιηκέναι πάντα, ὅσα ὁ πατὴρ αὐτῷ ἐνετείλατο. Καὶ ταῦτα λέγομεν οὐκ αὐτοὶ ἐπιβάλλοντες ἀλλὰ ταῖς παρὰ Ἰουδαίοις φερομέναις προφητείαις πιστεύοντες· ἐν αἷς λέγεται περὶ θεοῦ καὶ τῶν δημιουργημάτων αὐταῖς λέξεσι τὰ οὕτως ἔχοντα· "Ὅτι αὐτὸς εἶπε καὶ ἐγενήθησαν, αὐτὸς ἐνετείλατο καὶ ἐκτίσθησαν.' Εἰ γὰρ ἐνετείλατο ὁ θεός, καὶ ἐκτίσθη τὰ δημιουργήματα, τίς ἂν κατὰ τὸ ἀρέσκον τῷ προφητικῷ πνεύματι εἴη ὁ τὴν τηλικαύτην τοῦ πατρὸς ἐντολὴν ἐκπληρῶσαι δυνηθεὶς ἢ ὁ, ἵν᾽οὕτως ὀνομάσω, ἔμψυχος λόγος καὶ "ἀλήθεια" τυγχάνων;

'. . . and the Logos, having received the order, accomplished everything which the Father had commanded. We affirm it and we base it, not on conjectures, but on the faith of the prophets received by the Jews, where it is said in proper terms of God and of created things: "He spoke and things were, He ordered and things were created." If, therefore, God gave the order and creatures were made, what could it be from the perspective of the prophetic spirit, that which was capable of carrying out the sublime commandment of the Father, if not that which is, if I may so term it, the living Logos and the Truth?'

[132] *CCels.* VIII.15.22–6

Origen also returns to the question of *apokatastasis*, pointing out that this was posited by the Greeks. (He tries to present *ekpyrosis* as a Greek version of *apokatastasis* in order to respond to the criticisms of Celsus.):

καὶ τί ἄτοπον ἐπὶ τῇ χύσει τῆς κακίας ἐπιδημήσειν τὸν ἀποκαθαροῦντα τὸν κόσμον καὶ ἑκάστῳ κατ' ἀξίαν χρησόμενον; Οὐ γὰρ κατὰ τὸν θεόν ἐστι μὴ στῆσαι τὴν τῆς κακίας νομὴν καὶ ἀνακαινῶσαι τὰ πράγματα. Ἴσασι δὲ καὶ Ἕλληνες κατακλυσμῷ ἢ πυρὶ τὴν γῆν κατὰ περιόδους καθαιρομένην, ὡς καὶ Πλάτων που οὕτω λέγει· "Ὅταν δ' οἱ θεοὶ τὴν γῆν ὕδασι καθαίροντες κατακλύζωσιν, οἱ μὲν ἐν τοῖς ὄρεσι' καὶ τὰ ἑξῆς. Λεκτέον οὖν ὅτι ἆρ' ἐὰν μὲν ἐκεῖνοι ταῦτα φάσκωσι, σεμνά ἐστι καὶ λόγου ἄξια τὰ ἀπαγγελλόμενα, ἐὰν δ' ἡμεῖς τάδε τινὰ ὑπὸ Ἑλλήνων ἐπαινούμενα καὶ αὐτοὶ κατασκευάζωμεν, οὐκέτι καλά ἐστι ταῦτα δόγματα;

And what is absurd in believing that the flood of vice is stayed by the one who will purify the world and will treat each one according to his merit? It is not worthy of God to not stop the diffusion of vice by a renewal of things. The Greeks themselves know that the earth is periodically purified by flood and by fire, as Plato says: 'Whenever the gods, in order to purify the earth, submerged it under water, those in the mountains' etc. Is it then necessary to say that, while the Greeks affirm it, it merits respect and consideration, but when we ourselves establish some of these doctrines, which the Greeks approve, they lose all their value? (IV.20.11–22)

As Origen states at IV.21.24–38, the example of Sodom and Gomorrah reveals the partial destruction of the cosmos. However, here we are straying away from metaphysics, since Origen expresses *ekpyrosis* in eschatological terms. This is because of the context in which the *Contra Celsum* was composed. Origen represents Christianity as prefigured within the Graeco-Roman intellectual tradition, rather than as a religion which is alien. Interestingly, partial destruction is caused by sin, while complete destruction (in the sense of the dissolution of the created world) occurs due to the final salvation of all rational creatures. For Origen, this destruction is due to a continual law of retribution inherent in the nature of things, not a temporary loss of emotional control on the part of the Demiurge. This comes across when he attacks Celsus' misreading of the prologue to the Flood, when God is said to repent of His creation.[133]

Origen also defends the account of creation at *Genesis* against Celsus at IV.37. Celsus ridicules the description of man's creation, where he is presented as modelled by the hands of God, and the notion that God breathed into Man. Origen counters by pointing out that Celsus does

---

[133] *CCels.* IV.72

not understand the symbolic sense of the passage, since God should not be envisaged as possessing a form similar to our own. The description of God breathing into his creation is also symbolic; God passing on the incorruptible spirit to Man. For Origen, as for Plato, God is the creator only of what is immortal (including the soul), whereas what is mortal has been created by secondary, immortal creators.[134] From what is said here, it appears that animals are the work of the angels. Origen elsewhere sees them as the result of a secondary creation.[135] The mortal creatures that Origen is referring to here in any case seem to be corporeal bodies, rather than animals. Origen may be hinting at Rabbinic doctrine that the body of man was made by the angels. He is certainly drawing upon Platonic thought.[136] However, it seems that he is getting carried away with the force of his own polemic, since at IV.54.23–45 he again affirms his general view that there cannot be multiple Demiurges, but everything must have been created by a single one, who created the distinctions between the different varieties of created being. They are all composed from the same matter which continues to underlie (ὑποκειμένη, IV.56.10) the created world.

The *Contra Celsum* also expresses some remarks concerning divine Providence. It is responsible for everything that is good, but not for anything evil [*CCels*. VII.68.31–7]. Origen presents it as a hypostasis of God the Father: it is 'like a divine power which embraces everything which it contains' (ἀλλ᾽ ὡς δύναμις θεία καὶ περιειληφυῖα τὰ περιεχόμενα).[137] Divine Providence regulates the entire universe by permeating it. It is responsible for the creation of individuals who turn to evil (rather than evil individuals) so that it can subsequently save them (VI.56.1–24). This may appear to be a thoroughly pointless exercise, but it is all part of the divine plan, since by doing this God is purifying souls, and possibly preventing them from making immoral choices in the future.

Conclusion

Origen stands at the juncture of the Platonic and Christian traditions, a fact which is reflected in his account of demiurgy. He presents a real alternative to the Middle Platonist tradition, although at the same time

---

[134] *CCels*. IV.52.11–12: . . . ὁ θεὸς οὐδὲν θνητὸν ἐποίησεν· ἀλλα θεοῦ μὲν ἔργα ὅσα ἀθάνατα, θνητὰ δ᾽ἐκείνων, . . . 'God made nothing that is mortal, but all the immortal beings are the works of God, and the mortal beings are their works'.
[135] *Princ*. III.6.7 [136] E.g. *Tim*. 69c–d; Alcinous, *Didask*. 8, Atticus ap. Eus xv.6
[137] *CCels*. VI.71.12–13

he does not reject the best which that tradition has to offer.[138] His Christ functions like a second god, and does not proceed directly from the Father, but from His power,[139] a sequence which incorporates even the Chaldean Oracles into Origenian thought.[140] He avoids debasing the Logos, and unlike Philo, who claims that it pervades the parts of the cosmos, where it would be beneath God's dignity to go, he firmly locates it in the bosom of God. His *Logos* collaborates with the Father in a much more effective and dynamic way, for the purposes of demiurgy, than the Numenian First God collaborates with the Second, making both principles truly creators. However, understanding Origen's thought is problematic, since it has been subjected to varying degrees of misrepresentation by his opponents.

In spite of his opposition to the Gnostics, his motivation of creation leaves it as inherently evil for creatures, rather than merely pointless. As St Thomas observed, under this system corporeal creatures have no goal other than to atone for the consequences of sin; they were not created to participate in the bounty of the Lord.[141] Such an interpretation may be rather harsh on Origen and may unduly strain his meaning. (One could refute this claim by pointing out that God creates non-corporeal intelligences for no reason other than Himself and his own goodness.[142] Creation has a point if the end will be such a perfection of love that rational intelligences will not turn to sin again). After all, God does place Man at the centre of the universe, since the current cosmos will be dissolved once all rational creatures will be saved; although logically it would indicate that the devil has the power to dissolve the created universe, since presumably he will be the last to be saved. Origen attempts to avoid the extreme consequences of his doctrine, as presented by St Thomas. This is evinced by his interpretation of St Paul's words: 'Creation has been subjected to vanity, not of its own desire, but by the wish of him who submitted it, in the hope that it will be saved.'[143] This line was one of the great Biblical bastions of the Valentinians. Yet creation has greater purpose for Origen than for Valentinus; it results from the gift of free will, not from a split within the godhead itself.

---

[138] As he says at *CCels*. VII.45.6 (in relation to Celsus' use of the image of the Sun and Line of the *Republic*): 'We are careful not to raise objections to good teaching, even if the authors are outside the faith.'

[139] 'He (Christ) is the image of his goodness and a ray, not of God, but of his glory and of his eternal light and a breath, not of the Father but of his power, an unsullied emanation of his almighty glory, and an untarnished mirror of his activity (*energeia*). The mirror through which Peter and Paul and their like see God.' (*Comm. Jn.* 13.251–3 1 Preuschen)

[140] *Dunamis* is the middle term in the Chaldean version of an intelligible triad. Edwards: 2002, 75

[141] St. Thomas, *ST.* Ia, QXLVII, art. II

[142] *Princ.* II.9.6.183–98   [143] *Epist. Ad. Rom.* VIII.20

In fact, one of the merits of Origen's system is the means by which he posits multiple aspects of the *Logos* as the refraction of the indivisible Father. This allows him to maintain the unity of God and defend his monistic stance, since he does not view matter as a principle. Although God is not debased through contact with matter, the Father as First Principle is sufficiently removed from it, since He creates by means of the Son. At the same time, the Trinity as a whole is distinguished from the rest of creation, since it alone has no corporeal form and does not participate in the substrate. Origen's system may have problematic consequences if pursued to its ultimate conclusions, but it does represent a serious attempt to grapple with the problems of demiurgy, and express Christian theology in terms which would be acceptable (and even appealing) to a highly-educated elite; that is an elite with a training in Greek philosophy.

CHAPTER 10

Plotinus and the demise of the Demiurge

The disappearance of the Demiurge

It would be inaccurate to claim that the concept of the Demiurge simply disappeared and to a limited extent it has persisted into our own time, although mainly as a result of having captured the non-philosophical imagination. 'Demiurge' was a character in the 1988 novel *Overburdened with Evil* by the Soviet science fiction writers Arkady and Boris Strugatsky. (The title refers to matter). In 1996, Lucasart released a game in which the player is called the Demiurge and has to manage heaven and hell. Most famously of all, Christ-Michael, in Karlheinz Stockhausen's opera *Donnerstag aus Licht* was a trainee Demiurge, who had to be incarnated in seven levels of being before he was entitled to create his own universe. (Stockhausen was influenced by Gnosticism, which he encountered via *The Urantia Book*).[1] However, its importance as a philosophical concept declined with the emergence of Neoplatonism, which propounded an alternative model for generating the physical cosmos, while still remaining loyal to the essential elements of Platonism in drawing a distinction between the suprasensible and phenomenal realms.

Essentially one can claim that the Plotinian model is midway between Darwinianism and Deism, or as Dillon puts it in terms of an ancient perspective, between that of an atomistic generation, such as that advanced by Democritus, and the model of the Demiurge that we find in Plato's *Timaeus*.[2] The concept of the Demiurge effectively reached its postscript with the emergence of this new generational model propounded by Plotinus. However, Plotinus still shares sufficient similarities with Numenius to have been accused of having plagiarised his predecessor, a situation which

---

[1] This text is supposed to have been received in a series of trances from 1934–5 by Wilfred C. Kellogg, a Chicago businessman (from the Kellogg's Cornflakes family) and recorded by Dr William S. Sadler, a psychiatrist and Seventh Day Adventist minister. It was published by the Urantia Foundation in 1955.

[2] Dillon: 2005b, 263–6

prompted his disciple, Amelius, to compose a treatise, *The Doctrinal Differences Between Plotinus and Numenius*, in his defence.[3]

Although Plotinus advocates an alternative model for world-generation, he still attempted to answer the primary question of Greek metaphysics, which Plato had attempted to solve with the Demiurge; how can the multiplicity of the generated realm be derived from the Monad? While the classic response of Middle Platonism had been to propose some sort of duality, Plotinus responded in terms of radical monism. Just as the Middle Platonists reduced the principles from three to two, he reduced them further. Everything owed its existence to the One. While the Demiurge presumably needs to produce in order to be regarded as a Demiurge (and there is evidence to this effect in the *Timaeus*, where he has to ensure that every aspect of the intelligible realm is instantiated in its physical counterpart, or in Plutarch's *Quaestiones Convivales*, where he must continually engage in geometry), the One does not require his productions.

Plotinus describes this generative process in terms of the radiation of light in diminishing degrees. This has often been referred to inaccurately as emanation. In fact, this implies that the process is one way, whereas in reality it consists of two stages: 'procession' and 'creative contemplation'. Plotinus is under no obligation to insulate his First Principle from what it produces since it remains in its transcendent state, even when producing; although he acknowledges that the generated is always inferior to the generator (*cf.* V.4.[7] 2.19; V 5 [32] 5.1–7; VI 9 [9] 3.45–9; VI 9 [9] 9.1–7).[4]

The One differs from the Demiurge in that it does not order; it spontaneously produces a power which then orders itself in contemplation of the One.[5] This is illustrated in the case of *Nous*; the One generates what can best be described as intelligible matter, but in a formless state, although it shapes itself as a result of its *epistrophê*, this becomes Intellect, which in Plotinus' system contains the world of the Forms. *Enn.* II 9 [33] 2.1–18 highlights the unchangeability of this Intellect and connects it with the constancy of soul, which, for Plotinus, has an undescended part 'always directed to the intelligible realities' and links it to the constancy of the contemplative power.[6] (The intelligible matter which forms Intellect is different from the sensible matter which is ordered to form the world). Proclus would later comment that (sensible) matter was not brought into existence by the Demiurge, based on his interpretation of Plato *Tim.* 53d3–5 and is perhaps 'derived from another order of [causes], the one positioned

[3] *Vita Plotini* 17   [4] Dillon: 2005b, 266
[5] Plotinus, *Enn.* V 2 [11] 1.6, *cf.* V 2 [11] 1.1–18   [6] Narbonne: 2011, 126–7

above the Demiurge, whom he compares to a mother and father',[7] adding
that 'according to Plato, matter proceeds both from the One and from
the Unlimitedness which is prior also to the One Being',[8] a view which
Narbonne takes to be close to its Plotinian model.[9] Although this idea of an
indeterminate production ordering itself under the influence of a superior
entity is alien to the *Timaeus*, where Necessity dominates the account of
world-generation from below, it can be found in Plutarch's account of Isis
or indeed the Numenian Second God's continual contemplation of the
First.

While the Demiurge's production owes itself to his inherent goodness
and ungrudging nature, this is not the case with the One: 'And all things
produce upon attaining perfection, and the One is always perfect and it
everlastingly produces and it produces what is less than itself' (v 1 [10]
6.37–9). The One produces in the following manner: (1) everlastingly, (2)
from inexhaustible reality (vi 9 [9] 9.3–4), (3) without undergoing change
(iii 8 [30] 8. 46–8), (4) without deliberation or desire to generate (v 1 [10]
6. 25–7, v 3 [49] 12.28–33, cf. v 5 [32] 12.43–9) and (5) without knowledge
of products (vi 7 [38] 39.19–33). The One has generated all possibilities: 'it
is not possible now for anything to be generated. For since all things have
been generated, there is nothing else which might come into being' (v 5
[32] 12.46–7).

The subordinate hypostases are not produced from the substance of
the First Principle, since it does not flow to them, rather from its power.
Nous then produces its own matter which, turning back to contemplate
it, is generated as soul. At the extremity of this procession, the soul of the
universe (which for Plotinus represents *physis* or nature) generates sensible
matter.[10] Because of its distance ontologically from the One, it is unable to
contemplate nature and from its attempt to turn back the sensible realm is
produced.

The Plotinian model, in a sense, stands midway between the two
extremes of demiurgy. It envisages no role for the element of planning
prior to embarking on the world-production undertaken by the Demiurge of Plato or of Philo, even though the portrayal of world-generation
undertaken by the Intellectual-Principle in accordance with its vision of
the Good might seem to resemble the production of the Demiurge in
accordance with the Forms.[11] Conversely, although the sensible world is

[7] Proclus, *In Tim.* 1 384, 19–385, 13. Runia and Share: 2007, 253–4. *Cf.* the discussion of Narbonne:
2011, 39ff.
[8] trans. Runia and Share: 2007   [9] Narbonne: 2011, 40
[10] Gatti: 1996, 33   [11] *Enn.* vi 7 [38] 15

not planned, there is no sense in which it results from the mistake of a hypostasis, as with the Gnostic myth of Sophia. Rather, sensible matter is ethically neutral (although Plotinus acknowledges that the soul's obsession with the material world can be the cause of evil).

Plotinus makes explicit the ontological status of his generative principle, unlike Plato. It is true that the *Timaeus* never mentions any god superior to the Demiurge, but equally it never identifies him with the Good of the *Republic*. Plotinus makes this identification explicit, referring to his supreme principle as either the Good or the One depending upon the context. Although Plotinus denied the existence of demiurgy above the level of *Nous*, here I consider the One from the perspective of a generative principle, as it is the *father of the cause* (VI 1 [10] 8.5). While the Gnostics provide a detailed account of the Demiurge's ancestry, and Plato never troubles to explain where he came from (a moot point, if he was only introduced for 'the purposes of exposition'), Plotinus specifies the origin of the One: '(the Good) must not be classified as made, but as the maker and we must consider that his making is unconstrained' (VI 8 [39] 20.4–6), or 'the One is the cause of itself' (VI 8 [39] 13.55, 14.41; 16.13–15).[12] Unlike the Demiurge, who even in Plato's *Timaeus* was of rather limited resources, the One possesses infinite power to generate the suprasensible realm (V 4 [7] 1.23–6, V 5 [32] 10.18–23, VI 9 [9] 6.10–12, II 4 [12] 15.17–20, *cf.* V 5 [32] 11.1–2). However, Plotinus acknowledges that the analogies used in his account of world-generation are inaccurate: 'To say that it is the cause is not to assert something accidental of it, but of us' (VI 9 [9] 3.49–50).

The predominant trend of the negative association of matter was continued by Plotinus, who regards matter as 'evil itself' (I 8 [51] 8.37–44, I 8 [51] 13.21–5) and as responsible for evil in soul (I 8 [51] 14). Although he refers to it as 'non-being' (II 4 [12] 16.3, II 5 [25] 4–5), this is not a denial of its existence, but an assertion of how lowly on the ontological scale it ranks (and it is therefore comparatively evil). While Numenius declared that matter was not derived from the supreme principle (Fr. 52 Des Places), Plotinus could not accept that since it would posit more than one First Principle and the relationship between the two would result from chance (I 4 [46] 2.9–20). Matter is evil, for Plotinus, not because it is recalcitrant, but because of its lack of Form (I 8 [51] 10, II 4 [12] 16.16–25, III 6 [26] 11.15–45), although this evil can be seen in terms of deficiency, rather than as a positive principle (*cf.* I 8 [51] 3.16, II 4 [12] 16.10–24, III 6 [26] 14.5–15).

---

[12] Bussanich: 1996, 44

For Plotinus, matter never really takes on Form; rather its relation to the Form it adopts is comparable to that between an object and its reflection (III 6 [26] 7.23–43, 9.16–19, 13.18–55). Plotinus does state that each soul is dependent upon an individual archetype (IV 3 [27] 5, VI 4 [22] 4.35–46), which is an easier transition for him to make than for Plato, since he regards the Forms as God's thoughts, but he does note that it would be ridiculous to postulate a separate Form of fire for each individual fire (VI 5 [23] 8.39–46), though his position in this regard is ambivalent, since at V 7 [18], he entertains the possibility of Forms of individuals of some sort.[13]

Plotinus moves away from the dualism of the preceding period; since in his model of procession Form is adopted by the lower ranking entity in response to the One, it reflects poorly on matter that it should be unable to order itself, rather than on the One because he cannot order it. The Middle Platonist doctrine of the Forms as the thoughts of God has been rehabilitated by Plotinus. He identifies the noetic realm with the Living Animal of *Timaeus* 30cff. (V 9 [5] 9.3–8, VI 2 [43] 21.53–9, VI 6 [34] 7.14–19, VI 7 [38] 8.27–32). For Plotinus, Forms are living intelligences (VI 7 [38] 9.20) which do not require to be thought in order to exist (V 9 [5] 7.11–18, VI 6 [34] 6 *cf. Parm.* 132b–c). While Origen was at pains to maintain that the intelligible world had to be finite, since otherwise it would be unknown even to God (*De. Princ.* Frs. 24, 38), Plotinus similarly does not posit an infinite number of Forms, since he denies the existence of infinite number (VI 6 [34] 2.1) and although Intelligence has no external limitations, once it adopts Form, it imposes limitation upon itself (VI 6 [34] 18, VI 7 [38] 17.14–26, 33.7–12).

Plotinus' model breaks with the traditional one of demiurgy, since he no longer views the generative principle as partaking in Being, as had been the case with the Demiurge of the *Timaeus*. This had to some extent been anticipated by Numenius in his identification of Being with the First Principle, rather than with the Demiurge, or in the position of the Demiurge in the Gnostic and Hermetic traditions. However, in these systems the modification has the opposite effect; the creative principle is demoted. Plotinus, by moving away from the demiurgic model and linking

---

[13] The problem is that if there is no Form of an individual, it excludes the individual from the intelligible world and prevents him having knowledge of it. The Forms here, though partly intended to be Forms of individual souls, are embodied in an infinite series of particular physical individuals (V 7 [18] 1.13–18). To avoid positing an infinity of ideas, the same model can function for an infinity of individuals, each of which is reincarnated (according to the doctrine of metempsychosis) at a different period.

the supreme power with the demiurgic principle, raises the status of world-generation. Simultaneously, he elevates the ontological status of his First Principle by placing it beyond Being (III 8 [30] 10.26–35). The realm of the One is not a mere blueprint for the intelligible world, in the manner in which it serves as the paradigm for the phenomenal realm; rather it is its source.

Such an exalted principle can still be responsible for generating everything else in Plotinus' system, since the product is always less than the producer.[14] For Plotinus, there is no need to posit an instrument which the One requires to order to produce (III 8 [30] 2.1–15; V 9 [5] 6.20–4). However, Plotinus does posit a succession of Hypostases, which are generated before sensible matter is reached. Additionally, the One never contemplates the lower entities, but concentrates its attention upon itself. Generation is a spontaneous process caused when the energy generated by this contemplation overflows (III 8 [30] 3–4).

Plotinus is opposed to the notion of demiurgy, since regarding world-generation as having been preceded by deliberation would imply hesitation, which would lead one to locate doubt and ignorance in the godhead. For Plotinus, every aspect of the generative process occurs in the only possible way, because it is the best possible way (IV 4 [28] 12, V 7 [18] 1.21–5). Plotinus vocalises his opposition to demiurgy at *Enn.* IV 3 [27] 10.13–19 and IV 4 [28] 11, where he points out that the activity of the divine hypostases is more akin to the spontaneous processes of nature than the deliberations of human craftsmen.[15]

He does, however, make a concession to the *Timaeus* by acknowledging that the world is as good as if it had been planned with the best divine reasoning (III 2 [47] 14.1–6; VI 2 [43] 21.32–8; VI 7 [38] 1.28–32; VI 8 [39] 17.1–12), although he argues, like the majority of Platonists, that fixing a temporal origin to the world should not be taken literally (III 2 [47] 1.20–6, IV 3 [27] 9.16–20, VI 7 [38] 3.1–9). This Plotinian generation is continual and it does not terminate with intelligence, but must continue to matter (IV 8 [6] 6, V 2 [11] 2.1–5), just as the sensible cosmos must contain all possible living creatures (*Tim.* 30c–d, 39e). This leads Plotinus to postulate the Principle of Plenitude: as many beings as possible and every kind of being, even though not all beings are equally good (II 9 [33] 13.1–5, 25–33; III 3 [48] 3–4), but if they were, the universe itself would be less perfect, just as with a work of art, which for the beauty of the whole may

[14] One is reminded of the maxim later expressed by St. Thomas Aquinas as bonum diffusivum sui ('The good diffuses itself').

[15] Wallis: 1972, 62

require elements that are less beautiful when considered in isolation (III 2 [47] II).

Interestingly, although Plotinus criticises the demiurgic model, the force of it is such that he considers the generation of the cosmos in terms of the production of a work of art. While Christians or Platonists do not have much choice about whether they are created or not, all entities in the Plotinian system demonstrate some sort of creative volition; ordering themselves in response to their contemplation of the One to the best of their ability. This leads Plotinus to conclude that every being seeks to return to its cause (III 8 [30] 7.15–18). Yet the metaphysical contemplation required to achieve this is not based upon looking upwards to the heavens, but contemplating oneself in order to revert to the cause (VI 9 [9] 2.33–45, *cf. ibid.* 7.29–33). This leads to the two phases of Neoplatonist generation: procession (*prohodos*) and reversion (*epistrophē*).

Plotinus also adapts the *Logos* to his system. However, he is influenced more by the Stoic conception of the *Logos* as an entity regulating the soul's governance of the phenomenal realm, than the Platonic or Origenian sense in which it is a separate Hypostasis that aids in creation. The *Logos*, for Plotinus, is a rational formative principle which proceeds from Intellect.

> Now Mind, having given to matter something of itself wrought all things calmly and quietly. And it was the *logos* (ordering principle) which flowed from Mind. For the *logos* flows out from Mind and it always flows out as long as Mind is always present in the things that are ... For the noetic is only *logos* and there could not be another one which is not *logos*. If something else were to come into being, it would be necessary that it is inferior to the noetic cosmos and less than *logos* and not a type of matter. For that is disorderly. So it is a mixture and the points at which it terminates are matter and *logos* and it starts from soul presiding over the mixture, which we must not suppose to suffer evil as it administers this universe easily by means of a sort of presence. (*Enn.* III 2 [47] 2.15–42)

The notion of continual flowing here is reminiscent of Philo's comparison of the *Logos* with the cupbearer of Zeus. The *Logos*, despite the wide range of meanings which Plotinus bestows on the word, often refers to the relation of the Hypostasis to its source, products or both (III 2 [47] 2.15–42). The term is also used to refer to the causal principles in the divine mind; the same sense in which Origen uses it (*spermatikoi logoi*, III 2 [47] 2.15–17; V 9 [5] 6.20–4).

Another interpretation

According to Anton, the decline in the importance of the Demiurge can to a certain extent be linked to the rise of theurgy in Platonic circles; the role of the artist-demiurge as the revealer of divine beauty is replaced by the theurgist.[16] According to such a reading, Gnosticism would be responsible for the decline of the Demiurge, since it was accompanied by an increase in the significance of theurgy. As Damascius states in his *Commentary on the Phaedo*:

> Ὅτι οἱ μὲν τὴν φιλοσοφίαν προτιμῶσιν, ὡς Πορφύριος καὶ Πλωτῖνος καὶ ἄλλοι πολλοὶ φιλόσοφοι· οἱ δὲ τὴν ἱερατικήν, ὡς Ἰάμβλιχος καὶ Συριανὸς καὶ Πρόκλος καὶ οἱ ἱερατικοὶ πάντες.

> Some put philosophy first, such as Porphyry, Plotinus etc; others the priestly art, as Iamblichus, Syrianus, Proclus and all the priestly school. (Damascius, *In Platonis Phaedonem* i, sect. 172, trans. Dodds 1963, xxii)

Olympiodorus identified two stages in the development of Neoplatonic theurgy. In the first phase they began to conceptualise the demiurgic principle differently, exploring it dialectically.[17] Furthermore, since the Gnostics disassociated God from the sensible world, knowledge of him could not be reached by contemplating the heavens, as it could for a Platonist. In the Neoplatonist concept of the world, the soul could only know the *logoi* of the World-Soul, but not any higher entity.

The attraction of Anton's theory lies in the charge that Gnosticism was responsible for the decline of the Demiurge. While he proposes that it is because of the increase of theurgy that Gnosticism promoted (as well as the decline in the social importance of the artist), that demiurgy as a concept fell from favour, by demoting the Demiurge's ontological rank in the first place, Gnosticism was further responsible for the decline of the demiurgic concept. The social importance of the artist presumably played less of a role, since it was not particularly elevated when Plato chose to use his image.

Proclus

Numenius' attempts to distinguish between a supreme principle and a demiurgic intelligence (Fr. 16 Des Places) is echoed by his Neoplatonist successors. Numenius (in his surviving work) leaves the Third God as

---

[16] Anton: 1992, 12   [17] Anton: 1992, 14

something of a mystery; it appears to be a last vestige of the Platonic World-Soul, although since the Numenian Demiurge interacts with the phenomenal realm in a more immediate fashion than his ancestors, the World-Soul's role has disappeared.[18] Proclus identifies it with the cosmos, although Numenius himself regarded it as 'generated' (ποίημα, δημιουργούμενον).[19]

It would be wrong, however, to imply that Plotinus or his successors simply did away with the Demiurge. He survives, though occupying a role within a derivational, rather than demiurgic, model of world-generation. Additionally, the Neoplatonic systems tend to be more specific in delineating his ontological rank, not only identifying him with νοῦς, but in Proclus' case, equating each subdivision of demiurgy with a precise form of intelligence. Indeed, much was made in the period of *Tim.* 39e:

ἥπερ οὖν νοῦς ἐνούσας ἰδέας τῷ ὃ ἔστιν ζῷον, οἷαί τε ἔνεισι καὶ ὅσαι, καθορᾷ, τοιαύτας καὶ τοσαύτας διενοήθη δεῖν καὶ τόδε σχεῖν.

According, then, as Mind perceives forms existing in the living being, he thought it necessary that this world should contain these, as many as exist there.

According to Proclus, *In. Tim.* I p. 306 1*ff.*, Amelius read this as referring to a demiurgic triad: 'he who is, he who possesses, and he who sees' (ὁ ὤν, ὁ ἔχων, ὁρῶν, based on ὁ ἔστι ζῷον, ἐχούσας and καθορᾷ). This idea of a demiurgic triad is incorporated by Proclus into his metaphysical system (although it was previously used by Iamblichus – *In. Tim.* I. p. 308. 18*ff.*). Proclus outlines his views on demiurgy in his *Commentary on the Timaeus*. He adopts the distinction drawn between the suprasensible and phenomenal realms at *Tim.* 27d–28a 'that which always is and which does not have becoming and that which is always becoming but never is', positing an increasing level of multiplicity as ontological levels become more remote from the One. When Plato prefaces his remarks on causation by ὑπ'αἰτίου τινός (*Tim.* 28a4–6), Proclus takes this to mean that the demiurgic cause is only one amongst several efficient causes (efficient is illustrated by the preposition ὑπό).[20]

As the Demiurge is identified with Intellect, this places it third in the primary Neoplatonist triad of Being, Life and Intellect. This accords, incidentally, with the function of the Demiurge. As he is the conduit between the higher and sublunar realms, he requires proximity (ontologically) to the physical world. Demiurgic activity needs to be mediated if the Intellect

---

[18] On the basis of *In. Tim.* III p. 10.3.28*ff.*, where it seems to represent the lower 'dianoetic' aspect of the Demiurge. *Cf.* Dillon: 2000, 341.
[19] Dillon: 2000, 341   [20] Opsomer: 2000, 115

is to remain transcendent. Proclus saw in Plato's comments at *Tim.* 29a6, that the Demiurge is the best of causes, an assertion that it is superior to the other forms of demiurgic causes. Opsomer has analysed in-depth the structure of the intellective hebdomad,[21] which can be subdivided into two triads and an entity that functions as a membrane separating the hebdomad from the other realms and providing internal divisions within its own hebdomad. (This echoes the ὑπεζωκώς of the *Chaldean Oracles*). The second triad duplicates the activity of the first, but at a less exalted level, thereby insulating it from matter. As the first member of a Proclean triad is usually concerned with inner activity and the Demiurge's activity by its very nature needs to be external, he cannot occupy this position. The second member of a triad is typically associated with Life, though in the *Timaeus* account, the Demiurge is not principally associated with this, since he resorts to the mixing-bowl to produce soul at 41d4–5, but is able to impart intellect to the universe (30b4) by himself, so he logically occupies the third (intellective) position as intellective intellect.[22]

Proclus draws upon the *Philebus'* statement that royal soul and royal intellect pre-exist in Zeus to posit two separate roles for the intellective triad as the fatherly cause of eternal beings, but as the demiurgic cause of mortal beings, with various distinctions drawn between the intermediary entities, which have combined titles. The 'father and maker', therefore, (in which the fatherly element dominates) ranks above the 'maker and father'.

Another distinction drawn by Proclus amongst the entities of his intellective hebdomad is amongst the four forms of demiurgic causes (*TP* 5.13; *in. Tim.* 1.310.18–24). It is the 'one demiurge' who produces universal beings in a universal way (τῶν ὅλων ὁλικῶς δημιουργικοὶ αἴτιον), while the demiurgic triad produces partial beings in a partial way (τῶν μερῶν ὅλικῶς), a Monad (Dionysos) produces universal beings in a partial way (τῶν ὅλων μερικῶς), and the lower triad (the Titans) produces partial beings in a partial way (τῶν μερῶν μερικῶς) [*in Tim.* 1.310.15–18]. Opsomer concludes that the main distinction being drawn is not in terms of what is actually being created, but between a universal and partial mode of creation.[23] As has been observed, the triads dealing with universal and partial demiurgy

---

[21] Opsomer: 2000, 117*ff.*

[22] Opsomer: 2000, 117. Dillon: 1969 discusses the four principal Neoplatonist theories concerning the ontological rank of the Demiurge (those of Amelius Gentilianus, Porphyry, Iamblichus and Proclus, arising from open-ended interpretations of Plotinus, *Enn.* III 9 [13] 1, which itself was stimulated by Plato, *Tim.* 39e (and also *Tim.* 28c).

[23] Opsomer: 2000, 119

exhibit the same internal structure. Unfortunately, the section of the *Platonic Theology* which would have dealt with encosmic demiurgy (if this was actually composed) has been lost.

The hypercosmic demiurgic triad (that responsible for the production of parts in a universal way) finds Platonic authority in the *Gorgias* myth with the division of Cronos' kingdom between Zeus, Poseidon and Hades (523a3–5). Zeus is more than just one of the three rulers, who divides the world, but in his role as the sovereign ruler, he is also the universal Demiurge. The second Zeus is a lower Demiurge, but still part of the chain originating with the first Zeus. The hypercosmic-demiurgic triad is responsible for existence, life and intellective reversion (the process whereby beings turn towards the ontological level which precedes them), activities which all exist causally in the universal Demiurge.[24] The problem Proclus faces in advocating such intermediary levels of demiurgy is not one of 'contaminating' his Demiurge through proximity to matter, but one of 'declension' (ὕφεσις), the decline of unity down through the ontological scale, which is why this hypercosmic triad is only responsible 'for parts'.

The first triad at the hypercosmic-encosmic level consists of the third Zeus, second Poseidon and Hephaistos, who are 'drawn into multiplicity by the Young Gods' (*TP* 6.15 p. 73. 17–19), and who separate the upper two levels of Proclus' four levels of demiurgy from the lower ones. They form an intermediate realm between the hypercosmic and encosmic *diakosmoi*. Next follows the encosmic demiurgic gods, headed by Dionysus (a Monad), who ensures the unity of the cosmos at the 'inner-worldly' level. Dionysus represents the indivisible (held together by a totality) and divisible (a multitude of separable parts) nature of the universe. The encosmic Demiurges are Proclus' equivalent of the Young Gods of the *Timaeus*. Dionysus is followed by a triad of Titans, who engage in partial demiurgy. Dionysus himself, as noted above, produces universal beings in a partial way while the Titans produce partial beings in a partial way. The partial Demiurges also delegate some of their tasks to a plethora of lesser entities (such as heroes and *daimones*). The main distinction between universal and partial demiurgy is that the universal Demiurge can produce while remaining motionless ('he remained in his own accustomed nature', *Tim.* 42e5–6), while the encosmic demiurges produce through their activity.

---

[24] Opsomer: 2000, 120

The identification of the first god of the hypercosmic-encosmic triad with Dionysus has Orphic associations. It draws upon a tale in Orphic mythology, whereby the young Dionysus, placed upon his father's throne, is torn to shreds by the Titans. The Titans are struck down by Zeus' thunderbolt in revenge, and the human race is reborn from their ashes, while Dionysus is reborn to Semele. This was interpreted as symbolising Dionysus' divisible and indivisible nature (and by extension, as outlined above, the divisible and indivisible nature of the universe). His rebirth symbolises the regeneration of the universe, while the birth of mankind from the ashes of the Titans represents the demiurgy of man. Proclus regards the Titans as identifiable with the celestial, aquatic and chthonic aspects of Dionysus, paralleling these three divisions observable elsewhere. It is beyond the scope of our analysis to comment in detail on these Proclean refinements, beyond observing that in his attempts at job demarcation, the lesser Demiurges have their activities confined to a particular division of the cosmos. Such a tripartite division of demiurgy raises questions concerning its interrelation with the fourfold division which Proclus suggests elsewhere. For all its complexity, the essential distinction being drawn is that made by Plato himself at *Tim.* 41a, between the Demiurge and the Young Gods.

As Opsomer notes, Proclus' scheme displays the tension inherent in two separate generative models; demiurgy and derivation.[25] Plotinus did not draw such sharp distinctions between the primary hypostases, though equating the Demiurge with intellect, but transferring his activities to soul. Porphyry finalises this process in his system, where matter is ordered by soul. The numerous intermediaries, then, inserted in Proclus' demiurgic scheme are not solely insulation against the evil of matter, but preserve the image of continuous transition.

Proclus explains at *PT* v 13 p. 42.14–22 why he ranks the demiurgic function so comparatively humbly on the ontological scale:

> Then where are we to place it? For all the partial entities arising subsequent to the intellective realm are more partial than the single and whole demiurgy, for the division of the whole into three and the leaders of the partial fabrication manifest themselves at this level of cosmic order. However, the beings which are superior to the intellective realm are marked off by the proper characteristics of the gods, as has been demonstrated before, and generally, they have been conceived according to unity and they are superior to the distinctiveness of the Forms of the intellective realm. Therefore, it only remains that the single Demiurge of everything is stationed in the intellective realm.

[25] Opsomer: 2000, 273

Pleroma and noetic cosmos

The ordering model of demiurgy and the creative Judaeo–Christian model start to coalesce to some extent. This is not solely due to the activities of Platonising members of the Judaeo–Christian tradition, such as Philo and Origen, but also due to the emergence of Christian Gnosticism. Originally in Jewish or Christian thought, there was no notion of God creating according to a pre-existent model; the concept which we find in Philo and Origen has been imported from Platonism. This model, the *autozoōn* (Essential Living Being), becomes highly speculative as one descends through the Platonic tradition, with hierarchies of genera and species, leading Plotinus to describe it as a 'globe or a thing all faces, radiant with living faces' (*Enn.* VI 7 [38] 15.25–6). This concept of the paradigm, according to which the world is constructed as the contents of the divine mind, can be traced back to Xenocrates' assertion that the supreme principle is an Intellect (which is necessarily engaged in thinking) and the Forms which Xenocrates equates with numbers (Fr. 34 Heinze) could be regarded, perhaps, as the contents of this Intellect.[26]

Though I have suggested above that Philo may be the first to have used the term 'noetic cosmos', I do not believe he was the first to develop this concept, as the identification of Forms with the *logoi spermatikoi* of Stoicism would easily have given rise to this theory. A comparable theory exists in Valentinianism with the view that the Aeons are the 'thoughts of the Father'. The difference here is that the Aeons can be deficient in varying degrees, whereas this notion is never articulated in Middle Platonism. A related point is the rank accorded to the various Aeons, whereas the Forms are all on the same level (although subordinate to the Form of the Good). The imagery applied to the concept is similar in both cases – God is the 'place' of the Aeons (*cf.* Philo, *Opif.* 20) and he is an undiminished spring (*Trip. Treatise*; Philo. *Opif.* 2, *Leg. All.* II. 87, *Cher.* 86, *Post.* 136; Plotinus, *Enn.* III 8 [30] 10.5; VI 7 [38] 12.24–5).[27]

From the *Gospel of the Egyptians*, we learn that there are a mass of 'thrones, powers and glories' which have not been characterized (54). The version of the Pleroma expressed at *Zostrianos* 48 shares some correspondences with the Platonic noetic realm:

---

[26] Dillon: 1982, 101. It must be noted that based on the extant evidence, Xenocrates himself does not actually draw this conclusion.

[27] Dillon: 1982, 102

Corresponding to each of the Aeons, I saw a living earth and a living water and (air) made of light and fire that cannot burn ... all being simple and immutable with trees that do not perish in many ways and tares ... this way and all these and imperishable fruit and living men and every form and immortal souls and every shape and form of mind, and gods of truth and messengers who exist in great glory and indissoluble bodies and an unborn begetting and an immovable perception. (trans. J. N. Sieber)

In the *Poimandres* 8, the *kalos kosmos* functions as a noetic archetype which God contemplates prior to producing the world. A major difference between the Pleroma and the noetic realm, however, is that the Pleroma is not meant to serve as a model upon which the world is based, since the world results from an error in the godhead.[28] However, even here there is evidence of the traditions coalescing. Man serves as the archetype of mankind. In the *Second Treatise of the Great Seth* (*NHC* 53–4), Adam is the image of 'the Father of Truth, the Man of the Greatness'. In the *Apocryphon of John* (*NHC* II, I, 2, 5–14), 'the perfect man', the Barbelo, is the archetype for Adam. In the Sethian system additional archetypes of all the pneumatics exist in the Pleroma. The Pleroma, then, reveals some traces of Platonic influence.

---

[28] Dillon: 1982, 106

CHAPTER II

Concluding remarks

Based on the evidence of the *Timaeus* dialogue itself, it seems apparent that Plato intended the Demiurge myth simply for the purposes of exposition, although I acknowledge that such a position is disputed, even in modern scholarship. Once the Demiurge re-emerges in the first to third centuries, though, he is taken as a literal figure and the discussion concerns the precise nature of his activity, rather than whether he existed or not. Via Stoicism and its speculations regarding the *Logos*, the motif of the Demiurge became of importance for Philo of Alexandria, as well as those who can more unequivocally be described as Middle Platonists. The mythological account of an anthropomorphised, generative intelligence had an obvious utility for Christian intellectuals. Faced with attacks on their religion's lack of philosophical sophistication, it provided a mechanism whereby the account of *Genesis* could be reconciled with Greek philosophy, with some of the foundations of this line of approach having already been laid by Philo.

Gnostic (and Hermetic) usage of the demiurgic motif simply reveals the ultimate evolution of the concept that the Demiurge was a secondary god or divine mediator, who was in some way less good than the First Principle (a means of accounting for the imperfections of the generated realm and of accommodating dualistic beliefs). The trend of placing the demiurgic power lower on the ontological scheme as a means of insulating the First Principle from matter finally led to the point where both entities were placed in a state of antagonism. Neoplatonism did not really require a Demiurge in its alternative generational model, but it still found a minor position in its ontological scheme which could be occupied by demiurgic figures.

It is clear that we are dealing with the same motif, rather than simply alternative accounts concerning the origin of the universe. These systems involve a generative entity using some sort of model (which may be the contents of his mind or something external) to produce the world and often involves some sort of ordering activity in which the world is constructed on geometrical principles and frequently the Demiurge does not create the matter out of which he generates the cosmos. Usually the desire to produce is the result of the goodness of the Demiurge and the aim is to produce the best kind of world possible. While Gnosticism is an obvious exception, even there, in several accounts, the true God conspires to ensure that Man's position is somehow better than that envisioned by the Demiurge. The accounts also frequently make use of artisanal imagery or language which described the secondary god as a craftsman or fabricator.

The intense debate generated during more recent times between proponents of Darwinianism and rational design can perhaps be paralleled in terms of the rival creational or demiurgic models of the first to third centuries AD. That there clearly is a difference between creation (whether or not one wants to insist on *creatio ex nihilo*) in a Judaeo–Christian sense and demiurgy is beyond question. In a similar manner, the biochemist Michael Behe has attempted to demonstrate that Darwinianism and rational design are not necessarily incompatible; the same may perhaps be said for creation and demiurgy.[1] Behe argues for intelligent design as the best possible means of explaining 'irreducible complex systems', systems such as the bacterial flagellum. According to Behe, such systems are only capable of functioning in their entirety and because of this he claims that Darwinism cannot adequately explain how they came about.[2] For him, this suggests a designer who knew in advance the outline of the completed system. Indeed we could see the conflict of Darwinianism versus rational design as represented in the ancient world by the difference of opinion between Democritus and Plato.[3]

Origen and Philo, to take the case of the 'creationalists', were prepared to incorporate elements of demiurgy. Most notable in this regard is the notion that God should create from a model, clearly not a Jewish or Christian concept. Conversely, Maximus of Tyre asserts that Zeus' nod is enough for demiurgy to occur – a notion closer to Origen than to Plato. Additionally, the notion that God requires 'tools' to create is not to be found in the Biblical account (although there he seems to require time). Since these 'tools' are for the most part insulating hypostases, their origin can be traced back to the Young Gods of the *Timaeus*, but also to the winnowing-fan (πλόκανον) at *Tim.* 52e, which is used to separate out the different atoms, similar to Philo's division of atoms on the part of the

---

[1] Behe: 1996
[2] Behe's claims have been contested within the scientific community, e.g. by Ussery: 1998.
[3] Dillon: 2005b, 263

Logos-Cutter. This πλόκανον is perhaps a reaction to the sieve (κόσκινον) which Democritus uses as an analogy to explain world-generation.

Creation and demiurgy, then, seem to differ more in the nature of the mechanism they posit (a necessity when one proposes an omnipotent creator and the other a less exalted entity), rather than in terms of their original causality. Both are propositions along deistic lines, differing from the mindless 'evolution' propounded by atomism or indeed the repeated generation of the cosmos found in Stoicism. In a sense, the Plotinian model can be viewed as midway between atomism and the deism advanced in different ways by creationalism and 'demiurgism' (if one can indeed posit such a term, since the existence of the Demiurge was not a doctrine that even many Platonists believed in) – for Neoplatonists the universe was produced according to rational principles, but this had occurred spontaneously, not thanks to the zealous concern of a Demiurge.

The metaphysical systems exhibited by those traditions which posit a Demiurge appear to become increasingly elaborate and in the case of some of the Gnostic sects, almost tortuous. This can be viewed as part of an increasing tendency of various traditions to either insulate the First Principle from the phenomenal realm or as part of a growing anxiety to increase his transcendence, as well as part of a drive for 'one-upmanship', claiming to accept, for example, the entities of a preceding intellectual figure and then going further back in tracing the cause of the universe. Plato may have had difficulty in finding the Father of the universe, but Numenius seems to have had no trouble in discovering its Grandfather! Additionally, Numenius' tampering with the Platonic 'trinity' of the Demiurge, the Young Gods and the World-Soul, did not form a particularly satisfactory division, with the Third God a metaphysical hybrid formed from a lower demiurgic aspect, a World-Soul and a generated cosmos.

A related problem emerges in Plutarch's attempts to express his view of the *Timaeus* in terms of Egyptian mythology; the correspondences do not quite work consistently, given his combination of the Receptacle and matter in the form of Isis. His double-Demiurge is indicative of the tendency to strive for a greater degree of sophistication (or unnecessary complexity) than that of Plato's *Timaeus*. With the Valentinian desire to make their Platonic inheritance compatible with Christianity, the incentive for developing Plato's triad into something outrageously complex is easy to observe.

All cultures (presumably) speculate on the origin of the cosmos. There is nothing inherently 'Greek' in that, nor does one require Plato in order to observe rationality and order in the created world. If God in the Old

Testament can be regarded as a builder, then perhaps the thesis that the thinkers assembled here are part of the development of the demiurgic concept (rather than merely speculation on creation) requires some defence. Against this I would contend that they are all attempting to various extents to respond to the nature of demiurgy, as advocated in the *Timaeus*. On a superficial level, all these systems make use of the entities (or modified version of them) drawn from the demiurgic myth. More importantly, the nature of demiurgy is similar in broad outline – ordering of disorderly matter by an entity of limited powers in accordance with rationality, or 'a beautiful model'. The nature of this limitation varies, from the negative influence of Necessity in the *Timaeus*, to the ignorant Gnostic Demiurge. Even in systems which envisage an omnipotent creator (such as the Judaeo–Christian one), the work of demiurgy is assigned to a lower-ranking entity or hypostasis, such as the *Logos* or Son-*Logos*, (even if the title is applied to God the Father). Although the entities of Gnosticism can be viewed as caricatured or distorted versions of their Platonic originals, their ancestry from the *Timaeus* (or the subsequent philosophical tradition) cannot be disputed. The Middle Platonist or Gnostic Demiurge might be an imperfect creator, but to a lesser degree so is his counterpart in the *Timaeus*, who is limited by Necessity. The *Logos* of the *Poimandres* may not be found in the *Timaeus*, but it does occupy a mediating role between the elements, though it evidently lacks the sophistication of its counterpart in Philo. The Gnostic Pleroma adopts the language used to describe the Platonic realm of the Forms.

This point can be made to a lesser degree regarding other interpretations of the *Timaeus*. It is clear that the Numenian account of the generation of the soul, enmattered as it is by the Second God, but with production supervised at some level by the First God, is influenced by the co-production of the Demiurge and the Young Gods. The mixing-bowl used by the Demiurge of the *Timaeus* is, in some sense, the ancestor of the elaborate system of hypostases, which are often envisaged as tools, from the representation of the *Logos* as a saw in Philo, to the mechanical imagery used by Maximus. The trend could also find justification in the description of the Young Gods, which led to positing various associates who aid the Demiurge during the process of world-generation. Such a trend was no doubt reinforced as it coincides perfectly with the unnamed associates who aid God in the Biblical account.

The pervasiveness of the demiurgic concept lies evidently in Plato's philosophical importance and the esteem in which the *Timaeus* was held amongst the Platonic dialogues as a source for Plato's metaphysics. In developing such powerful philosophical imagery to recount 'a likely story' which 'accounted for appearances', Plato produced a myth which could easily be adapted by other thinkers for their own ends (who could still have a legitimate claim for producing the more accurate story that *Timaeus* mentions as possible at some stage in the future). Plato's own ambivalence on certain points (especially the precise ontological status of the Demiurge), raised interest amongst those keen on systematising his thought, but also meant that the imagery was flexible enough to be welcomed by other traditions and manipulated to suit their particular interpretations. Even Christianity, with its radically different heritage and fundamentally different vision of 'creation', was able to accommodate and indeed contribute to the debate on demiurgy (though this is largely indebted to the Jewish philosopher Philo's attempt to rewrite *Genesis* in philosophical language).

Of course, Platonism, Gnosticism, Hermetism and Christianity are separate intellectual traditions, but this does not mean that they should be conceived of as hermetically-sealed units. They responded to each other (even if the direction of the influence is sometimes difficult to discern). Analysing all four traditions allows the complex nature of the demiurgic concept to be revealed, from its more strict metaphysical usage through to various mythological permutations. Between all four traditions, a clear development can be observed, primarily centering on the Demiurge's declining ontological status and the functioning of lesser entities in various ancillary or insulating roles, such as *daimones* or the Archons of Gnosticism.

Another question concerning demiurgy is whether it should be viewed as a continual, or a once-off event. While Plato was vague concerning this, Plutarch clearly views the Demiurge as continually ordering. Not enough of Numenius survives to make a definitive assessment, and the division of the Second and Third Gods may be a single occurrence. Still, one could argue that the Second God is continually instantiating the Intelligibles, as received from the First God. There is no doubt that Philo envisages the *Logos* as continually dividing (although much of the influence which this exterted on Christianity was mediated via the New Testament concept of the *Logos*). For Gnosticism and Hermetism, this can evidently not be the case. Since the world is generated in these systems by a cataclysmic event, namely the fragmentation of the godhead itself, it has to be a single occurrence. This does not mean that both traditions have merely appropriated the language of demiurgy to describe a different process. Rather, they have accommodated certain elements of the Demiurge into their overall structure. After all, if one wanted to push the matter, the *orexis* (lust) of the Numenian Second God could be claimed as the ancestor of the sublunar Demiurge of Gnosticism.

The double-edged problem facing those propounding the demiurgic model of world-generation is allowing the Demiurge to remain transcendent while still sufficiently immanent to order matter. This is evidently more acute for those who regard the Demiurge as the First Principle; the Gnostics have no such concern. The νεῦμα (nod of Zeus necessary for world-generation to occur) proposed by Maximus of Tyre or the 'other contacts and attachments' which Plutarch is so vague about, helps to preserve this transcendence. However, it is not necessary to conceal aspects of the Demiurge's causality merely to preserve his transcendence. Philo and Origen have more pressing demands to maintain divine transcendence and still develop a detailed model of how creation actually works, in spite of Origen's claim that the will of God is sufficient. Indeed, they are additionally forced to posit the unity of the godhead, which can be compromised when positing numerous hypostases. As the Demiurge is by definition responsible for transmitting the Forms to the sensible world, he has to be placed quite close to it. This helps to explain his comparatively low ontological rank.

Perhaps the success of the demiurgic concept, and its impact even in our own time on popular culture (although in an extremely limited way) lies in Timaeus' assertion that what he was expounding was only 'a likely story' designed to account for appearances, and his admission that it would be superseded at some stage by a more accurate version, which would equally show that the world had been fashioned by a rational intelligence. Ultimately that is what occurred and 'the likely story' became one influenced by Judaism, Christianity or a more modern version of Platonism. That it lapsed from the forefront of even Platonist (or Neoplatonist) systems is largely because it had no response to the cogent argumentation of Plotinus that the world's generation could not be the result of deliberation, but must be spontaneous.

Bibliography

ANCIENT SOURCES: EDITIONS, TRANSLATIONS, COMMENTARIES

Alcinous, *The Handbook of Platonism*, trans. and comm. Dillon, J. M., Oxford: Clarendon Press, 1993.

Aristotle, *Generation of Animals*, ed., trans. and comm. Peck, A., Cambridge MA: Harvard University Press, 1942.

Aristotle's De Motu Animalum. Text with Translation, Commentary and Interpretative Essays, ed., trans. and comm. Nussbaum, M. C., New Jersey: Princeton University Press, 1978.

Damascius, *In Platonis Phaedonem*, in ed. Westerink, L. G. *The Greek Commentaries on Plato's Phaedo*, vol. 2, Amsterdam: North Holland Publishing Company, 1977.

Doxographi Graeci, ed. Diels, H., Berlin: G. Reimer, 1879. Reprinted De Gruyter, 1976.

Epictetus, *Discourses, The Handbook, Fragments*, ed. Gill C. and trans. Hard, R., London: Everyman's Library/Random House, 1995.

Gnostic Texts, *The Coptic Gnostic Library: A Complete Edition of the Nag Hammadi Codices* Vol. 1–5, ed. Robinson J. M., Leiden: E. J. Brill, 1975–96.

The Gnostic Scriptures: Ancient Wisdom for the New Age, ed., trans. and comm. Layton, B., New York: Doubleday & Co., 1987.

The Nag Hammadi Library in English, ed. Robinson, J. M., Leiden: E. J. Brill, 1988.

Testi gnostici in lingua greca e latina, ed., trans. and comm. Simonetti, M., Milan: Mondadori, 1993.

Hermes Trismegistus, *Hermetica: The Ancient Greek and Latin Writings which Contain Religious or Philosophic Teachings ascribed to Hermes Trismegistus*, ed., trans. and comm. Scott, W., vols I–III. Oxford: Clarendon Press, 1924–6.

Corpus Hermeticum – Tomes I–XII, ed. and trans. Nock, A. D. and Festugière, A. J., Paris: Belles Lettres, 1946 (repr. 1972).

Hermetica –The Greek Corpus Hermeticum and the Latin Asclepius, ed. and trans. Copenhaver, B. P., Cambridge University Press, 1992.

The Way of Hermes: New Translations of The Corpus Hermeticum and The Definitions of Hermes Trismegistus to Asclepius, trans. Salaman, C., van Oyen, D., Wharton, W. D. and Mahé, J. P., London: Duckworth, 1992.

Corpus Hermeticum. Edizione e commento di A. D. Nock e A. J. Festugière. Édizione dei testi ermetici copti e commento di I. Ramelli. Testo greco, latino e copto a fronte. Il pensiero occidentale. Milan: Bompiani, 2005.

Iamblichus, *The Platonic Commentaries*, ed., trans. and comm. Dillon, J. M., 2nd rev. edn, Wiltshire: The Prometheus Trust, 2009.

De Anima, ed. and trans. Finamore, J. F. and Dillon, J. M., Leiden: E. J. Brill, 2002.

Inscriptiones Graecae, *Inscriptions Phocidis, Locridis, Aetoliae, Acarnaniae, insularum maris, Ionii*, vol. IX, ed. Dittenberger W., Berlin: Reimer, 1897 (= *Corpus Incriptionum Graecarum Graecae Septentrionalis*, vol. III).

Justinian, *Sacrorum conciliorum nova et amplissima collectio*, ed. Mansi, G. D. Florence/Venice, (31 vols.) 1758–98.

Maximus of Tyre, *Dissertationes*, ed. Trapp, M. B., Leipzig: B. G. Teubner, 1994.

The Philosophical Orations, trans. Trapp, M. B., Oxford: Clarendon Press, 1997.

Numenius, *Fragments*, ed. and trans. Des Places, E., Paris: Belles Lettres, 1973.

Origen, *Commentaire sur Saint Jean*, ed., trans. and comm., Blanc, C., Paris: Sources Chrétiennes, CERF, 1966.

On First Principles, trans. Butterworth, G. W., New York: Harper and Row, 1966.

Commento al Vangelo di Giovani, ed., trans. and comm. Corsini, E., Turin: Unione Tipografico-Editrice Torinese, 1968.

Contra Celse, Tomes I–IV, trans. and comm. Bourret, M., Paris: Sources Chrétiennes, CERF, 1967–9.

Homilies on Genesis and Exodus, ed. and trans. Heine, R. E., Washington, D. C.: Catholic University of America, 1982.

Traité des Principes, trans. Harl, M., Dorival, G. and Le Bouilluec, A., Paris: Études Augustiniennes, 1976.

I principi di Origene (Classici delle Religioni), ed., trans. and comm. Simonetti M., Turin: Unione Tipografico-Editrice Torinese, 1968.

Traité des Principes, Tomes I–IV, ed. trans. and comm. Crouzel, H. and Simonetti, M., Paris: Sources Chrétiennes, CERF, 1978.

Philo of Alexandria, *Opera*, ed. and trans. Colson, F. H., Whitaker, G. H. *et al.*, *Philo Judaeus Volumes I–X & Supplement Volumes I–II*, London & New York: Loeb Classical Library, 1929–61.

Quis rerum divinarum heres sit, trans. and comm. Harl, M., Paris: Éditions du Cerf, 1966.

On the Creation of the Cosmos According to Moses, Introduction, Translation and Commentary, trans. and comm. Runia, D. T., Leiden: E. J. Brill, 2001.

Philodemus, *De Stoicis*, in ed. Dorandi, T. *Filodemo, Gli Stoici* (PHerc 155 e 339), *Cronache Eroclanesi* 12, 91–133.

Plato, *Timée, Critias*, trans. Brisson, L. and Patillon, M., Paris: G. F. Flammarion 1992.

Plato's Cosmology – The Timaeus of Plato, trans. and comm. Cornford, F. M, London: Routledge and Keegan Paul, 1937, reprinted Indianapolis: Hackett, 1997.

A Commentary on Plato's Timaeus, comm. Taylor, A. E., Oxford: Clarendon Press, 1998.

Der Platonismus in der Antike V, ed., trans. and comm. Baltes, M., Stuttgart-Bad: Cannstatt, 1928.

Der Platonismus in der Antike VI 1/2, ed., trans. and comm. Baltes, M., Stuttgart-Bad: Cannstatt, 2002.

Timeo, ed., trans. and comm. Fronterotta, F., Milan: BUR Biblioteca Universale Rizzoli, 2003.

Plotinus, *The Enneads*, ed. and trans. Armstrong, A. H., vols 1–7, Cambridge, MA/London: Harvard/Heineman, 1978–87.

Plutarch, *Lives: Lycurgus and Numa*, ed. and trans. Perrin, B., Cambridge, MA: Loeb Classical Library, 1982.

Moralia Volumes I–XV, ed. and trans. Babbitt, F. C., Cherniss, H. *et al.*, London and New York: Loeb Classical Library, 1927–76.

Œuvres Morales, Tomes I–XV, ed. and trans. Flacelière, R., Froidefond, C. *et al.*, Paris: Belles Lettres, 1972–2004.

Le generazione dell' anima nel Timeo, ed., trans. and comm. Ferrari, F. and Baldi, L. Naples: D'Auria, 2002.

Presocratics, *Die Fragmente der Vorsokratiker*, 3 vols, Greek and German by H. Diels, ed. by W. Kranz, 6th rev. edn, Berlin: Weidmann, 1951–2.

Proclus, *The Elements of Theology, a Revised Text with Translation, Introduction and Commentary* by Dodds, E. R. 2nd edn with addenda and corrigenda, Oxford: Clarendon Press, 1963.

Commentaire sur le Timée, trans. Festugière, A. J., Paris: Libraire Philosophique J. Vrin, 1966.

Théologie Platonicienne, ed. and trans. Saffrey, H. D. and Westerink, L. G., Paris: Belles Lettres, 1987.

Teologia Platonica ed. and trans. Abbate M., Milan: Bompiani, 2005.

Commentary on Plato's Timaeus, Volume 2, Book 2: Proclus on the Causes of the Cosmos and its Creation, ed. and trans. Runia, D. T. and Share, M., Cambridge University Press, 2008.

Syrianus, *In Metaphysica Commentaria* ed. G. Kroll, *Acad. Litt. Reg. Borus* 6.1.1079a4, Berolini, 1902.

Valentinus, *Summer Harvest*, ed. Heitsch, E., *Die griechischen Dichterfragmente der römischen Kaiserzeit*, vol. 1, 2nd edn, Göttingen: Vandenhoeck & Ruprecht, 1963.

Varro, M. Terentius, *Antiquitates Rerum Divinarum*, Akad. der Wissenschaften und der lit., Abhand. der Geistes und Soz. kl. Einz, ed. Cardauns, B., Weisbaden: F. Steiner, 1976.

Xenocrates, *Testimonia, doctrina et Fragmenta*, in ed. Parente, M. I. *Senocrate-Ermodoro, Frammenti*, Naples: Bibiliopolis, 1982.

Zosimus, M. Berthelot and C. E. Ruelle, *Collection des anciens alchimistes grecs*, Paris, 1887–88, ii.P.245, 6–7 = *Zosimo di Panopoli, Visconi e risvegli*, ed. A. Tonelli, Milan, 1988.

SECONDARY WORKS

Abbate, M. (2008a), *Il divino tra unità e moltiplicità. Saggio sulla teologica di Proclo* (Collana Hellenica), Alessandria: Edizioni del Orso.
  (2008b), *Il "male" dai commentari al Timeo di Platone-Proclo*. Caserta: Saletta dell Uva.
Af Hällström, G. (ed.) *Människan i Universum: Platons Timaios och dess tolknings-shistoria (Man's Place in the Universe. Plato's Timaeus and the History of its Interpretation)*, Åbo Akademi University Press.
Alt, K. (1993), *Weltflucht und Weltbejahung – zur Frage des Dualismus bei Plutarch, Numenios, Plotin*. Stuttgart: Franz Steiner Verlag.
Andron, C. I. (2001), 'Numenius' Fragment 13 (E. Des Places)- A Response to M. J. Edwards.' www.neoplatonism.org;groups.yahoo.com/group/neo-platonism.
Anton, J. P. (1992), 'Theorgica-Demiourgica: A Controversial Issue in Hellenistic Thought and Religion', in Wallis, R. T. and Bregman J., (eds.), *Neoplatonism and Gnosticism*. New York: SUNY Press, 9–32.
Armstrong, A. H. (1978), 'Gnosticism and Greek Philosophy', in Aland, B. (ed.) *Gnosis–Festschrift für Hans Jonas*, Göttingen: Vandenhoek and Ruprecht, 87–124.
Arruzza, C. (2012), 'Plato's World-Maker in Origen's *Contra Celsum*', in Song, E. (ed.) *Demiurge: The World-Maker in the Platonic Tradition (= Horizons: Seoul Journal of Humanities* 3.1), 61–80.
Babut, D. (1969), *Plutarque et le Stoicisme*, Paris: Presses universitaires de France.
Baer, R. A. (1970), *Philo's Use of the Categories Male and Female*, Leiden: E. J. Brill.
Behe, M. J. (1996), *Darwin's Black Box: The Biochemical Challenge to Evolution*, Free Press: New York.
Bénatouil, T. (2009), 'How Industrious can Zeus be? The Extent and Objects of Divine Activity in Stoicism', in Salles, R. (ed.) *God and Cosmos in Stoicism*. Oxford University Press, 23–45.
Berchman, R. M. (1984), *From Philo to Origen – Middle Platonism in Transition. Brown Judaic Studies* Chico, CA: Scholar's Press, 69.
Bianchi, U. (1978), 'Religio-Historical Observations on Valentinianism', in Layton, B. (ed.), *The Rediscovery of Gnosticism, Proceedings of the Conference at Yale (March 1978), Volume I, The School of Valentinus*. Leiden: E. J. Brill, 103–17.
  (1987a), 'An Imperial Heritage: The Religious Spirit of Plutarch of Chaironeia', *ANRW* II. 36.1, 248–349.
  (1987b), 'Plutarch und der Dualismus', *ANRW* II. 36.1, 350–65.
Bignone, E. (2007), *L'Aristotele perduto e la formazione di Epicuro*. Milan: Bompiani.

Billings, T. H. (1919), *The Platonism of Philo Judaeus*, University of Chicago Press.

Black, D. L. (2005), 'Psychology: Soul and Intellect', in Adamson, P. and Taylor, R. C. (eds.) *The Cambridge Companion to Arabic Philosophy*, Cambridge University Press, 308–26.

Bostock, G. (2007), 'Origen's Doctrine of Creation', *The Expository Times* 118, 222–7.

Bousset, W. (1907), *Hauptprobleme der Gnosis*, Göttingen: Vandenhoeck & Ruprecht.

Boys-Stones, G. (2001), *Post-Hellenistic Philosophy: A Study of its Development From the Stoics To Origen*, Oxford University Press.

(2007), '"Middle" Platonists on Fate and Human Autonomy', in Sharples, R. W. and Sorabji, R. W. (eds.), *Greek and Roman Philosophy 100 BC–200 AD*, Vol. 2, Bulletin of the Institute of Classical Studies Supplement 94, London, 431–47.

Brakke, D. (2010), *The Gnostics. Myth, Ritual and Diversity in Early Christianity.* Cambridge, MA: Harvard University Press.

Brenk, F. E. (1977), *In Mist Apparelled – Religious Themes in Plutarch's Moralia and Lives*, Leiden: E. J. Brill.

(1987), 'An Imperial Heritage: The Religious Spirit of Plutarch of Chaironeia', *ANRW* II. 36.1, 248–349.

Brisson, L. (1994), *Le Même et l'Autre dans la Structure Ontologique du Timée de Plato. Un commentaire systematique du Timée de Platon.* International Plato Studies, St. Augustin: Academia Verlag.

Büchli, J. (1987), *Der Poimandres. Ein Paganisiertes Evangelium: sprachliche und begriffliche Untersuchungen zum 1. Traktat des Corpus Hermeticum*, Tübingen: J. C. B. Mohr.

Bussanich, J. (1988), *The One and Its Relation to Intellect in Plotinus*, Leiden, E. J. Brill.

(1996), 'Plotinus' Metaphysics of the One', in Gerson, L. P. (ed.) *The Cambridge Companion to Plotinus*, Cambridge University Press, 38–65.

Cadiou, R. (1932), *Introduction au système d'Origène*, Paris: Belles Lettres.

Chadwick, H. (1960), *Early Christian Thought and the Classical Tradition – Studies in Justin, Clement and Origen*, Oxford: Clarendon Press.

Cherniss, H. (1944), *Aristotle's Criticism of Plato and the Academy.* Baltimore: Johns Hopkins Press.

D'Ancona Costa, C. (1996), 'Plotinus and later Platonic Philosophers on the Causality of the First Principle', in Gerson, L. P. (ed.) *The Cambridge Companion to Plotinus.* Cambridge University Press, 356–85.

Daniélou, J. (2012), *Philon d'Alexandrie*, Paris: Éditions du Cerf.

Dechow, J. F. (1988), 'Origen and Early Christian Pluralism: The Context of his Eschatology', in Kannengiesser, C. and Petersen, W. L. (eds.) *Origen of Alexandria – His World and His Legacy*, Indiana: University of Notre Dame Press, 337–53.

Deck, J. N. (1967), *Nature, Contemplation and the One.* University of Toronto Press.

De Ley, H. (1972), *Macrobius and Numenius – A Study of Macrobius In Somn.* 1, *c. 12*, Collection Latomus, Vol. 125, Brussels: Latomus.

Deuse, W. (1985), *Untersuchungen zur mittelplatonischen und neuplatoniuschen Seelenlehre*; Mainz & Wiesbaden: Akademie der Wissenschaften und der Literatur, Mainz/Franz Steiner Verlag GMBH, Wiesbaden.

Dillon, J. M. (1969), 'Plotinus Enn. 3.9.1 and Later Views on the Intelligible World', *TAPA* 100, 65–70, reprinted in Dillon, J. *The Golden Chain: Studies in the Development of Platonism and Christianity*, Aldershot: Variorum.

(1977), *The Middle Platonists: A Study of Platonism (80 BC–AD 220)*, London: Duckworth, (see also 2nd rev. edn, Ithaca: Cornell University Press).

(1979), 'Ganymede as the Logos: Traces of a Forgotten Allegorization in Philo', in *Studia Philonica – Studies in Hellenistic Judaism*, Vol. 6, 37–40.

(1980), 'The Descent of the Soul in Middle Platonism and Gnostic Thought', in Layton, B (ed.) *The Rediscovery of Gnosticism*, Vol. 1, Leiden: E. J. Brill, 357–64.

(1982), 'Origen's Doctrine of the Trinity and Some Later Neoplatonic Theories', in O'Meara, D. J. (ed.) *Neoplatonism and Christian Thought*, New York: SUNY Press, 19–23.

(1988a), 'Looking on the Light: Some Remarks on the Imagery of Light in the First Chapter of the Peri Archon', in Kannengiesser, C. and Petersen, W. L. (eds.), *Origen of Alexandria – His World and His Legacy*, Indiana: University of Notre Dame Press, 215–30.

(1988b), 'Orthodoxy and Eclecticism – Middle Platonists and Neopythagoreans', in Dillon, J. M. and Long, A. A. (eds.) *The Question of Eclecticism – Studies in Later Greek Philosophy*, Berkeley and Los Angeles: University of California Press, 103–27.

(1992a), 'Pleroma and Noetic Cosmos: A Comparative Study', in Wallis, R. T. and Bregman, J (eds.) *Neoplatonism and Gnosticism*, New York: SUNY Press, 99–110.

(1992b), 'Plotinus at Work on Platonism', *G&R*, 2nd Series, Vol. 39, 189–204.

(1993), 'A Response to Runia and Sterling', in *Studia Philonica Annual V*, 151–5.

(1995), 'Reclaiming the Heritage of Moses. Philo's Confrontation with Greek Philosophy', in *Studia Philonica VII*, 108–23.

(1997), 'The Riddle of the Timaeus: Is Plato Sowing Clues?', in Joyal, M. (ed.) *Studies in Plato and the Platonic Tradition: Essays Presented to John Whitaker*, Aldershot: Ashgate, 3–7.

(1999), 'Monotheism in the Gnostic Tradition', in Athanassiadi, P. and Frede, M., *Pagan Monotheism in Late Antiquity*, Oxford: Clarendon Press, 69–79.

(2000), 'The Role of the Demiurge in the Platonic Theology', in Segonds, A. P. and Steel, C. (eds.) *Proclus et le Théologie Platonicienne: Actes du Colloque International de Louvain (13–16 mai 1998). En l'honneur de H. D. Saffrey et L. G. Westerink*, Leuven and Paris: Leuven University Press/Belles Lettres, 339–72.

(2003a), *The Heirs of Plato – A Study of the Old Academy (347–274 BC)*, Oxford: Clarendon Press.

(2003b), 'The Timaeus in the Old Academy', in *Plato's Timaeus as Cultural Icon*, Reydams-Schils, G. J. (ed.), Indiana: University of Notre Dame Press, 80–94.

(2005a), 'Cosmic Gods and Primordial Chaos in Hellenistic and Roman Philosophy: The Context of Philo's Interpretation of Plato's Timaeus and the Book of Genesis', in Van Kooten, G. H. (ed.), *The Creation of Heaven and Earth: Reinterpretations of Genesis 1 in the Context of Judaism, Ancient Philosophy, Christianity, and Modern Physics*, Leiden: E. J. Brill, 97–107.

(2005b), 'Design in Nature: Some Comments from the Ancient Perspective' in Van Kooten, G. H. (ed.) *The Creation of Heaven and Earth: Reinterpretations of Genesis 1 in the Context of Judaism, Ancient Philosophy, Christianity, and Modern Physics*, Leiden: E. J. Brill, 263–6.

(2007), 'Numenius: Some Ontological Questions' in Sorabji, R. and Sharples, R. W. (eds.), *Greek and Roman Philosophy 100 BC–200 AD*, London, 397–402.

(2009), 'How Does the Soul Direct the Body After All: Traces of a Dispute in Mind-Body Relations in the Old Academy', in Frede, D. and Reis, B. (eds.) *Body and Soul in Ancient Philosophy*, Berlin/New York: De Gruyter, 349–58.

(2013), 'Towards the Noosphere: Plotinus, Origen, Teilhard de Chardin and the Striving for a Rational World', in Dillon, J. M. and Clark, S. R. I. *Towards the Noosphere; Futures Singular and Plural*, Wiltshire: Prometheus Trust, 1–23.

Dillon, J. M. and Elkaisy-Friemuth, M. (eds.). (2009), *The Afterlife of the Platonic Soul. Reflections of Platonic Psychology in the Monotheistic Religions*, Leiden: E. J. Brill.

Dodd, C. H. (1935), *The Bible and the Greeks*, London: Hodder & Stoughton.

Dodds, E. R. (1960), 'Numenius and Ammonius', *Entretiens Hardt V, Les Sources de Plotin*, Vandoeuvres-Geneva: Fondation Hardt, 1–61.

Doherty, K. F. (1960), 'Location of the Platonic Ideas', *The Review of Metaphysics* 14, 57–72.

Donini, P. (1988), 'Science and Metaphysics: Platonism, Aristotelianism and Stoicism in Plutarch's *On the Face in the Moon*', in Dillon, J. M. and Long, A. A. (eds.), *The Question of Eclecticism. Studies in Later Greek Philosophy*, Berkeley and Los Angeles: University of California Press, 126–44.

D'Onofrio, G. (2013), *Vera philosophia. Studi sul pensiero cristiano in età tardo-antica, alto-medievale e umanistica*, Rome: Editrice Città Nuova.

Dorandi, T. (2007), *Nell'officina dei classici. Come lavoravano gli autori antichi*, Rome: Carrocci.

Edel, A. (1982), *Aristotle and His Philosophy*, London: Croom Helm.

Edwards, M. J. (1989a), 'Gnostics and Valentinians in the Church Fathers', *JTS* n.s. 40, 161–85.

(1989b), 'Numenius, Fr. 13 (Des Places): A Note on Interpretation', *Mnemosyne* 42, fasc. 3–4, 478–82.

(1990), 'Numenius, Pherecydes and The Cave of the Nymphs', *CQ*, n. s. 40, 258–62.

(2002), *Origen Against Plato* (= Ashgate Studies in Philosophy and Theology in Late Antiquity), Aldershot: Ashgate.

(2010), 'Origen's Platonism: Questions and Caveats' in Turner, J. D. and Corrigan, K. (eds.) *Plato's Parmenides and Its Heritage, Volume 2. Reception in Patristic, Gnostic and Christian Neoplatonic Texts*, Atlanta: Society of Biblical Literature, 199–216.

Fabricius, J. A (1693), *Exercitatio de Platonismo Philonis Iudaei*, Leipzig: Zeidler.

Fakhry, M. (1968), 'A Tenth-Century Interpretation of Plato's Cosmology', *JHI* 6, 15–22.

Fattal, M. (1998), Logos *et Image chez Plotin*, Paris and Montréal: L'Harmattan.

(2010), 'Bild und Weltproduktion bei Plotin. Eine Kritik des gnostischen Bildes', in Grave, J. and Schubbach, A. (eds.), *Denken mit dem Bild*, Munich: Wilhelm Fink Verlag, 43–73.

Ferber, R. (1997), 'Why did Plato Maintain the "Theory of Ideas" in the Timaeus?' in Calvo, T. and Brisson, L. (eds.), *Interpreting the Timaeus-Critias – Proceedings of the IV Symposium*, International Plato Studies 9, Sankt Augustin: Academia Verlag, 179–86.

Ferrari, F. (1995a), *Dio, idee e materia – La struttura del cosmo in Plutarco di Cheronea*, Naples: M. D'Auria.

(1995b), 'E' nata prima la gallina o l'uovo? Un problema cosmologico in Plut. *Quaest. Conv.* II 3', *Sandalion* 18, 121–132.

(1996a), 'La generazione precosmica e la struttura della materia in Plutarco', *Museum Helveticum* 53, 44–55.

(1996b), 'Il problema della trascendenza nell'ontologia di Plutarco', *Rivista di filosofia neoscolastica* 88, 363–89.

(1996c), 'La teoria delle idee in Plutarco', *Elenchos* 17, 121–42.

(2010), 'Der entmythologisierte Demiurg', in Koch, D., Männlein-Robert, I. and N. Weidtmann, N. (eds.), *Platon und das Göttliche*, Tübingen: Attempto Verlag, 62–81.

Filoramo, G. (1990), *A History of Gnosticism*, Oxford: Basil Blackwell.

Fossum, J. E. (1982), *The Name of God and the Angel of the Lord: The Origins of the Idea of Mediation in Gnosticism*, Utrecht: Druckereij Elinkwijk.

Fowden, G. (1986), *The Egyptian Hermes: A Historical Approach to the Late Pagan Mind*, Cambridge University Press.

Frankfort, H. (1951), *The Problem of Similarity in Ancient Near Eastern Religions*, Oxford: Clarendon Press.

Frede, D. (2002), 'Theodicy and Providential Care in Stoicism', in Frede, D. and Laks, A. (eds.) *Traditions of Theology – Studies in Hellenistic Theology, its Background and Aftermath, Philosophia Antiqua*, Vol. LXXXIX, Leiden: E. J. Brill, 281–316.

Frede, M. (1987), 'Numenius', *ANRW* II. 36.2, 1034–75.

Froidefond, C. (1987), 'Plutarque et le Platonisme', *ANRW* II. 36.1, 184–233.

Gatti, M. L. (1996), 'Plotinus: The Platonic Tradition and the Foundation of Neoplatonism', in Gerson, L. P. (ed.) *The Cambridge Companion to Plotinus*, Cambridge University Press, 10–37.

Gentile, S. and Gilly, C. (2000), *Marsilio Ficiono e il Ritorno di Hermete Trismegisto*, Florence: Centro Di.

Gonzalez Blanco, A. (1984), 'Hermetism. A Bibliographical Approach', *ANRW* II.17.4, 2240–84.

Gorday, P. J. (1988), 'Moses and Jesus in *Contra Celsum* 7.1–25: Ethics, History and Jewish-Christian Eirenics in Origen's Theology', in Kannengiesser C. and Petersen, W. L. (eds.) *Origen of Alexandria – His World and His Legacy*, Indiana: University of Notre Dame Press, 313–36.

Gourinat, J. B. (2009), 'The Stoics on Matter and Prime Matter: "Corporealism" and the Imprint of Plato's Timaeus', in Salles, R. (ed.), *God and Cosmos in Stoicism*, Oxford University Press, 46–70.

Grafton, A. (1983), 'Protestant versus Prophet: Isaac Casaubon on Hermes Trismegistus', *Journal of the Warburg and Courtauld Institutes* Vol. 46, 78–93.

Greer, R. (1978), 'The Dog and the Mushrooms: Irenaeus' View of the Valentinians Assessed', in Layton, B. (ed.), *The Rediscovery of Gnosticism, Proceedings of the Conference at Yale (March 1978), Volume I, The School of Valentinus*, Leiden: E. J. Brill, 146–75.

Hahm, D. E. (1977), *The Origins of Stoic Cosmology*, Columbus: Ohio State University Press.

Halfwassen, J. (1994), *Geist und Selbstbewußtsein – Studien zu Plotin und Numenios (= Abhandlung der Geistes- und Sozialwissenschaftlichen Klasse, Jahrgang 1994, No. 10)*, Mainz and Stuttgart: Akademie der Wissenschaften und der Literatur/Franz Steiner Verlag.

(1999), *Hegel und der Spätantike Neuplatonismus – Untersuchungen zur Metaphysik des Einen und des Nous in Hegels spekulativer und geschichtlicher Deutung (= Hegel Studien, Beiheft 40)*, Bonn: Bouvier Verlag.

(2000), 'Der Demiurg: Seine Stellung in der Philosophie Platons und Seine Stellung im Antiken Platonismus', in Neschke-Hentschke, A. (ed.) *Le Timée de Platon- Contributions à l'histoire de sa Reception/Platons Timaios – Beiträge zu Seiner Rezeptionsgeschichte (= Bibliothèque Philosophique de Louvain 50)*, Louvain-La-Neuve/Paris: Éditions de l'Institut Supérieur de Philosophie/Éditions Peeters, 39–62.

(2002), 'Ewigkeit und Zeit bei Plotin', in Angehrn, E., Iber, C., Lohman, G and Pocali, R. (eds.) *Der Sinn der Zeit*, Weilerswist: Velbrück Wissenschaft.

(2004), *Plotin und der Neuplatonismus*, Munich: C. H. Beck, 222–34.

(2005), 'Seele und Zeit im Neuplatonismus', in Kelin, H. D. (ed.) *Der Begriff der Seele in der Philosophiegeschichte*, Würzburg: Königshausen und Neumann, 101–116.

Hay, D. M. (1973), 'Philo's Treatise on the Logos-Cutter', in *Studia Philonica* Vol. 2, 9–22.

Helderman, J. (1998), 'A Christian Gnostic Text: The Gospel of Truth', in Van den Broek, R. and Hanegraaf, W. J. (ed.) *Gnosis and Hermetism – From Antiquity until Modern Times*, New York: SUNY Press, 53–68.

Hershbell, J. P. (1992), 'Plutarch and Stoicism', *ANRW* II.36.5, 3336–52.

Hobein, H. and Kroll, W. (1930), 'Maximus (37) von Tyrus', *RE* 14, 2555–62.

Holzhausen, J. (1994), *Der mythos vom Menschen im hellenistischen Ägypten: eine Studie zum Poimandres (= CH I), zu Valentin und dem gnostichen Mythos.* Bodenheim: Athenäum-Hain-Hanstein.

Johansen, T. K. (2010), 'Should Aristotle Have Recognised Final Causes in Plato's Timaeus?' in Mohr, R. D. and. Sattler, B. M. (eds.). *One Book, The Whole Universe: Plato's Timaeus Today*, Las Vegas: Parmenides Publishing, 179–200.

Jonas, H. (1963), *The Gnostic Religion: The Message of the Alien God and the Beginnings of Christianity*, Boston, MA: Beacon Press.

(1967), 'Delimitation of the Gnostic Phenomenon-Typological and Historical', in Bianchi, U. (ed.) *Le Origini Dello Gnosticismo, Colloquio di Messina*, 13–18 Aprile 1966, Studies in the History of Religions (*Supplements to Numen* 12), Leiden: E. J. Brill, 90–108.

Jones, R. M. (1918), 'Chalcidius and Neoplatonism', *CPh* 13, 194–208.

(1926), 'The Ideas as the Thoughts of God', *CPh* 21, 317–26.

Jung, C. G. (1969), 'Gnostic Symbols of the Self', *Aion*, Ch. 13, republished in Segal, R. A. (ed.) *The Gnostic Jung: Selections from the Writings of C. G. Jung and His Critics*, Princeton University Press, 1992, 55–92.

Kees-Geijon, A. (2005), 'Divine Infinitude in Gregory of Nyssa and Philo of Alexandria', *VChr* 59.

Kenny, J. P. (1991), *Mystical Monotheism: A Study in Ancient Platonic Theology*, Providence RI: Brown University Press.

Keyt, D. (1971), 'The Mad Craftsman of the *Timaeus*', *Philosophical Review* 80, 230–5.

King, K. L. (2005), *What is Gnosticism?*, Cambridge MA: Belknap Press/Harvard University Press.

Kingsley, P (1993), 'Poimandres: The Etymology of the Name and the Origins of the Hermetica', *Journal of the Warburg and Courtauld Institutes*, Vol. 56, 1–24.

Kirk, G. S., Raven, J. E. and Schofield, M. (eds.) (1983), *The Presocratic Philosophers*, 2nd edn, Cambridge University Press.

Klotz, F. and Oikonomopoulou, K. (eds.) (2011), *The Philosopher's Banquet: Plutarch's Table Talk in the Intellectual Culture of the Roman Empire*, Oxford University Press.

Köckert, C. (2009), *Christliche Kosmologie und Kaiserzeitliche Philosophie. Die Auslegung des Schöpfungsberichtes bei Origenes, Basilius und Gregor von Nyssa vor dem Hintergrund kaiserzeitlicher Timaeus-Interpretationen*, Tübingen: Mohr Siebeck.

Kritikos, A. (2007), 'Platonism and Principles in Origen', in Sorabji, R. and Sharples, R. W. (eds.) *Greek and Roman Philosophy 100 BC–200 AD, Bulletin of the Institute of Classical Studies*, London: Institute of Classical Studies, University of London, 403–17.

Kutash, E. (2011), *Ten Gifts of the Demiurge. Proclus on Plato's Timaeus.* London/New York: Bristol Classical Press/Bloomsbury.

Lapidge, M. (1973), 'ἀρχαι and στοιχεῖα: A Problem in Stoic Cosmology', *Phronesis* 19, 240–78.

(1978), 'Stoic Cosmology', in Rist, J. M. (ed.) *The Stoics*, Berkeley and Los Angeles: University of California Press, 161–85.

Lisi, F. (1997), 'La Construcción del Alma del Mundo en el Timeo (35a–b) Y La Tradición Indirecta', in Calvo, T. and Brisson, L. (eds.), *Interpreting the Timaeus-Critias – Proceedings of the IV Symposium* (International Plato Studies 9), Sankt Augustin: Academia Verlag, 251–9.

Logan, H. B. (1996), *Gnostic Truth and Christian Heresy: A Study in the History of Gnosticism*, Edinburgh: T & T Clark.

Long, A. A. (2010), 'Cosmic Craftsmanship in Plato and Stoicism', in Mohr, R. D. and Sattler, B. M. (eds.) *One Book: The Whole Universe. Plato's Timaeus Today*, Las Vegas and Zurich: Parmenides Publishing, 37–53.

Lyman, J. R. (1993), *Christology and Cosmology – Models of Divine Activity in Origen, Eusebius and Athanasius*, Oxford: Clarendon Press.

Lyons, J. A. (1982), *The Cosmic Christ in Origen and Teilhard de Chardin: A Comparative Study*, Oxford University Press.

Macrae, G. W. (1970), 'The Jewish Background of the Gnostic Sophia Myth', in *Novum Testamentum* 12, 86–101.

Mahé, J. P. (1978), *Hermès en Haute-Égypte-Les Textes Hermétiques de Nag Hammadi et leurs Parallèles Grecs et Latins- Tome I*, Québec: Les Presses de l'Université Laval.

Majercik, R. (1989), *The Chaldean Oracles*, Leiden: E. J. Brill.

Markschies, C. (2000), 'New Research on Ptolemaeus Gnosticus', *Zeitschrift für Antikes Christentum* 4, 225–54.

Meijer, P. A. (1992), *Plotinus on the Good or the One. An Analytical Commentary*. Amsterdam: J. C. Gießen.

Metry, A. (2002), *Speusippos – Zahl – Erkenntnis – Sein*, Bern-Stuttgart-Vienna: Verlag Paul Haupt.

Migliori, M. (2002), 'Ontologia e materia. Un confronto tra il Timeo di Platone e il De generatione et corruptione di Aristotele', in Migliori, M. (ed.) *Gigantomachia, Convergenze e divergenze tra Platone e Aristotele*, Brescia: Morcelliana, 35–104.

(2003), 'Il problema della generazione nel Timeo', in Maso, S. and Natali, C. (eds.), *Plato Physicus, Cosmologia e antropologia nel* Timeo, Amsterdam: Adolf M. Hakkert Editore.

Mohr, R. D. (1985), *The Platonic Cosmology*, Leiden: E. J. Brill.

(1989), 'Plato's Theology Reconsidered: What the Demiurge Does', in Anton, J. P. and Preus A. (eds.), *Essays in Ancient Greek Philosophy III*, New York: SUNY Press, 293–307.

Mohr, R. D. and Sattler, B. M. (eds.) (2010), *One Book: The Whole Universe. Plato's Timaeus today*, Las Vegas and Zurich: Parmenides Publishing.

Mühlenberg, E. (1966), *Die Unendlichkeit Gottes bei Gregor von Nyssa. Gregor's Kritik am Gottesbegriff der klassichen Metaphysik* (= Forschungen zur Kirchen- und Dogmengeschichte 16). Göttingen: Vandenhoek & Ruprecht.

Narbonne, J. M. (2011), *Plotinus in Dialogue with the Gnostics* (= Studies in Platonism, Neoplatonism and the Platonic Tradition, Vol. 11), Leiden: E. J. Brill.

O'Brien, C. S. (2007a), 'The Origin in Origen: Platonic Demiurgy or Christian Creation?', *Freiburger Zeitschrift für Philosophie und Theologie 54 Band, Heft 1/2*, 169–77.

(2007b), 'Platonism and the Tools of God', *Trinity College Dublin Journal of Postgraduate Research Volume 6*, 60–72. Electronic version available at tcdgsu.ie/wp-content/uploads/2014/01/full_jpr_2007_vol_6.pdf

(2009), 'The Descent of the Demiurge from Platonism to Gnosticism', in Af Hällström, G. (ed.) *Människan i Universum: Platons Timaios och dess tolkningshistoria*, Åbo Akademi University Press, 113–32.

(2011), 'St Basil's Explanation of Creation', in Af Hällström, G. (ed.) *The Actuality of St Basil the Great*, Åbo Akademi University Press.

(2012), 'The Middle Platonist Demiurge and Stoic Cosmobiology', in Song, E. (ed.) *Demiurge: The World-Maker in the Platonic Tradition* (= *Horizons: Seoul Journal of Humanities* 3.1), 19–39.

(in press), 'Calcidius on Fate and the World-Soul' in Helmig C. and Markschies, C. (eds.), *The World Soul and Cosmic Space – New Readings on the Relation of Ancient Cosmology and Psychology*, Berlin: De Gruyter.

O'Brien, D. (1996), 'Plotinus on Matter and Evil', in Gerson, L. P (ed.), *The Cambridge Companion to Plotinus*, Cambridge University Press, 171–95.

O'Meara, D. J. (1975), *Structures Hiérarchiques dans la pensée de Plotin. Étude Historique et Interprétative*. Leiden: E. J. Brill.

(1976), 'Being in Numenius and Plotinus: Some Points of Comparison', *Phronesis* 21, 120–9.

(1993), *Plotin – Une Introduction aux Ennéades* (= *Vestigia 10, Pensée Antique et Médiéval*), Fribourg and Paris: Academic Press/CERF.

(1996), 'The Hierarchical Ordering of Reality in Plotinus', in Gerson L. P (ed.), *The Cambridge Companion to Plotinus*, Cambridge University Press, 66–81.

(2004), 'Dire le vrai chez Héraclite', in O'Meara, D. and Schüssler, I. (eds.), *La Vérité*, GENOS, Cahiers de Philosophie, Lausanne: Éditions Payot.

(2012), 'Who is the Demiurge in Plato's Timaeus?' in Song, E. (ed.) *Demiurge: The World-Maker in the Platonic Tradition* (= *Horizons: Seoul Journal of Humanities* 3.1), 19–39.

O'Neill, J. C. (2002), 'How Early is the Doctrine of *Creatio ex Nihilo*?', *Journal of Theological Studies* 53, 449–65.

Opsomer, J. (2000), 'Proclus on Demiurgy and Procession in the Timaeus: a Neoplatonic Reading of the Timaeus', in Wright, M. R. (ed.), *Reason and Necessity. Essays on Plato's Timaeus*, London: Duckworth and the Classical Press of Wales, 113–43.

(2003), 'La démiurgie des jeunes dieux selon Proclus', *Les Études Classiques* 71, 5–49.

(2004), 'Plutarch' *De Animae Procreatione in Timaeo*: Manipulation or Search for Consistency?' in Adamson, P., Baltussen, H. and Stone, M. W. F. (eds.),

Philosophy, Science and Exegesis in Greek, Arabic and Latin Commentaries, Volume I (= Bulletin of the Institue of Classical Studies Supplement 83.1), London: Institute of Classical Studies, School of Advanced Study, 137–62.

(2005), 'A Craftsman and His Handmaiden: Demiurgy According to Plotinus', in Leinkauf, T. and Steel, C. (eds.), *Platon's Timaios als Grundtext der Kosmologie in Spätantike, Mittelalter und Renaissance/Plato's Timaeus and the Foundations of Cosmology in Late Antiquity, the Middle Ages and Renaissance*, Leuven University Press, 67–102.

(2006), 'To Find the Maker and Father. Proclus' Exegesis of Plato *Tim.* 28c3–5 in *Études Platoniciennes* 2, 261–83.

Orbe, A. (1966), *Estudios valentinianos. Vol. 4: La teología del Espíritu Santo*. Rome: Pontificia Università Gregoriana.

(2012), *Introduction à la théologie des IIe et IIIe siècles*. Paris: Éditions du Cerf.

Ostenfeld, E. (1997), 'The Role and Status of the Forms in the *Timaeus*: Paradigmatism Revisited', in Calvo, T. and Brisson, L. (eds.), *Interpreting the Timaeus-Critias – Proceedings of the IV Symposium*, (= International Plato Studies 9), Sankt Augustin: Academia Verlag, 167–77.

Pearson, B. A. (1990), 'Jewish Elements in *Corpus Hermeticum* I (*Poimandres*)', in *Gnosticism, Judaism and Egyptian Christianity*, Minneapolis: Fortress Press, 136–47.

Pépin, J. (1964), *Théologie Cosmique et Théologie Chrétienne*, Paris: Université de France.

Perkins, P. (1976), 'Irenaeus and the Gnostics', *VChr* 30, 193–206.

(1980), 'On the Origin of the World (CG II.5): A Gnostic Physics', *VChr* 34, 36–46.

Pétrement, S. (1947), *Essai sur le dualisme chez Platon, les Gnostiques, et les manichéens*, (Thesis), Paris: Presses universitaires de France.

(1991), *A Separate God: The Christian Origins of Gnosticism* London: Darton, Longman and Todd.

Puiggali, J. (1983), *Etude sur les dialexeis de Maxime de Tyr – Conferencier Platonicien du IIème siècle*, Lille: Atelier National de Reproduction des Thèses/Université de Lille III.

Quispel, G. (1951), *Gnosis als Weltreligion*, Origo: Zurich.

Radice, R. (1989), *Platonismo e Creationismo in Filone Di Alessandria (= Metafisica del Platonismo nel suo Sviluppo Storico e nelle Filosofia Patristica 7)*, Milan: Pubblicationi delle Università Cattolica del Sacro Cuore.

(1991), 'Observations on the Theory of the Ideas as the Thoughts of God in Philo of Alexandria', in *Studia Philonica Annual-Studies in Hellenistic Judaism*, Vol. 3, 126–34.

Ramelli, I. and Konstan, D. (2007), *Terms for Eternity: Aiônios and Aïdios in Classical and Christian Texts*, Piscataway: Gorgias Press.

Reale, G. (1997), 'Plato's Doctrine of the Origin of the World, with Special Reference to the *Timaeus*', in Calvo, T. and Brisson, L. (eds.), *Interpreting the Timaeus-Critias – Proceedings of the IV Symposium*, International Plato Studies 9. Sankt Augustin: Academia Verlag, 149–64.

Reitzenstein, R. (1904), *Poimandres – Studien zur Griechisch-Ägyptischen und Frühchristlichen Literatur*, Leipzig: B. G. Teubner.

Renehan, R. (1987), 'Some Passages in Maximus of Tyre', *CPh* 82, 43–9.

Reydams-Schil, G. (1995), 'Stoicized Readings of Plato's *Timaeus* in Philo of Alexandria', in *Studia Philonica* 8, 85–102.

(1999), *Demiurge and Providence – Stoic and Platonist Readings of Plato's Timaeus*, Monothéismes et Philosophie, Turnhout: Brepols.

Rist, J. M. (1965), 'Monism: Plotinus and some Predecessors', *HSCP* 69, 329–44.

Rudolph, K. (1983), *Gnosis*, Edinburgh: T & T Clark.

Runia, D. T. (1981), 'Philo's *de aeternitate mundi*: The Problem of its Interpretation' *VChr* 35, 105–51.

(1986), *Philo of Alexandria and the Timaeus of Plato*, (= *Philosophia Antiqua* Vol. XLIV), Leiden: E. J. Brill.

(1993), 'Was Philo a Middle Platonist – A Difficult Question Revisited', in *Studia Philonica Annual V*, 112–40.

(1997), 'The Literary and Philosophical Status of Timaeus' Prooemium', in Calvo, T. and Brisson, L. (eds.), *Interpreting the Timaeus-Critias – Proceedings of the IV Symposium*, (= International Plato Studies 9), Sankt Augustin: Academia Verlag, 101–18.

(2007), 'The Rehabilitation of the Jackdaw: Philo of Alexandria and Ancient Philosophy', in Sorabji, R. and Sharples, R. W. (eds.) *Greek and Roman Philosophy 100 BC–200 AD*, London, 483–500.

(2012), 'God the Creator as Demiurge in Philo of Alexandria', in Song, E. (ed.) *Demiurge: The World-Maker in the Platonic Tradition (= Horizons: Seoul Journal of Humanities* 3.1), 41–59.

Sagnard, F. M. (1947), *La Gnose Valentienne et le Témoignage de Saint Irénée* (= Études de Philosophie Médiévale. Vol. XXXVI), Paris: Librarie Philosophique J. Vrin.

Salles, R. (2009), 'Introduction', in Salles, R. (ed.) *God and Cosmos in Stoicism*, Oxford University Press, 1–20.

Sambursky, S. (1959), *Physics of the Stoics*, London: Routledge and Kegan Paul.

Schelling, F. W. J. (1856–61), *Sämmtliche Werke*, ed. K. F. A Schelling, I Abteilung Vols. 1–10, II Abteilung Vols. 1–4, Stuttgart: I. G. Cotta..

Schenke, H. M. (1962), *Der Gott 'Mensch': Ein religionsgeschichtlicher Beitrag zur Diskussion über die paulinische Anschauung von der Kirche als Leib Christi*, Göttingen: Vandenhoeck und Ruprecht.

Schoonenberg, P. (1968), *Covenant and Creation*, London & Sydney: Sheed and Ward.

Schott, J. M. (2008), *Christianity, Empire and the Making of Religion in Late Antiquity*, Philadelphia, PA: University of Pennsylvania Press.

Sedley, D. (2002), 'The Origins of Stoic God', in Frede, D. and Laks, A. (eds.) *Traditions of Theology – Studies in Hellenistic Theology, its Background and Aftermath*, (= *Philosophia Antiqua*, Vol. LXXXIX), Leiden: E. J. Brill, 85–117.

(2007), *Creationism and its Critics in Antiquity*, Berkeley and Los Angeles: University of California Press.

Segal, A. F. (1977), *Two Powers in Heaven. Early Rabbinic Reports about Christianity and Gnosticism*, Leiden: E. J. Brill.

Segal, R. A. (1986), *The Poimandres as Myth: Scholarly Theory and Gnostic Meaning*, Berlin and New York: Walter De Gruyter.

Sharples, R. (1995), 'Counting Plato's Principles' in Ayres, L. (ed.) *The Passionate Intellect. Esasys on the Transformation of the Classical Traditions* (= Rutgers University Studies in Classical Humanities, Vol. VII), New Brunswick and London: Transaction Publishers, 67–82.

Simonetti, M. (2004), *Origene esegeta e la sua tradizione* (Collana Letteratura Cristiana Antica), Brescia: Morcelliana.

Smith, M. (1980), 'The History of the Term Gnostikos', in Layton B. (ed.) *The Rediscovery of Gnosticism*, Leiden: E. J. Brill, 796–807.

Smulders, P. (1968), *The Fathers on Christology. The Development of Christological Dogma from the Bible to the Great Councils*, De Pere, Wisconsin: St Norbert Abbey Press.

Solmsen, F. (1957), 'The Vital Heat, the Inborn Pneuma and the Aether (*De gen. an.* II, 3, 736b30–737a11', *JHS* 77, 119–23.

(1961), 'Greek Philosophy and the Discovery of the Nerves', *Museum Helveticum* 18, 150–97.

(1963), 'Nature as Craftsman in Greek Thought', *Journal of the History of Ideas* 24, 473–96. Reprinted in F. Solmsen, *Kleine Schriften*, Hidesheim: Olms, 332–55.

Song, E. (2012), "Plotinus on the World-Maker", in Song, E. (ed.) *Demiurge: The World-Maker in the Platonic Tradition* (= Horizons: Seoul Journal of Humanities 3.1), 81–102.

Spence, A. J. (2008), *Christology: A Guide For the Perplexed*, London and New York: T & T Clarke/Continuum.

Stead, G. C. (1969), 'The Valentinian Myth of Sophia', *JTS* n.s. 20, 75–104.

(1978), 'In Search of Valentinus', in *The Rediscovery of Gnosticism*, 75–102.

Sterling, G. E. (1992), 'Creatio Aeterna vel Continua? An Analysis of the Thought of Philo of Alexandria', in *Studia Philonica Annual* 4, 15–41.

(1993), 'Platonizing Moses – Philo and Middle Platonism', in *Studia Philonica Annual* IV, 96–111.

Svendsen, S. N. 'Origen and the Possibility of Future Falls', Copenhagen: Naturalism and Christian Semantics Research Group, unpublished data.

Tanner, K. (1988), *God and Creation in Christian Theology*, Oxford: Basil Blackwell.

Tarán, L. (1971), 'The Creation Myth in Plato's Timaeus', in Anton, J. P. and Kustas, G. L. (eds.), *Essays in Ancient Greek Philosophy*, New York: SUNY Press, 372–407.

(1982), *Speusippus of Athens: A Critical Study with a Collection of the Related Texts and Commentary*, Leiden: E. J. Brill.

Tarrant, H. (1985), *Scepticism or Platonism: The Philosophy of the Fourth Academy*, Cambridge.

Tobin, T. H. (1993), 'Was Philo a Middle Platonist? Some Suggestions', in *Studia Philonica Annual* 5, 144–50.

Todd, R. B. (1978), 'Monism and Immanence – The Foundations of Stoic Physics', in Rist, J. M. (ed.), *The Stoics*, Berkeley & Los Angeles: University of California Press, 137–59.

Torjensen, K. J. (1986), *Hermeneutical Procedure and Theological Method in Origen's Exegesis*, Berlin & New York: Walter De Gruyter.

Trapp, M. B. (1991), 'Some Emendations in the Text of Maximum of Tyre, *Dialexis* 1-21 (H.)', *CQ* 41, 566–71.

(1992), 'More Emendations in the Text of Maximus of Tyre', *CQ* 42, 569–75.

(1997), 'Philosophical Sermons: The "Dialexis" of Maximus of Tyre', *ANRW* II. 34.3, 1945–76.

Turner, J. D. (1992), 'Gnosticism and Platonism. The Platonizing Sethian Texts From Nag Hammadi In Their Relation To Later Platonic Literature', in Wallis, R. T. and Bregman, J. (eds.) *Gnosticism and Neoplatonism* (= Studies in Neoplatonism VI), Albany, NY: SUNY Press, 425–59.

Tzamalikos, P. (2006), *Origen: Cosmology and Ontology of Time* (= Supplements to *Vigiliae Christianae* Vol. 77), Leiden: E. J. Brill.

(2007), *Origen: Philosophy of History and Eschatology* (= Supplements to *Vigiliae Christianae* Vol. 85), Leiden: E. J. Brill.

Ussery, D. (1998), 'A Biochemist's Response to "the Biochemical Challenge to Evolution"', *Bios Magazine*. Electronic Version available at http://www.cbs. dtu.dk/~dave/Behe.html

Vallejo, A. (1997), 'No, It's Not a Fiction', in Calvo, T. and Brisson, L. (eds.), *Interpreting the Timaeus-Critias – Proceedings of the IV Symposium*, International Plato Studies 9, Sankt Augustin: Academia Verlag, 141–8. *Philosophy, Christianity, and Modern Physics* (= Themes in Biblical Narrative 8), Leiden: E. J. Brill, 245–61.

Van Den Broek, R. (1998a), 'Gnosticism and Hermetism in Antiquity: Two Roads to Salvation', in Van den Broek, R. and Hanegraaf (eds.) *Gnosis and Hermetism – From Antiquity until Modern Times*, New York: SUNY Press, 1–20.

(1998b), 'The Cathars: Mediaeval Gnostics', in Van den Broek, R. and Hanegraaf, (eds.) *Gnosis and Hermetism – From Antiquity until Modern Times*, New York, SUNY Press, 87–108.

Van Den Broek, R. and Hanagraaf, W. J. (eds.) (1997), *Gnosis and Hermetism – From Antiquity until Modern Times*, New York, SUNY Press.

Van Meurs, J. (1998), 'William Blake and his Gnostic Myths', in Van den Broek, R. and Hanegraaf, W. J. (eds.) *Gnosis and Hermetism – From Antiquity until Modern Times*, Albany: SUNY Press, 269–309.

Van Winden, J. C. M. (1959), *Calcidius on Matter – His Doctrine and Sources A Chapter in the History of Platonism*, Leiden: E. J. Brill.

Van Woudenberg, R. (2005), 'Design in Nature: Some Current Issues', in Van Kooten, G. H (ed.) *The Creation of Heaven and Earth: Reinterpretations of Genesis 1 in the Context of Judaism, Ancient Philosophy, Christianity and Modern Physics*, Leiden: E. J. Brill, 245–261.

Verbeke, G. (1982), 'Some Later Neoplatonic Views on Divine Creation and the Eternity of the World', in O' Meara, D. J. (ed.) *Neoplatonism and Christian Thought*, Albany: SUNY Press, 45–53.

Vlastos, G. (1965), 'The Disorderley Motion in the Timaeus', in Allen, R. E. (ed.) *Studies in Plato's Metaphysics*, London: Routledge and Keegan Paul, 379–99.

(1975), *Plato's Universe*, Oxford: Clarendon Press.

Von Harnack A. (1900), *Des Wesen des Christentums, Sechzehn Vorlesungen vor Studierenden aller Fakultäten im Wintersemester 1899/1900 an der Universität Berlin*, Leipzig, J. C. Hinrichs. (English Translation: *What is Christianity?* New York and London: G. P. Putnam's Sons and Williams & Norgate, 1901).

Vorwerk, M. (2010), 'Maker or Father? The Demiurge From Plutarch To Plotinus', in Mohr, R. D. and. Sattler, B. M. (eds.) *One Book, The Whole Universe: Plato's Timaeus Today*, Las Vegas and New York: Parmenides Publishing, 79–100.

Wallis, R. T. (1972), *Neoplatonism*, London: Duckworth.

Waszink, J. H. (1964), *Studien zum Timaioskommenter des Calcidius, Band I: Die Erste Hälfte des Kommentars*, Leiden: E. J. Brill.

(1965), 'Porphyrois und Numenios', *Fondation Hardt pour L'Étude de L'Antiquité Classique, Entretiens, Tome XII, Porphyre*, Vandoeuvres-Geneva, 35–83.

Whittaker, J. (1967), 'Moses Atticizing', *Phoenix* 21, 196–201.

(1969), 'Ammonios on the Delphic E', *CQ n.s.* 19, 185–92.

(1978), 'Numenius and Alcinous on the First Principle', *Phoenix* 32, 144–54.

(1987), 'Platonic Philosophy in the Early Centuries of the Empire', *ANRW* 11. 36.1, 81–123.

Widdicombe, P. (1994), *The Fatherhood of God from Origen to Athanasius*, Oxford: Clarendon Press.

Williams, M. A. (1996), *Rethinking "Gnosticism" – An Argument for Dismantling a Dubious Category*, Princeton University Press.

Wilson, R. McL. (1993), 'Philo and Gnosticism', *Studia Philonica Annual* 5, 84–92.

Winston, D. (1973), 'Freedom and Determinism in Greek Philosophy and Jewish Hellenistic Wisdom', *Studia Philonica-Studies in Hellenistic Judaism* 2, 40–50.

(1974–5), 'Freedom and Determinism in Philo of Alexandria', *Studia Philonica-Studies in Hellenistic Judaism* 3, 47–70.

Witt, R. E. (1931), 'The Hellenism of Clement of Alexandria;' *CQ* 25, 195–204.

Wolfson, H. A. (1968), *Philo – Foundations of Religious Philosophy in Judaism, Christianity and Islam*, Cambridge MA: Harvard University Press.

Wüst, E. (1939a), 'Ophion 1', in RE XVIII, 1, 645.

(1939b), 'Ophion 2', in RE XVIII, 1, 645.

(1939c), 'Ophioneus 2', in RE XVIII, 1, 646.

Zeller, E. (1919–23), *Philosophie der Griechen in ihrer geschichtlichen Entwicklung*, Leipzig: Fues/R. Reisland.

Index

Index locorum

Lightning Source UK Ltd.
Milton Keynes UK
UKHW020736150622
404452UK00019B/353